C000261238

The
History
of
Bodmin Jail
New Edition

Compiled, edited and arranged from
Contemporary Sources

by

Bill Johnson

Published by Bodmin Town Museum,
Mount Folly, Bodmin, Cornwall, PL31 2HQ

The Title

The institution for criminals in Bodmin has been known as Bodmin Gaol; the County Gaol, Cornwall; H.M. Prison at Bodmin; and Bodmin Jail. The latter spelling has been chosen as the book title for two reasons, firstly, the Act of Parliament, published in 1778, was entitled *'An Act for building an additional Jail...'* and, secondly, in recent times, the *Jail* spelling has been used for the night club and later the tourist attraction and restaurant. Throughout the book the alternate spelling, *gaol,* has been used as this is the most common spelling in published documents.

About the Author

Bill Johnson, Ph.D., is a graduate with degrees in chemistry who has spent his working life in the pharmaceutical industry, researching auto-immune diseases and potential new treatments. He has published many research papers, articles, and patents and given many lectures in Europe and the United States, on the subject of enzyme inhibitors. Now retired, he has lived in Bodmin since 1998 and does voluntary work for Bodmin Town Museum, involving photography, art-work for exhibits and publishing.

This book is the result of many queries from both locals and visitors regarding the buildings and life in Bodmin Jail. It is also by way of a challenge issued many years ago by a friend and colleague, the late Dr Antonin Kroehn of Prague, who claimed that the education of British scientists was too narrow and that scientists were not able to talk or write about non-scientific issues. Well Toni, if you are watching, this is the author's attempt at a piece of social history.

First published 2006. Reprinted 2007. Second Edition 2009.

©William Henry Johnson, 2009
All rights reserved. No part of this publication may be reproduced, stored in a retrieval system, or transmitted in any form or by any means electrical, mechanical, photocopied, recorded or otherwise, without prior permission of the author.

Published by:
Bodmin Town Museum, Mount Folly, Bodmin, Cornwall, PL31 2HQ.
Manuscript prepared for publication by W H & J M Johnson, the publishing team.

ISBN 978-0-9549913-5-7

Printed by MPG Books Ltd, Bodmin, Cornwall

Contents

Chapter 1	Introduction	5
Chapter 2	The Design and Building of the First Bodmin Gaol	13
Chapter 3	The Expansion of Bodmin Gaol	19
Chapter 4	The New Bodmin Gaol	25
Chapter 5	Inside the Buildings	37
Chapter 6	Position of the Old Gaol	43
Chapter 7	English Gaol Administration	47
Chapter 8	Courts, Crimes and Sentences	51
Chapter 9	The People – Staff	65
Chapter 10	The People – Inmates	75
Chapter 11	Gaol Life – Rules and Punishments	89
Chapter 12	Prisoners' Employment	101
Chapter 13	Hard Labour Machines at Bodmin	109
Chapter 14	Prisoners Diets	115
Chapter 15	Welfare of Prisoners	125
Chapter 16	Ins and Outs	135
Chapter 17	Death Sentence and Executions	143
Chapter 18	In their Own Words	169
Chapter 19	Naval Prisoners at Bodmin	183
Chapter 20	Establishment of H.M. Naval Prison	195
Chapter 21	Life in the Naval Prison	203
Chapter 22	The Closure of the Prisons	215
Appendix 1:	Sir John Call, Bart., J.P., M.P. (1732-1801)	224
Appendix 2:	Haden Warm-air Stove Systems	225
Appendix 3:	Regulations and Rules 1867	226
Appendix 4:	Quarter sessions sentences for 1812, 1822 & 1832	234
Appendix 5:	List of staff employed in Bodmin Gaol	237
Appendix 6:	Numbers of Prisoners	241
Appendix 7:	Prisoners in the Gaol on 12th July 1850	243
Appendix 8:	Notes on Gaol Budgets	246
Appendix 9:	Records removed from PRO to Bodmin Prison (1918)	250
References		251
Index		255

Dedicated to my family,
Jan & Kiki
and to the
Future of the Jail

I would like to thank the following people and organisations:

Mrs Maureen Tooze, curator of Bodmin Town Museum, for access to documents and photographs, including *'The State of Prisons'* by Howard and the Victorian Statute Books. The John Soane's Museum, London, for permission to publish the *'John Call Engraving'*. Councillor Frank Stone, Mr Peter Davies, Mr Dudley Prout, Mr Christopher Smith and Mr & Mrs Ken Allen for useful discussions and permission to publish photographs and documents. The Cornish Studies Library, Redruth, for permission to use a photograph from the *'Ellis Collection'* and the Cornwall Records Office for providing copies of broadsheets, Quarter Sessions records and many other documents. Ms. Suzanne Rix, Social Policy section, British Library, for providing an index to Parliamentary Papers and the staff at Bodmin Library for their help in obtaining these Papers. The National Archive, Kew, and the House of Lords Records Office for providing copies of documents. The owners of Wildish's Builders for permission to photograph the buildings from their premises.

A book about the gaol would not be possible without the free access to the buildings provided to me by the owners of the gaol, Simon, Helen and David Wheten and their family and staff. I am grateful to them for their interest and discussion.

W H Johnson, January, 2006.

In addition to the Organisations and people mentioned above, this new extended edition would not have been possible without photographs and documents provided by the following: Malcolm McCarthy of Padstow, Shaun Babb, Gary James, Margaret Nott, Richard Diodge, Paul O'Callaghan (Bodmin Town Clerk) and Messrs. R Clark and D J Mossop. I would also like to thank members of the CIBSE Heritage Group, for discussion about Victorian heating and ventilation systems and the booksellers, particularly, *Empire Books of York,* who have found many documents which have contained information about the history of the gaol. Special thanks to Skytrax Aviation Ltd., for permission to use their copyright image on the cover.

W H Johnson, 2009.

CHAPTER 1

Introduction

Bodmin Gaol, built in 1779, was one of the first modern prisons built in England and was designed according to the reformist ideas of John Howard (1726-1790).

Howard,[1] a philanthropist, embarked for Lisbon in November 1755, 'for the purpose of assisting to alleviate the suffering caused by the great earthquake, that had recently laid the city in ruin'. However, the ship was captured by a French privateer, and the crew and passengers were taken into Brest, where they were treated with extreme cruelty. The sufferings which he underwent and witnessed during his captivity appear to have made a deep impression on him. When he was released he brought the case of the prisoners of war to the notice of the English Commissioners of sick and wounded seamen and induced them to take measures for an exchange of prisoners.

Later, when Howard became Sheriff of Bedford, he was already aware of the existence of abuses in the management of criminals and, as soon as he started the duties of his office, he commenced an inquiry into the horrible corruptions of the English prison system. On examining the three prisons in Bedford, he found that they were not only miserably deficient in decent accommodation, in cleanliness, air, food, and water, but that the gaoler and his subordinates had no salary, and were entirely dependent on the fees they could wring from the wretched prisoners, who were, after their acquittal by the court, detained in the gaol, in some cases for years, until they paid the fees of gaol delivery. In order to put an end to these gross abuses, Mr. Howard proposed that a salary should be given to the gaoler in lieu of these fees; but the magistrates were startled at such an innovation, and refused to adopt it without a precedent.

In 1773, Howard started the first of several tours of public gaols in Great Britain and Ireland, all of which he found in a state disgraceful to a civilized country. He ultimately extended his investigation to the prisons and houses of correction in twelve foreign countries. Details of his journeys and the distance travelled later appeared in one of his memorandum books.[2]

Howard, who had called attention to the miserable state of the prisons, many of which he had visited, appeared as a witness before a House of Commons committee to support proposed legislation introduced by Alexander Popham MP for Taunton. This led to two prison reform bills being passed by Parliament in 1774. The first declared that all prisoners against whom no bill of indictment had been found by the grand jury, or who should be discharged by proclamation for want of prosecution, should be immediately set at large in open court, without any payment of any fee or sum of money to the sheriff or gaoler in respect of such discharge; and abolishing all such fees for the future, it directed the payment, in lieu of them, of a sum not exceeding 13s. 4d. out of public funds for every prisoner discharged (The Discharged Prisoners Act, 14 George III. cap. 20).

The other bill was concerned with health and sanitation in the prisons (The Health of Prisoners Act, 14 George III. cap. 59). It required the Justices to see that all prisons within their respective jurisdictions, be scraped and whitewashed once a year at least - that the rooms be regularly washed and ventilated, that infirmaries be provided for the sick, and proper care be taken of them - to order clothes for them when needed - whenever possible to prevent their being kept in underground dungeons - and, generally, to take such measures as shall tend to restore and preserve their health.

When the acts passed into law, Howard immediately took energetic measures for carrying out the reforms, including having copies of the acts printed and sent to every prison in the land. The justices and gaolers generally ignored the new laws, except in Sussex and Cornwall. In 1775 the 3rd Duke of Richmond started planning a new fully cellular county gaol at Horsham, Sussex, based on the new Howard principles. Building was stared in 1776 and the gaol opened in 1779.[3] Also in 1775, the Justices of the Peace in Cornwall started discussions on the building of a new county gaol.

AN ACCOUNT OF THE NUMBER OF MILES TRAVELLED ON THE REFORM OF PRISONS.

JOURNEYS	MILES
In Great Britain and Ireland, 1773-6	10,318
First Foreign Journey, 1775	1,400
Second Ditto, 1776	1,700
Third Ditto, 1778	4,636
In Great Britain and Ireland, 1779	6,490
Fourth Foreign Journey, 1781	4,465
In Great Britain and Ireland, 1782	8,165
Fifth Foreign Journey, 1783	3,304
To Ireland	715
To Worcester	238
To Hertford, Chelmsford, and Warrington	602
TOTAL	42033

'To God alone be all praise! I do not regret the loss of many conveniences of life, but bless God who inclined my mind to such a scheme.'

In 1777, Howard published the results of his investigations in 'The State of Prisons in England and Wales with Preliminary Observations, and an Account of some Foreign Prisons.'[4] This volume contains, in addition to detailed descriptions and remarks on all the gaols in the country, a section on proposed improvements in the structure and management of prisons and a generic plan for building a county gaol:

State of the Gaols in Cornwall (before 1776).[4]

COUNTY GAOL AT LAUNCESTON for felons

Gaoler: John Mules, Deputy, under Coryndon Carpenter Esq. Constable of the Castle.

Salary, lately augmented by the County from £8 to £12 p.a.

Prisoners: Allowance, Felons, a three-penny loaf each in two days; white or brown at their option (weight in Dec. 1775, white bread 1 lb 10 oz. and brown 2 lb 2oz.)

Number of Felons: 19th Feb.1774 11; 13th Sep.1774 8; 23rd Dec.1775 6.

Chaplain: Rev. Mr. Lethbridge. Duty: Tuesday and Friday. Salary, lately reduced from £50 to £30.

Surgeon: Mr. Bennet. Salary, £15.

Remarks: This gaol, though built in a large yard belonging to the old ruinous Castle, is very small; house and court measuring only fifty two feet by forty four; and the house not covering half that ground. The Prison is a room or passage twenty three feet and a half by seven and a half, with only one window two feet by one and a half:—and three Dungeons or Cages on the side opposite the window: these are about six and half feet deep; one nine feet long; one about eight; one not five: this last for women. They are all very offensive. No chimney: no drains: no water: damp earth floors: no **Infirmary**. The yard not secure; and Prisoners seldom permitted to go out to it. Indeed the whole Prison is out of repair, and yet the Gaoler lives distant. I once found the Prisoners chained two or three together. Their provision is put down to them through a hole in the floor of the room above (used as a Chapel); and those who serve them there, often catch the fatal fever. At my first visit I found the Keeper, his Assistant, and all the Prisoners but one, sick of it: and heard that a few years before, many Prisoners had died of it; and the Keeper and his wife in one night.

I learned that a woman who was discharged just before my first visit (by the Grand Jury making a collection for her Fees) had been confined three years by the Ecclesiastical Court; and had three children in the gaol. There is no Table of Fees. The King, of his Royal Bounty, has offered TWO THOUSAND POUNDS towards a new Gaol; but nothing is done by the County.

I WAS edified by the serious behaviour of the Chaplain at Prayers. The Prisoners respect him, and were very attentive. He has a large family: I was sorry for the late reduction of his Salary. The Mayor sends weekly one shilling's worth of bread.

COUNTY BRIDEWELL AT BODMIN.

The County pays £10 a year for this Prison. It is much out of repair; and the walls round the yard not safe enough to let Prisoners use it. The night rooms are two garrets, with small sky-lights seventeen inches by twelve, close glazed. I was informed that a few years ago the Gaol-Fever was very fatal, not only in the Prison, but also in the Town.

Keepers Salary lately raised from £20 to £28. Allowance a three-penny loaf in two days; (weight, Dec. 1775, 31 oz.) No employment.

A **Surgeon** to this Bridewell; his Salary £20.

Prisoners: 14th Sep.1774   19; 22nd Dec.1775   29.

SHERIFF'S WARD AT BODMIN, (The County Prison for Debtors)

Keeper: Joseph Catty. Salary, £25. Fees, Debtors, £0 : 13 : 4, Besides   £0 : 4 : 1 to the Sheriff. **Prisoners**: Allowance, none.

Number of Debtors: 14th Sep. 1774   19; 22nd Dec. 1775   18.

Chaplain: None. **Surgeon:** None.

Remarks: This prison, for which the Sheriff pays £20 a year, is out of repair. A spacious back-yard; with a stream running through it. The Keeper pays Window-tax £3 : 7 : 0, and I saw some windows were stopped up.—He said he had been Keeper above twenty years; and during the whole time had but four Prisoners who obtained from their Creditors the allowance commonly called the Groats.

County Bridewell, (for minor offenders) also known as the House of Correction, at Church Stile. After 1779, it became 'Bodmin Brewery'. Demolished in 1898.

Sheriff's Ward at Bodmin, in Prison Lane (now Crockwell Street). In use between 1749 and 1779.

TRURO TOWN GAOL.

Built about two years ago upon a good plan. Two houses in front, for the two Sergeants at Mace who are the Keepers. Cross the yard is the Prison; which consists of four convenient rooms, two of them vaulted: no pump. 18th Dec. 1775, **Prisoners** none.

FALMOUTH TOWN GAOL.

Two rooms: no court-yard: no water. 19th Dec. 1775: **Prisoners** none.

PENZANCE TOWN GAOL.

Two close rooms: no court-yard: no water. 19th Dec. 1775, **Prisoners** none.

AT PENZANCE is also A PRISON for the Hundred and Liberties of PENWITH,

The Property of Lord Arundel. Two rooms in the Keeper's stable-yard; but distant from his house, and quite out of sight and hearing. The room for men is full eleven feet square, and six high: window eighteen inches square: no chimney. Earth floor; very damp. The door had not been opened for four weeks when I went in; and then the Keeper began shoveling away the dirt.—There was only one Debtor, who seemed to have been robust, but was grown pale by ten weeks close confinement, with little food, which he had from a brother, who is poor and has a family. He said, the dampness of the Prison, with but little straw, had obliged him (he spoke with sorrow) to send for the bed on which some of his children lay. He had a wife and ten children, two of whom died since became thither, and the rest were almost starving. — He has written me a letter since, by which I learn that his distress was not mitigated, and that he had a companion, miserable as himself. — No allowance. **Keeper** no Salary: Fees 8s. 4d. every action, no Table. A year or two ago five **Prisoners**, I was informed, grew desperate by what they suffered in this wretched Prison, and broke out. 21st Dec. 1775, Prisoners 1.

LOSTWITHIEL GAOL for debtors

Is the Property of the Duke of Cornwall, Lord of the Stannaries. It was lately repaired and whitewashed. The Rules extend over the whole Borough. The Keeper told me that he lately had a Prisoner who was arrested for £6: the man had a large family, and not a bad Character; yet the Plaintiff paid him his groats for two years; and dying then, bound his Estate for the continual Payment of them: but the Insolvent Act freed the Prisoner and the Estate. **Keeper** no Salary: Fees 13s. 4d.
Debtors: 14th Sep 1774 4; 18th Dec. 1775 2.

PENRYN GAOL for debtors

ST. LEONARD'S Chapel: the Property of the Earl of Godolphin. One room thirteen feet square, six high: window about two feet by one foot four inches. **Keeper** (a woman) complained of paying Rent £4, and of the Prison window being taxed with those in her house. Dec. 19th Dec. 1775, **Prisoners** none.

At this time Bodmin had the County Bridewell, which housed prisoners who had committed misdemeanours; it was situated at Church Stile. However there are two documents, which suggest that felons were also imprisoned in the bridewell. A lease dated 5th December, 1791, contains the following description:

'... of all buildings and premises lying opposite to and against the South side of the church, abutting North on a street or road leading from Honey Street, otherwise Church Street, to the Priory, known as the Old Prison, together with the large walled courtledge adjoining the same premises, all of which buildings were formerly used as the Sherrif's(!) Ward Bridewell and **County Gaol**.'[5] The second document, dated 1772, is a decision of the Justices: *'As a result of the bridewell being used to hold prisoners for capital offences……. The salary of the bridewell keeper to be increased to £28 p.a.'*[6]

The Sheriff's Ward at Bodmin, The County Prison for Debtors, was in Crockwell Street, at that time known as Prison Lane. The building still exists as the 'Hole-in-the-Wall' public house. The name derives from the time when relatives and friends passed food through the 'Hole-in-the-Wall' to the imprisoned debtors.

Proposed Improvements in the Structure and Management of Prisons.[4]

Situation: A County-gaol, should be built on a spot that is *airy*, and if possible near a river, or brook. I have commonly found prisons situated near a *river*, the cleanest and most healthy. They generally have not (they could not well have) subterraneous dungeons, which have been destructive to thousands: and by their nearness to running water, another evil, almost as noxious, is prevented, that is, the stench of **sewers**. I said a Gaol should be near a stream but I must annex this caution; that it be not so near as that either the house or yard shall be within the reach of floods. This circumstance was so little thought of at Appleby in Westmoreland, when their new Gaol was built, that I saw the walls marked from nine inches to three feet high by floods. IF it be not practicable to build near a stream, then an eminence should be chosen: for as the walls round a prison-yard must be so high as greatly to obstruct a free circulation of **air**; this inconvenience should be lessened by a rising round: and the prison should not be surrounded by other buildings, nor built in the middle of a town or city.

Plan: The annexed engraving represents a plan for a prison as, according to my ideas, unites the greatest advantages with regard to health, order, and security.

That part of the building which is detached from the walls, and contains the men-felons ward, may be square, or rectangular, *raised on arcades*, that it may be more **airy**, and leave under it a dry walk in wet weather. Wards over arcades are also best for safety, for I have found that escapes have been most commonly effected by undermining cells and dungeons.

I wish to have so many **small rooms or cabins** in this ward, that each criminal may sleep alone. If it be difficult to prevent their being together in the day-time, they should by all means be separated at night. Solitude and silence are favourable to reflection; and may possibly lead them to repentance. Privacy and hours of thoughtfulness are necessary for those who must soon leave the world.

The **separation** I am pleading for, especially at night, would prevent escapes, or make them very difficult: for that is the time in which they are generally planned, and effected. Another reason for separation is, that it would free gaolers from a difficulty of which I have heard them complain: they hardly know where to keep criminals admitted to be evidence for the King. These would be murdered by their accomplices if put among them; and in more than one prison, I have seen them, for that reason, put in the women's ward.

10

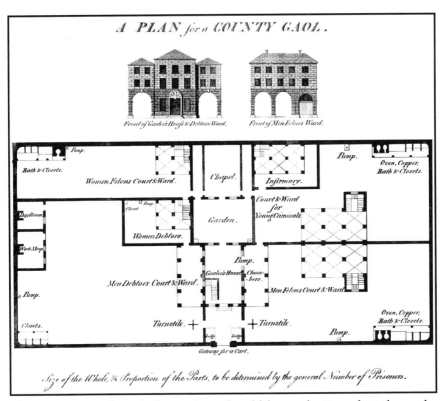

A PLAN for a COUNTY GAOL.

Front of Gaoler's House & Debtors Ward.   Front of Men Felons Ward.

Size of the Whole, & Proportion of the Parts, to be determined by the general Number of Prisoners.

Where there are opposite windows they should have shutters; but these should be open all day. In the men-felons ward there should be no glass; nor should the prisoners be allowed to stop the windows with straw, &c.

The women-felons should be quite **separate** from the men: and young criminals from old and hardened offenders. Each of these three classes should also have their day-room or kitchen; and their court-yard and offices all separate.

Every court should be paved for the more convenient washing it; and have a good pump or pipes laid in; both if possible: and the *Pump* and *Pipes* should be repaired as soon as they need it; otherwise the Gaols will soon be offensive and unwholesome, as I have always found them to be in such cases. A small **stream** constantly running in the yard is very desireable. In a room or shed near the pump or pipe, there should be a *Bath* to wash prisoners that come in dirty, or grow dirty afterwards. It should be filled every morning, and let off in the evening through the privies into the drains. There should also be a copper in the shed, to heat a quantity of water sufficient to warm that in the bath; for washing those that are sickly. There should likewise be an *Oven*: nothing so effectually destroys vermin in cloaths and bedding, nor purifies them so thoroughly when tainted with infection, as being a few hours in an oven moderately heated.

The *Infirmary* or sick wards should be in the most airy part of the yard, quite detached from the rest of the Gaol, and raised on arcades. In the middle of the floor of each room there should be a grate; of twelve or eighteen inches square, for a current of air; covered with a shutter or hatch at night. The same contrivance might also be convenient the other wards.

Debtors and **felons** should have wards totally **separate**: the peace, the cleanliness, the health and morals of debtors cannot be secured otherwise. The Act 22 & 23 Charles II, cap. 20, requires this separation at night; that debtors may not be disturbed by the curses and other profane language of felons. This would also remove the objection that is now made against permitting debtors to work: that is, the danger of their furnishing felons with tools for mischief, or escape.

In the debtors ward there should be a day-room or kitchen; also a large **Work-shop** for such as are willing to work. Some few Gaols have the latter and in them I have seen chair-makers, shoe-makers, &c. employed in their several trades; preserving their habit of industry; contributing to the support of their families.

Prisoners indicted for felony should not be compelled to work. But I have heard many of them wishing they might be permitted to earn something for their more comfortable support.

Women debtors should have a ward, a court, a pump &c. to themselves: and no communication should be allowed between the two sexes.

The **Ward for Men-Debtors** should also be over arcades, and placed on one side of the gaolers house. This house should be in or near the middle of the Gaol, with windows to the felons and the debtors court-yard.

A **Chapel** is necessary in a Gaol, I have chosen for it what seems to me a proper situation. It should have a **gallery** for debtors or women; and the rest may be separated below. Bibles and prayer-books should be chained at convenient distances on each side: those who tear or otherwise damage them should be punished.

It was these ideas and designs which formed the basis of the plans for the building of the new Gaol at Bodmin.

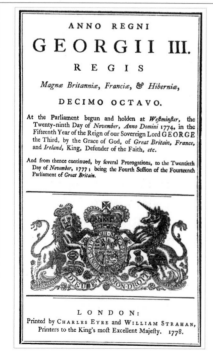

The 1778 Act of Parliament which established The County Gaol at Bodmin
Bodmin Town Museum

CHAPTER 2

The Design and Building of the First Bodmin Gaol

The poor conditions at Launceston had been recognised by the Justices of the Peace in 1775, when they had written[7] to Lord North, the Lord Treasurer, *"We beg leave to represent to your Lordship how cruel the delay has already been to the unhappy wretches confined in so deplorable a place; which has at times been so bad as that the Justices of the Peace have not thought themselves justified in committing thither such persons as have been brought to them."* Lord North had offered £2,000 to the Lord Warden of the Stanneries for the building of the new gaol but no action was taken. It was nearly two years later that the Justices were informed of the offer from Lord North. They then decided that a new gaol was needed.

Launceston was ruled out as the site for the new gaol for the same reasons that the Summer Assizes had been moved to Bodmin. Launceston, 'gateway to Cornwall', was isolated from the rest of the county and the cost of transporting prisoners, paid by the parishes rather than the government, was considered a discouragement to justice. This decision confirmed Bodmin as the County Town and the site of the new gaol. *(The assizes moved to Bodmin in 1838 and the County Gaol at Launceston closed in 1829.)*

In 1778 an Act of Parliament was passed entitled**, 'An Act for the building of an additional Jail, and also a Prison and House of Correction within the County of Cornwall; and for other purposes therein mentioned'.**[8]

The Act recommended Bodmin for its clean air and pure water, early recognition that this would help in reducing disease. The Mayor and Burgesses of Bodmin had agreed to give up 'a piece or parcel of ground known by the name of Berrycombe for the site of the intended gaol'. In addition to the accommodation for criminals the new buildings were to include a new bridewell (house of correction for those found guilty of minor offences) and a new Sheriff's Ward (prison for debtors).

The gaol, which opened in 1779, was built under the supervision of John Call, J.P. *(appendix 1)*. The architects and builders were Philip Stowey and Thomas Jones of Exeter, their foreman, James Chapple, later became governor. A post he held for nearly fifty years. The design of the prison was based on the *'Proposed Improvements in the Structure and Management of Prisons'* by Howard.

The only plans available are on a 1779 engraving (see pages 16-17),[9] sent to John Howard by John Call, which contained the following message:
To John Howard *Esq. This* PLAN, ELEVATION *and* SECTION *of the* GOAL(!), Bridewell *and* Sheriff's Ward, *lately Built at* BODMIN *in the County of*

CORNWALL, *is most gratefully inscribed by his very obedient humble Servant Jn. Call.*

As a small Token of the high Esteem, in which he holds his very indefatigable perseverance, and humane Enquiries, in behalf of his fellow Creatures unhappily deprived of Liberty during the course of many Years at the most imminent risque of his Life; and as **a Tribute justly due to him, from whose Ideas given to the Publick the plan has been principally formed.**

The bottom section of the engraving consists of a description of the site and explains the principles behind the design of the gaol:

This Goal(!) is built on the side of a steep Hill facing the South on a spot rather too confined in Extent but as no more commodious Situation for Air and Water could be got, the Plan was with no small difficulty adapted to the Ground and at length so happily contrived that the Steepness of the Ground which at first appeared a great obstacle seems to be of advantage in many points, by placing the several Buildings above each other, and thereby giving each a full Sun, and fresh Air. A copious Stream of the purest fresh Water is brought in above the Goalers(!) House, and divided through every Ward to supply the Baths and other uses, and ultimately carried off through the Bog Houses. The leading principle in the disposal of the several parts of the Building is to prevent any communication of Speech or otherwise, between the different kinds of Criminals, and to keep each sex distinct by Day, and every individual separate from one another by Night. All are lodged up stairs and the Lodgings have no contact with the outer Wall so that no escape can be concerted or effected by mining. One Hundred Men and Women may be lodged in the several Wards at the same time.

The gaol was airy and had a stream of pure water coming in at the top of the site which was piped throughout all the buildings for drinking and sanitation. There were separate areas for felons, debtors, and the bridewell. Men and women were segregated and each person had an individual cell for sleeping. All cells were built on arcades above the ground floor. This was for security and also gave a dry walk in wet weather. This arrangement was also considered more healthy because of improved circulation of air. There was an infirmary area, consisting of five rooms with a surgeon in daily attendance and as required, a chapel, dayrooms (one for each type and sex of prisoner) and a workshop.

In the Infirmary Court there were three condemned cells. In all courts there were stone troughs with a pipe and cock to supply a constant run of water. In addition there were baths, boilers to heat the water and ovens to bake the cloathes, to prevent infection and destroy vermin.

The gaoler was provided with accommodation in the main house, which contained a hall, parlour, kitchen and seven rooms for master debtors from whom he could exact fees for the privilege of living in the best part of the gaol. The turnkeys each had a chamber.

The *Call Engraving* gives a good impression of the design of the buildings but there are some problems. Firstly, the gaol was intended to house 100 inmates in single sleeping cells (except for debtors) but from the detailed plans the number of cells for each type of prisoner is as follows: Common Debtors rooms, each for two people (D) 7; Chambers for Master Debtors (E) 7; Women Felons (a) 7; Women Bridewell (b) 7; Men Felons (c & e) 16; Men Bridewell (d & f) 16: Other cells included; Infirmary (B) 5 and Condemned Cells (C) 3. This only gives a total of approximately seventy inmates.

There are inconsistencies between different parts of the engraving. The elevations show a beautiful symmetrical building but the ground plan includes the addition of a workshop and a 'Vagrants Ward for Boys'. The 'Court for Women Felons' on the first floor plan is incorrectly labelled on the ground floor plan as 'Women Debtors Court'.

These discrepancies suggest that the engraving was a piece of art-work designed to impress Howard, and not an accurate plan of the gaol.

Howard's response to the new gaol was recorded after his visit to Bodmin in 1782:

"By a spirited exertion, the gentlemen of this county have erected a monument of their humanity, and attention to health and morals of prisoners."

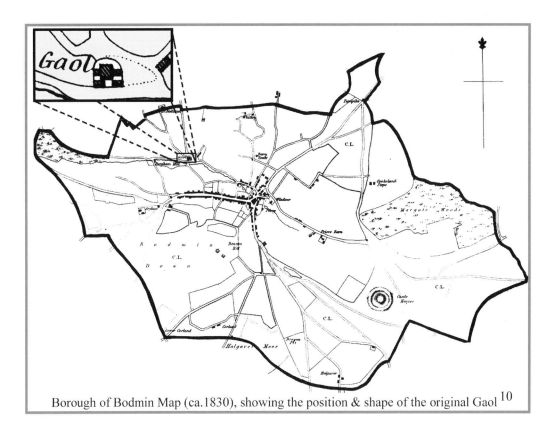

Borough of Bodmin Map (ca.1830), showing the position & shape of the original Gaol [10]

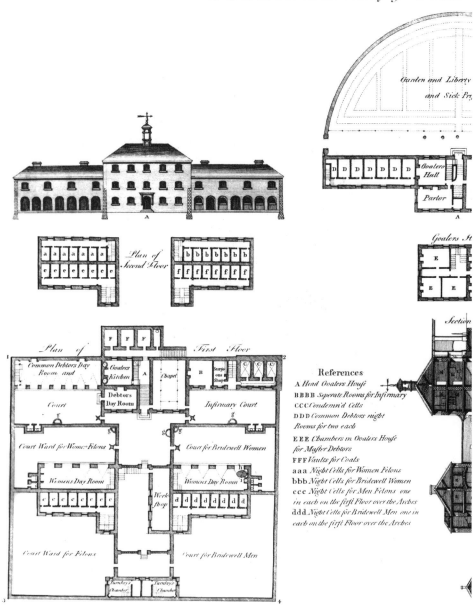

The 'John Call' Engraving

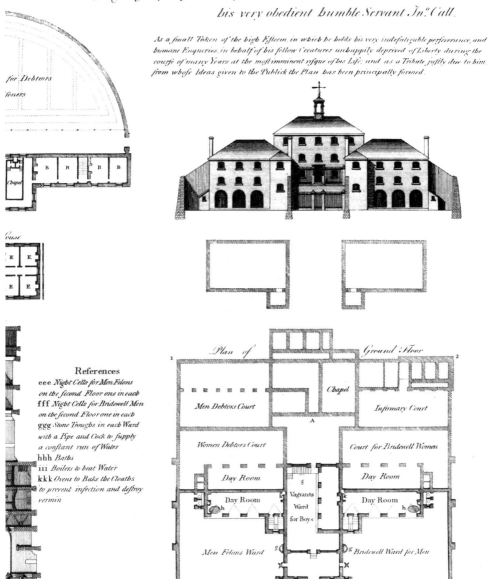

SECTION of the Goal, Bridewell and Sheriffs Ward, lately Built at WALL, is most gratefully inscribed by

his very obedient humble Servant Jnᵒ Call.

As a small Token of the high Esteem, in which he holds his very indefatigable perseverance, and humane Enquiries, in behalf of his fellow Creatures unhappily deprived of Liberty during the course of many Years at the most imminent risque of his Life, and as a Tribute justly due to him, from whose Ideas given to the Publick the Plan has been principally formed.

for Debtors
ioners

B   B   B   B

Chapel

ouse

E E
E E

References

eee *Night Cells for Men Felons on the second Floor one in each*
fff *Night Cells for Bridewell Men on the second Floor one in each*
ggg *Stone Troughs in each Ward with a Pipe and Cock to supply a constant run of Water*
hhh *Baths*
iii *Boilers to heat Water*
kkk *Ovens to Bake the Cloaths to prevent infection and destroy vermin*

Plan of   Ground Floor

1   2

Men Debtors Court   Chapel   Infirmary Court
                           A

Women Debtors Court   Court for Bridewell Women

Day Room   Day Room

Day Room   Vagrants   Day Room
             Ward
             for Boys

Men Felons Ward   Bridewell Ward for Men

3   4

South Front

ation for Air and Water could be got, the Plan was with no small difficulty adapted to the Ground and at length so happily ing the several Buildings above each other, and thereby giving each a full Sun, and fresh Air. A copious Stream of the tely carried off through the Bog Houses. The leading principle in the disposal of the several parts of the Building is to prevent individual seperate from one another by Night. All are lodgd up stairs and the Lodgings have no contact with the outer Wall the same time.

Feet

all Esqᵉ one of ye Justices of the County 1779.

Architectural Library Nᵒ 36 Holborn.

H   Darling sculp Newport Street.

(Published by kind permission of The John Soane's Museum, London)

17

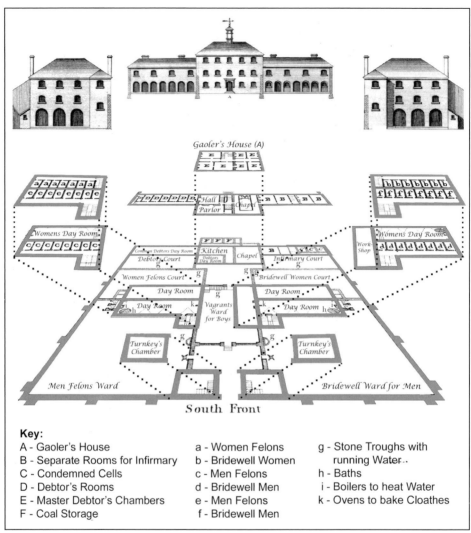

Gaoler's House (A)

Hall D Parlor | Chapel

Womens Day Room

Common Debtors Day Room
Kitchen
Debtor's Court
Debtors Day Room
Debtor's Day Room
Chapel
Infirmary Court
Work Shop
Womens Day Room

Women Felons Court
Bridewell Women Court

Day Room
Day Room
Day Room
Vagrants Ward for Boys
Day Room
Day Room

Turnkey's Chamber
Turnkey's Chamber

Men Felons Ward
Bridewell Ward for Men

South Front

Key:

A - Gaoler's House	a - Women Felons	g - Stone Troughs with
B - Separate Rooms for Infirmary	b - Bridewell Women	running Water
C - Condemned Cells	c - Men Felons	h - Baths
D - Debtor's Rooms	d - Bridewell Men	i - Boilers to heat Water
E - Master Debtor's Chambers	e - Men Felons	k - Ovens to bake Cloathes
F - Coal Storage	f - Bridewell Men	

Detailed Floor Plans of the First Bodmin Gaol
(Adapted from the 'John Call' Engraving)

Computer Generated Image derived from the John Call Engraving

CHAPTER 3

The Expansion of Bodmin Gaol

The new gaol consisted of a set of elegant buildings and was considered a great advance in the care and rehabilitation of offenders. When it was built, Bodmin was one of only five gaols in the Country designed for 100 inmates. However there were problems with the function of the buildings right from the start and this led to a series of new buildings and changes. The inclusion of a workshop and a vagrants' court for boys seem to have been added to the plans before the gaol was completed. In 1780, Cornwall Quarter Sessions Records contain the following entry: ***Proposed alterations to Bodmin jail and Bridewell submitted by Mr James Chappell, keeper: stopping up 2 arcades, making a partition across the hall and adding 2 grates in the chimney there, in the women's section; stopping up 1 arcade, making a partition across the hall, making a window in each end of the passage leading to the cells, and whitewashing the cells in the men's section.*** *(QS/1/4/282-291,1780).*

The arcades, a key feature in the original plan, had lasted about one year. Other changes, including repairs, alterations and rebuilding, recorded in the Quarter Sessions records include:

1791 Additional buildings to the Sheriff's Ward at Bodmin completed by Joseph Beard, Architect. *(QS/1/6/168/1-182/1).*

1784 Following attempts at escape by prisoners at Bodmin Gaol, repairs to be carried out to defective walls. *(QS/1/5/1-34).*

1785 Authorisation given for the completion of repairs at Bodmin Gaol. (QS/1/5/35-63).

1805 James Chapple produced plan and estimate for alterations of turnkey's lodges at Bodmin Gaol. *(QS/1/7/317-334).*

1814 Visiting magistrates of Bodmin Gaol to consider need for erecting an additional ward at the prison for separate confinement of young persons, to procure estimates for building, and to produce their report to the court. *(QS/1/8/171-187).*

1818 Addition and alterations to Bodmin Gaol to be carried out by James Chapple, in accordance with plan and specification produced in court, not to exceed £60 in cost. *(QS/1/9/80-116).*

1820 Sum not exceeding £400 granted to improve and enlarge Bodmin Gaol, to be administered by a committee and according to plan already produced. *(QS/1/10/28-61).*

1824 Committee of magistrates appointed to consider new requirements for Bodmin Gaol and house of correction, made necessary by recent Act (QS/1/10/500-531).

1825 New Sheriffs Ward to be erected adjacent to Bodmin Gaol to house thirty male debtors. *(QS/1/10/609-636).*

1827 On 1 Feb. next debtors confined in Bodmin Gaol to be removed to new building recently erected at western end of gaol, and the building to become integral part of the prison, together with such part of the gaoler's house as the sheriff shall see fit. *(QS/1/11/192-224).*

1828 Visiting magistrates of Bodmin Gaol reported that drains, ordered last year, nearly finished, greatly improved atmosphere in the gaol, and consequently in the health of the prisoners.

Since appointment of new governor many necessary repairs had been made and a contract to repair the dilapidated roof drawn up.

A new kitchen provided, where all prisoners to be served with allowance of food instead of cooking for themselves at large Fires which were kept constantly burning in their day rooms.

A laundry wash-house had been provided, where women sentenced to hard labour, would wash for the prisoners.

The apartment, previously occupied by the matron, to become the governor's office.

By building up the doorway of the Debtors' Ward and opening a way through into the gaol, the entrance to the debtors' prison would also be under the surveillance of the governor. *(QS/1/11/339-369).*

1829 Repairs of old Bridewell progressing and separate sleeping cells being built.

Gaol yard divided into three, for separate classes of prisoners. *(QS/1/11/502).*

1830 Governor, having reported on confined state of the chapel, too small for the increased number of prisoners, and having suggested adding an adjoining room, previously a kitchen but now vacant, for reception of female prisoners, and rearrangement of benches for the men, probable expense not to exceed £60.

Completion of all new buildings. Some repairs and alterations to old buildings remain to be done. New buildings in men's gaol now occupied. *(QS/1/11/614-657).*

1831 Addition to turnkeys' lodges estimated at £35 but needs a further £56 as internal work had not been included.

Cast iron drop for executions ready but cannot be fixed until increased expenditure approved.

Garden wall to be raised. *(QS/1/12/60-99).*

1832 The visiting justices hoped that the gaol expenses might have been less but noted that many repairs had been necessary to both gaol and Bridewell "built not much more than fifty years ago". *(QS/1/12/150-153).*

1834 Visiting Justices to Bodmin Gaol empowered to buy small piece of land adjoining western end of gaol. *(QS/1/12/430-452).*

There were further additions to the gaol in 1842 and 1847 supervised by the architect, George Wightwick of Plymouth.[11]

Some of the above reports mention sums of money but one report[12] gives an indication of the cost of the major reorganisation of the gaol: *'The justices made comparison of expenditure on gaol for four years from year ending Easter 1828 showing amounts spent on building, totalling £18,087.16s.6d.'* For comparison, the *'repairs, alterations and additions'* costs for 1843 and 1846, were £613.6s.7d. and £167.17s.5½d.[13, 14]

There are three reasons for the increase in the number of buildings and the other changes in the use of buildings between 1779 and 1855.

1.   The number of committals to the gaol increased markedly during the early part of the nineteenth century. According to Redding[15], there were 105 committals in 1805, 378 in 1829 and 293 in 1839. The difference between 1805 and 1829/1839 is partly explained by an increase in the population. Redding reports that the population in 1805 was 188,369. This had risen to 302,440 in 1829 and 341,269 in 1839.

This was a period of industrialisation in Cornwall which led to larger towns, easier movement of people with the improved road system (and later rail system) and, in general, and an increase in wealth. The change in the Cornish economy coincided with the arrival of large numbers of ex-servicemen returning from the Napoleonic wars and seeking work. Both of these factors led to a higher prison population and caused overcrowding. In 1820, the maximum capacity of the gaol was reported as 183 (common gaol 70, bridewell 75 and debtors 38)[16], however several prisoners were moved to Launceston because Bodmin was full. When Launceston closed down in 1829, prisoners were transferred to Bodmin. In July, 1830, the Governor reported[17] that 'number of prisoners now *"unusually great"'*.

2.   In addition to the increase in population and the closure of Launceston Gaol, the Act of Parliament in 1823, which emphasised separate confinement and the five-fold classification of prisoners, also meant that the gaol needed significant change. There were now five classes of prisoners in both the gaol and the house of correction. The sexes were to be separated at all times, this meant the gaol required separate accommodation and work facilities for up to twenty different classes of prisoners. The rebuilding of the prison, from 1828 to 1833, was supervised by the new Governor, Mr. Everest. The changes resulted in the number of day-rooms and courtyards increasing to 14 and the number of cells rose from 63 to 147 single and 15 double cells.[18]

The following table also shows the large increase in cell numbers between the opening of the gaol in 1779 and 1836. The number of cells increased from 46 single and 14 double to 166 single and 11 double. The maximum number of prisoners that could be accommodated increased from 100 to 210 including double occupancy. The numbers of Wards and court yards doubled due to the increase in the separation of different classes of prisoners.[20]

Recorded changes in the maximum gaol population from 1779 to 1836						
	1779[9] & 1815[19]			1836[20]		
		M	F		M	F
Cells where one prisoner sleeps		32	14		136	30*
Cells where more than one prisoner sleeps (debtors)	14				10	1
Prisoners the prison is capable of containing	100#				176	33 / 34
Refractory cells - Dark				3		
Refractory cells - Light				2		
Apartments below ground				0		
Wards or divisions in the prison	6 or 7			15		
Day-rooms	6			16		
Work-rooms	1			0		
Tread-wheel houses				1		
Receiving rooms or cells (1 room and 6 cells)				7		
Divisions in the chapel				11		
Infirmaries or rooms for the sick	5				3	3
Warm and cold-baths, or bathing tubs	3 or 4			1		
Airing yards (courts)	7			15		
* In the gaol the female cells are in a state of disorder. The females sleep in the House of Correction.						
# Only achievable with two prisoners per cell.						

3.   The 1841 census gives a total of 195 people. In addition to the 137 prisoners, it lists 13 staff members and 45 others. This represents 30% of the inhabitants of the gaol. As the original gaol had only a few chambers for the governor and the turnkeys it would seem that additional accommodation for staff and their families must have been made available.

Plan of the Extended Gaol (1840)

The Tithe map of 1840,[21] although generally to scale, the gaol buildings and adjacent roads were hand drawn and are therefore not very accurate. The buildings on the right hand side of the site extend into the road and the building is distorted in an attempt to make it fit. The walls of some of the buildings are curved and the walls are not parallel.

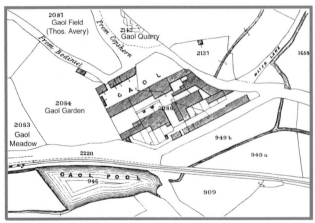

Tithe Map showing the County Gaol at Bodmin.

A comparison of the Tithe map plan with the 1779 Call Engraving shows that the site has been increased in area and now uses parts of both the gaol garden and the garden for debtors and sick prisoners. All the original 1779 gaol buildings can be identified. The gaoler's house, with both the debtor's and the Infirmary wings is still present. The two central blocks, one with the workshop, and the two gatehouses which have been extended. Many additional buildings are present and the wards have been sub-divided. The walls in the area from the gatehouse to the Governor's house seem to be identical in both plans but the walls on the left and right of the original gaol have been removed during the extensions. One of the three sets of buildings on the left of the site must be the new debtors' prison but none of the additional buildings on the tithe map have been identified.

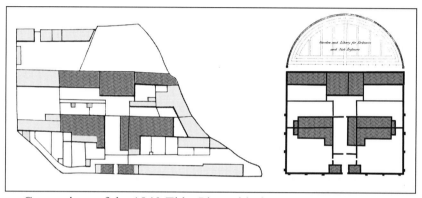

Comparison of the 1840 Tithe Plan with the 1779 Call Engraving

Water-colour entitled 'An Execution at Bodmin Gaol in 1841.'

This very colourful painting[22] is accompanied by the following text: *"Bodmin Gaol 1841 – The fields and house behind it was called 'Copshorn', which belonged to my grandfather Thomas Pearce. (Rich? W?) P. Jago, 1865."*

The painting seems to be an accurate representation of the gaol, as judged by its position in relation to the Pearce house and the Copshorn Road. It also clearly shows the angular section of the front wall. The darker coloured building and the building to the right of it are the Governor's House and the Infirmary block from the original gaol. Many of the extended and new buildings are in the same relative positions as those shown on the Tithe map plan. This painting is a three-dimensional representation of the gaol in 1840-41.

After about 1848, the Inspectors of Prisons started to criticise the conditions in the gaol and bridewell. In the report of 1851[23], the buildings were declared 'unfit for purpose' in the following statement:

The details of the defective construction and insufficient accommodation of this prison have been fully described in the Fourteenth Report (1849). The only material addition since that period was in progress at the time of my visit on the 12th July last, namely, the construction of a large tank and force-pump at the eastern side of the prison for the supply of spring water, in place of that of the leat already described, by which the prison is now supplied, and which had been subject to be fouled by cattle. This improvement when complete will, it is hoped, remove for the future all ground for complaints of the nature of those made to me by some of the prisoners, of the occasional impurity of the water supplied to them, and which I had an opportunity of ascertaining from my own observation.

*In the prison buildings no alterations have been made, nor is it desirable, as I have before remarked, that any expense which can be avoided should be incurred in upholding a prison which is allowed on all hands **to be so unfit for its purposes as to stand in need of being replaced by an entirely new building**. As long as the construction remains as it is, the prisoners, even of different sexes, will continually seize opportunities of conversation, giving rise to the constant infliction of punishments on those who are discovered, while a still larger number probably escape detection altogether. The utmost energy and the most judicious management on the part of the governor must be insufficient to maintain good discipline under such disadvantages.*

Since the publication of the Fourteenth Report a sum of £5,000 has been voted by the Court of Quarter Sessions for the erection of a new building for 48 male prisoners in cells capable of being certified for separate confinement. It was intended previously to the erection of this building to have added to the prison enclosure a piece of freehold land lying to the north and east of the present buildings, and it has only been from some difficulties as to the title of the land, and the consequent delay in the completion of the purchase, that the building has not yet been proceeded with. On the west side of the prison, however, there is an acre of ground which might, I am informed, be purchased on reasonable terms, and which would seem to be at least as convenient an addition as the one originally contemplated. Before quitting this subject I think it right to observe that the roofs of the present building are much out of repair, admitting both wind and rain.

It is very sad that the beautiful original 1779 Georgian buildings had become the totally unplanned random collection of buildings shown after 1840. The original designers could not have foreseen the increase in population, the resulting crime wave and increase in prison population but there must have been other factors which resulted in some of the changes. The addition of the workshop and 'Vagrant Ward for Boys' were very early changes, closely followed by the stopping up of the arcades in 1780. This would indicate that the original plan was very idealistic and elegant but it did not fulfil the function of a gaol.

In the mid 1850s the 'old gaol' was abandoned and a new gaol was built.

CHAPTER 4

The New Bodmin Gaol

It was noted in the Governor's and Chaplain's Report of October 1854 that overcrowding in the gaol had encouraged association of prisoners.[18] The total separation of different types of prisoners, sexes and individuals, who were not allowed to communicate, even when working together, was one of the main principals of the John Howard proposals for prison reform. The themes of separation and silence had been reinforced in Robert Peel's Gaol Act of 1823 and were still in favour in the 1850s. The separation of prisoners was probably more important to the Authorities than the dilapidated state of the gaol and the overcrowding.

In 1855, the Visiting Justices Report on the building of a new County Gaol stated that plans should be produced for a new gaol to accommodate the maximum numbers of prisoners. £25,000 was allocated by the County Authorities. The architect of the building was a Mr. F W Porter of London and the gaol was to be built on the same site at Berrycombe but using the old gaol site, the gaol gardens and other pieces of adjacent land. Initial quotations for the work were all significantly over the £25,000 available. The plans were modified and by using less granite and cheaper materials, a new lower estimate of £26,650 was obtained from Goodyear and King of Devon.[24] This quotation did not include fittings, gas and water services or architects fees. The final cost of the building was reported in 'The Royal Cornwall Gazette" as "upwards of forty thousand pounds".

The building work started in 1856 and Inspectors of Prisons reports cover the progress of the building work:

1856:[25] *A very extensive improvement was in progress at the time of my visit in the erection of a new prison.* **The foundation was laid of the new boundary wall,** *which will enclose an area of much larger extent than that now occupied by the prison. The stone for the new buildings is being quaried upon the premises, and the labour of prisoners (for which the contractors will pay the county) will be extensively employed on the buildings.*

1859:[26] *This prison is on the eve of being removed out of the category of those in which the association of prisoners is permitted. .A new building is being erected upon the same site, in which every attention has been paid to fitting it in all respects for the separate confinement of prisoners; and* **it is confidently expected that the division for male prisoners will be fit for occupation in the course of the summer.** *As soon as this shall be the case, another installment of* *the old building will be removed, and the females' prison will be immediately proceeded with.*

The accommodation for male criminal prisoners in the building now approaching completion, will be as follows:—

Ordinary cells on the ground floor and 2 galleries	124
Reception cells in basement	7
Punishment cells in ditto	6
Cells for condemned prisoners	2
Baths in the basement	3

The basement will also contain a kitchen, scullery, several store-rooms, workshops, the heating and ventilation apparatus, a lift for raising the food from the kitchen to the several floors, not only of the males' prison, but also of the females' to be hereafter erected at right angles to it.

1860:[27] ***The reconstruction of this prison was rapidly advancing towards completion at the time of my last inspection on the llth September last (1860).** At the end of the year 1859, I had the satisfaction of certifying 141 cells for the adoption of separate confinement in a wing which will eventually be devoted to male prisoners, a part of which is however now used for prisoners of the other sex during the erection of their proper building. The inclination of the ground upon which the prison is erected, formerly the site of that which it has superseded, is so steep that much excavation and levelling will be necessary to obtain convenient airing yards at the back of the prison which will be safe against escape, and not overlooked from the surrounding country. This was in progress at the time of my visit and **was being carried on entirely by prisoners, some of whom were also employed, in a manner less to be commended, without the walls of the prison. Granting the desirableness of saving the county the expense of hired labour in the performance of works on the exterior of the prison, I cannot admit the propriety of the practice of taking out the prisoners for that purpose, whatever may be the care and discrimination with which they are selected for the duty.***

1865:[28]   *It is needless to say that no alteration has been necessary either in the buildings or the discipline.*

The new gaol was built of local stone *(Gaol Quarry)* until it was exhausted. Additional material was bought by tender. It had been suggested that stone from the old buildings should be reused in the new buildings to save money but this idea proved impractical because of the poor quality of the stone recovered. The old gaol was finally removed by a contractor at a cost of £50. Labour was not a problem as quarrying just became another form of hard labour. Perhaps the prisoners enjoyed the new task as it gave them the opportunity to work outside the prison.

Plan of H. M. Prison, Bodmin from the Sale Document, 1929.

Description of gaol (1929)

No original plans of the site have been found but there is general agreement that the gaol buildings changed very little between 1860 and the sale in 1929. The sale documents, prepared by Messrs. D. Ward and Son of Plymouth,[29] contain a full plan of the gaol, the adjoining properties and a detailed description of each of the buildings on the site.

From the plan, the gaol consisted of the following buildings. The main civil prison block contained four separate sections: offices, prison administration and chapel; male prison; female prison; and laundry. The Naval Prison block was joined to the main block at the first and second floor levels. A building, linked to the Naval Prison by covered walkway on the first floor, contained: store rooms; offices and naval administration; and a naval infirmary. The kitchen, mill and workroom block of the civil prison. A kitchen and laundry attached to the Naval Prison. The main gateway and staff quarters, stables and the execution shed. Two houses for the Naval Officers. The houses for the Governor and Chaplain were outside the prison. The sale document contained the following details of the buildings.

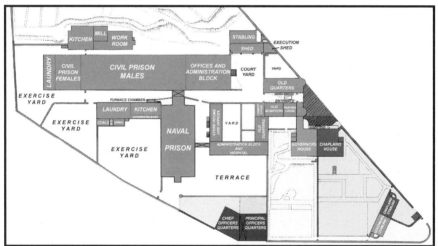

Plan of the Gaol Buildings 1929.

Main Gateway and Staff Quarters

This building formed the main entrance to the gaol and is still in use today. Through the archway can be seen the original double storey staff quarters, which were removed after the sale in 1930. Opposite these quarters is a similar block, which contained the gatekeepers lodge and more staff quarters, which is still in use.

Originally the area between the two sets of quarters was kept secure by two sets of gates.

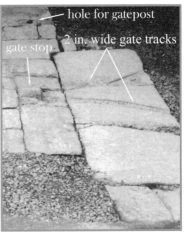

The outside gates are shown in the adjacent photograph. The other pair of gates, at the end of the two staff blocks, was made of iron. It is believed locally that these gates were sold and used at the Apex Garage in Scorrier but those gates were very ornate for a Victorian prison. The gates at the garage have been reported to come from Tehidy, Cornwall and not Bodmin Gaol.[30] Recently, the site of the inner gates has been unearthed. The gates were 48in. wide and each had a 2in. wheel or roller to enable easier opening and closing.

(F.G.Stone Collection)

hole for gatepost

2 in. wide gate tracks

gate stop

The Main Block (Administration section)

This was the largest building on the site. Viewed from the gatehouse the first part of the block was used for administration and offices on the ground/first floor. Above this was the chapel and on the third floor were storage space and

the access to the turret. There was also a large basement, which extended under the male prison. In the link between the administration section and the male prison on the ground/first floor was the large condemned cell with the iron gates.

(F.G.Stone Collection)

(F.G.Stone Collection)

The Main Block (Male Civil Prison)

(F.G.Stone Collection)

The prison was on four floors. The ground floor area was 6,700 square feet. The lowest floor contained offices, bathrooms, a kitchen etc. together with 16 cells and a punishment cell fitted with iron gates. The ground/first floor contained 31 cells and the top two floors, each had 33 cells. These floors had slate slab galleries supported on steel girders and protected by iron railings. The floors were connected by two circular stone stairways. All the cell doors were 6ft 3in x 2ft 3in and 2½ inches thick. They were lined internally with iron. This part of the prison had a total of 114 cells. There was a lift to take food from the basement to the cells.

There is an extra area below ground which contained the heating and ventilation system and coal storage areas.

The Main Block (Female Prison)

The third section of the main block was for women prisoners. In general, it was similar to the male prison. It was on four floors and had galleries on the top two floors and the same size cells. There were 31 cells, arranged with seven on the lowest floor and eight on each of the other three floors. The ground floor area was 2,000 square feet.

The Main Block (Laundry)

This was a single storey with a floor area of 700 square feet. It contained five washing cubicles, each fitted with washing trays and water supply and a bathroom with a boiler.

Kitchen, Mill and Workroom

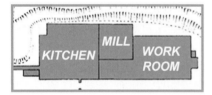

The kitchen covered an area of 810 square feet had a 60ft high chimney stack and was fitted with skylights. The workroom and mill, area 1,400 square feet, had wooden flooring and a lavatory.

Naval Prison Block

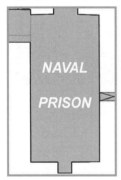

The 1929 sale document describes the Naval Prison as having five floors with a ground floor area of 4,600 square feet. The ground floor had 18 cells (13 feet x 7 feet), the first floor 21 cells and a gallery of slate slabs, supported on iron beams and protected with iron railings. The second, third and fourth floors each with 22 cells.

Naval Administration Block and Infirmary

The building was approached from the Naval Prison by overhead passage and covered an area of 2,150 square feet. It had three floors and a large basement. These premises were connected to store rooms and offices covering an area of 825 square feet, which together formed two sides of an enclosed yard.

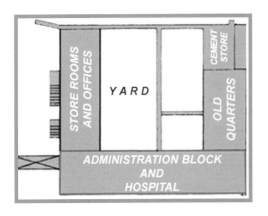

Kitchen and Laundry (Naval Prison)

This block connected to the Naval Prison contained: kitchen, floor area 900 square feet, with slate flooring; two bathrooms and a laundry, area 1,100 square feet, which contained copper furnace and boiler. The picture also shows the coal store.

Naval Officers Houses, Governor's House and Chaplaincy

Two villas were built, before 1891, to house Officers of the Naval prison. In 1929, they were sold as private houses as were the Chaplaincy and the Governor's House. The properties are still privately owned.

Stables and Shed

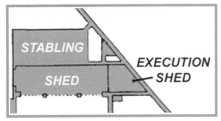

The stables contained six stalls with wooden partitions, mangers and iron racks, together with a hay loft and an open shed. Total floor area 950 square feet. In the 1890s, the right hand side of the shed was converted into an execution shed.

Bodmin Gaol, 1894.

(F.G.Stone Collection)

Bodmin Gaol, about 1900.

(F.G.Stone Collection)

Changes to the Buildings between 1860 and 1929

In addition to the detailed description of the buildings in 1929, there are photographs dating from the turn of the twentieth century, which show most of the main buildings and the walls. The details are generally consistent with the later plan. From various sources, a number of changes to the buildings between the 1860s and the sale in 1929 have been identified.

To conform with the rules of the 1865 Gaol Act, a new treadwheel house was built in part of the garden (1868).

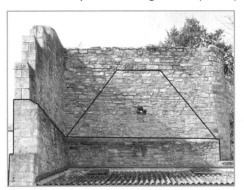

In 1882/3, the male officers quarters, later called the 'old quarters', were separated from the prison by a new boundary wall with a second set of gates. It has recently been realised that two sections of the new wall were, in fact, part of the quarters, the remainder of the North-South section of the 'L' shaped building was demolished. The photograph shows the original walls of the building and the approximate position of part of the roof line. The work was done by the prisoners and had advantages to the prison officers and their families, they were now outside the prison and the double gate system increased security.[31]

An Act of Parliament of 1868 ruled that executions *'must be screened from the public'*. In 1897, part of the shed in front of the stables, used for carts, was converted into a new private execution area.[32]

The 1901 Commissioners of Prisoners report[33] states *'The steam boilers and cooking apparatus in the old kitchen have been removed, the floors and walls repaired, and the whole place whitewashed and painted.'* This means that the new kitchen, shown on the sale document, had been built in the extended treadwheel house, probably after the treadwheel went out of use in 1899.

The major change in the buildings and their use was the transfer of two of the main blocks from the County Gaol to the Admiralty. The number of prisoners in the gaol had been falling and the gaol had occasionally been used to house naval prisoners from about 1855. The numbers increased after 1873 and in 1887, two prison blocks, which had been previously used to house female prisoners and debtors, were handed over to form H.M. Naval Prison, Bodmin. This change resulted in the building of new walls to separate the two prisons. The only facility used by both the naval and civil prisons was the chapel.

Other changes in the Civil prison included: Female prisoners were moved to the end of the male prison and a new internal wall was build to give complete separation between the men and women; The male washhouse at the end of the main block was converted into a new laundry and drying room for the females.

Extensive changes were required to form the new naval prison in 1887.

The Debtors prison, which originally also contained both female and male staff quarters, was joined to the main naval block by a bridge, and converted into store-rooms, offices, administration and an infirmary. Part of the original laundry building was converted into a kitchen. A new naval prison entrance was built with accommodation for two officers and their families. This building was later referred to as the *'naval villas'*.

A photograph, which is dated ca.1901, shows the building of an extension on the southern end of the naval block. The poor quality picture shows scaffolding, many pieces of stone, a ladder and a man building a new wall. It would suggest that the extension was built with the granite quoins being removed from the main building as the wall was increased. The quoins were then used to 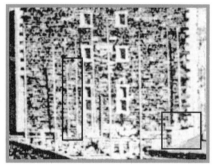 make the corners of the extension. The outside shell was built and secured before the original end wall was removed. By this strategy the prisoners could remain inside a secure building.

Changes in Number of Cells between 1860 and 1929

The change in use of the buildings is reflected in an analysis of the Certified numbers and uses of the prison cells.

Number of Certified Cells in each Section of the Gaol													
	Males				**Females**				Civil Total	Naval Total	Total Cells	Ref.
Year	Cells	Punish.	Recept.	Total	Cells	Punish.	Recept.	Total				
Planned:												
1855	150	6	?	**156+**	50	2	?	**52+**	**208+**		**208+**	*34*
New County Gaol:												
1866	141	6	7	154	59	2	5	66	**220**		**220**	*28*
1877	141	6	7	154	59	2	5	66	**220**		**220**	*35*
HM Prison:												
1878				152				61	**213**		**213**	*36*
1884				150				59	**209**		**209**	*37*
1884				146				59	**205**		**205**	*37*
HM Prison & HM Naval Prison:												
1889									**129**	75	**204**	*38*
1901				106				14	**120**	(75)	**195**	*33*
1916				105				14	**119**	105	**224**	*39*
After Closure:												
1929				114				31	**145**	105	**250**	*29*

The original plan for the gaol was for 200 cells of which 50 were for females and an additional 8 punishment cells (6M and 2F). When the gaol was completed, the total number of cells had increased to 220 by the addition of 12 reception cells. This is the number of Certified cells for criminals. The Debtors' Prison, which is not contained in the above Table, consisted of 20 male sleeping rooms, 5 female rooms and 4 day-rooms, two for each sex.

The data from the 31st Report on Prisons (1866) gives the most detailed accommodation data: 141 male cells, 59 female cells, 8 (6M + 2F) punishment cells and 12 (7M & 5F) reception cells. These numbers are also included in the 39th Report (1875)[40] and the 42nd Report of 1878.[35]

The number of Certified cells gradually reduced after Nationalisation in 1878[36,37] and by 1884, the total cell number had reduced from 220 to 205, that is, 146 male and 59 female cells. The establishment of the Naval Prison had little effect on the total number of cells, in 1889 there were 129 civil cells and 75 for naval personnel. A total of 204.[38]

The civil prison continued to reduce its capacity. By 1901,[33] there were only 120 cells, including 14 for female prisoners. At the same time, an addition of 29 or 30 new cells was being provided in an extension to the naval block.

When the gaol was sold the number of cells in the civil block was reported as 114 cells for males and 31 cells for females, a total of 145. The Naval prison contained 105 cells, giving the total number of cells in both prisons as 250. Excluding the naval extension, the cell number is 220, identical to the earlier years. However, the capacity of the civil prison had been reduced by 15 cells between 1877 and 1884 and a further 10 cells from 1889 to 1916. It would appear that cells, which could include reception and punishment cells in both the male and female sections of the prison, went out of use and must have been closed or used as work-rooms or for other purposes.

In the Commissioners of Prison Report for 1901, under the heading of 'accommodation for prisoners' it is reported that there are 5 rooms, 4 for males and one for females, and in 1916, three rooms (2M & 1F). The nature and use of these rooms is not reported.

The plans for the gaol have not been found but from the 1929 Sale plan, two block plans, dated 1884, prepared by the Admiralty for the Naval Prison and the several reports of building changes listed above, it is possible to speculate on the layout and use of the buildings on different dates. The following plans are proposed for the gaol (a) when it was completed in the early 1860s and (b) in the late 1880s, after the establishment of the naval prison and the building of the new inner boundary wall and gates.

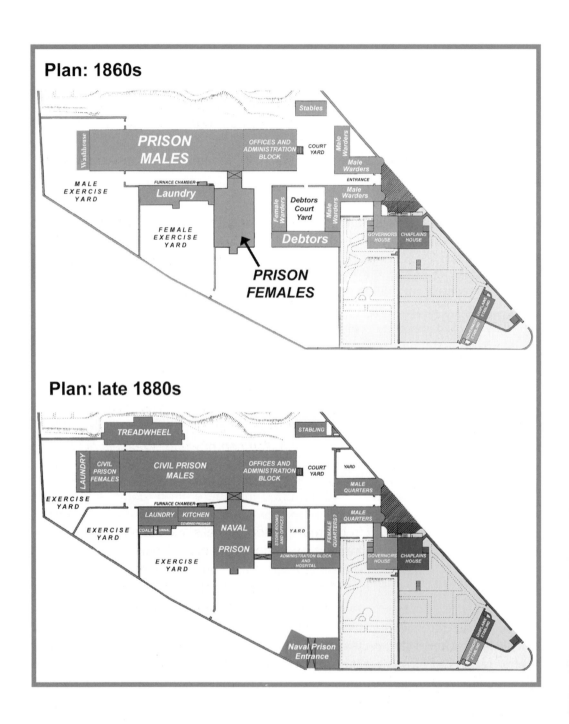

Plan: 1860s

Stables

Washhouse

PRISON
MALES

OFFICES AND
ADMINISTRATION
BLOCK

COURT
YARD

Male Warders

Male
Warders

ENTRANCE

MALE
EXERCISE
YARD

FURNACE CHAMBER

Laundry

Female Warders

Debtors
Court
Yard

Male
Warders

Male Warders

FEMALE
EXERCISE
YARD

Debtors

GOVERNORS
HOUSE

CHAPLAINS
HOUSE

*PRISON
FEMALES*

CHAPLAINS
STABLING

Plan: late 1880s

TREADWHEEL

STABLING

LAUNDRY

CIVIL
PRISON
FEMALES

CIVIL PRISON
MALES

OFFICES AND
ADMINISTRATION
BLOCK

COURT
YARD

YARD

MALE
QUARTERS

EXERCISE
YARD

FURNACE CHAMBER

LAUNDRY

KITCHEN

COVERED PASSAGE

MALE
QUARTERS?

EXERCISE
YARD

COALS

URINAL

NAVAL

STORE ROOMS
AND OFFICES

YARD

FEMALE
QUARTERS?

EXERCISE
YARD

PRISON

ADMINISTRATION BLOCK
AND
HOSPITAL

GOVERNORS
HOUSE

CHAPLAINS
HOUSE

Naval Prison
Entrance

CHAPLAINS
STABLING

CHAPTER 5

Inside the Buildings

The 33rd Report of the Inspectors of Prisons (1868)[41] contains the following comment on the physical conditions in the gaol: *'All the certified cells for criminals are warmed and ventilated, and all cells, occupied by criminal prisoners except punishment cells, are lighted with gas. All the cells are furnished with bells.'* This comment had led to research into the building services and physical conditions, required by law, for housing prisoners in the gaol.

The Cells

To be certified, a cell had to be of a certain size. The average size of cells at Bodmin was 13 ft long x 7ft wide. All the doors were 6ft 3in x 2ft 3in x 2½in thick, lined internally with iron sheets. The sleeping rooms in the Debtors prison were not certified as cells because of size. They could not be used even when they were transferred to the Navy. Each cell contained two small corner shelves on the outside wall. There was a list of the allowed contents in a cell. In 1901, it contained the following items: *Bed with wooden slats and mattress. Pillow with slip, sheets, blankets and coverlet rolled-up. Books, including Bible, Prayer book, Hymn book and other allowed books, for example, 'Pilgrim's Progress' by Bunyan or 'The Newcomes' by Thackeray. Wooden stool. Mirror. 1 gallon can of water. Washing bowl. Slop pot. A salt cellar. Wooden spoon. Cleaning rags for shining-up the metal vessels. Very small hand brush for sweeping. Copy of gaol regulations on a board.*

Lighting

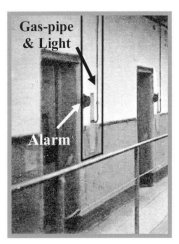

In the male prison, all cells, except punishment cells, were lit by a gas light placed outside each cell. A thick piece of glass prevented the prisoner from interfering with the light. The shape of the '*light window*' was tall and narrow. Punishment cells had no lighting, except for the window. A different system was used in the original women's prison, either they were allowed candles or the gas lights were inside the cells.

Outside each cell was a device, which could be activated by a prisoner requiring assistance. By pulling a rope or lever inside the cell, a bell would ring and an indicator arm would be raised.

The Lower Ground Floor

There were several different types of rooms and cells on this level. This floor contained *reception cells,* where the new prisoners stayed until they were processed and examined by the surgeon; they were later transferred to the main cell block and *punishment cells*, with no gas lighting and one or more padded cells. There were three *bathrooms* of which one or two have been identified. These were the only bathrooms in the male block.

Opposite the food-lift and staircase was a *Warder's room*. This feature is present on all floors of the block. It enables one warder to control access to the stairs, lift and the cross corridor, which separated prisoners and cells from services.

On the east of the cross corridor was the *kitchen,* with its connected *scullery* and the kitchen *store* opposite. The remainder of this section consisted of offices and store rooms.

While attempting to identify the function of various rooms, it was realised that a double cell and two other 'cells' had a special function. The rooms (A & B), which had normal cell doors, contained large square windows and no gas lighting. There is a connecting door-way between the double cell and 'Cell A'. 'Cell B', contains an outside door. These facts suggest that these rooms are a *condemned cell suite*.

The door-way between Cell A and the double cell was the 'secret door', usual covered by a wardrobe, which would be the route the prisoner was taken to be executed. He would cross the floor, it is not known whether there were additional walls or features between 'A' and 'B', out through the door in 'B', past the female prison to the 'drop' on the south wall.

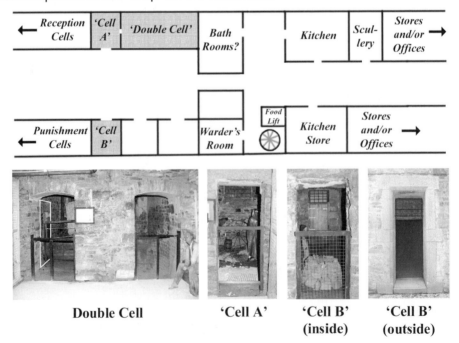

Double Cell   'Cell A'   'Cell B'   'Cell B'
                                        (inside)   (outside)

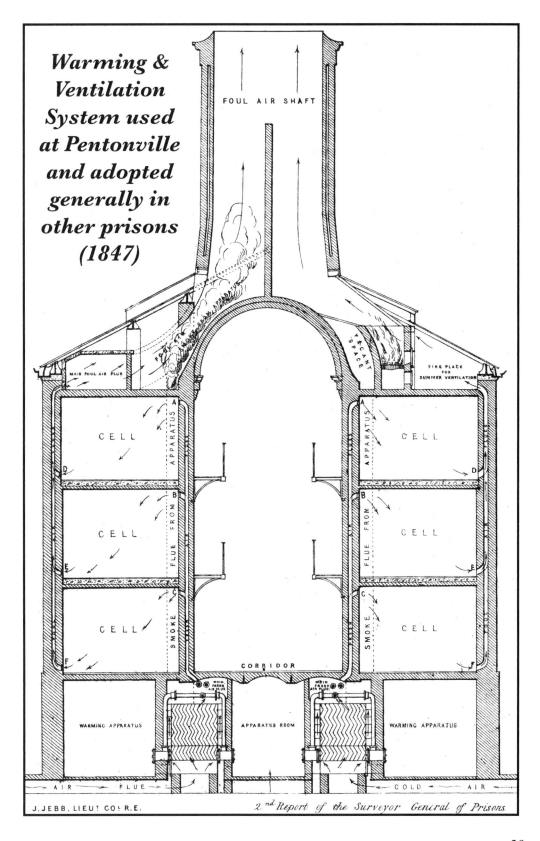

Warming & Ventilation System used at Pentonville and adopted generally in other prisons (1847)

FOUL AIR SHAFT

MAIN FOUL AIR FLUE

VACANT SPACE

FIRE PLACE FOR SUMMER VENTILATION

CELL

APPARATUS

CELL

A

FLUE FROM

CELL

B

FLUE FROM

SMOKE

CELL

C

SMOKE

D

E

F

CELL

CELL

CELL

APPARATUS

A

B

C

D

E

F

CORRIDOR

MAIN FRESH AIR FLUE

MAIN FRESH AIR FLUE

WARMING APPARATUS

APPARATUS ROOM

WARMING APPARATUS

AIR FLUE

COLD AIR

J. JEBB, LIEUT COL R.E.

2nd Report of the Surveyor General of Prisons

39

Warming and Ventilation

It is a little surprising to find that prisons in the early 1840s were built with heating and ventilation systems which kept the temperature in every cell between 12 and 15° C both in the Winter and Summer. The system, later used in many prisons including Bodmin, was pioneered in Pentonville prison,[42] built around 1843.

The heating was provided by cold air travelling between the inner and outer cases of a hot-air stove, which was placed in the basement of the building. The warmed air was then distributed to every cell by ducts inside the cell walls. Stale air was removed by ducts in the outside walls of the cells into the plenum tower. Each cell also contained a fresh air inlet. In Summer, the stove would not be used but a fire would be made in a fire-room in the roof of the building which would draw outside air though each cell and out via the tower.

The warming system for the main Male block at Bodmin, build 1859, is a variation on the Pentonville system. Only one stove was used and the cold air inlets were much larger that those at Pentonville. At Bodmin the cold air came from the two 'rooms' on either side of the stove, whereas at Pentonville, the air entered though a small under floor duct. In both systems, the air entered below the stoves.

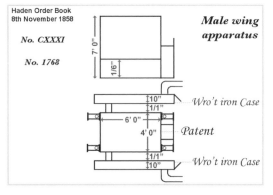

The adjacent diagram, dated 8th November, 1858, copied from the Order Book of Hadens of Trowbridge,[43] shows the details of the main male-block heating system at Bodmin. The stove was 7' high, ca. 8' wide and deep. Details of the Haden's *Patent* referred to on the drawing are shown in *Appendix 2*.

Identified Features of the System at Bodmin

The stove room is in the basement of the building. It is at the end of a corridor which contains other rooms, some of which have chutes to the outside. These rooms are now believed to be coal store areas. The dimensions of the room and the stove, suggest that it would have been in the centre of the room with an area in front for charging the stove with coal and removing the ashes. The room itself contains other features, arches at the floor level (air inlets), and two large hot air outlets, which would have been connected to the brickwork containing the stove. There are two other features which could be for smoke and coal.

Above: Left-hand side of Stove room
Above Centre: Right-hand side hot Air Outlet
Right: Coal shute?

Top: Smoke pipe going through wall to flue.
Bottom: Inspection hatch in corridor showing the smoke flue.

The two warm-air ducts from the basement continued to the ceiling of the floor above. This was the main floor of the building and contained many ducts, which transferred the hot-air to individual cells. The photograph shows the thickness of this floor and its similarity to a Roman hypocaust system.

Each cell contained three vents, the warm-air inlet above the door, the stale-air outlet on the ground under the window and a fresh-air vent. The fresh air vent was constructed with the grill in the cell above the outside grill. This prevented prisoners seeing or passing small objects to people on the outside. In the Pentonville plan, the vent was covered by a wooden slide which could be adjusted by the prisoner but in Bodmin an adjustable metal vent was used.

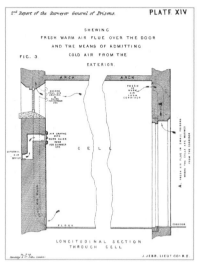

Warm-air Inlet

Fresh-air Inlet

Stale-air Outlet

The system of bringing the warm-air at the top of the cell and taking the cooler air out at the bottom appears to be inefficient; however, the Victorians had their reasons. They are stated in the 2nd Report of the Surveyor General on the Construction of Prisons (1847):[42] *Among other reasons, it may be stated that the effect of introducing the air at a low level would be, that when the fires were not lighted, the prisoner would be sensible of the draught of cold air, and would devise some means of stopping up the grating; and during the cold weather, when the air would be warmed, he would probably sit or lie down close to it, and be enervated by its effects.*

The above description covers only one of the four Haden warming systems in the gaol. The Chapel, Women's Prison and one other (Debtors' Prison?) are also found in the Haden Order Books. [43-44]

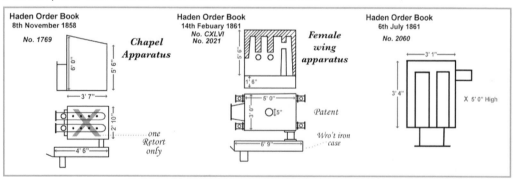

Although the drawings are all different, two are related to the same 'Patent' equipment.[45] The Chapel Apparatus is a different *'Early Form of Steam Apparatus'*, in which steam from a boiler is condensed in a retort. The heat from the retort is transferred to the cold air which goes over its surface.[46]

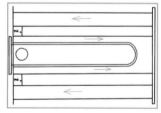

There is no information on the fourth system.

CHAPTER 6

Position of the Old Gaol

Although the old gaol was built on the same site as the new gaol, its position in relation to the later buildings is not recorded. In an attempt to position the original buildings the following documents have been used:

1. Ground plan of gaol from the Call Engraving (page 18).[9] This plan is to scale.
2. Bodmin Town and Bodmin Borough Tithe maps, 1840.[21] Hand drawn buildings.
3. 'Plan and Sections of the proposed Alteration of Roads for the enlargement of the County Gaol, Bodmin, Cornwall'.[47a,b] Architect's drawing.
4. Ordinance Survey map, 1881.[48] This map contains only the outline of the boundary of the gaol.
5. The Sale Document plan, 1929.[29] Architect's drawing (page 27).
6. Ordinance Survey map,1970.[49]

Documents 1 to 5 were digitised, edited, scaled and overlaid. The gaol boundary walls on the documents 4, 5 and 6 are identical. The walls had not changed from before 1881 until many years after the gaol was closed. It is possible that the walls shown in the 1881 plan are the original 1859 walls as the 1853 document is only a proposal and not an agreed plan.

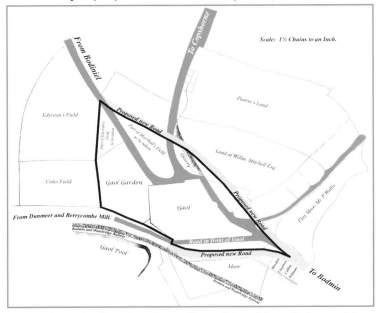

Document 3 (1853): Showing the outline of the old gaol, the position of the old roads (dark grey), proposed new roads (light grey) and the new wall (black).

The key step in finding the site of the old gaol was to fix the position of *'the road in front of the gaol'* onto the 1929 document and to confirm that the *'Proposed new road'* was in the same place in 1853 and 1929.

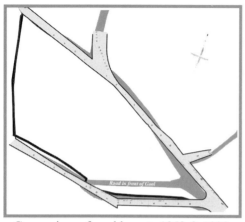

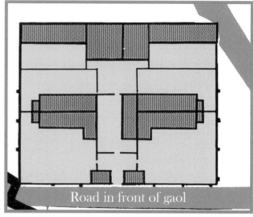

Comparison of road layouts 1853 & 1929.   Old gaol overlaid onto the 1853 plan.

The new roads show some differences to the original proposals. The main change is in the curved corner at the bottom right of the diagram in place of the strange pointed feature. Bodiniel Road is straighter than in the proposal but the junctions are in the same places. This overlay now allows the *'road in front of the gaol',* and therefore the old gaol, to be fixed onto the 1929 sale document plan. In addition, the 1779 gaol, which was 172 ft wide by 144 ft, fits the 1853 road plan, including the small portion which extends into the road. Both of these plans are to scale.

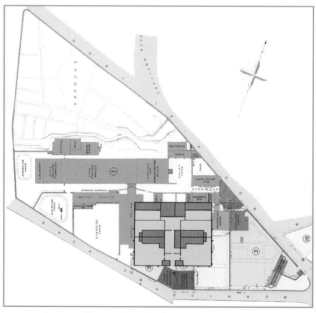

The diagram above shows both the position of the old gaol on the 1929 sale plan and the great increase in the gaol area between 1779 and 1929.

The Position of the Original Gaol

EXECUTION SHED

OLD QUARTERS

YARD

STABLING

SHED

COURT YARD

OFFICES AND ADMINISTRATION BLOCK

CIVIL PRISON MALES

WORK ROOM

MILL

KITCHEN

CIVIL PRISON FEMALES

LAUNDRY

EXERCISE YARD

EXERCISE YARD

EXERCISE YARD

FURNACE CHAMBER

LAUNDRY

KITCHEN

COALS

W.C.

URINAL

COVERED PASSAGE

EXERCISE YARD

WEIGH BRIDGE

ENTRANCE

OLD PORTERS LODGE

CEMENT STORE

OLD QUAR...

STO...ROOMS

AD...NISTRATION BLOCK

ADMINISTRATION AND HOSPITAL

NAVAL PRISON

GOVERNORS HOUSE

CHAPLAINS HOUSE

GOVERNORS STABLING

CHAPLAINS STABLING

PRINCIPAL OFFICERS QUARTERS

CHIEF OFFICERS QUARTERS

This diagram is an edited version of the previous overlay.

It shows the buildings and walls of the old gaol in relationship to the buildings present in 1929.

The Position of the Extended Gaol

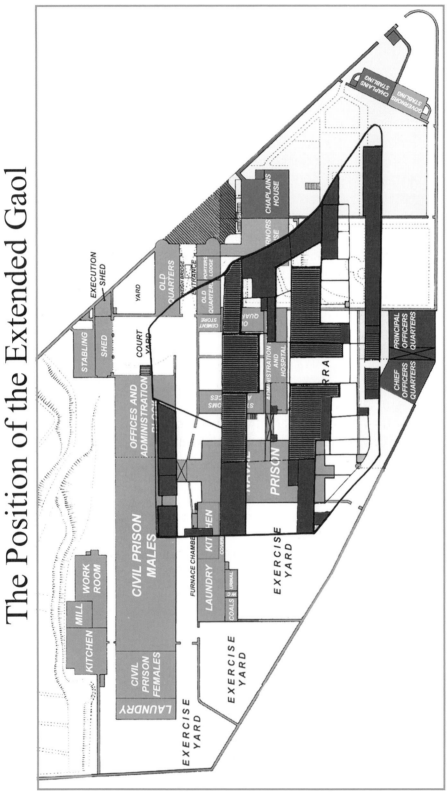

This diagram shows the approximate position of the 1840 extended gaol in relationship to the 1929 buildings (not scaled)

CHAPTER 7

English Gaol Administration

For most of the eighteenth century no one cared very much about what happened to felons. Many were hanged, thrown into dungeons or transported to work in the American plantations. The American War of Independence (1778 - 1783) put an end to the transportation and the government had to provide accommodation for about 1,000 convicts per year. The simple solution was to house the convicts in the ships previously used as transports. They were moored in places like Portsmouth, Chatham and London and the prisoners were employed on local public works. Planned as a temporary measure, the use of prison hulks lasted until 1858. The Government's stated intention was to build new prisons and there was much discussion of the reformist ideas of Howard after the publication of his book in 1777. Some of the Howard principles were included in Sir William Blackstone's Penitentiary Act of 1779,[50] and the further Acts of 1782 and 1784.[51,52] These Acts all failed as there were no new prisons built and the old places of detention were in no state to be converted into the new Howard type establishments. The Prison Act of 1791,[53] which stated that the principles of cellular confinement and enforced silence, both mentioned in the earlier Acts, should apply to all prisons. However, the Act was not compulsory and no inspection system was initiated. This Act was largely ignored. From 1791 to 1815 the country was too involved in the Napoleonic Wars to worry about convicts. The hulks were still in use and, after 1787, convicts were now transported to Australia. These solutions to the prisoner problem were much cheaper than building expensive new prisons.

After the war, with an increasing gaol population, conditions in gaols moved higher up the agenda. In 1815,[54] all prison fees were abolished and exacting money from prisoners became a penal offence but there was no inspection to see that the new measures were effective. In 1823 Peel, then Home Secretary, introduced and passed the 'The Gaol Act'.[55] This was largely a consolidating act, reaffirming the four Howard principles which had previously been enacted and neglected in 1779 and 1791:

1. Provision of secure, roomy and sanitary prisons.
2. Change gaoler from profit-maker into a salaried public servant.
3. Subjection of prisoners to a reformatory regime of diet, work and religious exercises.
4. Systematic inspection of the prison by outside public authority.

The objectives of the Act were 'effectively to preserve the health and improve the morals of the prisoners as well as to ensure the proper punishment to convicted offenders'.

The Act included the following Rules and Regulations:

i)   The male & female prisoners shall be confined in separate buildings, so as to prevent them from seeing or conversing with each other.

ii) The prisoners of each sex shall be divided into distinct classes, care being taken that when at labour they only associate with other members of the same class:

In Gaols:

1st	Debtors / contempt of court or civil process
2nd	Convicted of Felony
3rd	Convicted of Misdemeanours
4th	Charged with Felony
5th	Charged with Misdemeanours or for Want of Sureties

In Houses of Correction (formerly Bridewells):

1st	Convicted of Felony
2nd	Convicted of Misdemeanours
3rd	Charged with Felony
4th	Charged with Misdemeanours
5th	Vagrants

These are the same classifications, which were used in the design of the Bodmin Gaol, with the addition of vagrants and the separation of prisoners charged with a crime and those convicted.

iii) Female supervision of female prisoners

iv) Gaolers, surgeons and chaplains must inspect the prison at regular intervals, keep records and to present them to the justices at the Quarter Sessions. The justices must then report to the Home Secretary

v)   Dietaries.

This Act only applied to prisons under the control of the justices. Some 150 others, used largely for the confinement of debtors, were unaffected. The main weakness of the Act was that there was no provision for inspectors. The Home Office demanded of the justices a certain standard but the only reports required by law were from the justices themselves.

In a further attempt to get uniformity of punishments and conditions in all gaols, a further Act was passed in 1835,[56] which allowed the appointment of five *'Inspectors of Prisons'*, who visited all gaols and reported directly to the government. The inspectors were allowed to give advice to the local authorities but they had no power to enforce the provisions of Peel's 1823 Act.

From about this time, there was a tendency toward the 'separate system', not only for different types of prisoners but for individuals. The idea was that a prisoner was confined to a cell, which was his workshop by day and his bedroom by night. This prevented prisoners talking, or even being recognised by each other. It was believed that continuous solitude would result in the reformation of the prisoner but in practice it often resulted in the prisoner's insanity. The Prisons Act of 1839 [57] provided for *'individual separation of prisoners during the whole or*

48

any part of their imprisonment and that this separation shall not be deemed solitary confinement.'

In 1863, deficiencies in the local administration of gaols were catalogued by a Select Committee of the House of Lords. This led to the Prison Act of 1865,[58] which was the last great measure for penal administration while the prisons were under local control. The Act, which covered all aspects of prison life, contains 82 clauses and three Schedules containing a further 104 regulations, a list of prisons to be closed and a list of 18 Acts to be wholly or partially repealed, including those mentioned above. It was the final attempt by central government to unify the prison system and included the following provisions:-

i)   All difference between gaols & houses of correction *(formerly bridewells used for Misdemeanours)* were abolished.

ii) Justices still retained control but now under strict control from headquarters.

iii) Justices must build prisons according to government plans.

iv) Penal labour must be in defined form.

v)   Dietaries must be submitted to the Home Office.

vi) New code of prison regulations.

vii) New classifications for Hard Labour class 1 and 2.

viii) Government powers to close inadequate local gaols. *(For Cornwall, this meant the closure of the local gaols in Falmouth, Penzance and Helstone by the 1st February, 1866.)* [28]

ix) Every local prison should have separate cells equal to the average greatest number of prisoners held at any time in the previous five years.

Four years later an Act to abolish prison for debtors was passed.[59] This Act came into operation on the same day as the 'Bankruptcy Act 1869'.[60] Debtors could still go to prison for defaulting on a court settlement or for fraud in a bankruptcy settlement. Leaving England with over £20 after being declared bankrupt was a felony carrying a sentence of two years. Before this Act, creditors could have their debtors imprisoned under 'The Lords' Act of 1759' and should have provided the debtor with 4d. per day allowance (groats) but this was rarely paid.

Even with all the above Acts of Parliament, the government was still not convinced that a truly uniform prison system existed in England. So they enacted the 1877 Prison Act [61] which resulted in the total nationalisation of the prison system and transferred all aspects of prison administration, including the costs, to the Secretary of State and the Prison Commissioners from the local justices. Bodmin Gaol ceased to be the County Gaol and became H.M. Prison, Bodmin.

The final Act of Parliament enacted during the life-time of the gaol, was the Prison Act of 1898.[62] In addition to changes in the employment of prisoners, a new classification of prisoners was introduced. This consisted of three divisions and was intended to prevent contamination of low level prisoners by 'those who are depraved or of criminal habits':

First Division: Intended for strictly limited classes of prisoners, for example, those committed of contempt of court or offences loosely described as 'political'. This division was non-punitive and as reasonably comfortable that the conditions of prison life and discipline would allow.

Second Division: For prisoners, who in the opinion of the court should be separated from hardened criminals.

Third Division: All prisoners who were not in the above divisions.

Unlike earlier Acts, the work and general treatment of the prisoners in the 2nd and 3rd Divisions were identical.

Against the national background of no new prison buildings and the use of hulks and transportation, the Justices in Cornwall, had totally accepted Howard's reforms and had built the new gaol in Bodmin to his designs. The gaol was probably the only prison which was able to comply with the Acts of Parliament and all the government's stated ideals up to the start of the nineteenth century. Later, the Justices enforced all the Acts of Parliament. After the Peel Act, they planned the big expansion of the gaol to allow the 'separation system' to be implemented and issued new Rules & Regulations from the Act. Changes in the treatment of prisoners including employment, diets, prison offences and punishments always resulted after new legislation.

There was always a conflict between the Government, which wanted uniformity in the treatment of prisoners nationally and the Justices and tax-payers in local areas, who actually paid for all aspects of their local prisons, including the buildings, staffing and the maintenance of the prisoners.

Recently a document has been donated to Bodmin Town Museum entitled, ***'Regulations and Rules for the Government of the Gaol and House of Correction for the County of Cornwall at Bodmin, 1867'.***[63] This document, reproduced in *Appendix* 3, was prepared by the Quarter Sessions Justices and contained new rules for the management and treatment of prisoners. All these new Rules & Regulations had to conform to the new *'Prison Act'* passed by the Government in 1865. To confirm that the local justices had arrived at the 'right answer', the final document was sent to Whitehall to be approved and signed by the Home Secretary, Gathorne Hardy. Copies were then issued to all members of staff, initialled by the Governor, H G Colvill.

Although this appears to be a document issued by the local justices it was in fact dictated totally by the Home Secretary!

CHAPTER 8

Courts, Crimes and Sentences

In the early 19th century, before the police force was formed in 1856, any person suspected of a crime was taken by the parish constable or the person who caught the suspect to the magistrate. He could:

(a) discharge the suspect, if he believed that there was no case to answer.

(b) If it was a minor offence, for example, poaching or vagrancy, he could be summarily tried on the spot by the magistrate and sent to gaol, or he could be sent to the Petty Sessions, a court consisting of two magistrates with no jury.

(c) If the magistrate thought that the offence was indictable, the prisoner would be sent to gaol until the next Quarter Sessions and tried by a bench of magistrates and a jury or, for the most serious crimes, before a judge and jury at the Assizes.

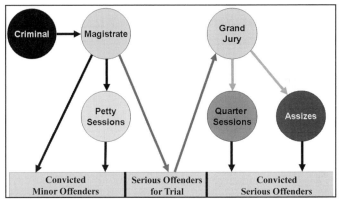

This system resulted in several different classes of criminal prisoners being housed in the local gaol.

Petty Sessions

The Petty Sessions, later known as the Magistrates Court, was the Court which handled minor crimes. The crimes prosecuted in this court included, vagrancy, common assault, trespass, drunkenness, poaching and breaches of the licensing and bye-laws.

A transcript from two volumes of *'Bodmin Borough Justices – Minutes'* has recently been produced.[64] The books cover Bodmin Borough Magistrates cases from March 1885 to April 1901. They contain 950+ criminal cases, excluding licensing applications and cases involving the non-payment of the Poor Rate, an average of ~60 per year.

There were many different types of crime tried by the Justices. The most

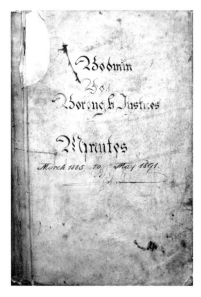

frequent being Drunkenness & Vagrancy, including related crimes of begging, living-rough, prostitution & peddling without a license. Bodmin, being a garrison town, also had a significant number of Army offences such as Fraudulent Attestation, False Attestation and Absent without leave. The list includes several examples of: Assault; Fighting; Cruelty & neglect of wife and/or family; Trespass; Cruelty to animals; Allowing animals, cows, horses, etc., to stray and none payment of dog license. Less common offences included *'Leaving a locomotive on the highway'*, *'Damaging the bell at the Police Station'* and *'Riding a bicycle furiously'*.

Most of the sentences involved payment of a fine but over the sixteen years, the Court sentenced 164 people to gaol and 3 were committed 'until the next Quarter Sessions'. In addition, 30 were committed directly to gaol for being unable to pay fines (NPF), giving a total of 197. The sentences ranged from 2 to 30 days in gaol and 3 to 90 days at Hard Labour.

Offence	Male		Female		Total
	Gaol	NPF	Gaol	NPF	
Vagrancy/Begging	75	2	13		90
Army/Navy	31	3	0		34
Drunk (& Disorderly)	4	16	3	7	30
Neglect Fam.	10		5		15
Hawking/Peddling	7	1	1		9
Stealing	5		0		5
Trespass	2		0		2
Assault	1		0		1
Others	3		4	1	8
To QS	2		1		3
Total	**140**	**22**	**27**	**8**	**197**

The offences resulting in the longest sentences were: False attestation (4 cases: 2-3 months); Cruelty / neglect of family (3 cases: 6-8 weeks) and Stealing (1 case: 2 months).

Although the number of committals to gaol appears small for a period of 16 years, they only cover Bodmin Magistrates Court, just one of many similar courts in the county.

In 1908, there were 898 committals to the gaol this included 119 cases of non-payment of fines and 508 vagrants. Most of these prisoners came from the Magistrates' Courts throughout Cornwall.[65]

Quarter Sessions

The Quarter Sessions dealt with many different crimes. The following table lists both the indictable felonies and misdemeanours taken from QS records for 1812, 1822 and 1832 (see Appendix 4). The data for 1816 is from a court return [66] and the remainder (*) come from single 'Calendars of Prisoners'. [67-69]

The number of cases increased rapidly between 1812 and 1832. It remained high in the late 1860s but dropped markedly by 1903. The common feature of the list is the number of cases of Taking, later called stealing, which is

	1812	1816	1817*	1822	1832	1867*	1903*
Indictments:	26	32	19	66	152	43	12
Offences:							
Taking / Stealing	22	30	11	43	123	25	5
Assault	5		8	15	16	2	2
Disorderly House				4	1		
Poaching Game				1			
Receiving Goods				1		6	1
Disturbing peace				1			
Begging				1			
False Pretences		2			3	3	
Misdemeanor					3		
Breaking & Entering					3	5	
Embezzlement					2	1	
Criminal Damage					1		
Wounding						1	
Grievous Bodily Harm							1
Killing a Cow (Steal)							1
Maiming Mare							1
Incorrigible Rogue							1
Verdicts:							
Acquitted /No Bill	7	10		13	29	3	5
Guilty	19	22		52	123		7
% Found Guilty	*73*	*69*		*79*	*81*		*58*
Sentences:							
Fined	6			7	3		
Whipped					1		
Transported					13		
Inebriate Home (3yrs.)							1
County Asylum							1
Gaol	13	22		45	106		5
% of Guilty Gaoled	*68*	*100*		*86*	*86*		*71*

by far the main offence dealt with by the Quarter Sessions Court. Assault was the second most common offence, with all the other contributing occasional cases.

Between 58-81% of those indicted were found guilty and 68-100% of those convicted were returned to the gaol.

There are two groups of offenders not contained in the above figures; they are vagrants and the bastardy cases.

The Calendar for the Quarter Sessions, April 15th, 1817 contains nineteen Bastardy cases. This was a crime for men who had fathered an illegitimate child or women who would not name the father. They were imprisoned by the Magistrates until they could guarantee, by way of sureties, to indemnify the local parish for supporting the child. The Quarter Sessions Order books for the same Session, contain 'Bastardy Orders' but no names or details of the prisoners before the court. Similar entries are found for 1812, 1822 and 1832.

The same 1817 Calendar also contains 10 cases under the heading of Vagrancy. This offence was usually dealt with by the Petty Sessions but those appearing at the Quarter Sessions seem to be repeat or serious offenders. They were committed for the following reasons: being a rogue & vagabond & leaving his family chargeable to the Parish; under suspicion of stealing geese and not giving a satisfactory account of himself (3 males); lewd, idle, disorderly person, wandering in the Parish (3rd time); charged with being a common whore (3rd time); convicted of wandering and begging in the Parish; for Want of Sureties for her good behaviour; charged with having threatened to burn the Alms House of the Parish.

In 1812, five and in 1822, ten vagrants were brought before the Court from the Bridewell, thirteen were discharged by the Magistrates and 'sent to place of last legal settlement', one who was deemed to be a 'Rogue & Vagabond' was sentenced to one month at Hard Labour. A female vagrant was sentenced to one month solitary confinement.

Assizes

The Assizes dealt with the most serious crimes, which included arson, burglary, felony, fraud and murder. Typical examples of the crimes tried at the Assizes are contained in the 'Calendar of Prisoners for the Assizes'.

Details from several individual Calendars are compiled in the table.[70-75]

Date of Assizes	Mar 1794	Aug 1803	Aug 1829	Mar 1869	Nov 1905	1914	Oct 1915
Prisoners:	7	10	16	41	11	26	12
Charges:							
Murder & Infanticide	1	1		3	1	2	
Attempted Murder					1		
Manslaughter				1			
Wounding	1			1			3
Arson					3	1	1
Bigamy					2		
Disposal of dead baby				3		1	
Abortion					1		
Assault & Ravish			1	1		1	1
Intent to Rape (8 yr.old)			1				
Carnal Know. (under 16)						5	1
Buggery						1	
Stealing	3	1	6	26		5	
Breaking in & Stealing	1	4	6	3		3	1
Housebreaking					2		
Breaking Windows						3	
Receiving				1			
Uttering Counterfeit		1	1				
Embezzled Kings Stores		1					
Fraud		1				1	4
Embezzlement			1	1			
Forgery				1	1	1	
Stabbing Heifers		1					
Demanding Money						1	
False Statement						1	
Unlawful Assembly	1						
Verdicts:							
No Bill Found		2	1			2	
Ignoramus	2						
Acquitted	1				3	3	1
Discharged							
Guilty	4				8	18	
Sentences:							
Bound Over							5
Whipped	1						
Transported	1						
Sent to Asylum					1		
Death	2						
Gaol					7	18	3

The numbers of cases is smaller but similar to the Quarter Sessions, in that, there was an increase in cases up to the late 1860s and then a decline in the twentieth century. The three Calendars for 1914 contain a total of 26 cases, much less than the one Calendar for 1869.

With regard to the crimes, stealing was still a serious problem up to and including 1869 but in the later records there appears to be a more varied set of offences being tried by the Assize Courts. Offences against the person, for example, wounding, murder, carnal knowledge and fraud and arson. There is little information on sentences but from the small amount available, it would seem that crimes which led to the death penalty before 1840, now only resulted in a short gaol sentences or even being 'bound over'.

The Calendar for 23rd October, 1915, the last Assizes before the closure of the gaol, contains a list of twelve cases. The copy of this document held in Bodmin Town Museum, has been annotated with the outcome of the trials and the sentences.

No.	Name, Age and Trade.	Particulars of Offence	Sentence
		PRISONERS FOR TRIAL	
1	**George Martin,** 40, Soldier	At Falmouth, on the 3rd June, 1915, did feloniously forge a Banker's Cheque for the payment of £2 with intent to defraud. Also Committed:-	**Bound over for 12 months in £5.**
2	**Alfred Smith,** 38, Soldier	At Falmouth, on the 5th June, 1915, did feloniously forge a Banker's Cheque for the payment of £1-10-0 with intent to defraud.	**Bound over for 12 months in £5.**
3	**Stephen Henry Stratton,** 48, Soldier	At Trewen, on the 16th June, 1913, did feloniously marry Frances Caroline Allen, his former wife, Henrietta Rosetta, to whom he was previously married, being then alive.	**3 years Penal Servitude**
4	**Alfred Vellanoweth,** 16, Labourer	At Camborne, on the 25th June, 1915, did unlawfully assault with intent to feloniously ravish and carnally know, against her will, Olive Pearce.	**Bound over for 12 months in £5.**
5	**Frederick Taylor,** 25, Labourer	At Poundstock, on the 29th June, 1915, did feloniously set fire to a stack of oat and barley straw, the property of James Trathen.	
6	**William Alfred Bray,** 24, Labourer	At St. Stephens-in-Bramwell. on the 2nd July, 1915, did unlawfully and carnally know Hilda Ann Trethewey, she being a girl above the age of 13 years and under the age of 16 years.	**Not Guilty**
7	**Arthur Edward Heath,** 34, Agent	At Camborne on the 6th May, 1915, being entrusted by the National Amalgamated Approved Society with the sum of ten shillings for payment to Andrew Hocking, did unlawfully and fraudulently convert the sum of five shillings, part thereof, to his own use and benefit.	**Bound over for 12 months in £5.**
8	**William Brailsford,** 31, Miner	At Gwennap, on the 11th August, 1915, did feloniously and maliciously wound Albina Brailsford with intent to do her some grievous bodily harm.	**12 months**
9	**Annie Ethel Jenkin,** 21, Servant	At Bodmin, on the 22nd May, 1915 did feloniously, forge a cheque for £3 purporting to be signed by A. S. Lund and drawn on the Capital and Counties Bank, Bodmin, with intent to defraud.	**6 months (2nd Division)**
10	**Gordon Abel,** 19, Labourer	At Mabe, on the 3rd October, 1915, did feloniously break and enter the shop of Mary Jane Williams and steal the sum of 2s. 5d., also 4 packets of cigarettes; 3 collar studs and some roll tobacco, the monies and goods of Mary Jane Williams.	**Bound over for 12 months in £5.**
11	**Mads Peter Mortensen,** 22, Mate	At St. Blazey, on the 16th September, 1915, did feloniously and maliciously wound, with a knife, and break the leg of Frank Louis Pittaway, with intent to do him some grievous bodily harm.	
12	**John Nathaniel Lewis,** 45, Seaman		

National Court Statistics

There are some early National statistics for the numbers of persons committed to gaols for trial at the Sessions and Assizes.[76] There is no data for the separate types of court.

National Statistics	1805-11		1822-28	
	Number	%	Number	%
Committed for Trial				
Males	24246	71.4	86530	83.8
Females	9699	28.6	16758	16.2
	33945	100.0	**103288**	100.0
Trial Results:				
Acquitted	7930	23.4	20074	19.4
No Bill/Not prosecuted	5868	17.3	12018	11.6
Convicted	20147	59.3	71196	69.0
	33945	100.0	**103288**	100.0
Sentences: (% of Guilty)				
Death*	***2628***	*13.0*	***7980***	*11.2*
Transported: Life	51		1139	
14 years	258		1384	
7 years	3631		11776	
Other Terms	0		5	
Total Transported	***3940***	*19.6*	***14304***	*20.1*
Imprisonment: < 6 months	9321		36269	
6 months - 1 year	2391		8368	
1 year - 5 years	875		2317	
Total Imprisoned	***12587***	*62.5*	***46954***	*66.0*
Whipping - and Fine	***992***	*4.9*	***1958***	*2.7*
	20147	100.0	**71196**	100.0

For England and Wales, the number of committals for 1805 to 1811 inclusive was 33,945. For the years 1822 to 1828 the corresponding number had increased threefold. This seems to show the differences in crime levels between the time of the Napoleonic wars and peacetime. The number of females committed was relatively much higher when the males were away at war. The numbers for Cornwall were 273 cases (0.8%) in 1805-11 and 713 (0.7%) for 1822-28. This shows that the crime wave and thus the increase in the gaol population was national and not a local Cornish event.

Of the prisoners brought before the Courts, around 60-70% were found guilty and sentenced to Death (11.2-13%); Transportation (ca.20%); Imprisonment (ca.64%) and Whipping and/or Fine (2.7-4.9%).

Crimes were classified into over forty different types of offence. For the years 1811[77] and 1827[76b], the number of convictions were 3,163 and 12,564. The main crime recorded for both years was Larceny (stealing goods from person, or from houses, to value of 40/-; shops 5/-; rivers 40/-) 2503 (79.1 and 78% of all convictions). The next most common convictions were for Uttering (passing counterfeit coins) (2.8 & 1.8%) and Burglary (2.4 & 2.9%). Murder, including Attempted Murder and Concealing the Birth of Infant, accounted for 23 cases (0.73%) and 52 (0.41%). There are no significant differences in the types of crimes reported between the two selected years.

Which Crimes went to which Court?

Petty Sessions	Quarter Sessions	Assizes
Poaching	Stealing	Stealing
Vagrancy	Vagrancy	Break/Enter.
Trespass Act	Bastardy	Forgery
Revenue Laws	False Pretences	Receiving
Assault	Assault	Violent Assault
	Begging	Wounding
	Disorderly House	Fraud
		Murder

Generally different offences were tried in Petty Sessions, Quarter Sessions and Assizes Courts, depending on the seriousness of the crime and the corresponding sentences that could be handed down. Some offences were restricted to a court type, for example, drunkenness was tried in the Petty Sessions and resulted in a fine or a few days in gaol, whereas Murder, Manslaughter etc., were tried at the Assizes where the sentences could include long terms in gaol or even death. Some crimes like stealing (larceny, taking) appear in all the Courts depending on the value of the goods. Repeat offenders would gradually move up the system so that the sentences for the crimes could be increased.

The Courts in Bodmin

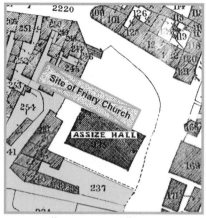

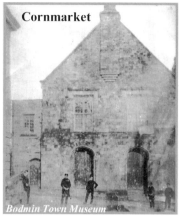

Cornmarket

Bodmin Town Museum

In the 18th & early 19th Centuries the Assizes were held in the Friary Church and the judges had lodgings in other Friary buildings. After a private Act of Parliament passed in 1836, most of the church was demolished for the building of the new Assize Hall (Shire Hall). The western portion of the church was still in use as a cornmarket until the building of the Public Rooms in 1891. The Act also allowed for the building of new judges' lodgings, The Mayoralty (Shire House).

The Assizes, Quarter Sessions and later the Crown Court were all held in the Shire Hall from 1837 until 1988 when the Courts were moved to Truro.

The building contained two courts. One is now used as a Tourist Information Centre and the other, Courtroom 1, with its original fittings, is used for a reenactment of the Matthew Weeks' trial for murder in 1844.

The lower floor of the building still contains the holding cells where prisoners waited for their cases to be heard in Court and if found guilty, waited to be returned to the gaol. These cells are very small (5'10"h x 28"d x 21"w) and contain a simple bench (15" above the floor). The only other facility for prisoners was a single lavatory at the end of the holding corridor.

In 1844, the body of Charlotte Dymond was found near Rough Tor. Matthew Weeks, her boyfriend, was accused of her murder. But was he guilty? In the *'Courtroom Experience',* visitors hear the evidence and vote as members of the jury.

The Elizabethan Guild-hall, now a bakery & tea-room, was used as the Council Chamber and Magistrates Court.

The above image shows the inside of the building during a Mayor Choosing Ceremony (1981).

The old-stocks were exhibited in the Guildhall after the closure of the old Museum in 1956.

© *Cornish Studies Library*
(Ellis Collection)

Permission to photograph the inside of the Shire Hall and Guildhall picture by kind permission of
Bodmin Town Clerk, Mr Paul O'Callaghan.

Other Sentences from the Courts

In addition to sending convicted prisoners to gaol or giving them a Fine, the Judges and Magistrates could add additional punishments and even more serious sentences.

Whipping:

The following details are whippings as part of the court sentence and are different from the punishment for breaking the *'Rules & Regulations'* while in the gaol.

Period	Cases	Whipping Only	Whipping + gaol	% Whipping only
1740s	59	57	2	97
1750s	61	61	0	100
1760s	71	71	0	100
1770s	103	100	3	97
1780s	51	18	33	35
1790s	25	16	9	64
1800s	22	5	17	23
1810s	31	1	30	3
1820s	58	15	43	26
1830-6	62	9	53	15

From the QS records,[78] it can be seen that there was a major change in the mid-1780s from using whipping as an individual court sentence to using it as an additional punishment for those sentenced to a period in gaol.

Sentences on individuals who were to be whipped also contained severity, number, time and place that the punishment would be carried out or repeated. Before 1786 between 62% and 85% were whipped in public. Later, the punishment was generally carried out in the gaol but for prisoners who had stolen from a mine they were whipped at the mine.

The variations in sentences are shown in the following examples:

*Thomas Cary, a vagabond held in bridewell: found to be an incorrigible rogue, 3 months with hard labour and the correction of the house, and to be **publicly whipped at Truro next Saturday and Bodmin the following Saturday between the hours of twelve and two. 1741***

*Honor Hayman widow and Ann, wife of Will Bray, both of St. Stephens by Launceston, petty larceny: **to be moderately whipped. 1743***

*Mary Ann Hugo of Kenwyn, single woman; stealing one handkerchief and one bed sheet, value 6d., the property of the parish, pleaded guilty: to serve 3 months hard labour, separate from the rest of the prisoners, **and be whipped privately on the first Monday of each such month. 1787***

*William Jeffery of Gwinear, labourer; convicted for taking one pair of brass buckles, value 1d., the property of William Pearce: W. J. to be **publicly whipped on Wednesday next at the Butter Market in Bodmin till his body is bloody. 1793***

*James Coleman, late of East Looe, labourer, and wife Elizabeth; tried for taking one silver teaspoon, the property of Thomas Bond gent: James Coleman convicted and sentenced to **be publicly whipped in Truro between 8 and 10 in the morning. 1798***

Practice of committing vagrants, rogues and vagabonds to gaol or house of correction until next sessions found insufficient deterrent, and also too great a charge on rates. **Recommended to justices that all such persons be publically whipped** in future or committed to hard labour in house of correction. **20th April 1819**

> *Thomas Dunstan of Penryn, lab., indicted for taking a waistcoat, value 6d., property of Joseph Tree: 3 months in Bodmin gaol **and to be "privately and severely whipped". 1822***

> *Joseph Cook of St. Austell, lab., indicted for stealing a copper-bottomed sieve, value 16s., property of Thomas Blamey. Joseph Cook **to be taken to Lanescot Mine and whipped on the dressing-floor of the mine** and then discharged. 1828*

There are numbers for whippings in some *Inspectors of Prisons Reports*: **1836:** 15 (2 females); **1838:** 16; **1843:** 12 (young males) and **1846:** 12.

Solitary Confinement:

The sentence of Solitary Confinement was rare, only 11 examples have been found in QS papers, with dates from 1822 to 1834 and a total of 37 in Inspectors Reports, covering the years 1836,[20] 1838,[79] 1843[13] and 1846.[14] The punishment was limited to two weeks, for example, for a 1 month sentence in gaol, only the first and last weeks would be in solitary.

Hard Labour:

Period	Gaol Sentences per Year	% at Hard Labour
1816-17	36	42
1818-25	35	64
1826-29	55	74
1830-35	70	91

The table, with data from the QS records, shows the average number of gaol sentences for selected periods and the average number of sentences with hard labour. From 1826, the number of gaol sentences started to increase and doubled by 1835, while the percentage of prisoners at Hard Labour increased from 42% in 1816 to 91% in the 1830s.

The percentage of prisoners at Hard Labour in the gaol was in the range 42-57% for four years between 1836 and 1846. This number is lower than in the QS records as many of the prisoners were sentenced by the lower Petty Sessions courts or on summary conviction. Later in the century, under the Four Stage System, all fit prisoners did the equivalent of Hard Labour in Stage 1.

Transportation:

Transportation to the colonies and plantations was an alternative punishment to hanging for felons. It was originally called banishment and was later placed on the statute book as transportation in the reign of Charles II (13 & 14 Car. II, cap. 12) and George I (4 Geo. I, cap.2). The American War (1778-83) prevented the government from sending convicts to America and the government had to accommodate about 1000 extra convicts per year. The simple solution was to house the convicts in the ships previously used as transports. The 'Hulks' were moored in places like Portsmouth, Devonport, Chatham and London and the prisoners were employed on local public works. Planned as a temporary measure, the use of prison hulks lasted until 1858, even though Australia was conveniently discovered in 1770 and the penal colony of Botany Bay was established in 1788.

The Quarter Sessions records for Cornwall show that from 1736 to 1776, 88 convicts from Cornwall were each transported for 7 years to America, the American Colonies and American Plantations. Their crimes were petty larceny (84), that is taking items valued at less than 12 pence, obtaining goods by false pretences (2) and being a rogue and vagabond (2). No transportation was recorded between 1776 and 1788. From 1788 to 1830, 54 people were transported for 7 years, including 17 *'transported to New South Wales or one of the adjacent islands'.* Between 1830 and 1836, 76 were sentenced to transportation, however the sentence was being increased, 49 were sentenced to 7 years, 18 for 14 years and 9 for life. It is not known whether these prisoners served their time in the hulks or actually went to Australia. Howard[2] recorded that between 1st November 1769 to 1st November 1776, Cornwall sentenced 78 convicts to transportation, 25 from Quarter Sessions and 53 from the Assizes. This is an average of 12 per year. He also noted that the practice of transportation (to America) having in great measure ceased before the 1st May, 1776.

The Governor's reports for 1832 & 1833 state that 32 & 33 prisoners were transported and sent to the Hulks. In 1843, 31 were sentenced to between 7 years and life and for 1846 the number was 20. These gaol numbers include both Quarter Sessions and Assize cases. In other reports, up to 1857, receipts for the 'removal of transports' are included but the convict numbers are not included.

The numbers of prisoners both on the hulks and transported are included in two parliamentary papers, printed on the 17th February, 1830.[80] They are two six monthly reports for 1829, from John Henry Capper, Superintendent of Ships and Vessels employed for the Confinement of Offenders under Sentence of Transportation, to The Right Hon. Robert Peel.

The national statistics are summarised in the following statement: On the 1st January 1829, there were 4,185 Prisoners on board the Convict Hulks in England, since which there have been received at the respective depots 4,230; of whom 1,672 were of 20 years of age, and under. Of the whole number, 3,608 have been transported to New South Wales and Van Diemen's Land (Tasmania), (being an excess of the preceding year of 800); 392 have been discharged; 7 have escaped; 158 have died; and 4,250 remained in the Hulks at home, on the 1st January instant.

The hulk used for convicts sentenced in Cornwall was probably "Captivity", which was moored at Devonport. The annual numbers (1829) for this ship are as follows:

Daily average number of prisoners on board	407
Number of Days on which Labour was performed	310
(Convicts were not employed on Sundays,	
Christmas Day & Good Friday)	
Total Convict Days Worked (Artificers) (Trades)	3060
Total Convict Days Worked (Labourers)	109,175

Estimated Value of Convicts public work:	
Artificers @ 1/9d. per day	£267-15-0d.
Labourers @ 1/3d. per day	£6,823-8-9d.
Total Estimated Value	£7,091-3-9d.
Total Cost of running "Captivity"	£7,312-16-4d.

The total cost of the English hulks for the year 1829 was £79,516-15-3d.

Transportation to New South Wales was stopped in 1840 but continued to Tasmania until 1852. Transportation to the Swan River Settlement (Western Australia) finally stopped in 1867. By the Acts of 1855 (16 & 17 Vict. cap. 99) and 1857 (20 & 21 Vict. cap. 3) provision was made for the alternative sentence of 'penal servitude' which the convict was allowed to undergo in this country.

Penal Servitude:
The essential features of Penal Servitude were a combination of:

(a) the enforcement, for a fixed period of rigorous cellular isolation and complete non-intercourse, day and night, accompanied by a plank bed, a restricted diet, a prescribed task of isolated labour, and deprivation of all humanizing privileges; with

(b) a subsequent period of associated labour under the Silent System, originally upon public works in the open air; at first with increased diet, and, later, with opportunities for "progressive stages" of improvement in conditions, and for earning a partial remission of the original sentence; and

(c) conditional discharge on a "Ticket of Leave," originally to an overseas colony, and subsequently at home under police supervision for a prescribed period.[81]

In 1868,[41] 1874 [40] and 1877,[35] four, eight (including one female) and four prisoners respectively were sentenced to 'Penal Servitude' at Bodmin gaol.

Death Penalty:
This topic is discussed in chapter 17 , page 143 'Death Sentence and Executions'.

Bodmin Town Museum

Henry Leonard Browett
Last Governor of H M Prison, Bodmin

Richard Amos Doidge (1860-1945)
Chief Warder, H M Prison, Bodmin.
*(Picture and Medal kindly provided by his
grandson, Richard Doidge of Redruth)*

Service Medal awarded to
Richard A. Doidge

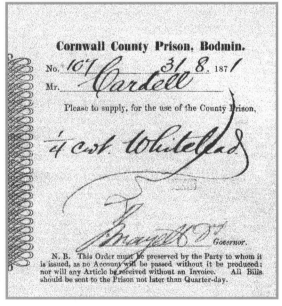

Order Signed by James Mayell
Principal Warder, 1871

Bodmin Town Museum

CHAPTER 9

The People – Staff

Details of staff members have been found in Census records (C),[82] Prison Inspectors reports (IR), Quarter Sessions records (QS),[78] Post Office Directories (PO),[83] Kelly's Directories of Cornwall and Devon & Cornwall (K) [83] and newspapers, for example, Bodmin Guardian (BG).[84] The lists are not comprehensive as the reports are usually several years apart; however, they do allow trends in staff numbers to be seen and, in some cases, details of the careers of individual people during the life-time of the gaol.

The earliest report of staff numbers is contained in an 1815 document:[19] *"The governor is allowed a salary of £30 p.a., and if his profits of the prisoners' work (and fees), with the salary do not amount to two hundred pounds, the County pay the deficiency. There are also two Turnkeys, who are paid by the County twelve pounds, with sundry allowances to make up their salaries one hundred pounds per annum each."* These staff numbers are in agreement with the accommodation described in the 1779 Call engraving, that is, the governor's house and two turnkey's chambers in the gatehouse. The chaplain and surgeon both lived in the town.

In 1828, the new governor, Everest, appointed Thomas Dungey as Head turnkey (£50 p.a.), Richard Holman as second turnkey (£35 p.a.) and Peter Every, third turnkey (£30 p.a.), in addition, four turnkeys were appointed at a salary of £25 per annum.[85] The 1831 census quotes seven families living at the gaol; Governor, Dungey, Dungey, Harris, Holman, Mules and Hill. In addition, there was a Chaplain, surgeon and messenger living off-site. Later reports, suggest that Thomas White, turnkey/shoemaker, also worked at the gaol at this time. The 1831 staff count is a minimum of eleven but could be higher as the Dungey and Holman families could have provided more than one family member to the staff.

In the Inspectors of Prisons report for 1837 [20] (returns for the year to Michaelmas 1835) the Job titles and salaries are: Keeper (£400), Chaplain (£200), Surgeon (£80), Matron (£18), Head Male Turnkey (£50), 3 x Male Turnkey (£35), Female Turnkey (£18), Taskmaster/Shoemaker (£35), Miller (£35), Porter (£35), Watchman (14/- per week) and Sunday Schoolmaster (£4). This gives a total of 14.

For the reports issued in 1839 [79], 1843 [13] and 1846 [14] and the 1841 census return, the staff numbers are constant at 15. An additional post of 'Superintendent of Treadwheel' was created before 1837 and in the 1843 Report the turnkeys are described as Debtor's Turnkey, Gaol Turnkey and House of Correction Turnkey. The female Turnkey now has the title of Assistant Matron and the Schoolmaster has been replaced by a full time Clerk. All staff other than

Governor and Chaplain have increased salaries and, except for the Chaplain, Surgeon and Watchman, receive free lodging, fuel and candles. The matrons also had free washing and the Governor had a house, free washing and soap. The 1851 census reports 16 staff and most of the job titles have changed. The title Turnkey has been replaced by Warder. The staff lists for the 1846 return and the names and titles from the 1851 census are contained in the following table:

Name	Office (1846)	Office (1851)	Salary	Allowances
John Bentham Everest	Governor	Governor	400 0 0	House, fuel, candles, washing,
Nicholas Kendall	Chaplain	Chaplain	200 0 0	
Joseph Hamley	Surgeon		90 0 0	
William Peter	Clerk	Clerk / School.	40 0 0	Lodging, fuel and candles.
Thomas Dungey	Principal Turnkey	Principal Warder	55 0 0	Ditto.
Joseph Whetter	Debtor's Turnkey		40 0 0	Ditto.
John Martin	Gaol Turnkey	Gateporter	40 0 0	Ditto.
William 0sborne	H.of C. Turnkey	Warder	40 0 0	Ditto.
William Hill	Superintendent T/W		40 0 0	Ditto.
James Holman	Gate Porter	Debtors Warder	40 0 0	Ditto.
Thomas White	Shoemaker	Warder Corn	40 0 0	Ditto.
James Tucker	Miller	Warder	40 0 0	Ditto.
Sampson Hill	Watchman		36 8 0	Ditto.
Ann Dungey	Matron	Matron	30 0 0	Lodging, fuel, candles and
Jane Peter	Assistant Matron	Assist. Matron	25 0 0	Ditto.
Surgeon		Surgeon		
John Thomas Bramble		Warder		
George Harrison		Warder		
William Beard		Watchman		
James Ranger		Messenger		
Total	**15**	**16**		

In the five years between the two reports, four staff: Surgeon, Debtor's Turnkey, Superintendent of Treadwheel and Watchman, have left. By 1851 they have been replaced with a new surgeon, two warders and a new watchman. The additional post is that of messenger.

In 1861, the staff of the new gaol consisted of Governor, Chaplain, Surgeon, Clerk, Matron, 6 male warders and 2 assistant warders, 3 female assistant matrons, 2 watchmen, a baker and an engineer. The same number of staff (20) is recorded in 1871 but there are now eight warders and a principal warder and 2 assistant matrons. One watchman has been replaced by a schoolmaster. The other positions remained the same.

The report for 1874 [40] states *the staff of subordinate prison officers consists of 10 male warders and 4 other male sub-officers and 3 female warders, with schoolmaster and clerks.* To this should be added Governor, Chaplain, Surgeon and Matron. This gives a total staff of 24, which is four higher than the census data for 1871. In 1877 [35], the four main posts are supported by 16 males and 3 females, giving a total staff of 23. There were 19 staff in 1881 consisting of Governor, Chaplain, Surgeon, Clerk, Matron with 3 assistants, Chief Warder with 6 Warders and 3 Assistant Warders and a Watchman. The Naval Prison was established in 1887 and this event caused a reduction in staff at the Civil Prison. The 1891 census shows a staff of 16. The four main posts are the same, except for the Surgeon, who became Medical Officer and the Governor who became Warder-in-Charge. The staff consisted of 8 male warders, a clerk/storekeeper, a schoolmaster and two female warders. In 1894, the Secretary of State at the Home Office considered that 8 warders, a chief warder and a night watchman were adequate security staff for H.M. Prison Bodmin.[86] In spite of this comment, the staff numbers increased and the 1901 census records 20 staff in the Civil Prison. The full Establishment list for H.M. Prison Bodmin on the 31st March, 1901,[33] was Chief Warder-in-Charge, Chaplain, Roman Catholic Priest, Medical Officer, Clerk, Discipline Officer, acting as Clerk or Schoolmaster, Principal Warder, 5 Warders and 6 Assistant Warders. The matron had 1 Assistant Warder. One of the female officers acted as Schoolmistress.

There are two lists of staff for the Naval Prison, the 1891 & 1901 census returns. In 1891 the staff consisted of Governor, Principal Warder, Chief Warder, 3 Warders, 3 Assistant Warders and a Clerk/storekeeper. By 1901, the Principal Warder, 1 Warder and 1 Assistant Warder had left and the only replacement was a Schoolmaster.

Summary of Staff Numbers

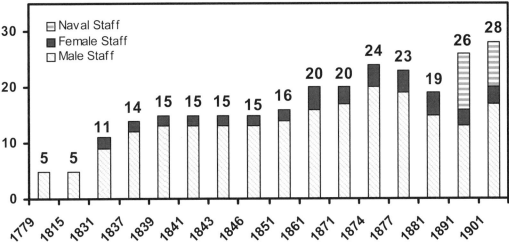

Before 1828 the gaol had a small number of turnkeys. It is probable that the number of posts reported is an under-estimate as other members of the families, particularly the women, would have helped with the women prisoners. From before 1837 until the old gaol closed in 1860/61 the staff remained constant at about 15 (ranging from 14 to 16). In 1861, the staff of the new gaol increased to 20. There were further increases in the mid 1870s but after the nationalisation of the gaol the number decreased to 19 in 1881. The opening of the Naval Prison in 1887 resulted in a decrease in civil staff to 16 in 1891 but this returned to 20 in 1901. The Naval Prison had a staff of 10 in 1891 and 8 in 1901.

A preliminary search of the 1911 Census has identified 14 staff members for the Civil Prison and 6 for the Naval Prison. It is anticipated that these numbers will increase when 'job title' searches become available.

Staff Accommodation

Originally the gaol accommodation consisted of the Governor's House, most of the rooms of which were used by master debtors, and two chambers for warders. The Chaplain and Surgeon lived in the town. The Inspector's Report of 1837[20] states that the five Turnkeys 'All reside in the prison and may have their families with them'. Several later reports indicate that most staff with their families were living within the gaol. The exceptions were the Chaplain, Surgeon, Watchman, Schoolmaster or Clerk. In 1851, 13 of the 16 staff were living in the gaol. The Chaplain, Surgeon and Watchman were living in the town.

This policy seems to have created a problem. In 1831, the 7 staff had 17 other family members living in the gaol and the 1841 census lists 12 staff members and 45 others. They included spouses (8), children (32), other relatives (2) and servants (3). The corresponding numbers for 1851 are: 13 staff and 47 other people. The staff and dependants represent between 13% (1831) and 35% (1851) of the total gaol population. Therefore, additional accommodation for staff and their families must have been made available inside the gaol site.

The building of the new gaol gave the planners the opportunity to solve this problem. In addition to the prisoner accommodation, they built two large houses outside the wall for the Governor and the Chaplain and provided staff accommodation in two parts of the Debtors prison block (male and female) and two sets of cottages near the gate, later known as the 'old quarters'. Six houses for warders were later built across the road from the gaol. According to residents, the houses were erected in 1872. (F Stone, personal communication)

The table shows the staff numbers and correlates the census entries with the available accommodation.

	1861	1871	1881	1891	1901
Staff	20	20	19	16	20
in Gov. House	1	1	1	2	1
in Chap. House	1	1	1	1	1
in W. Houses	-	-	6	6	7
Others on Site	13	11	5	1	2
Total on Site	15	13	13	10	11
Total in Town	5	7	6	6	8

One individual was not found in the 1901 census but other evidence[87] confirms that he worked in the gaol in 1901. There were only six Warder's houses, the 7 warders in 1901 include a husband and wife who were both warders. In 1861 & 1871 there were 7 or 8 warders with families living at the gaol. It is assumed that they and their families lived in the cottages, while the married staff with no children and single people lived in the warders' quarters. In the sale document of 1929, part of the cottage building is labelled 'porters lodge' and the description states *'Main entrance flanked on either side by various offices and stores arranged on two floors'*. These buildings were named the 'Old Quarters', which indicates that they went out of use when the warders' houses were built.

From the opening of the new gaol in 1861, some staff and their families were living in the town. The number varied from 5 to 8 over the five census returns from 1861 to 1901. In addition to the surgeon, schoolmaster, and watchman, there were between 2 and 5 warders living away from the gaol. The addresses of staff living in the town include: Gaol Lane (later called Berrycoombe Road), Higher & Lower Bore Street, Pool Street, Orange Terrace, Downing Terrace, Fore Street, St Leonards Terrace, Cribbage Terrace, St Nicholas Street, Burnards Terrace, Elm Grove, Honey Street and Quarry Park Terrace.

In 1911, the Surgeon and 4 warders were living in the town. The Governor's House, Chaplaincy, 6 Warder's Houses were all occupied and the Chief Warder's family were living inside the prison.

When the new gaol was built did the planners get the staff accommodation right? It would seem from the numbers that the planned accommodation at the gaol in 1861 was for a staff of fifteen, the average number employed in the old gaol. However the new gaol required a staff of twenty, requiring at least five staff and their families to live in town.

The accommodation for staff in the Naval Prison was very simple. As part of the main gateway into the new Prison, constructed in 1887, were two sets of living quarters. These were occupied by two naval warders and their families. All other members of the naval prison staff lived in the town. Their addresses are almost identical to those of the civil staff. It is possible that there were agreed lodgings for both civil and naval staff, particularly those in Gaol Lane, Elm Terrace and Cribbage Terrace.

In 1911, 3 warders were living in the town and the Naval Governor was resident in St Petroc's Hotel, St Nicholas Street. Both naval quarters were occupied.

Senior Members of the Staff

The main post in the gaol was that of Governor, also known earlier as Keeper of the gaol. The titles Warder-in-Charge (1891) and Chief Warder-in-Charge (1901) were government grades below that of Governor. In an attempt to save money, the government policy, after 1880, was that prisons with less than 101 prisoners on average in the previous year, were not large enough to have the higher grade of governor.[86] There was also a Matron, usually with an assistant, who was responsible for the women prisoners, a Chaplain, who lived on site (after 1861) and the services of a Surgeon or Medical Officer, daily and as required. During the time of the Naval Prison, a local Catholic Chaplain was available for both civil and naval prisoners.

Governors (County Gaol and H. M. Civil Prison)

The first governor of the gaol was Edmund Leach. In January 1780, he complained at the Quarter sessions,[88] that Thomas Jones, the contractor, had not completed the buildings in a proper, workmanlike way. The justices dismissed his complaint as groundless and discharged him from office, with immediate effect, because of several instances of misbehaviour. James Chapple, foreman of the builder of the gaol, was appointed temporary gaoler. A post he held for 48 years until his death in 1827. Frederick Chapple, son of James was appointed *'Keeper of the Common Gaol'* in October 1827 but at the next Quarter Sessions, John Bentham Everest, a professional gaoler who transferred from the prison hulk at Chatham, was appointed Governor of the House of Correction at Bodmin. There is no further mention of Frederick Chapple and Everest was recorded as governor of the gaol until his retirement in 1860. Effectively there were only two governors of the gaol between 1780 and 1860. This covers approximately 60% of the useful lifetime of the institution.

From Quarter Sessions records it would appear that the two governors were treated quite differently by the ruling Justices. In 1795, the Court noted that the expenses for the gaol were increasing but that no accounts had been received from Chapple since 1781. They ordered accounts to be prepared indicating costs for the subsistence of prisoners, repairs to buildings, expenses in conveying prisoners, fees for discharge, punishment etc., salaries and accounts of prisoner's labour. The Court also called upon Chapple to explain the use of advances made to him to purchase materials for the employment of prisoners. The court had provided £494/9/11¾d for this purpose, of which £218/11/3d had been used for labour on the gaol. Chapple claimed that prisoners might be more usefully employed in the growing and manufacture of flax. He had used some of the advance and his own money to cultivate 34 acres of flax and had made a considerable quantity of course linen called Dowlas. The Court considered that it was improper that the County should engage in such a speculative concern. It highly disapproved and ordered that the cultivation and manufacture should be discontinued.

Chapple's attitude to accounts did not change as judged by a report on the prison in 1821[89]. *'The Gaoler who enjoys the entire confidence of the magistrates says that some profit arises from the prisoners' work but he could not furnish me with any account – or reference to other accounts of former years. I observed that the gross amounts of earnings in 1800 and 1803 were £36.19.8 and £28.4.4 a regular account having been then kept.'*

After Everest became governor there is a marked change in the comments of the Court. The Visiting Justices report of April, 1832, noted *'four years have elapsed since total change in system made.'* Justices expressed their *'perfect satisfaction'. 'The new governor was appointed 12th February 1828'.* Everest organised a major building and repair programme from 1828 so that the gaol conditions conformed to various Acts of Parliament. The Court was so impressed with the running of the gaol, the behaviour of the prisoners and the rebuilding programme that in 1832, it ordered £100 or a piece of plate to that value to be presented to Mr. John Bentham Everest in recognition of his valuable service. By 1835, the Justices reported the gaol in excellent order and in a state of progressive improvement. The inspector of Prisons,[27] wrote the following tribute to governor Everest after his retirement:

"Advancing age and infirmity have deprived the County of the services of an officer who has long and deservedly enjoyed the reputation of being one of the best of prison governors. M. Everest has in that capacity had to struggle with the all but insurmountable obstacles presented by an ill-constructed prison, which, besides other disadvantages was far too small for the convenient confinement of its inmates, and it is not too much to say that his talent, energy, and activity so completely triumphed over these difficulties as to render the County prison of Cornwall one of the best conducted establishments of the kind in the kingdom, and to reduce the expenses quite as much as, the discipline was improved."

List of Governors. County Gaol and Civil Prison			
	From	**To**	**Recorded in:**
Edmund Leach	1779?	1780	QS1780
James Chapple	1780	1827	QS1827
Frederick Chapple	1827		QS1827
John Bentham Everest	Jan.1828	1860	QS1828, C1831, C1851
Hugh George Colvill	1860	post 1878	C1861, C1871, PO1873
Maj. E W Lane	pre 1881	1883	C1881
Vacancy	1883		K1883
Mr. Parr	1883		T 1/15534 (Nat.Arch.)
William Stevens	ca. 1883	1896	K1889, C1891, K1893
Wm. Repulsa Shenton	pre 1897	post 1901	K1897, C1901
Duncan, Jas. H			Ref.69 (1903)
Henry Leonard Browett	pre 1906	1916	K1906, K1914

Governors (H. M. Naval Prison)

After 1887, when the Naval Prison was established, there were separate governors for this prison. The official job title seems to have been Deputy Governor of H.M. Prison or H.M. Naval prison. The first governor was Commander Malcolm McNeile, followed by Captain G S McIlwaine, for three months and M B Cartwright for less than a year. Commander Pearson Campbell Johnstone served until ca.1910 and the final governor, Commander Thomas Brandreth remained until the closure of the Naval Prison.

It is believed that the 'Naval Governor' lived in one of the gaol villas but documents show that the holder of this position never lived on the gaol site.

Commander McNeile had a very famous son, Lt. Col. Herman Cyril McNeile, who under the pen-name 'Sapper', wrote books featuring *'Bulldog Drummond'*. As a character, Drummond has been compared with Sherlock Holmes, Raffles and the Saint. The character finally disappeared in the 1950s with the introduction of James Bond. There are published reports [90] that 'Sapper' was born in the Naval Prison on 28th September, 1888. In fact, his birth certificate states that he was born at his father's residence in Higher Bore Street. Of the other governors, for which we have details, Commander P C Johnstone lived in Windsor Cottage, Castle Street and Thomas Brandreth lived in 'Rockleigh', St Nicholas Street, Bodmin.

List of Governors. Naval Prison			
	From	To	Recorded in:
Comm. Malcolm McNeile	1887	1890	K1889
Captain G S McIlwaine	1890	1890	BG 7/1/1922, p4
M B Cartwright	1890	1890/1	BG 7/1/1922, p4
Comm. Pearson C Johnstone	1891	1910	C1891, K1893, K1906
Comm. Thomas Brandreth	1910	1922	K1914

Chaplains (County Gaol and H. M. Civil Prison)

In 1802, the appointment of Rev. Moses Morgan as chaplain to the County Gaol was revoked. The Court ordered that he be appointed chaplain to the gaol and bridewell at Bodmin at the yearly salary of £50. He died in 1810 and was replaced by George Thomas Plummer, who resigned in 1812. Joseph Fayrer, appointed 1812, was chaplain until 1822 when he was replaced by Leonard Jarvis Boor, who held the position until his death in 1835. In 1823 the

List of Chaplains. County Gaol, Civil & Naval Prisons			
	From	To	Recorded in:
John Lethbridge		1797	QS1797
Moses Morgan	1797	1810	QS1802
George Thomas Plummer	July 1810	Apr 1812	QS1810, QS1812
Joseph Fayrer	July1812	1822	QS1812
Leonard Jarvis Boor	1822	1835	QS1823, QS1835
Nicholas Kendall Francis John Hext Kendall	1835	1836	QS1835
Francis J H Kendall	10/1835	1845	QS1836, IR1844
Nicholas Kendall	1845	post 1851	IR1847
William Frederick Everest	pre 1861	post 1883	C1861, C1881, K1883
Charles Boutflower Simpson	pre 1891	post 1901	C1891, K1897, C1901
Samuel Percy Statham	post 1901	1907	K1906
Thomas Austin	13/11/1907	1922	K1914

salary had increased to £150 p.a. After the death of Boor, the services were taken alternately by Nicholas and Francis John Hext Kendall. Francis Kendall held the post from 1836 to 1845 when he was replaced by his brother, Nicholas. In 1847, the salary was £200 p.a. William Frederick Everest was chaplain from before 1861 to after 1883 and he was followed by Charles Boutflower Simpson (pre1891 to post 1901). Samuel Percy Hammond Statham and Thomas Austin held the position in 1906 and 1914 respectively.

Kelly's Directories contain the following names as Catholic chaplains: Felix Menchini (1889), Augustine H White (1893), Cuthbert McAdam (1897), Aloysius Smith (1906) and Alphonsus McElroy (1914).

Matrons (County Gaol and H. M. Civil Prison)

Date	Matron	Assistant	Date	Matron	Assistant
1831	Mary Ann Dungey		1871	Ann Dungey	Mary Dungey
1841	Mary Ann Dungey	Ann Dungey	1881	Mary Dungey	
1851	Ann Dungey	Jane Peter	1883	Harriet Simmons	
1861	Ann Dungey	Jane Peter	1891	Mary A Stevens	
		Edna Ann Dungey	1902	Lucy Curnick	
		Elizabeth White	1905	Adelaide Marshall	

Before 1891, most of the Matrons and Assistant Matrons were related to other members of the gaol staff. For example, Jane Peter was married to the gaol clerk William Peter and Elizabeth White was the wife of the warder Thomas White, but the Dungey family provided most of the matrons and assistants. A partial family tree shows the relationships in the family. Thomas (born ca.1770) was appointed turnkey in 1790 and his wife Ann was possibly Matron in 1831. The only record [79] of the matron in the 1830s states *'Matron, age 67, appointed 1822.'* Their son Thomas (born 1790), joined the staff in 1819, was promoted to Head Turnkey in 1828 and Principal Turnkey in 1841. His sister (?) Mary Ann was assistant matron in 1831 and matron in 1841, and his wife Ann, assistant matron from 1840 and matron in 1851, 1861 & 1871. Their daughter, Edna Ann, was assistant matron in 1861 and their other daughter, Mary, was matron in 1881. She retired in 1883, after 20 years service. Members of this family were employed in the gaol from 1790 to 1883. This covers over 93 years of the gaol's 137 year history.

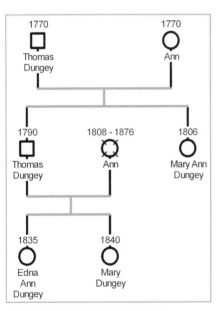

Surgeons & Medical Officers (County Gaol, Civil & Naval Prisons)

William Hamley was the surgeon to the gaol from before 1797 to 1810. From 1797 to 1803, Peter Edward Scobell was joint surgeon with Hamley. Joseph Hamley was appointed surgeon, in place of his father, in 1810. He remained in the post until after 1847. In 1810, his salary was £30 p.a.; it was gradually increased and reached £90 p.a. in 1847. Thomas Quiller-Couch, father of Sir Arthur Quiller-Couch, was surgeon in 1883. Bartholomew Gidley Derry was Medical Officer from the 1880s until after 1914.

List of Surgeons. County Gaol, Civil & Naval Prisons			
	From	To	Recorded in:
William Hamley	pre 1797	1810	QS 1797, QS 1810
Peter Edward Scobell (joint)	1797	1803	QS 1797, QS 1803
Joseph Hamley	1805	post 1847	QS 1810, QS 1823,
Thomas Quiller Couch			K1883
Bartholomew Gidley Derry	pre 1889	post 1914	K1889, K1906, K1914

List of Staff Employed in Bodmin Gaol

A list of people employed in the gaol (*Appendix 5*) contains over 130 names, including the governors, chaplains, matrons and surgeons mentioned above. The County Gaol was a place of stable employment; there are several examples of people working there for over 20 years. Included in this group are the governors Chapple (48) and Everest (32), the turnkey/messenger, Philip Corney (49) and Clerk William Peter (20). The turnkeys, Thomas Dungey (>40), James Holman (>43), John Martin (>30), Thomas White (>23), William Osbourn (27) and the watchman, Thomas Jago (>20). Surgeons Joseph Hamley (>47) and B G Derry (>25), the matrons, Jane Peter (>27), Mary Dungey (20), Ann Dungey (>31) and Chaplain William Frederick Everest (>22). The naval warder, Joseph Edmonds served for over 23 years. The officer Richard Doidge received a long service medal, possibly for 25 years service.

Family members were also employed, in addition to the Dungey family, there are several examples of fathers and sons/daughters working in the gaol. They are William & Joseph Hamley (surgeons), William & Sampson Francis Hill, James & Frederick Chapple, William & William H Angwin, William & John H Osborne, Thomas & Thomas, jnr. White and Thomas & Avis Wellington. There were also a number of married couples employed, Jane & William Peter (assistant matron & clerk), George J & Alice M Richards (assistant warder & female warder), Thomas, jnr. & Elizabeth White (warder & matron's assistant).

There are two people each called Holman (James & Richard), Sowden (William & Henry), Martin (John & John N), Beard (William & John), Stevens (William & Mary A) and Bound (Walter & Eliza). No relationship between them has been found.

CHAPTER 10

The People – Inmates

There are a number of documents, including census returns, Inspectors' reports, a few Governors' reports & Returns and the reports of Howard (1779 & 1787)[2,4] and Neild (1803),[91] which give the numbers of prisoners in the gaol. This is a very small sample of the population as the reports account for the number of prisoners on 42 days in the 136 years of the gaol history. The prisoner numbers available are not spread evenly across the life of the gaol but concentrated from about 1830 to 1878 when many statistics were included in the Inspectors of Prisons reports. The source data for prisoner numbers is contained in *Appendix 6*. In the early 1830s and for a few other years, multiple reports were published. These have been averaged.

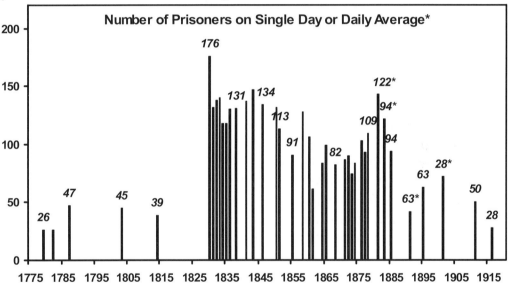

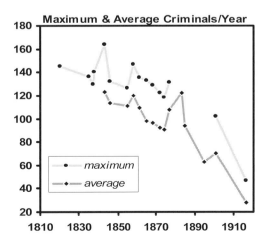

The second graph on the left shows the maximum number of prisoners on a single day in the year and the average number of prisoners per day over the year.

Debtors are not included.

The increase in the numbers in the mid 1870s was due to naval prisoners. Both graphs show a steady decline in prisoner numbers after the peaks in the early part of the nineteenth century.

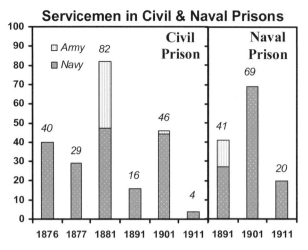

Servicemen in Civil & Naval Prisons

From November 1873, the prison was used to house servicemen from both the army and navy. The Inspectors' report covering 1874 recorded only convicts and did not give separate counts for civil and service personnel. The 1881 census clearly marks naval/ military prisoners by indicating the regiment or Royal Navy. After the transfer of the two buildings to the Admiralty, the practice of keeping naval prisoners in the civil prison continued. There were two types of naval prisoners in the gaol; those prisoners sentenced to *'dismissal from the service'* had to be housed in a Civil Prison, rather than a Naval Prison. For 1893 [92] the average civil prison population was 41 males, including 15 discharged navy personnel and 3 females. The 1891 census again identified naval/army prisoners in the civil block but the 1901 enumerator assumed that only civil prisoners were housed in the civil gaol. This error was partially corrected by the census supervisor. He marked 13 marines and a Naval Clerk in the civil section as 'Navymen' but failed to notice 9 stokers and 21 seamen. These people are counted as navymen in the civil prison.

The census data for the naval prison shows 27 Navy and 14 Army prisoners in 1891, 69 Navy prisoners in 1901 and only 20 in 1911.

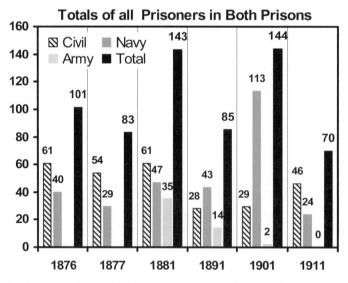

Totals of all Prisoners in Both Prisons

This chart shows the number of civil prisoners compared with army and navy prisoners for the years between 1876 and 1911.

The number of civil prisoners dropped from about 60 to below 30 and after 1877, Naval & Army prisoners outnumbered the civil prisoners. The number of servicemen was higher in 1881, before the Naval Prison was established, than in 1891 and it increased in 1901 to over twice the 1891 level. There were only 24 navy prisoners and no army prisoners in 1911.

The above data consists of 'one off' counts of prisoners and do not give an accurate picture of the total number of prisoners that went through the gaol. For some years, data is available for the total number of committals. For others the *'total number of Prisoners in the year'* is recorded (*).

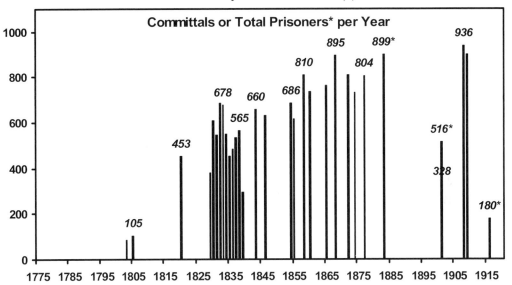

Some reports are incomplete, for example, they only contain a total, which may or may not include debtors and Army and Navy personnel.

The following chart contains a selection of the above data from reports which give more details of the prisoner types.

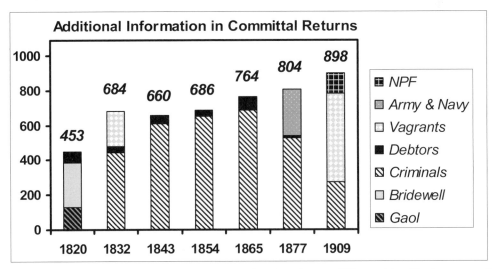

The earlier returns gave counts for the three different institutions on the gaol site, that is, Gaol, House of Correction (Bridewell) and Debtors' Prison. After 1830, the two classifications were Criminals and Debtors. Large groups of prisoners have been reported separately for example, vagrants in 1832 & 1909, naval/army prisoners (1877) and non-payment of fines in 1909.

Some of the numbers are explained in Governor's and Chaplain's reports. In 1829, the Chaplain stated that there was a greater proportion of juvenile offenders *"chiefly for robbing orchards and gardens".*[93] The Governor stated, in October, 1832, *"that 90 vagrants were committed since his last quarterly report, being exactly half the total of all prisoners."* The vagrant problem was largely moved from the gaol to the work-house after 1842[94] but re-appeared at the start of the twentieth century. For example, in 1909, the total number of prisoners received was 898. This included 508 vagrants, 119 in default of payment of fines and only 8 courts-martial prisoners.

In addition to the data in the charts, there are other sets of numbers. Howard reports that between 13th January 1780 and 27th July 1782, there were 261 committals, consisting of 75 debtors, 92 felons, etc. and 94 petty offenders. L E Long in *'An Old Cornish Town'*[34] states that during the first 27 years of its existence, 3,877 prisoners passed through the gaol, of whom 1,258 were criminals, 773 were debtors and the remaining 1,846 had been confined in the Bridewell.

Description of Gaol Population by Sex and Age

The charts of 'single day' returns show the steady decline in the number of male prisoners in the gaol but the situation with women prisoners is more complex. The ratio of male to female prisoners, derived from averaging the numbers from reports in each decade, starts at 4.3, declines in the 1840s and 1850s, reaches a low of 2.5 in the 1860s and then increases rapidly. The first phase, that is, the reduction in the ratio, was caused by an increase in the number of women prisoners, while the second phase was due to a rapid reduction in the number of women prisoners sent to the gaol. In 1901, the population consisted of 1 female and 28 male prisoners. For the years between 1843 and 1877 (11 reports) the ratio of male to female committals was 2.8 with a range from 2.2 in 1860 to 3.4 in 1843. Of the 189 debtors reported from years between 1830 and 1876 only 14 were women.

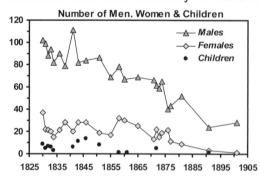
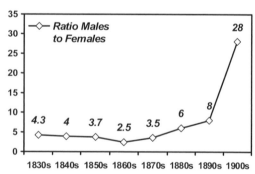

The definition of child prisoners has varied over the years, in different reports they are referred to as children, juveniles and 'under 17'. The children numbers in the above chart are for prisoners under 17 years of age, except for the 1841 census (14 years and below) and 'children' in the early 1830s Governors' reports, where no ages are given. (The age 15 in the 1841 census, includes all ages between 15 and 19). In some reports there are cases of infants with their mothers but they are not included.

In 1841, 1851 & 1861 the youngest child prisoner in each census was 12 years old and the prisoner in 1891 was 14. In six reports covering the years 1835 – 1872, there was a total of 341 committals of under 17 year olds, 286 males and 55 females and they included 15 boys and 3 girls under the age of twelve.

These numbers for children seem to be lower than the national averages. Although after the Reformatory School Act of 1864, imprisonment of children was reduced, it was not until the Children Act of 1908, that it was abolished.

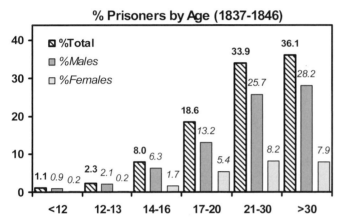

% Prisoners by Age (1837-1846)

The ages of prisoners in the gaol were reported for the years 1837, 1843 and 1847 they included prisoners either tried or for trial by the Quarter sessions and Assize Courts. In addition, the age classification for summary conviction prisoners was also included. The six sets of numbers are very similar and have been combined. The results in the table are derived from a population of 1668 prisoners, 1275 males and 393 females. The largest group was prisoners over 30 but 52.5% of the prisoners were aged between 17 and 30. Over eleven percent of the prisoners were under 17, this corresponds to 155 males and 35 females, including 15 males and 3 females under the age of 12.

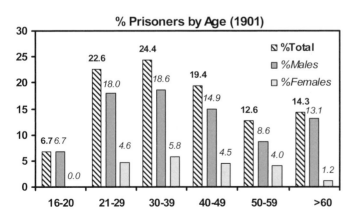

% Prisoners by Age (1901)

The Return of Convicted Prisoners for the year ending 31st March, 1901, contained 262 males and 66 females, a total of 328. The age of the population had changed, when compared to the earlier data. 70.3% of the prisoners were now over thirty, compared to 36.1% earlier. There were no female prisoners below the age of twenty-one or males below the age of sixteen. The number of prisoners under twenty-one was reduced to 6.7% from 30%. This is a much older population of prisoners.

Description of Gaol Population by Type of Prisoner

The population of the gaol did not just consist of convicted prisoners; some were waiting to go to trial while others, like debtors, were not even criminals. The prisoners were also felons or misdemeanants, that is, serious or minor offenders.

For the years 1830 to 1834, the governor John Bentham Everest, prepared a series of reports for the Quarter Sessions.[96] The reports contained the numbers for each of the different types of prisoner.

Prisoner Type	Number	%	Number	%
	Male		Female	
Convicted Misdemeanour	45.4	35	13	10
Convicted Felony	24.2	19	3.6	3
Charged Felony	17.6	14	4.4	3
Debtors	12.8	9.8	0.8	1
Charged Misdemeanour	6.8	5.2	1	1

The average numbers for each group, over the five years and the percentage of the gaol population are shown in the table. The groups are debtors, male and female representing 9.8% and 0.6% of the total prisoners; convicted of felony (18.7 & 2.8%) and charged with felony (13.6 & 3.4%). The largest group, convicted of misdemeanours and imprisoned for want of sureties (35 & 10%) and the smallest group, charged with misdemeanours (5.2 & 0.8%).

	1836	1838	1843	1846	1855	1858	1860	1865
Felons for Trial		9				4		
Misdem. for Trial		1				1		
Felons Covicted	25	38				41		
Misdem. Convicted	79	59				17		
Committed for Trial	7		27	30	7		12	20
Convicted			47	51	43		46	43
Summary Convictions:								
Under Crim. Justice Act					5	12	6	5
Under Vagrant Act								14
Under Game Laws								1
Assault								4
For Sureties								1
Other Summ. Convictions			47	45	31	36	33	6
Debtors:	19	24	26	8	5			
Superior/Sheriffs Court						6	1	1
County Court						11	8	4
Total Prisoners	130	131	147	134	91	128	106	99

After 1835, the Inspectors of Prisons not only counted the prisoners on the day of their visit but also gave the status of each prisoner. The early reports gave the same information as the 'Governors' Reports' quoted above. However, the system varied, some reports classified the prisoners as 'Committed for trial', 'Convicted', 'Summary convictions' and 'Debtors', while others, for example, the data for 1858 and 1865, gave more detailed information.

Later in the 19th century, debtors were not imprisoned and the distinction between felons and misdemeanants was removed. This gave a classification system of prisoners which contained only two groups, those charged with a crime and those sentenced by the courts.

The Reports of the Inspectors of Prisons, published in 1844 [13] and 1847/8,[14] contained a full account of the gaol population and the disposal of the prisoners for the years ending September 1843 and September 1846.

Number of Prisoners.	1843			1846		
	M	F	Total	M	F	Total
Prisoners at start of year	30	11	41	20	8	28
Committed for trial during year	158	65	223	143	45	188
Rendered in court for trial in year	57	6	63	55	15	70
Total	**245**	**82**	**327**	**218**	**68**	**286**
How Disposed of.						
Bodmin Prison	115	33	148	105	36	141
Transportation	25	6	31	17	3	20
Sentence deferred				1		1
Whipped, Fined or Surities	5		5	3	1	4
Aquitted at the Bar	55	13	68	36	11	47
No Bills Found	21	16	37	23	7	30
Not Prosecuted	5	4	9	4	1	5
Aquitted as Insane				1		1
Gave Crown Evidence				3		3
Left at end of year	19	10	29	25	9	34
Total	**245**	**82**	**327**	**218**	**68**	**286**

Summary Convictions	M	F	Total	M	F	Total
Commencement of year	32	15	47	37	11	48
By Courts Martial	10		10			
Deserters	1		1	1		1
Under the Game Laws	4		4	5		5
Under the Revenue Laws	5		5	1		1
Under the Bastardy Laws				21		21
Under the Vagrant Act	88	44	132	70	40	110
Under the Trespass Act	23	2	25	14	15	29
Under the Larceny Act	25		25	15	7	22
For Assaults	44	14	58	33	8	41
For want of Sureties	10		10	12	2	14
Others	49	7	56	63	24	87
Total	**259**	**67**	**326**	**235**	**96**	**331**

Debtors	M	F	Total	M	F	Total
Commencement of year	12	1	13	6		6
In Execution	41	2	43	19	3	22
In Execution from Courts of Request	3		3	4		4
Forfeitures or Contempt	1	1	2	8	1	9
Total	**45**	**3**	**48**	**31**	**4**	**35**

This data shows that of the prisoners brought to trial only about 50% were returned to serve a sentence in Bodmin Gaol.

Terms of Imprisonment for Convicted Prisoners																		
Sentence	1812		1822		1832		1837		1843		1846		1868		1874		1877	
	M	F	M	F	M	F	M	F	M	F	M	F	M	F	M	F	M	F
7 days or less	1		5	2	5								78	33	67	30	51	34
14 days or less							13	4	8	1	4	4						
> 7 days to 14 days		1	3	2	7	4							102	46	39	35	88	36
> 14 days to 1 month	1	1	8	1	20	2	29	14	47	10	29	17	168	63	109	36	112	34
> 1 m to 2 months	3	0	2	0	5	3	138	38	127	36	138	61	58	15	71	12	53	17
> 2 m to 3 months	4	1	6	2	13	1	54	13	71	19	45	20	27	7	26	2	34	8
> 3 m to 6 months			8	2	17	6	38	14	68	20	80	18	38	11	22	8	20	4
> 6 m to 1 year			2		16	2	22	6	37	9	39	9	16	1	10		8	
> 1 y to 2 years	1				2		18	1	15	5	12	2			3		1	1
> 2 y to 3 years							1		1		1	1						
Total	10	3	34	9	85	18	313	90	374	100	348	132	487	176	347	123	367	134

This table contains the numbers of prisoners sentenced to different lengths of imprisonment for nine selected years between 1812 and 1877. The 1812 to 1832 numbers are from Quarter Sessions records. The data for later years cover all prisoners from all courts and include all age groups.

Bodmin Gaol was a local prison and generally only accepted prisoners serving two years or less. In addition, it housed prisoners before trial, prisoners sentenced to transportation and those to be hanged. Prisoners sentenced to periods of imprisonment over two years would be sent to a Convict prison, for example, Dartmoor.

Time on Remand	1837		1843		1846	
	M	F	M	F	M	F
14 days or less	69	9	51	10	34	13
> 14 days to 1 month	33	12	22	23	38	8
> 1 m to 2 months	54	11	50	13	38	15
> 2 m to 3 months	20	8	25	17	25	7
> 3 m to 6 months	3	1	16	2	3	1
> 6 m to 1 year			5	1	0	1
Total	179	41	169	66	138	45

The reports for the years 1837, 1843 and 1846, contain 'Terms of Imprisonment before Trial'. The average time on remand was 4 - 7 weeks but a total of seven prisoners, 5 male and 2 female, waited 6 months to a year before they were brought to court.

Changes in the Gaol Population

Number of Prisoners on Single Day or Daily Average

Committals and/or Total Prisoners per Year

The two simplified charts above show how the population of the gaol changed with time. Using the 'number of prisoners in the gaol on single days or daily averages' graph, it is clear that after 1815 there was a massive increase in the population, peaking in the 1820s or 1830s, followed by a decline until the gaol closed in 1916. The spike in the population after 1874 was caused by the admission of Army and Navy prisoners.

The second chart gives the total number of prisoners sent to the gaol per year. The shape shows a steady but continuous increase in numbers from 1803 up to 1868 and then a small drop. From 1874 there was an increase due to the influx of Service personnel followed by a massive fall to the closure of the gaol in 1916. The peak in 1908 & 1909 was due to large numbers of vagrants being imprisoned. The following factors are believed to of importance in explaining the shape of the graphs and the large difference between them:

Population

The increase in the population of the gaol, from 1815 to the early 1830s, was much higher than the increase in the Cornish population.[96] The reason for the increase seems to be related to the growth in the mining industry. At the end

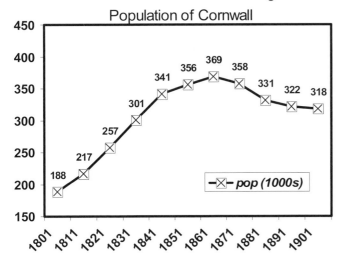

of the Napoleonic wars in 1815, many unemployed soldiers and sailors returned, searching for work and this led to an increase in crime and a massive increase in the gaol population. The exact time of the peak is not known but in a Return for 1820,[16] the gaol was reported as being full, having a population of 183 (145 criminals and 38 debtors). There was a second peak in 1830, caused by the closure of the County Gaol at Launceston. After this there was a slow steady decrease during the remainder of the 19th century. Again the population statistics do not explain the fall in prisoner numbers after about 1841 as the total population of the county was still increasing at this time.

New Laws and Practices

Reasons for the decrease in the gaol population could include new Acts of Parliament, for example, the Debtor's Act of 1869, which virtually ended imprisonment for debt and later in the century, the practice of issuing 'fines' rather than sending guilty people to prison.

Sentencing Policy

The main explanation for the difference between the two sets of population statistics, that is, the decrease in prisoner numbers after 1840 and, at the same time, the continuing increase in the number of people being sent to the gaol, lies in the length of the sentences.

For example, in the years from 1837 to 1877, the number of committals to the gaol was increasing, and the number of prisoners sentenced to Gaol remained constant but, over the same years, the number of prisoners in the gaol, on single day counts, dropped from 147 to 54.

Number of Prisoners Sentenced

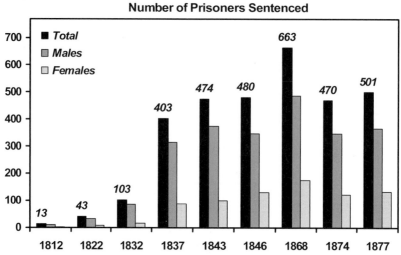

The explanation for this lies in the lengths of sentences handed down by the magistrates and judges. The length of sentence data for 1812, 1822 & 1832 are an under-estimate as they refer only to the QS courts. They do not include the longer sentences imposed by the Assize courts for serious offences.

Average Length of Sentence (weeks)

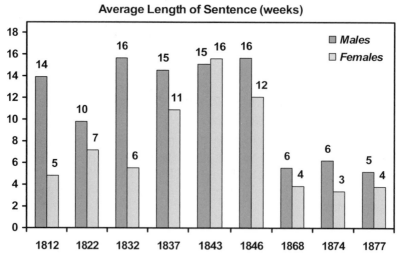

The 1812 data is from a very small sample and the average sentences for that year are probably not reliable. There was an increase between 1822 and 1832 and from 1837 to 1846 the length of sentence for males remained constant at 15 or 16 weeks. The corresponding number for females varied from 6 weeks (1832) to a high of 16 weeks in 1843. At some time between 1846 and 1868, there was a major change in sentencing policy, the average length of sentence for males decreased from 15/16 weeks to only 5 or 6 weeks. For females, the sentence was now only 3 to 4 weeks.

Summary

The following chart contains only data for Civil prisoners and Debtors, it does not include the Army and Naval prisoners who were housed in the Civil Prison.

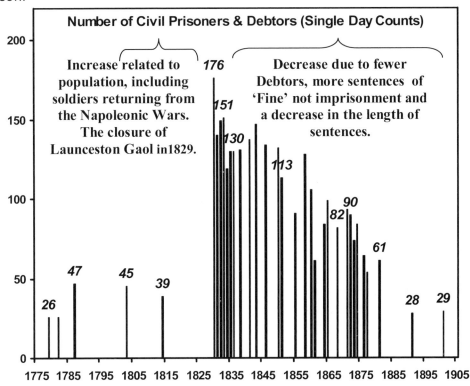

The increase in the gaol population in the early nineteenth century was caused by an increase in the County population and the large number of servicemen seeking work in the mining industry. The decrease in prisoner numbers, which started before 1850, was not due to l ess crime but to a significant reduction the number of debtors, more 'Fines' and a significant reduction in the length of sentences handed down by the judges and magi strates.

By the mid 1870s there was no need for a prison of this size in Cornwall.

Analysis of a Single-day Prisoner Return

The Inspector of Prisons report, published in 1851,[23] contained a full list of prisoners in the Gaol and House of Correction on the 12th July, 1850. The return contained prisoners, identified by initials and age, offences, dates of committal and trial, the type of court, that is, assizes (Ass.), sessions (Sess.) or summarily conviction (Sum.) and full details of the sentences. It contained information on felons, misdemeanants, prisoners for trial, at the assizes, and debtors (appendix 7).

The Prisoners:

Type of Prisoner	Adults		16 and under		Total
	M	F	M	F	
Felons	47	9	4	1	61
Misdemeanants	34	4	1	1	40
Under Juvenile Act	0	0	2	0	2
For Trial (Assizes)	11	3	1	0	15
Debtors	13	1	0	0	14
Total Prisoners	105	17	8	2	**132**

The population of the gaol consisted of 113 males and 19 females, including 10 prisoners aged 16 or under. The youngest prisoner, age 11, was awaiting trial on a charge of burglary.

The two largest groups were male convicted felons and misdemeanants. There were 15 felons for trial at the next Assizes and 14 debtors sentenced by various bodies, including Exchequer, Queen's Bench, County and Stannery Courts.

The Crimes:

Felonies				Misdemeanours			
	M	F	T.		M	F	T.
Tried.				*Tried.*			
Stealing	46	8	54	Assault / rape	10		10
Receiving	1	2	3	Vagrancy	5	1	6
Stabbing	2		2	Breach of Peace	2	2	4
Burglary	1		1	Uttering	3		3
Arson	1		1	Fraud	3		3
Assault / rape	1		1	Bastardy	3		3
Housebreaking	1		1	Smuggling	2		2
For Trial				Maintain family	2		2
Stealing	7	2	9	Disob. in Union	1	1	2
Burglary	1	1	2	Forgery	1		1
Stabbing	1		1	Rogue	1		1
Arson	1		1	Tax Evasion	1		1
Rape	1		1	Furious riding	1		1
Housebreaking	1		1	Damage		1	1
Total	65	13	**78**	**Total**	35	5	**40**

The table contains the full list of crimes committed by the prisoners. Of the 78 felony charges, 63 were for stealing (81%). The remainder were for Burglary (3), Stabbing (3), Receiving (3), Assault/rape (2) Arson (2) and House breaking (2).

There were many more types of crimes described as misdemeanours.

The most common charges were: Assault/rape, 10 cases (25%), Vagrancy (6: 15%) and Breach of the peace (4: 10%). The remaining 50% of charges were accounted for by 11 different offences, including 'Disobedience in the Union Workhouse', Smuggling, Tax Evasion and Furious Riding.

The Courts:

The prisoners were sentenced to time in gaol by the three different types of Courts. Of the 103 sentenced, 32 came from the Assizes (31%), 39 from the Sessions (38%) and the remaining 32 (31%) from Summary Conviction by the Magistrates.

	Ass.	Sess.	Sum.	Total
Felons	26	35	0	61
Misdemeanants	6	4	30	40
Under Juvenile Act	0	0	2	2
Total	32	39	32	103

The Sentences:

The sentences from all the Courts ranged from 14 days to two years in gaol and 10 years transportation.

The Assizes issued sentences of between 4 months and 2 years. Although the group numbers are small and therefore may not be accurate, the average sentence of this court was 49 weeks for males and 41 weeks for females.

The Sessions sentences ranged from 1 to 18 months. Average 24 weeks (males) and 19 weeks (females). This court sentenced two prisoners to 10 years transportation. Summary Magistrates sentences ranged from 14 days to one year.

Terms of Imprisonment for Prisoners

Sentence	Ass.		Sess.		Sum.		Total
	M	F	M	F	M	F	
14 days					1	1	2
21 days					2		2
1 month			3	1	5	1	10
2 months			5		5		10
3 months			6	1	6	1	14
4 months	3	3	2				8
5 months			1				1
6 months	5	1	11		4		21
7 months					1		1
9 months	3		1	1			5
12 months	9	1	3		2	2	17
18 months	2	2	2				6
20 months	1						1
24 months	2						2
Total	**25**	**7**	**34**	**3**	**26**	**5**	**100**
Until Fine Paid					1		1
Transported			2				2
Average Sentence (weeks)							
	49	41	24	19	15	25	

In addition to a sentence in gaol, the courts could add additional punishments. All but two prisoners before the Assizes and Sessions were sentenced to hard labour. The sessions sentenced 5 prisoners to 2-4 weeks in solitary confinement and one to a whipping. The sentences of

Additional Punishments

	Ass.		Sess.		Sum.	
	M	F	M	F	M	F
Hard Labour	23	7	34	3	15	3
Sol. Conf.			5			
Whipping			1		1	
Alternative Punishments						
Surities					2	2
Fines					15	1

the Magistrates are more complex. Fourteen prisoners sentenced to imprisonment and six sentenced to hard labour were offered an alternative of 'finding sureties' or paying a Fine. For example, 'sentence of 6 months at hard labour or pay £21-12-0d.' An offer for tobacco smuggling was 6 months imprisonment or pay £100.

Details of Prisoners

The majority of the *'Registers of Prisoners'* for Bodmin Gaol and Bridewell, which were found in the Devon Records Office, have been transferred to the Cornwall Records Office. A team from the Cornwall Family History Society, led by Sally Pocock, has now published transcripts of these registers.

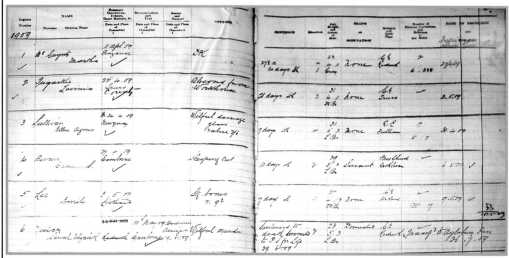

Part of page from Register (Female Prison 1909).

Entry 6 is the murderer, Sarah Elizabeth Visick, who was sentenced to Death at Bodmin Assizes (commuted to Penal Servitude for Life, served in Aylesbury Prison).

Later pages of this Register contain 11 entries for a 60 year old from Camborne (E.F.). They are listed as the 33rd to 43rd convictions for Drunkenness and date from 26th January to the 26th October 1910! *Photograph published by kind permission of Anne Hicks of Bodmin*

Prisoners in Cornwall County Gaol
Indexed alphabetically and chronologically with full introduction and explanations. Entries include place of birth and abode, age, occupation, aliases, brief details of charge, discharge date, and sundry notes regarding physical appearance, religious persuasion, etc. Later Volumes include how employed in the Gaol.
Vol 1: 1831-1836 (1,409 entries). Vol 2: 1836-1841 (1,410). Vol 3: 1846-1851 (1,770). Vol 4: 1851-1857 (1,770). Vol 5: 1856-1859/60 (1,836). Vol 6: 1860-1863 (1,891). Vol 7: 1862-1865 (970). Vol 8: 1863-1867 (1,930). Vol 9: 1866-1870 (2,030). Vol 10: 1869-1872 (2,472). Vol 11: 1872-1875/6 (2,250). Vol 12: 1875-1879 (2,290). Vol 13: 1878-1879 & 1895-1899 (2,656).

Bodmin Bridewell and its Inmates
Details include full names, occupations, age, marital status, number of children, place of birth and abode at the time of imprisonment, year of discharge and some personal descriptions. 1821-1848 (ca.7500 entries)

Debtors Imprisoned in Bodmin Gaol
Details included are place of birth, Age, approximate amount of debt, date of discharge and some personal descriptions. 1831-1853 and 1868-1879

Prisoners in Cornwall County Gaol & Bridewell – Master Index
This Index contains 32,340 entries from 1821 to 1899. (N.B. Registers for the gaol 1880-1894 and Debtors 1854-1867 have not survived.)

CHAPTER 11

Gaol Life - Rules and Punishments

"The distress of prisoners, of which there are few who have not some imperfect idea, came more immediately under my notice when I was sheriff of the county of Bedford; and the circumstance which excited me to activity in their behalf was, the seeing, some - who by the verdict of juries were declared not guilty; some - on whom the grand jury did not find such an appearance of guilt as subjected them to trial; and some - whose prosecutors did not appear against them; - after having been confined for months, dragged back to gaol, and locked up again till they should pay sundry fees to the gaoler, the clerk of assize, etc."

This quote from Howard describes the unjust treatment of prisoners who were found *not guilty* of the crime. They were kept, like those who had been convicted; some in dungeons, without regular food or a supply of water, in airless dark quarters, windows were blocked up due to the window tax, payable by the gaoler. All types of prisoners, debtors, felons and bridewell, were together and they had to pay charges to the gaoler, turnkeys and court clerks and for all services, including beds, straw, fees chargeable on arrival (garnish) and discharge and even fees for punishments, such as whipping and 'being put in irons'. It was legal at the time for prisoners to earn money by working, however, in many gaols there were no tools or suitable work spaces.

How different were the conditions in the new Bodmin Gaol in the late 18th Century? A prisoner arriving at Bodmin would see a set of prison buildings, unlike any seen before - buildings which would not be out of place in some of our famous Georgian cities. He would never have seen a gaol which had individual cells, baths, running water, an infirmary and chapel. Life would still be hard, charges had not been abolished but he would have opportunities to earn money to pay them. He would be forced to work hard, the food would be limited, as the cost of the food had to be below that spent by local poor families, he would have to be silent at all times, even when working with others and to attend chapel. On the other hand, he would be kept healthy, the services of the surgeon were not available to most of the population, and he would probably be in better condition on leaving the gaol than on arrival. This is a great difference to earlier institutions, where the chances of dying of gaol fever, smallpox or malnutrition were very high.

There is a contemporary document by Howard,[2] published in the third edition of his book *'The State of Prisons'*. This covered his journey of Great Britain and Ireland in 1782. In this edition, there is a report on the new County Gaol at Bodmin. In addition to a description of the facilities, it lists a table of fees and rates to be taken by the gaoler and turnkeys and a set of Articles,

Regulations and Allowances. These documents define the conditions and the daily life of the prisoners in the gaol.

County Gaol at Bodmin (1782)

'This new gaol is built on a fine eminence, at a little distance from the town, where there is a constant current of water. Here is a good house for the gaoler, in which there are apartments for master's-side debtors, and a chapel. There are separate rooms and courts for each sex of debtors, of felons, and of petty offenders or bridewell prisoners; and each prisoner has a separate lodging-room (about eight feet two inches by five feet eight, and seven and a half feet high), which is furnished with a bedstead, straw-bed, two blankets and a coverlet. There are two rooms for an infirmary, and under them three condemned cells. In two of the courts are baths. In the centre of the gaoler's house there is a turret with an alarm-bell and clock. The men who are confined for petty offences, are employed in sawing and polishing stone, and, as they have the county allowance (food and necessities paid for by the county), keep only one-sixth of what they earn. Clauses against spirituous liquors are hung up. The Act for preserving the health of prisoners is not hung up, but the gaol is now kept very neat and clean.

A table of fees and regulations were printed and hung up, though not signed. The majority of the fees and rates applied to debtors. The only charge for felons and persons committed to the bridewell was a discharge or acquittal fee of 13s.4d'.

The Rules and Regulations (1782) defined the conditions and the daily life and diet of the prisoners. All prisoners were employed for 10 hr. per day in the summer and 8 hr. in winter. The keeper kept one sixth of their earnings, the prisoner one sixth plus the full amount for extra work, the rest went to the county toward the expense of their maintenance. The working day started with a bell rung at sunrise, from the 1st November to 31st March, and at 6 a.m. for the rest of the year. Locking-up time was 6 p.m. from 1st October – 31st March and 8 p.m. during the remainder of the year.

The list of offences against prison rules included:- Abuse, ill-treatment or affray between prisoners; playing games for money or liquor; entering a cell during the day, except for cleaning; bad behaviour and failing to attend divine service. These offences were punishable by close confinement, harder labour or reduction in diet. Irons were provided, at the county expense, and kept ready to be used, when absolutely necessary for punishment.

The head gaoler kept a register containing the following details of each prisoner: Date of confinement – Person's name - Place of abode - By whom confined - For what offence - Stature, complexion, etc. - Where discharged or how disposed of – Remarks on behaviour, etc. The justices of Bodmin sessions, the grand jury at the assizes and all justices of the peace and the sheriff and his deputy, were all requested to visit the gaol and bridewell, as often as possible, to inquire into the state and treatment of all prisoners and debtors.

The situation of debtors in prison was complex. They were imprisoned by their creditors, who were expected to support them. Master or principle debtors of property could choose their room in the keeper's house and their bed and diet at the rates fixed by the keeper. Ordinary debtors were housed over the arcades according to their choice or ability to pay the established rates. Debtors were allowed to work and to keep all of their earnings.

The design of the new gaol, together with reasonable charges and defined regulations and allowances demonstrate that Bodmin was the first modern prison built in Britain. At the same time in Launceston, the prisoners were still in a dungeon and were fed through a hole in the ceiling!

After the death of Howard in 1790, the work of inspecting prisons was taken over by James Neild. In his report, after his visit in 1803,[91] he repeats many of the comments made by Howard but there are differences. He states that the prisoners keep one-half of their earnings, rather than one-sixth and that they work in a large work-room, in which there are several looms for weaving and a court, 46 yards by 32 yards, to work in. All the apartments were whitewashed twice a year and the sleeping cells, four times. The floors of the dayrooms and sleeping-cells were washed once a week in winter, and twice in summer, and swept every day. He had two complaints about the gaol, firstly, there was association between committed prisoners and those sentenced and, secondly, there was no separation of *young beginners* from *old offenders*.

Some interesting references to the gaol and bridewell are contained in a report printed by order of the Honourable Court of Aldermen of the City of London, on September 26th, 1815.[19] The report was drawn up by a committee which set out from London on July 29th, 1814, to visit the gaol of Gloucester, and such other gaols as they deemed expedient, so that they might become acquainted with their main features and compare them with those of some of the gaols in the City of London.

Describing the prison at Bodmin, the report of 1815 states:

'that it was built upwards of thirty years ago. It stands on the side of a hill near the town of Bodmin, so that the buildings range one above another; and every part is well supplied with excellent water distributed throughout for the supply of baths and for other purposes.

The Governor's house is in the centre of the Prison, as is also the Chapel, the seats of which are so placed, that the men are kept distinct from the women, and entirely out of sight of each other, and the Debtors as placed in the Gallery.

This Prison will contain thirty-six men, besides women, and thirty Debtors. There were at the time of the Committee's visit nineteen men in the Gaol, and sixteen men and four women in the Bridewell, and the average number in the two Prisons is stated to be forty-two.

The criminals are generally placed two in a cell, and are sometimes, ironed, and no preference whatever is allowed to be given to any prisoner by paying for it. Innocent exercises, conducive to health, are allowed; but all sorts of games for money or liquor are entirely prohibited. The prisoners are all employed in some work, and those committed to hard labour are strictly kept thereto. One-sixth part of their earnings is given to the Governor, one-sixth to themselves, and the remainder is paid into the County-stock towards the expenses of their maintenance.

The Debtors are allowed to work, and have all their earnings; and visitors are admitted generally to them during the day. The Allowance of Bread to the Debtors is the same as to the other prisoners; but they are restricted to the purchase of one quart of beer or cyder each day.'

This report confirms that the cell numbers are the same as those identified on the John Call engraving and that the comment on the bottom of the document, *'One Hundred Men and Women may be lodged in the several Wards at the same time'* could not be achieved without placing more than one prisoner in each cell.

The multiple occupancy of sleeping cells was later confirmed in the Inspector's Report, published in 1837. *'During the late governor's time (before 1828) …….. The sleeping rooms, which were originally intended for one, were always occupied by either three or five.'*

In accordance with the Prison Act of 1823, the Justices published a new set of Rules & Regulations in October, 1823.[97] The rules included: the keeper must have no financial interest in prison supplies or sell anything to prisoners; he must inspect every cell and see every prisoner daily; he must record all punishments and other 'occurrences of importance'. The chaplain to read selected prayers every morning and all convicted prisoners to attend divine service. Prisoners not to be put in irons, except when absolutely necessary.

The daily life of prisoners in the gaol was described in two Inspectors of Prisons reports published in 1837 [20] and 1839.[79] Extracts of these reports are reproduced below:

This prison lies near a public road, but it is not overlooked. An important change has been accomplished here by the exertions of the present keeper: the prisoners here, both men and women, are all sleeping in separate beds, and in separate night-cells; and have so slept for seven years, except in the infirmary. These cells are, however, too small for separate confinement during the day, nor are they sufficiently well lighted and ventilated for that purpose. The cells are almost all about 8½ feet long, 2½ wide, and 8½ high. This was foreseen; but it was justly deemed essential to separate the prisoners at night, although more could not be conveniently accomplished at the time.

The gaol part consists of seven wards (exclusive of that for debtors), each containing a distinct class viz. four for males, and three for females, with day-rooms, airing-yards, and dormitories to each. The House of Correction part also contains seven wards possessing the same accommodations as the Gaol. The building cannot be extended or increased within the present walls.

In the gaol the female cells are at present in a state of disorder: the magistrates had resolved to convert this part into single sleeping cells, as is the case for the males; but this was suspended from an idea of some further alterations which might be contemplated by the Legislature in prison discipline. The number of female inmates is usually small. They sleep at present in the House of Correction

Some additional means of ventilation may be advantageously adopted here; all of which I have pointed out on the spot. There are no measures in existence for warming the cells in winter. (Since my last visit gas has been introduced into the passages at night. Air holes have been made in some places, according to my recommendation, in order to improve the ventilation.[79]

Silence is enjoined upon all the prisoners, both the tried and the untried. The day-rooms are still in use; there is a fire kept up in them in winter, but no cooking is allowed in any of them. The untried prisoners are not locked up during the day, excepting as a punishment. The prisoners sentenced to hard labour remain in their day-rooms when not engaged in work.

The untried prisoners have no other occupation than the cleaning of their own cells, day-rooms, and courts. They associate in their day rooms, but they are narrowly watched, and kept in their airing-yards as much as possible, where they are not permitted to associate.

The convicted prisoners are separated by day according to classes, and by night in separate cells.

Intercourse must, from the construction of the day-rooms, take place at meals to a greater extent than at other times, as the turnkeys are present at locking and unlocking, washing, and at chapel, when all intercourse is prevented. The prisoners take their meals in their respective day-rooms.

They are not allowed to receive visits or letters oftener than once in three months after conviction.

The number of prisoners assembled on Sunday for instruction averages between 20 and 30, who are under the superintendence of a schoolmaster and a turnkey. When taking air and when at labour they are under the superintendence of a turnkey: but, at their meals, they are not under any constant superintendence beyond that of the turnkey walking backwards and forwards in the passages.

There are fire-places in each day-room The fires are put out every evening before the prisoners go to their respective sleeping cells.

Each ward has a towel, combs, and a brush but no paper. There are no wardsmen. All the prisoners clean the prison by turns.

Every week a piece of soap is distributed to each ward, varying in size according to the number of inmates. Every morning the prisoners are mustered before labour for the purpose of washing. The whole prison is remarkably neat, clean, and well arranged, as far as the nature of the building permits. There is a common kitchen in which only one prisoner is suffered to remain.

Prisoners convicted of felony are clothed in a prison dress, which consists of a woollen jacket, waistcoat, and trousers for the males, and a suitable clothing for the females. The cost of a suit of the former is about 7s. 9d. and of the latter about 5s. Shoes, stockings, handkerchiefs, &c., are supplied when necessary, and clean shirts and shifts are furnished every week. Other prisoners are allowed shirts, shifts, and such other clothing as they absolutely require.

The bedding consists of a straw mattress and three blankets to each prisoner, the cost of which is about 11s.

This prison is very clean, neat, and well-ordered, and reflects credit on the keeper, officers, and all employed in managing it.

New sets of 'Prison Rules & Regulations' were produced at various times throughout the history of the gaol. The Rules, introduced in July, 1832 [98] and a later set, undated but probably late Victorian are reproduced below. The breaking of any of these Rules resulted in punishment.

Rules and Regulations for Treatment of Prisoners in Bodmin Gaol and House of Correction at Bodmin (July 1832).

1. On arrival all prisoners to be cleansed and examined. Money, watches, knives and articles likely to be of use in escape attempts to be taken from them and listed by principal turnkey in a book kept for that purpose, all to be restored to owners on discharge.
2. Prisoners with no money, whose behaviour has been good, to be allowed a small sum on discharge, at discretion of governor.
3. Convicted prisoners not to receive any food, clothing or "necessaries" other than gaol allowance.
4. Established diet to be maintained. No wines, spirits or beer to be allowed except by direction of visiting justices, or by surgeon in case of prisoner's sickness.
5. Prisoners on remand to be allowed food, clothing and necessaries subject to examination.
6. Prisoners sentenced to hard labour and employed on hand mill, treadwheel or other work to be allowed up to extra ½lb of bread.
7. Prisoners not sentenced to hard labour to be set to work "not severe" and if able to earn their own subsistence. If more than subsistence amount earned by a prisoner, the surplus money to be paid on prisoner's discharge, subject to good conduct.
8. Prisoners on remand to be allowed to work for remuneration with their own consent.
9. All letters written by, or sent to prisoners to be read by Governor or principal turnkey but prisoners on remand not subject to this rule, and to be allowed pens, ink and paper.
10. Prisoners on remand to be allowed to see their friends and legal advisers.
11. Turnkeys forbidden to strike prisoners or to use abusive language. Cases of misconduct to be reported to governor.

Rules to be observed by prisoners
1. To be respectful to prison officers, and to obey turnkeys' orders. To be clean and "peaceable and orderly".
2. No gaming, fighting or wrestling, or abusive language.
3. No money to be extracted from fellow prisoners, nor to ill treat them.
4. To observe strict silence whilst working or locked in sleeping cells. No shouting or unnecessary noise at other times.
5. No clothes to be destroyed. No damage to county property.
6. No water to be boiled "in your Tin pots" and no cooking in dayrooms. No smoking or use of tobacco.
7. Wards-men to be responsible for clean state of their ward and good order.

Rules for prisoners confined for debt in Sheriff's Ward.

1. Debtors not to be subjected to any more regulations other than that necessary for their safe custody, and the discipline and hygiene of the prison.

2. Debtors paying their own expenses may occupy the best apartments, but those not paying to be allocated other accommodation.

3. Debtors' bedrooms to be opened at the same time as those of other prisoners and occupants to vacate their bedrooms by 9 a.m. unless prevented by sickness, and be locked up at 10p.m. at lights out.

4. Each debtor to make his/her bed, and clean the room by 11 a.m., and wash it at least once a week. Bedding to be aired. If more than one debtor in a bedroom to take turns with cleaning. Dayrooms to be cleaned daily.

5. No food to be prepared in bedrooms. Food to be cooked to be "dressed" in dayroom or at the lodge by permission of the turnkey.

6. No tobacco to be smoked in bedrooms or galleries. No tippling in the ward.

7. Debtors may receive from their friends, or purchase, a pint of wine or a quart of strong beer or cider daily, to be received between 8 a.m. and 1 p.m. Any attempt to obtain more liquor to lose the privilege of his allowance.

8. Debtors, "destitute of friends" or unable to support themselves, may receive the county allowance on production of a certificate from the parish to which they belong, stating their need. Debtors receiving their 6d. or allowance from their creditors not entitled to allowance until their means exhausted.

9. All clothing, liquor, bundles and parcels brought into prison liable to inspection by governor or turnkeys.

10. Debtors permitted to follow their professions, providing their own tools, may keep any earnings therefrom; "except dissenters".

11. All debtors to attend divine service in gaol chapel on Sundays and when held on other days. Those who refuse to be locked in their bedrooms during the service and to be deprived of their liquor allowance next day.

12. No gaming. Any cards or dice found will be destroyed.

13. Debtors to keep themselves clean. Those maintained by county to be allowed soap and towels and their linen to be washed in the prison wash kitchen.

14. Debtors' friends may visit them on any day except Sunday, Christmas day and Good Friday, between 10 a.m. and sunset. No visitor except a wife, husband, parent or child to stay more than an hour or be admitted more than twice a day. No visitors allowed in galleries, bedrooms, or even day rooms when a visiting room provided.

15. Visitors refusing to leave, or misbehaving in any way to be refused admission in future.

16. Disobedience to the rules subject to punishment or privation determined by visiting justices.

17. Female debtors to be kept in a separate ward under control of the matron, and subject to foregoing rules.

ABSTRACT OF THE REGULATIONS
RELATING TO THE
TREATMENT AND CONDUCT
OF
CONVICTED PRISONERS

1. Prisoners shall preserve silence.
2. They shall not communicate, or attempt to do so, with one another, or with any strangers or others who may visit the Prison.
3. They shall keep themselves clean and decent in their persons and shall obey such regulations as regards washing, bathing, and in the case of male prisoners, hair-cutting, as may from time to time be established, with a view to the proper maintenance of health and cleanliness.
4. They shall keep their cells, utensils, clothing, and bedding, clean and neatly arranged; and shall, when required, clean and sweep the yards, passages, and other parts of the prison.
5. If any prisoner has any complaint to make regarding the diet, it must be made immediately after a meal is served. Frivolous and groundless complaints, repeatedly made, will be dealt with a breach of Prison discipline.
6. A prisoner may if required for purposes of justice, be photographed and measured on reception and subsequently.
7. A prisoner committed to Prison for non-payment of a sum adjudged to be paid by the conviction of any court of summary jurisdiction, may obtain a reduction of a part of the sentence by paying part of the sum for which he is liable, viz., the fine, costs, and cost of commitment. No such
8. Prisoners shall attend Divine Service on Sundays and on other days when such Service is performed, unless they receive permission to be absent. Prisoners shall not be compelled to attend the religious service of a Church to which they do not belong.
9. If any Prisoner who is of a religious persuasion different from that of the Established Church specially so requests, the Governor shall permit a minister of that persuasion to visit him at proper and reasonable times under regulations approved by the Commissioners.
10. The following offences committed by prisoners will render them liable to punishment:—
1. Disobeying any order of the Governor or of any other officer, or any Prison regulation.
2. Treating with disrespect any officer or servant of the Prison, or any visitor, or any person employed in connection with the Prison or works.
3. Being idle, careless, or negligent at work, or refusing to work.

4. Being absent without leave from Divine Service, or prayers, or school instruction.
5. Behaving irreverently at Divine Service of prayers.
6. Swearing, cursing, or using any abusive, insolent, threatening, or other improper language.
7. Being indecent in language, act, or gesture.
8. Committing a common assault upon another prisoner.
9. Conversing or holding intercourse with another prisoner without authority.
10. Singing, whistling, or making any unnecessary noise, or giving any unnecessary trouble.
11. Leaving his cell or other appointed location, or his place or work, without permission.
12. In any way disfiguring or damaging any part of the Prison, or any article to which he may have access.
13. Committing any nuisance.
14. Having in his cell or possession any article he is not allowed to have.
15. Giving to or receiving from any prisoner any article whatever without leave.
16. In any other way offending against good order and discipline.
17. Attempting to do any of the foregoing things.
18. Personal violence to a fellow prisoner.
19. Grossly offensive or abusive language to any officer or servant of the Prison.
20. Wilfully or wantonly breaking the Prison windows, or otherwise destroying the Prison property.
21. When under punishment, wilfully making a disturbance tending to interrupt the order and discipline of the Prison.
22. Any other act of gross misconduct or insubordination requiring to be suppressed by extraordinary means.
23. Escaping or attempting to escape from Prison.

11. The following offences committed by male prisoners will render them liable to corporal punishment:—
1. Mutiny or incitement to mutiny.
2. Gross personal violence to any officer or servant of the Prison.

12. Prisoners may, if they desire, have an interview with the Governor or Superior Authority, to make complaints or prefer requests; and the Governor shall redress any grievance or take such steps as may seem necessary.

13. Any prisoner wishing to see a member of the Visiting Committee shall be allowed to do so on the occasion of his next occurring visit to the Prison.

Punishments for Prison Offences.

The following table is a compilation of the numbers of prison punishments for breaking the Rules and Regulations (Debtors & Civil Process prisoners are not included):

Year	Prisoners	Solitary confinement	Dark cells	Stoppage of diet	Whipping	Irons/handcuffs	Other punishments	Loss of Stage	Punishments (M & F)	Total Punishments	Prisoners Punished	Ref.
1830	555	115								115		95
1831	513	31								31		95
1832	650	44				20				64		95
1835	406	32			2		291			325		20
1837	M 373 / F 100 — 473	60 / 8	76 / 6	422	3	1	72		634 / 14	648		79
1843	M 474 / F 138 — 612	32 / 11	86 / 55	240 / 81			130 / 21		488 / 168	656		13
1846	M 441 / F 156 — 597		57 / 31	206 / 35	1		23 / 4		287 / 70	357		14
1850	M 563 / F 160 — 723	29 / 1	90 / 5	128 / 7	2	1	142 / 2		392 / 15	407		23
1865	M 539 / F 151 — 690								310 / 18	328		28
1868	M 521 / F 181 — 702	24 / 1		675 / 16	2	1	9 / 2		711 / 19	730		41
1871	M 679 / F 227 — 906	13 / 9		669 / 24	1	1			684 / 33	717		99
1872	M 525 / F 187 — 712	28 / 1		601 / 26	1				630 / 27	657		100
1874	M 600 / F 132 — 732	20		461 / 27	4				485 / 27	512		40
1877	M 652 / F 139 — 791	12 / 2		394 / 36	2				408 / 38	446		35
1883	M 783 / F 116 — 899	7		102 / 1	1			109	219 / 1	220	130 / 1	31
1901	M 446 / F 70 — 516	14 / 2		13 / 2				17 / 2	44 / 6	50	31 / 2	33
1916	M 180	8		8				10		26	13	39

The punishments include solitary confinement, sometimes in dark cells, whipping, being handcuffed or put in irons, but the most common punishment was reduction or stoppage of food. In the report for 1835, the Inspector described *'other punishments'* as a double turn at the tread-wheel or a reduction of diet. He also stated: *'Among other suggestions which I have made, I have recommended the disuse of the punishment called putting on the bars, which, however, was very seldom used, and was, I believe not a particularly severe one. The arms were extended and the wrists handcuffed to the bars. It will be no longer practised here'.*

The detailed reasons for the punishments are not recorded, except for the 20 prisoners in irons, who took part in an attempted escape. Governor Everest stated in 1835 that the *'silent system'*, which was directed by the justices, had been implemented to good effect, however it was impossible to maintain silence whilst prisoners congregated in the day rooms. He reported an increase in punishments arising from enforcement of the silent system.

In 1839, the Inspector reported: *'the punishment by solitary confinement has generally been for refusal to work, pilfering, assaults, profane swearing, repeated talking, and other acts of in-subordination. The whipping has been for mutinous and violent conduct; and irons have only been once used, which was for an attempt to break out of prison'.*

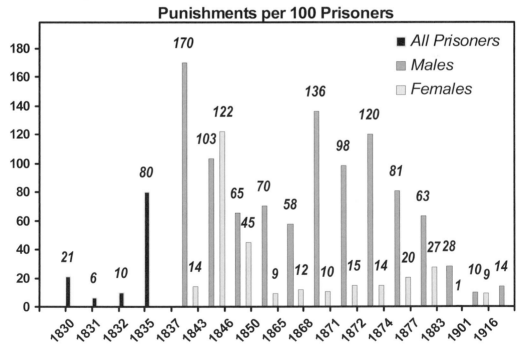

Punishments per 100 Prisoners

There was a large change in the number of punishments between 1833 and 1835 and it then doubled in 1837. For males in 1837 & 1843, there were more punishments handed out than there were prisoners, and then there was a slow decline until the Prison Act 1865. After this Act, which confirmed a harder regime, there was a large increase, followed by a decline until the prison closed. Part of the decline after 1872 may be due to the presence of naval prisoners. It would be expected that this category of prisoners would be much more disciplined than civil prisoners. If the naval prisoners are not included in the population, the percentage of punishments increases to 130% and 105% for the years 1874 & 1877. The number of punishments for females was generally much lower than for males except for the year 1843.

For the Victorian period, after 1837, the figures show that it was a hard regime in which, on average, most males received at least one punishment and between 10-45% of the women were punished for a breach of the Rules and Regulations.

One serious prison offence was recorded in the Governor's journal: [28]

20th Jan, 1865.—A savage and unprovoked assault was made on a warder, by a prisoner undergoing imprisonment for house-breaking, and who was engaged in the stone yard. Whilst the officer's back was towards him, he struck him on the leg with a sledge hammer, used for breaking the larger blocks of stone. The warder's leg was broken, and the man's murderous intention to have again struck him on the head was providentially prevented by the gallant behaviour of another prisoner, who seized the hammer and eventually took it from the man. (Nine months of this man's punishment has been remitted by Her Majesty.)

In less than an hour the case was investigated by two Visiting Justices, and the would-be murderer committed for trial at the assizes, where he was sentenced to twenty years' penal servitude.

And another by the Inspector of Prisons (1850): [23]

No prisoner was under punishment at the time of my last inspection, but a man had been flogged on the previous day to the extent of 36 lashes with a cat, for refusing to go upon the treadwheel, and insulting the governor with abusive language. He was duly sentenced by a Visiting Justice, after evidence of his offence given on oath: but he erroneously protested against the power of a single justice to inflict the punishment.

CHAPTER 12

Prisoners' Employment

At the end of the eighteenth century, prison was solely for the detention of offenders and not a place of punishment. This meant that the justices could allow the gaol to be used as a commercial, profit making concern. In the time of governor Chapple all prisoners could do useful work, which earned money for the county, the gaoler and the prisoner. The work for men consisted of cutting and polishing stone and slate, cutting wood, shoemaking and working in the garden. The women were employed in spinning, weaving and knitting. The gaoler would supply the raw materials and sell the finished objects. The prison workshop was a 'house of Industry', which kept the prisoners out of mischief and allowed them to earn as much as possible for their fees and maintenance and their families. Many prisoners, who had never been taught any trade before, were provided with the means of earning a livelihood after their discharge from the Prison.[19]

In the early nineteenth century the prison system came under criticism,[101] it was pointed out that it did not deter criminals from re-offending, in fact, *'under the system of profitable employment, the prison became, for many a poor labourer, a rather comfortable place. The healthy surroundings, ample but simple food, and regular employment compared favourably with his lot when out of gaol'.* It was alleged that the great increase in the numbers committed to prison was due to their positive attractiveness. This led to the suggestion that any productive labour in prison was bad, because it was too pleasant for the inmates. Useless labour was considered a great deterrent because the prisoner hated it for its uselessness; indeed, it was even argued that the knowledge that his work accomplished nothing had a reformative effect. These new ideas were accepted by the governor at Bodmin and led to the introduction of the treadwheel and other hard labour machines. Details of the new regime are contained in the 2nd Report of the Inspectors of Prisons published in 1837, covering the period Easter Sessions 1835 to Easter Sessions 1836.[20]

Labour is generally regarded as a punishment, particularly by the idle; but the industrious prisoner views moderate labour as an alleviation of his imprisonment.

There are two tread-wheels, both connected with the same shaft. The treadmill is employed during every month of the year, from 7 to 10 hours, according to the length of the days. The wheels will hold 26 prisoners at one time: each step is 7 inches in height. The ordinary velocity of the wheels per minute is from 48 to 60. The proportion of prisoners to the total number thus employed is about two-thirds. There is no application of the power.

There are two apartments, containing each a crank. Each crank will employ three men at one time. The ordinary velocity of the cranks per minute varies from 40 to 50. The power is applied to grinding corn for the prison and for the County Lunatic Asylum. A certain quantity of corn is put into the mill to be ground within a certain time; if it is ground before the expiration of that time the prisoners derive the benefit. The mill grinds in 10 hours 15 imperial bushels of corn, which, divided among the 12 men who are employed (6 on and 6 as relays), will yield a bushel and a quarter of corn as the daily amount of labour performed by each prisoner who works at the crank.

The other employments are sawing and breaking stones, carpentering, painting, shoemaking, tailoring, &c., for the males, and washing, ironing, needlework, &c., for the females.

It is not productive, except for county purposes, as far as regards the hand-mill grinding corn for the prison and County Asylum, and the labour of shoemakers, &c., for the use of the prison.

The report of the next inspection of the gaol,[79] covering Easter 1837 to Easter 1838, contains details of which prisoners work and states that the power generated from the treadwheel is now used to grind corn in place of the less efficient cranks.

The men work at the tread-wheel and crank, all except about three, who are incapable. The tread-wheel is used to grind corn for the prison and County Lunatic Asylum.

The male prisoners work at the tread-wheel, hand-mill, breaking and sawing stones, carpentering, blacksmith's work, mason's work, shoemaking and tailoring. Washing, ironing, needlework, and other suitable employment is provided for the females. Baking is not performed by the prisoners.

The unemployed prisoners are those for trial, those not sentenced to hard labour, and cripples.

In the summer months the prisoners labour ten hours daily; at other seasons of the year the hours of labour vary according to the length of the days. Prisoners for trial and those not sentenced to hard labour take as much exercise in their respective airing-yards as they please.

The labour of the prisoners being applied to county purposes, their earnings are nominal. They are paid a small sum at discharge, varying in amount according to behaviour and other circumstances.

For 1843 [13], of the 734 criminal prisoners confined during the previous year, 310 (42.2%), including 13 boys under 17 years of age, were employed at hard labour, 275 (37.5%), including 31 boys and 10 girls, had employment and the remaining 149 (20.3%), were unemployed. For 1846 [14] twenty-six percent of the prisoners were not employed. These two documents also report what appears to be a change in the two treadwheels. The machines now hold a total of 60 prisoners at a time compared to the earlier reports of 26. The height of each step has also increased from 7 to 7½ inches. The details of the use of these new wheels is contained in the table '*Scale of Treadwheel Labour*'.

Each prisoner 'ascended' between 7,800 and 12,000 feet in each working day. The total for a six-day week was between 46,800 and 72,000 feet depending on the time of year. For comparison Everest is 29,000 feet!

Scale of Treadwheel Labour

Months Employed	Number of Working Hours per Day	Number of Prisoners the Wheels will hold at a time	Height of each Step	The Number of Steps per Minute	Proportion of Prisoners off wheels to Number on Wheels	Number of Feet in Ascent per Day	Daily Ascent, in Feet, performed by every Prisoner	How recorded with precision	Application of its Power
Jan	7					12,600	8,400	The account here-given is from daily observation	Grinding corn for the use of the Prison and County Lunatic Asylum
Feb	8					14,400	9,600		
Mar	9					16,200	10,800		
Apr-Aug	10	60	7½	48	One-third	18,000	12,000		
Sep	9½					17,100	11,400		
Oct	8					14,400	9,600		
Nov	7					12,600	8,400		
Dec	6½					11,700	7,800		

The same employment system was followed into the mid-1850s.[25] Prisoners under sentence of hard labour, worked on the treadmill but some were now employed on the works appertaining to the new buildings. Those who were not under sentence of hard labour and the untried prisoners were employed on breaking stones and cleaning the prison.

The Inspector commented that it would be very desirable to have oakum to pick, but until the completion of the railway from Plymouth, the difficulty of obtaining the junk (old rope) to pick would continue to be very great. One man was employed as a tailor, one as a shoemaker and one as a maker of scrubbing brushes.

Details of the employment of all prisoners were published in reports covering selected years between 1858 and 1877, for the County Gaol and 1878 to 1916, for H.M. Prison, Bodmin. The numbers are included in the two tables 'Employment of Prisoners'. Some entries are figures for the single day on which the Inspector visited the gaol. The remainder, shown as ranges, are daily averages for the year quoted. The original documents contain the accurate but complex fractions, based on the number of working days in the year. For the year ending 31st March 1901, whole numbers were used.

In all reports, employment for females consisted of cleaning, knitting, needlework and working in the laundry. For males, there were a small number of tradesmen and a larger number of males employed at cleaning and 'working in the service of the prison' but the main hard labour changed over time. In 1858, the treadwheel and was still in use but a number of prisoners were now working on the new buildings. By 1860, the treadwheel was out of use and 'digging & excavating', connected with the new gaol, was the main employment. When the new gaol was complete, oakum picking was introduced, this was later replaced by coir picking, which was used to make brushes and mats. The Inspector reported in 1865 [28]: *The male prisoners are employed at the hand corn-mills, oakum picking, stone-breaking, gardening, carpentering, mason's and smith's work, stone-cutting, shoemaking, tailoring, cleaning the prison, painting, brush-making, &c. The hand corn-mills are worked by prisoners in separate cells. There is a single hard-labour machine (Crank) in the prison, which is only worked by men out of whom no other work can be got: it is very seldom used, but when, it is 10,000 revolutions are required in the day.*

After the 1865 Act, which in addition to abolishing the distinction between the house of correction and the gaol, all prisoners had to be subjected to penal labour in prescribed form, either hard labour 1st Class on the tread-wheel, the crank, the capstan or at shot-drill or stone breaking or hard labour 2nd Class which consisted of any labour approved by the Secretary of State. Most prisoners started in 1st Class and after three months, became eligible to transfer to 2nd Class.

HARD LABOUR, 1st CLASS. The treadwheel, 32 on the wheel, and 32 in waiting, working four hours and resting four hours by alternate periods of 15 minutes, ascending 7,200 feet *(This was another new treadwheel, built after 1865.)* During rest the prisoners are employed picking oakum, rope beating and mat weaving with heavy looms, and occasional stone breaking for prison use.

HARD LABOUR, 2nd CLASS. Rope and oakum picking, mat-making, and trades employment for males; washing, needlework and oakum picking for females.

Those who by their amenability to prison discipline, and who had served the period required by the Prison Act, 1865, at 1st class hard labour, were employed at mat-making, and were allowed a small per-centage on the whole of the quantity man-ufactured by them, which was paid on discharge.

Employment of Prisoners in County Gaol, Bodmin						
	1858	1860	1865	1868	1874	1877
MALES:						
Tread-wheel	30			28	24-25	32
Hand corn mills		3	12			
Oakum/Coir picking & beating			16	17	8-10	14-15
Digging & excavating	12	29			2-3	3-4
Trades	4	5	5	2	3-5	3-4
Cleaning & Prison Service	23	25	25		10-12	14-15
Brush & Mat making			1	1	9-11	17-19
Gardening			1	1		
School			7			
Woodcutting, Stone breaking		4			1-2	1
Not Employed, Sick, etc.	10	8	7			6-7
No. of Males	79	74	74	49	61-62	93
FEMALES:						
Oakum picking				2		
Cleaning	9	8	8			1
Knitting & needlework	9	10	10	4	3-4	3-4
Laundry, mangling,	11	12	4	8	7-9	7-9
School			3			
Not employed, Sick, etc.	3	2	0			2-3
No. of Females	32	32	25	14	11-12	15

Employment of Prisoners in H M Prison, Bodmin										
Year (Ref.)	1883 (31)		1885 (102)		1891 (103)		1895 (104)		1901 (33)	
	M	F	M	F	M	F	M	F	M	F
NON-PRODUCTIVE										
Crank, Tread-wheel, &c.	14-15		8-9							
Crank					2		5			
Tread-wheel					1-2		9-10			
IN MANUFACTURES										
Grinding Wheat	7-8		5-6		1-2				10	
Weaving Mats, Cotton &c.	6-7		1-2							
Knitters		1-2		1-2		< 1		< 1		
Mat Making	**22-23**		**23-24**		**6-7**					
Oakum & Coir Pickers	**30-31**		**23-24**		**6-7**	< 1	**21-22**	< 1	5	
Washing		1-2								
Bed, pillow makers. &c.									4	
Bookbinders									1	
Hammock makers									3	
Labourers, &c.									1	
Mail-bag makers									**20**	
Needleworkers, &c.										1
Sack makers & menders									4	
Tailors, &c.									1	
Wood choppers									1	
Total	67-68	2-3	56-57	1-2	14-15	< 1	21-22	< 1	50	1
IN BUILDINGS, &c.:										
Trades & labourers	4-5				2-3		2-3		2	
Total	4-5		3-4		2-3		2-3		2	
EMPLOYMENT in the ordinary service of the prison:										
Baking	1		1		1		1		1	
Cooking	1		1		1		1		2	
Cleaning and jobbing	6-7	1	7-8	1	2-3		2-3	< 1	5	1
Nursing	1-2		<1		< 1		< 1			
Gardening					< 1		1-2			
Stokers	1		1-2		< 1				1	
Washing	< 1	4-5	1-2	2-3	> 1	1-2	< 1	1-2	1	1
Repairing clothing & shoes	1-2	1-2	1-2	1-2	1	< 1	2-3	< 1		
Total	13-14	7-8	13-14	4-5	6-7	2-3	8-9	3-4	11	2
NON-EFFECTIVE :										
Sick & Under punishment	4-5	< 1	1-2	< 1	1	1	4-5	< 1		
Awaiting trial / Debtors	4-5	< 1	1-2	< 1	3-4	< 1	4-5	< 1	2	
Not told off at unlocking .	2-3	< 1	1-2	< 1	< 1	< 1	1-2	< 1	1	1
Total	10-11	1-2	5-6	1-2	5-6	1-2	11	< 1	3	1
GRAND TOTAL	**110**	**12**	**87**	**7**	**33**	**4**	**58**	**5**	**66**	**4**

Sometime before 1878, the Hard labour system of the 1865 Act was changed to the *'Progressive Four Stage System'*. In this system prisoners started at hardest labour in their cells, slept on a plank bed and were allowed no exercise or privileges, when they had accumulated 224 points, earned at a maximum of 8 per day for being obedient and docile, they were transferred to the second stage. Similar times were spent in the 2nd and 3rd stages. The details of this system are described in the *'System of Progressive Stages'*. This system was designed for long term prisoners, as the 'perfect prisoner' took a minimum of three months to arrive at stage four, whereas eighty-nine percent of prisoners were sentenced to less than three months' imprisonment. Oakum picking was still used as hard labour, even after the time when ships were being built of iron and it could not be sold, because it could be imposed on prisoners of any physical strength or mental ability and it could be performed in silence in absolute cellular isolation.

SYSTEM OF PROGRESSIVE STAGES.

The following instructions will be followed in local prisons, with a view to give effect to Rule 24, made by the Secretary of State, as to the employment of prisoners.

1. A prisoner shall be able to earn on each week-day, eight, seven, or six marks, according to the degree of his industry; and on Sunday he shall be awarded marks according to the degree of his industry during the previous week.

2. A prisoner who is idle on any day will be reported, and be liable to punishment.

3. There shall be four stages, and every prisoner shall pass through them, or through so much of them as the term of his imprisonment admits.

4. He shall commence in the first stage, and shall remain in the first stage until he has earned 28 x 8 or 224 marks; in the second stage until he has earned 224 more marks, or 448 in the whole; in the third stage until he has earned 224 more marks, or 672 in the whole; in the fourth stage during the remainder of his sentence.

5. A prisoner whose term of imprisonment is 28 days or less, shall serve the whole of his term in the first stage.

6. A prisoner who is idle, or who misconducts himself, or is inattentive to instruction, shall be liable,—

(1.) To forfeit gratuity earned or to be earned; or,

(2.) To forfeit any other stage privileges.

(3.) To detention in the stage in which he is until he shall have earned in that stage an additional number of marks.

(4.) To degradation to any lower stage (whether such stage is next below the one in which he is, or otherwise), until he has earned in such lower stage a stated number of marks.

As soon as the prisoner has earned the stated number, then, unless he has in the meantime incurred further punishment, he shall be restored to the stage from which he was degraded, and be credited with the number of marks he had previously earned therein.

7. None of the foregoing punishments shall exempt a prisoner from any other punishment to which he would be liable for conduct constituting a breach of prison regulations.

8. A prisoner in the 1st stage will—

(a.) Be employed 10 hours daily in strict separation on 1st class hard labour, of which six to eight hours will be on crank, tread wheel, or work of a similar nature. (b.) Sleep on a plank bed without a mattress, (c.) Earn no gratuity.

9. A prisoner in the 2nd stage will—

(a.) Be employed as in the first stage until he has completed one month of imprisonment, and afterwards on hard labour of the second class. (b.) Sleep on a plank bed without a mattress two nights weekly, and have a mattress on the other nights, (c.) Receive school instruction. (d.) Have school books in his cell. (e.) Have exercise on Sunday. (f.) Be able to earn a gratuity not exceeding 1s.

10. The gratuity to a prisoner in this stage whose sentence is not long enough for him to earn 224 marks in it, may be calculated at 1d. for every 20 marks earned.

11. A prisoner in the 3rd stage will—

(a.) Be employed on 2nd class hard labour. (b.) Sleep on a plank bed without a mattress one night weekly, and have a mattress on the other nights, (c.) Receive school instruction. (d.) Have school books in his cell. (e.) Have library books in his cell. (f.) Have exercise on Sunday. (g.) Be able to earn a gratuity not exceeding 1s. 6d.

12. The gratuity to a prisoner in this stage whose sentence is not long enough for him to earn 224 marks in it, may be calculated at 1d. for every 12 marks earned.

13. A prisoner in the 4th stage will—

(a.) Be eligible for employment of trust in the service of the prison. (b.) Sleep on a mattress every night. (c.) Receive school instruction. (d.) Have school books in his cell. (e.) Have library books in his cell. (f.) Have exercise on Sunday. (g.) Be allowed to receive and write a letter, and receive a visit of 20 minutes,

and in every three months afterwards to receive and write a letter, and receive a visit of half-an-hour. (h.) Be able to earn a gratuity not exceeding 2s.

14. The gratuity to a prisoner in this stage whose sentence is not long enough for him to earn 224 marks in it may be calculated at Id. for every 10 marks earned.

15. The gratuity to a prisoner in this stage whose sentence is long enough to enable him to earn more than 896 marks may be calculated at the same rate, provided that it shall not in any case exceed 10s.

16. If any prisoner shall, during his imprisonment, perform work for the prison of special value to the public, he will be eligible to receive an addition to the gratuity he has earned, so that the gratuity with such addition does not exceed £2.

17. The above provisions as to the use of plank beds shall apply only to convicted criminal prisoners.

In 1891, hard labour of the 1st Class was carried out by means of the tread-wheel and by cranks in the cells, the latter being used when there were not enough prisoners in the 1st stage to work the wheel, which was frequently the case.[103]

The last major change in employment came with the Prison Act of 1898. The treadwheel and crank were abolished and all work now had to be productive. This created problems for the Prison Commissioners, who had to find work for both prisoners in association (now allowed but still to be in total silence) and also hard labour that prisoners could do in their cells. These changes created many difficulties. The goods produced could not be sold to the public as both companies and trade unions would not tolerate cheap prison labour as competitors. Therefore all goods produced were used in the prison system or other government departments. The domestic work included cleaning and maintenance of the buildings. The prison workshops made and repaired boots, clothing and various pieces of equipment. In addition, coal bag making, for use on Royal Navy steam powered warships, and mail bag sewing were introduced. These canvas goods were sold to the Forces during the Boer War (1899-1902). Bag making was a cellular activity but after one month, prisoners qualified for associated labour. The Governor's report for 1900-1901 contains the following statement:

Hard labour during the first 28 days was enforced by means of the treadwheel, which ground wheat for this and other prisons, until the discontinuance of treadwheel. After that period it consisted of cutting out and sewing mail-bags, coal sacks, seamen's bags, bolster cases, and hammocks; also fire-wood chopping, gardening, oakum picking, labouring, and the usual domestic employments of the prison. The female prisoners are employed at washing, knitting socks and repairing clothing.

During the Great War, prisons provided goods for the Navy & Army. In 1916 the Commissioners of Prisons reported:

The manufacture of war stores has been conducted with unabated vigour throughout the year. During the 20 months ended 31st March, 1916, orders were placed with the Commissioners for nearly 7¼ million articles for use in connection with the Navy and Army. The number of inmates engaged on war work averaged 5,000 per day.

It will always stand to the credit of the Department that these results have been obtained in the face of a rapid and unprecedented fall in the prison population. They have been rendered possible by an extension of the hours of labour, by various emergency regulations calculated to increase the individual output, by the untiring zeal of the officers and by the keen desire of the prisoners to do their utmost.

Dudley Prout Collection

108

CHAPTER 13

Hard Labour Machines at Bodmin

1. Treadwheel

Governor Chapple applied to the justices in October 1822 for permission to build a treadwheel.[105] This was granted and a Bill to control the use of it was issued in 1824.[106] The Visiting justices allowed a new, 'treadwheel without a corn mill' to be erected in the bridewell and an enlarged hand corn mill to grind sufficient corn for all prisoners in 1829.[107] At their next visit, the justices stated that a small additional cost would allow the mill machinery to be attached to the wheel 'if desired'. Were they unsure of making the treadwheel 'useful labour' and therefore too pleasant for the prisoners? The hand-mill did not supply the needs of the prison or provide adequate labour for the class of prisoners employed on it, so the two machines were united sometime between 1836 and 1838. In fact, two treadwheels were connected by a single shaft to the cornmill. They were probably similar in dimensions and design to the plan shown on page 111 but longer. The earliest Bodmin machine had capacity for 26 prisoners and the machine described in detail, dated 1843, accommodated 60 prisoners.[13]

The treadwheel was not a popular punishment, many prisoners were injured, some wounded their legs and feet, and applied poisonous metals in order to keep the wounds open, so that they might not be put to work and it even led to a riot:[108]

On Monday last, the prisoners in Bodmin prison, sentenced to hard labour, refused to go upon the tread-mill, and declared they were resolved to resist every attempt to compel them to resume their labour. Two of the visiting magistrates . . . were immediately sent for, and on their arrival they remonstrated with the rioters, but in vain; they tore up the railing that was round the wheel and arming themselves, prepared for resistance.

Finding every other means unavailing, the staff of the Cornwall Militia were called together, and being armed and provided with ammunition, were drawn up in the outer yard of the prison. As soon as their arrival was announced to the rioters, they gave three cheers, shouting—"death or victory." . . . The militia men were then directed to enter the inner yard; and as the first file were about to pass the gate, some of the most daring of the rioters attempted to wrest their muskets from them. This attack was spiritedly and successfully resisted without firing, and the rioters retreated, some of them having been knocked down by the butt end of the soldiers' firelocks, and five of the most refractory being secured, and lodged in separate cells, the others then submitted. Sowden, who was convicted at the late Truro Sessions of a violent assault on the constables of Camborne, being the ring-leader, was ordered by the magistrates to ascend the wheel, which he positively refused to do. The magistrates finding it absolutely necessary to shew the prisoners that they were resolved to enforce obedience, and to correct a notion they appear to have entertained, that the magistrates could not inflict corporal punishment on them, orders were given to flog Sowden, which were instantly carried into effect, in a manner that will for some time afford him a feeling proof of his error. The other rioters, who beheld the punishment of their leader, were then ordered to ascend the wheel, under pain of a similar infliction, when they wisely chose the lesser evil, and resumed the obnoxious operation and promised obedience. 18th May, 1827.

In 1843, the Inspectors in the general survey stated that *'the treadmill was prejudicial to health for some prisoners and it exposes the prisoners to serious accidents.'* They stated that treadwheel labour was improper for females and boys under the age of fourteen and that it should only be used for prisoners sentenced to hard labour, and only with the permission of the Medical Officer.

The treadwheel was not in use in 1860 and 1865 but in October 1866, the governor reported *'some considerable progress has been made in the preparations for the new treadwheel and corn mill, sanctioned by your honourable Court, to meet the requirements of the Prison Act of 1865'.* The new building, which cost £1,800, housed a treadwheel and corn mill. The new wheel was a revolving drum, about six foot in diameter and up to eighty foot long, having about 20-25 treadboards. This could accommodate 32 prisoners in four groups of eight. Each prisoner was screened from the next to prevent communication. The treadwheel was finally abolished in 1898.

www.learnhistory.org.uk

The photograph, taken in Pentonville prison in 1895, shows a wheel similar in design to the Bodmin treadwheel, built after 1865, except that the prisoners are in groups of six not eight.

PLATE XVIII

DETAIL

SHEWING

THE DIVISION OF A TREADWHEEL INTO SEPARATE COMPARTMENTS.

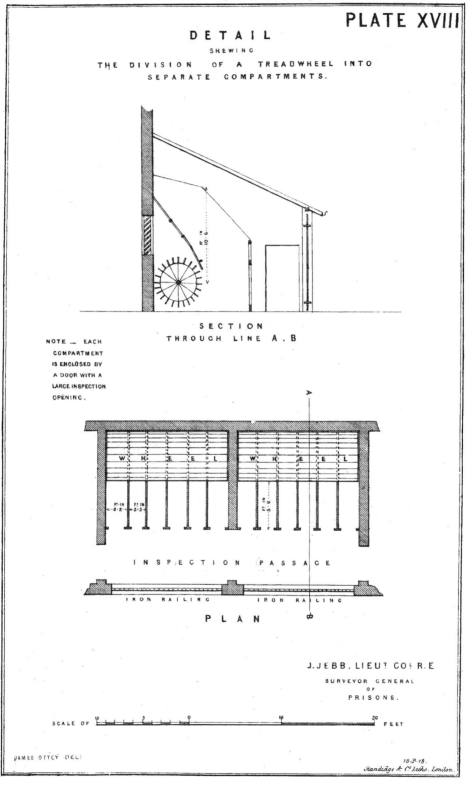

SECTION
THROUGH LINE A.B

NOTE — EACH COMPARTMENT IS ENCLOSED BY A DOOR WITH A LARGE INSPECTION OPENING.

WHEEL WHEEL

INSPECTION PASSAGE

IRON RAILING   IRON RAILING

PLAN

J. JEBB, LIEUT COL R.E

SURVEYOR GENERAL OF PRISONS.

SCALE OF   FEET

JAMES OTTEY DEL.

18-P-18.
Standidge & Co. Litho. London.

2. The Crank

There are many references in the literature to the hard labour machine called the Crank. It would appear that this is not a unique machine but any device which is driven by turning a handle. As it was used for hard labour, it was intended as a useless, measurable form of labour which could be used in cells.

One machine, devised by Gibbs of Pentonville in 1846, was recommended for use in the 2nd Report of the Surveyor General on the Construction of Prisons, 1847.[42] The cost of this machine was £5-6 in 1847.

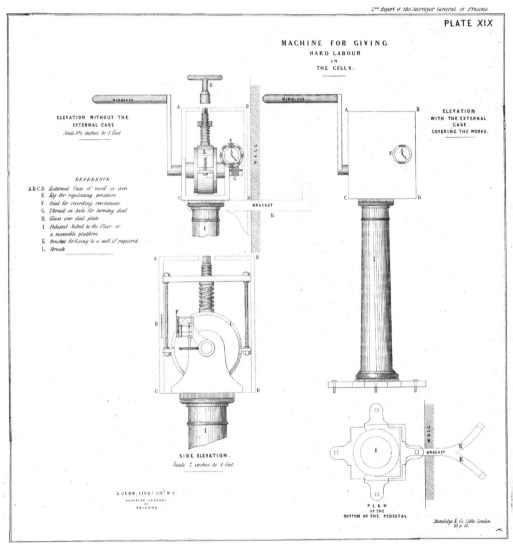

Another simpler crank consisted of a narrow metal drum, partially filled with sand, with a handle and a counter. When the handle was turned a series of scoops inside the machine filled with the sand and when they reached the top they emptied, similar in design to a dredger. Crank labour usually meant making 10,000 revolutions at the rate of 1200 revolutions per hour; this would last eight hours and twenty minutes. The amount of sand could be varied to make the task harder or easier, depending on the physical strength of the prisoner. Although recommended by Act of Parliament for hard labour, the only evidence that a crank was used in Bodmin is an Inspectors' report for 1860: *there is a single hard-labour machine in the prison, which is only worked by men out of whom no other work can be got; it is very seldom used, but when it is, 10,000 revolutions are required in the day.* The design of this machine is not recorded.

3. Hand Corn Mill

There is a statement in the report covering the year 1836 that: *There are two apartments, containing each a crank. Each crank will employ three men at one time. The power is applied to grinding corn for the prison and for the County Lunatic Asylum.* From 1838, the power to grind corn was provided by the tread-wheel but the hand-mills were still in use. In the 1840s no crank labour was employed in Bodmin [13,14] but in 1860 [27] and 1865,[28] the hand corn mills returned as the treadwheel was not being used. It would appear that the hand-mills were referred to as 'cranks' because they were worked by 'cranking a handle'.

However these hand-mills are not the same cranks or Hard labour machines described in the previous section. In support of this conclusion:

(a) The machines were worked by three prisoners at a time in an apartment not in a cell.

(b) In 1860, the hand corn mills were in use but the Hard Labour machine (Crank) was seldom used, and

(c) In an address given by Governor Everest, on the 3rd of April, 1838 [79] to the Chairman and other magistrates assembled at the General Quarter Sessions of the Peace held at Truro, the machines called cranks by the Inspector of Prisons in the same year were only referred to as hand-mills.

The address makes it very clear that Governor Everest did not agree with the use of hand-mills but his arguments had no effect on the Justices.

"In making this my quarterly report, I regret to state that, during the past quarter, there has been more cases of sickness amongst the prisoners than for a very considerable time; it has been confined almost exclusively to the male prisoners convicted of felony, particularly those who have laboured constantly at the hand-mill, which has evidently produced much debility and consequent illness; but by timely application to the surgeon, who ordered such nourishing diet as he considered their cases required, the men are fast recovering, and those who were getting weak; but who were not on the sick-list, have, by an alternate change of labour, and some extra food, improved in their strength.

"I have ever considered the hand-mill as a severe, as well as unequal kind of labour; but I have certainly never observed till the past winter its effects so manifest; and this I think may be attributed to one or two causes, viz. either the length and severity of the winter may have induced colds, and thus have rendered the men unequal to the labour, or they may have been kept more constantly employed at the hand-mill than heretofore, although I am not prepared to say that such has been the case. I feel it however, necessary to state to your Worships, that having for many months had a large number of prisoners of this class, I have, with a view of conforming as nearly as possible with the provisions of the Gaol Act, kept the felons more exclusively employed at the hand-mill, rather than mix them with other classes of prisoners, but there has not been more corn ground, nor has the mill been kept longer at work than heretofore; unless, therefore, the weakness and illness has been brought on in the way I have mentioned, I am quite unable to account for it; but it may be satisfactory to your Worships to be informed that the surgeon concurs in the opinion I have expressed. Before closing this part of my report, I respectfully beg leave to explain my objection to the use of the hand-mill as a prison labour. In the first place, the position of the body when so employed is unnatural, and likely to produce determination of blood to the head. In the second place, it frequently produces, faintness and giddiness, and instances have occurred of the prisoners having been thrown over the handles; and although no fatal consequences have ensued, yet they have sustained serious wounds and bruises; this is particularly liable to happen to the prisoners when first employed at it. And, finally, it is a decidedly unequal kind of labour, inasmuch as it is impossible to tell accurately whether every prisoner does his part; I have repeatedly watched them when at work with a view to detect the skulkers, but I confess I have never succeeded satisfactorily; and the prisoners themselves know they cannot be detected, and thus the willing man is worked off his legs, whilst the idler and skulker goes unpunished. I have made several alterations in the hand-mill within the last year or two, so as to regulate the motion and render the labour less irksome to the prisoners, and I am quite satisfied that it never worked better than at present; but worked as it now is, I am quite convinced it is objectionable for the reasons I have assigned. I therefore respectfully submit the subject to your Worships' consideration, and shall feel much pleasure in carrying into effect any determination you may come to, either as regards the continuance or abolition of this kind of labour."

In employment returns for 1883, 1885 & 1891, both a crank and 'grinding wheat' are listed. In 1901, after the crank went out of use, the grinding of wheat (for the prison and other prisons) was continued. The nature of the machine used was obviously not the Crank but was it a new version of the hand-corn Mill?

Oakum Picking	The following extract from the Governor's journal possesses sufficient interest to be recorded in this report[28]:—
This consisted of unravelling pieces of old rope into individual filaments, called oakum. This was sold to ship-yards where it was mixed with tar and used for caulking wooden ships. The tarred oakum was forced between the planks to make the ship watertight. Oakum picking was extremely tedious work and was very hard on the hands. All types of prisoners, including children, were employed in this task in their cells.	19th Nov. 1864.—Owing to the small number of female prisoners in confinement, it became necessary to select some male prisoners who could assist in the washing; four men were chosen and placed in the wash-house, without in the least degree having any communication with or having even to pass through the female department. These men washed the whole of the shirts, &c., which were then left in the wash-house to be dried and mangled by the female prisoners. This gave much relief, both on this and subsequently on one or two occasions.

CHAPTER 14

Prisoners' Diets

The quantity and cost of food provided to prisoners was always a contentious issue. Many people complained that prisoners were better fed than the generally poor, local population. The authorities, who were responsible for the health of the prisoners, had to provide sufficient food to enable the prisoners to work at hard labour, without them starving. During the nineteenth century, the Home Office gradually took control of the issue and published dietaries which depended on the length of sentence and the type of work done by the prisoners.

The diet for male prisoners in 1782 was 1lb. 3oz. of 'good wholesome bread' per day and 1lb. for women. All prisoners who attended divine service on Saturday were allowed, at the county expense, ½ lb. of meat made into broth for dinner on Sunday. Similar diets were reported for 1803 and 1814, although the amount of bread was stated as 1lb. 11oz. and later 1lb. 6oz.

The Gaol Act of 1823 ordered the following diet:

1. All prisoners who are entitled by law to receive food from the County shall be provided with the following diet:-
Two lbs. of bread, 2 oz. of cheese and one onion for four days in the week, and 2 lbs. of bread, ¾ lb. of suet puddings, three days in the week.
2. For prisoners under sentence of confinement, for terms not exceeding three months:-
Two lbs. of bread, 2 oz. of cheese, four days in the week, 2 lbs. of bread, 1 onion, three days in the week.
3. For prisoners whose term of imprisonment does not exceed six months:-
Two lbs. of bread, 2 oz. of cheese, four days, 2 lbs. of bread, ¾ lb. of suet puddings, three days.
4. For prisoners whose term of imprisonment does not exceed twelve months:-
For the first six months as above, for the remaining term a pint of small beer three days in the week in addition.
5. For those prisoners who shall be for twelve months and upwards:-
For twelve months as above, and after the twelve months an additional pint of beer per week.

This dietary was ignored by local authorities and even ten years later, different gaols still had different diets. The diet at the County Gaol at Bodmin was cited for having one of the worst diets in the country.[109]

To give one instance of the contrasts in prison diet, we may adduce the Somerset House of Correction at Shepton Mallet, where, in 1833, each prisoner had, daily, one pound of bread, one pound of potatoes, six ounces of beef without bone, and one-and-a-half pints of oatmeal gruel; and, when working on the tread-mill, also a pint-and-a-half of soup, or gruel when leaving work. On the other hand, at the Cornwall County Gaol, at Bodmin, the daily ration was, for the first month, only a pound-and-a-half of bread, with the addition, after that period, of a portion of gruel.

The diet at Bodmin was improved after this criticism by the addition of potatoes and soup. The details of the new dietary (1838) were:[79]

The male prisoners are allowed 1½lb.of bread (made from equal proportions of wheaten and barley flour), and 1 quart of oatmeal gruel daily; 4½ lbs. of potatoes and 4 pints of soup weekly. Those sentenced to hard labour are allowed ½lb. of bread extra at the discretion of the governor.

The female prisoners are allowed the same quantity of food, except bread and potatoes; of the former they have only 1lb. daily, and of the latter only 3 lbs. weekly, without any extra allowance for labour.

N.B. Vagrants are only allowed the above proportions of bread during the first month of their imprisonment, with the addition of gruel for the second month, after which they are allowed the full diet.

The cooking is performed by a prisoner who is sentenced for two years.

Analysis of the Dietary per week:-

N.B. The soup is made of ox heads and shins, thickened with peas, in the following proportions, viz., 1 ox head or 10 lb. of shin, with ten pints of peas, makes 20 quarts of soup. The gruel is made of Scotch oatmeal in the following proportions, viz. 2 oz. of meal to every pint. The bread is made of flour, from which the rough bran is taken out.

	Bread	Potatoes	Soup	Gruel	
	oz.	lbs.	Pints	Pints	Extra bread
Men	168	4½	4	14	for hard
Women	112	3	4	14	labour, 56 oz.
Boys	168	4½	4	14	

In 1842, Sir James Graham of the Home Office, instructed the inspectors of prisons to report on the question of prison dietaries. Their report was adopted and the Home Secretary informed the Chairmen of Quarter Sessions about the new dietaries, in a circular dated 27th February, 1843.[109]

The Graham Dietaries of 1843	Class 1	Class 2	Class 3	Class 4	Class 2	Class 3	Class 4	Class 5
	< 7 days	7-21 days	21 days - 4 months	> 4 months	7-21 days	21 days 6 weeks	6 weeks 4 months	> 4 months
		Without Hard Labour			With Hard Labour			
ozs.								
Bread	112	168	140	168	168	140	168	154
Potatoes	-	-	64	32	-	64	32	112
Meat	-	-	6	12	-	6	12	16
Total solid food	**112**	**168**	**210**	**212**	**168**	**210**	**212**	**282**
Pints								
Soup	-	-	2	3	1	2	3	3
Gruel	14	14	14	14	14	14	14	11
Cocoa	-	-	-	-	-	-	-	3
Total liquid food	**14**	**14**	**16**	**17**	**15**	**16**	**17**	**17**

There was considerable opposition in Cornwall to the new instructions.[110]

> The Chairman called the attention of the Bench to a recommendation from the Home Office for the erection in the gaol of a steam [cooking] apparatus . . . required in consequence of the alterations in the dietary . . . It was their [the magistrates'] opinion that a more unjust dietary was never passed. It was most unjust to the industrious labourer who did not get once a month so good a soup as the prisoners were to have three times a day . . . The Chairman said that the prisoners that were in gaol for a few days only were to have none of this soup—it was only those that were in for a long period, and had hard work to do. Before, the prisoners went out of gaol at the end of their confinement considerably reduced.
> 5 January 1844

The magistrates finally accepted the change as they had to comply with the order. These diets were used for about 20 years.

The next proposed changes were in parliamentary discussions of the Prison Act of 1865. A select committee proposed a new dietary (*Parliamentary Papers,1864,xlix,618*),[109] which included Cheese, Suet Pudding and Indian Meal Pudding in addition to Soup, Gruel, Bread and potatoes. There was no meat in this diet. This Act was the final attempt of the Government to get a uniform set of diets and employment across the country, while the prisons were still under the control of local authorities. There were changes in the diet at Bodmin after the Prison Act but the diet used was not that proposed by the select committee.

Dietaries used at Bodmin Gaol from before 1868 to 1878

Class	1st		2nd				3rd				4th				5th	
	> 14 days		14 days - 1 month				1 month - 2 months				2 months - 6 months				> 6 months	
Class of Labour			1st HL		2nd HL		1st HL		2nd HL		1st HL		2nd HL		1st HL	
	M.	F.	M.	F.	M.	F.	M.	F.	M.	F.	M.	F.	M.	F.	M.	F.
Bread	112	112	168	168	168	140	112	126	84	84	168	126	112	84	154	112
Potatoes							112	84	112	84	112	112	112	112	112	112
Meat							8	8	8	8	12	8	12	8	16	12
Total solid food (ozs.)																
Males: 1st Class HL	112		168				232				292				282	
Males: 2nd Class HL	112				168				204				236			
Females & under 16s: 1st Class HL		*112*		*168*				*218*				*246*				*236*
Females & under 16s: 2nd Class HL		*112*				*140*				*176*				*204*		
Gruel	14	14	14	14	14	14	14	14	14	14	14	14	14	14	14	14
Soup			2				2	2	2	2	3	2	3	2	3	3
Total liquid food (pints)																
Males: 1st Class HL	14		16				16				17				17	
Males: 2nd Class HL	14				14				16				17			
Females & under 16s: 1st Class HL		*14*		*14*				*16*				*16*				*17*
Females & under 16s: 2nd Class HL		*14*				*14*				*16*				*16*		

The starting diet consisting of bread and gruel (a very thin porridge) but after fourteen days, soup is added for males working at hard labour of the 1st Class. After one month, meat and potatoes are added to the diet. Male prisoners doing 1st Class hard labour get extra bread and after one month. Females who work in the Laundry receive extra bread in all classes after class 1.

An analysis of the new dietary, apparently shows some differences from the Graham dietary, for example, the length of time spent in each dietary class has changed but the weights and volumes of food covers the same range as the earlier system and the actual food served still consists of bread, potatoes, meat, gruel and soup. It seems that the new highly complex dietary was, in practice, very similar to the previous diet.

Sections of the 1874 Dietary

CLASS 3		
Convicted Prisoners for Terms exceeding One Calendar Month, and not exceeding Two Months.		
	Males over 16, years of age	Males under 16, and Females
Breakfast and Supper	1 pint gruel, 6 oz. bread	1 pint gruel, 6 oz. bread
Dinner — Sunday, Tuesday, Thursday, Saturday	2 oz. dressed meat 1 lb. potatoes	2 oz. dressed meat 12 oz. potatoes
Monday, Wednesday, Friday	⅔ pint soup 1 lb. potatoes	⅔ pint soup 12 oz. potatoes

Male Prisoners, if at Hard Labour of the 1st. Class, to have 4 oz. of Bread at Dinner. Women in the Laundry to have in addition 6 oz. Bread daily.

CLASS 4		
Convicted Prisoners at Hard Labour for Terms exceeding Two Months, and not exceeding Six Months; and Convicted Prisoners not at Hard Labour for Terms exceeding Two Months.		
	Males over 16 years of age	Males under 16, and Females
Breakfast and Supper	1 pint gruel, 8 oz. bread	1 pint gruel, 6 oz. bread
Dinner for 4 days	3 oz. dressed meat 1 lb. potatoes	2 oz. dressed meat 1 lb. potatoes
Dinner for 3 days	1 pint soup 1 lb. potatoes	? pint soup 1 lb. potatoes

Male Prisoners, at Hard Labour 1st. Class, to have 8 oz., and Females employed in the Laundry 6 oz. additional Bread at Dinner.

The above Classes to be Progressive.
Diets for other types of Prisoners.
Prisoners sentenced to Solitary Confinement to have the ordinary Diet of their respective Classes, without the addition for 1st Class Hard Labour.
Prisoners before Trial, when the period between Commitment and Trial.
      Shall not exceed one calendar month - - - - - - - - - - - - - - - -as Class 3.
      Shall exceed one month, but not exceed four months - - - as Class 4, with extra bread.
      Shall exceed four months -as Class 5.
Misdemeanants of the First Division who do not maintain themselves, the same as Prisoners before Trial.
Prisoners under Punishment for Prison Offences for Terms not exceeding Three Days.   1 lb. Bread per diem.
Prisoners in Close Confinement for Prison Offences for Terms exceeding Three Days.   The Diet of Class 2.
Debtors who do not maintain themselves. The Diet of Class 4, with extra Bread.

NOTE - 4 ozs. of split peas made into a pudding may be substituted for 1 Ib. of potatoes occasionally, but the change shall not be substituted more than three times a week. The soup to contain per pint 2 ozs. raw meat without bone, 3 ozs. potatoes, 1 oz. barley, rice or oatmeal, and 1 oz. of onions or leeks, with pepper and salt. The gruel to contain 2 ozs. oatmeal per pint and be seasoned with salt.

The most comprehensive dietary produced by the Prison Commissioners was published in 1878,[36] just after all the local prisons had been nationalised. The *Rules for the Dietaries of the Prisons in England and Wales subject to the Prison Acts 1865 and 1877 (Approved by the Secretary of State)* was signed by E.F.Du Cane. The document, reproduced below, contained not only the type and weight of food for each prisoner depending on age, sex, length of sentence and type of employment but also *'Ingredients and Instructions'; 'Substitutes for*

Cooked English Beef and Potatoes'; 'Diets for ill-conducted or Idle Prisoners'; 'Hospital Diets'; 'Allowed Extras and Substitutes'; 'Preparation Instructions' and a *'Dietary to be Provided for Infants in Local Prisons'.* In addition, the weekly shopping list, based on the diets per 100 prisoners, was included.

Rules for the Dietaries of the Prisons in England and Wales. (published in 1878)[36]

RULES for the DIETARIES of the PRISONS in ENGLAND and WALES subject to the PRISON ACTS, 1865 and 1877. (Approved by the Secretary of State.)

Meals	CLASS 1. Men, Women & Boys under 16, with or without Hard Labour.	CLASS 2. A: Men with Hard Labour. B: Men, without Hard Labour, Women & Boys under 16.		CLASS 3. A: Men with Hard Labour. B: Men, without Hard Labour, Women & Boys under 16. C: Prisoners awaiting Trial; Misdemeanants of the 1st Division and Destitute Debtors			CLASS 4. A: Men with Hard Labour. B: Men, without Hard Labour, Women & Boys under 16.	
		A	B	A	B	C	A	B
Breakfast	Daily- Bread 8oz.	Daily Bread 6 oz. Gruel 1 pint	5 oz. 1 pint	Daily Bread 8 oz. Gruel 1 pint Cocoa	6 oz. 1 pint	6 oz. 1 pint or ½ pint	Daily Bread 8 oz. Porridge 1 pint Gruel	6 oz. 1 pint
Dinner	Daily- Stirabout (containing 3oz. Indian Meal & 3oz. Oatmeal) 1½ pints	Sun.& Wed. Bread 6 oz. Suet Pudding 8 oz. / Mon.& Fri. Bread 6 oz. Potatoes 8 oz. / Tue., Thur. & Sat. Bread 6 oz. Soup ½ pint	5 oz. 6 oz. / 5 oz. 8 oz. / 5 oz. ½ pint	Sun.& Wed. Bread 4 oz. Suet Pudding 8 oz. Potatoes 8 oz. / Mon.& Fri. Bread 6 oz. Potatoes 8 oz. Cooked Beef 3 oz. / Tue., Thur. & Sat. Bread 8 oz. Soup ¾ pint Potatoes 8 oz.	4 oz. 6 oz. 8 oz. / 6 oz. 8 oz. 3 oz. / 6 oz. ¾ pint 6 oz.	4 oz. 6 oz. 8 oz. / 6 oz. 8 oz. 3 oz. / 6 oz. ¾ pint 6 oz.	Sun.& Wed. Bread 6 oz. Suet Pudding 12 oz. Potatoes 8 oz. / Mon.& Fri. Bread 8 oz. Potatoes 12 oz. Cooked Beef 4 oz. / Tue., Thur. & Sat. Bread 8 oz. Soup 1 pint Potatoes 8 oz.	4 oz. 10 oz. 8 oz. / 6 oz. 10 oz. 3 oz. / 6 oz. 1 pint 6 oz.
Supper	Daily- Bread 8oz.	Daily Bread 6 oz. Gruel 1 pint	5 oz. 1 pint	Daily Bread 6 oz. Gruel 1 pint Cocoa	6 oz. 1 pint	6 oz. 1 pint or ½ pint	Daily Bread 8 oz. Gruel 1 pint Porridge	6 oz. 1 pint

The beef is without bone. On Mondays beans and fat bacon maybe be substituted for beef. At the expiration of nine months, one pint of Cocoa, with two ounces extra bread may be given at breakfast, three days in the week in lieu of one pint of porridge or gruel, if preferred.

The terms to which the above diet shall he severally applied shall be those set forth in the following Table:

TERM	CLASS 1	CLASS 2	CLASS 3	CLASS 4
Seven days and under	Whole term.			
More than seven days and not more than one month	Seven days	Remainder of term		
More than one month and not more than four months		One month	Remainder of term	
More than four months			Four months	Remainder of term

119

INGREDIENTS AND INSTRUCTIONS.	
Bread	To be made with whole meal, which is to consist of all the products of grinding the wheaten grain, with the exception of the coarser bran.
Soup	In every pint 4 ounces clod (or shoulder), cheek, neck, leg, or shin of beef; 4 ounces split peas; 2 ounces fresh vegetables ; ½ ounce onions ; pepper and salt.
Suet pudding	1½ ounces mutton suet, 8 ounces flour, and about 6½ ounces water to make 1lb.
Gruel	2 ounces coarse Scotch oatmeal to the pint, with salt.
Porridge	3 ounces coarse Scotch oatmeal to the pint, with salt.
Stirabout	Equal parts of Indian meal and oatmeal, with salt. The Indian meal requires more cooking than the oatmeal. To make 1½ pint stirabout, boil 2½ pints water, to which a ¼ of an ounce of salt should be added; stir in 3 ounces of Indian meal, and afterwards 3 ounces oatmeal; keep constantly stirring, and when the meals are cooked, the required quantity of 1½ pint stirabout will be produced.
Cocoa	To every pint, ¾ ounce flaked or Admiralty cocoa. Sweetening : For flaked cocoa, ¾ ounce molasses or sugar to the pint. For Admiralty cocoa, ½ ounce molasses or sugar to the pint.
Meat liquor, or broth	The liquor in which the meat is cooked on Mondays and Fridays is to be thickened with ¼ ounce flour, and flavoured with ¼ ounce onions to each ration, with pepper and salt to taste.

TABLE of Substitutes for Cooked English Beef. (Meats weighed without Bone).

	Colonial Beef or Mutton Preserved by Heat	Beans and Fat Bacon	American or Foreign Beef Preserved by Cold	Cooked Fresh Fish	Cooked Salt Meat	Cooked Salt Fish
In lieu of 4 oz. cooked English Beef	5 oz.	Beans 9 oz. Fat Bacon 1 oz.	4 oz.	8 oz.	6 oz.	12 oz.
In lieu of 3 oz. cooked English Beef	3¾ oz.	Beans 7 oz. Fat Bacon ¾ oz.	3 oz.	6 oz.	4½ oz.	9 oz.

TABLE of Substitutes for Potatoes. (All Weighed after Cooking.)

	Cabbage or Turnip Tops.	Parsnips, Turnips, or Carrots.	Preserved (Dried) Potatoes.	Leeks.	Rice, steamed till tender.
	oz.	oz.	oz.	oz.	oz.
In lieu of 12 oz. potatoes	8	12	12	8	12
In lieu of 10 oz. potatoes	7	10	10	7	10
In lieu of 8 oz. potatoes	6	8	8	6	8
In lieu of 6 oz. potatoes	4	6	6	4	6

DIET FOR ILL-CONDUCTED OR IDLE PRISONERS.

No. 1. — BREAD AND WATER DIET.

MEN AND WOMEN,

1lb. Bread per Diem, with Water.

This diet to be limited, in the first place, to three days; after that, one of the under-mentioned stirabout diets, according to labour performed, for three days before its repetition, when it is again to be limited to three days, and a second interval on the stirabout diet is to elapse before it is again repeated. The entire period, including intervals, for which any single term of this diet may be ordered, is not to exceed 15 days. No task of labour is to be enforced on any one of the nine days on which the bread and water constitute the sole food supplied to the prisoner.

<table>
<tr><td colspan="2" align="center">No. 2.—STIRABOUT DIET.</td></tr>
<tr><td colspan="2" align="center">For Men and Women performing a Daily Task of any Labour not expressly defined as Hard Labour.</td></tr>
<tr><td>Breakfast</td><td>Bread 8 ounces.</td></tr>
<tr><td>Dinner</td><td>1 pint stirabout, containing 2 ounces oatmeal, and 2 ounces Indian meal, with salt.   Potatoes, 8 ounces.</td></tr>
<tr><td>Supper</td><td>Bread, 8 ounces.</td></tr>
<tr><td colspan="2">This diet to be limited, in the first place, to 21 days; after that, the diet of the class to which the prisoner belongs, for one week before its repetition, when it is to be limited to 14 days. The entire period, including the interval, for which any single term of this diet may be ordered, is not to exceed 42 days.</td></tr>
</table>

No. 3.—FULL STIRABOUT DIET.	
For Men performing a Daily Task of Hard Labour.	
Breakfast	Bread 8 ounces.
Dinner	1½ pint stirabout, containing 3 ounces oatmeal, and 3 ounces Indian meal, with salt. Potatoes, 8 ounces. Bread, 8 ounces.
Supper	Bread, 8 ounces.

This diet to be limited, in the first place, to 42 days; after that, the diet of the class to which the prisoner belongs, for 14 days before its repetition, when it is to be limited to 28 days. The entire period, including the interval, for which any single term of this diet may be ordered, is not to exceed 84 days.

HOSPITAL DIETS. MEN AND WOMEN. (Per Day)

Diets	Bread	Cooked Mutton (without Bone)	Cooked Fresh Fish.	Potatoes.	Rice Pudding	Arrowroot (made with Milk).	Tea.	Milk, additional to that in Arrowroot
	oz.	oz.	oz.	oz.	oz.	oz.	oz.	oz.
Ordinary	16	5		8	8		30	
Extra	20	6		8	8		30	
Fish	16		10	8			30	
Low	8					20	15	20

The following Articles maybe ordered as Extras or Substitutes in the Quantities deemed necessary by the Medical Officer:— **Ale. Bacon. Beef Tea. Biscuits. Butter. Cake. Cocoa. Corn Flour. Eggs. Fruit. Greens (or other Vegetables), in lieu of Potatoes. Ice.   Jam. Jelly. Lemonade (see below). Milk. Porter. Poultry. Rice (ground). Sago. Spirits. Stout. Sugar. Waters (Mineral). Wine.**

INSTRUCTIONS.

Rice Pudding - 2 ounces rice; 1 pint milk ; 1 ounce sugar; one egg and nutmeg, to produce 20 ounces.

Arrowroot - 1 ounce arrowroot: 1 pint milk; 1 ounce sugar, to produce 1 pint.

Beef Tea - 16 ounces of the lean parts of the neck of the ox to 1 pint water.

Tea - ⅛ ounce tea ; ¾ ounce sugar; 2 ounces milk, and water to make up ¾ pint.

Cocoa - ¾ ounce flaked or Admiralty cocoa to 1 pint water, sweetened with ¾ ounce molasses or sugar for flaked cocoa, and ½ ounce molasses or sugar for Admiralty cocoa.

Lemonade - ¼ ounce cream of tartar; ½ lemon (sliced); 2 ounces loaf suga; water 1½ pint. The water to be added hot to the other ingredients, and the whole to be allowed to stand till cold; then strain.

Mutton - To be roast or baked on four days in the week, and boiled on three days. On the days on which the mutton is boiled the meat liquor to be thickened with ¼ ounce flour, and flavoured with ¼ ounce onions per diet.

DIETARY PROVIDED FOR INFANTS IN LOCAL PRISONS.

The under-mentioned nursery dietary maybe provided for infants born in local prisons or received therein with their mothers, in cases in which the medical officer is of opinion that the nursing powers of the mother are defective.

SCALE.

Diet for infants under 3 months old	discretion of the medical officer.
Diet for infants from 3 to 6 months old	½ pint milk daily.
Diet for infants from 6 to 9 months old	6 oz. bread and 1 pint milk: daily ½ pint beef tea: 3 times a week

APPROXIMATE Quantity of Provisions that will be required under the Diet Scales for each 100 Prisoners per week.

Bread	900 Ibs.	Suet, Mutton	10 lbs.	Salt	21 Ibs.
Flour	56 lbs.	Oatmeal	200 lbs.	Potatoes	290 lbs.
Meal, Indian	9 lbs.	Peas, Split	56 lbs.	Onions	6 lbs.
Beef	56 lbs.	Pepper	3 ozs.	Vegetables	28 lbs.
Shins	56 lbs.				

The dietary headed *'Prisoners Sentenced to Hard Labour and Offenders of the Third Division',* is dated 1911. It appears different to the earlier documents but the food is basically the same with the addition of tea. In this dietary, meat, soup and suet pudding are each served on two days, and beans and fat bacon, which was a substitute for meat in the earlier diet, is now served once per week.

The terms to which the above diets shall be severally applied shall be those set forth in the following table:-			
TERM.	**DIET A.**	**DIET B.**	**DIET C.**
Seven days and under	Whole Term	———	———
More than seven days and not more than four months	Seven days	Remainder of term	———
More than four months.................................	———	Four months	Remainder of term

PRISONERS on Remand or Awaiting Trial who do not maintain themselves; Offenders of the First Division who do not maintain themselves; Offenders of the Second Division; Debtors:- DIET B, provided that they shall receive for breakfast one pint of tea in lieu of gruel, and for supper one pint of cocoa in lieu of porridge or gruel; and that when detained in prison more than four months they shall receive Diet C at the expiration of the fourth month.

The four classes of diet based on the sentence length have been reduced to three diets, labelled A, B and C. For a sentence of 7 days or less, Diet A was used; for between 7 days and four months, Diet A for seven days was followed by Diet B for the remainder of the sentence; over four months, Diet B used for four months and Diet C for the remainder of the term.

DIETARY FOR PRISONERS IN LOCAL PRISONS.

PRISONERS SENTENCED TO HARD LABOUR AND OFFENDERS OF THE THIRD DIVISON.

MEALS.	DIET A.			DIET B.			DIET C.		
	——	Men.	Women and Juvenile	——	Men.	Women and Juvenile	——	Men.	Women and Juvenile
BREAKFAST.	**Daily:-**			**Daily :—**			**Daily :—**		
	Bread	8 oz.	6 oz.	Bread	8 oz.	6 oz.	Bread	8 oz.	6 oz.
	Gruel......	1 pint	1 pint	Gruel......	1 pint	1 pint	Gruel......	1 pint	
							Tea.......		1 pint
DINNER	**Sunday:-**			**Sunday:-**			**Sunday:-**		
	Bread	8 oz.	6 oz.	Bread	6 oz.	6 oz.	Bread	6 oz.	6 oz.
	Porridge...	1 pint	1 pint	Potatoes...	8 oz.	8 oz.	Potatoes...	12 oz.	8 oz.
				Cooked Meat, preserved by heat	4 oz.	3 oz.	Cooked Meat, preserved by heat	5 oz.	4 oz.
	Monday:-			**Monday:-**			**Monday:-**		
	Bread	8 oz.	6 oz.	Bread	6 oz.	6 oz.	Bread	6 oz.	6 oz.
	Potatoes...	8 oz.	8 oz.	Potatoes......	8 oz.	8 oz.	Potatoes...	12 oz.	8 oz.
				Beans	10 oz.	8 oz.	Beans	12 oz.	10 oz.
	Tuesday:-			Fat Bacon...	2 oz.	1 oz.	Fat Bacon...	2 oz.	2 oz.
	Bread	8 oz.	6 oz.	**Tuesday:-**			**Tuesday:-**		
	Porridge...	1 pint	1 pint	Bread	6 oz.	6 oz.	Bread	6 oz.	6 oz.
				Potatoes...	8 oz.	8 oz.	Potatoes...	12 oz.	8 oz.
				Soup......	1 pint	1 pint	Soup......	1 pint	1 pint
	Wednesday:-			**Wednesday:-**			**Wednesday:-**		
	Bread	8 oz.	6 oz.	Bread	6 oz.	6 oz.	Bread	6 oz.	6 oz.
	Suet Pudding	8 oz.	6 oz.	Potatoes...	8 oz.	8 oz.	Potatoes...	12 oz.	8 oz.
				Suet Pudding	10 oz.	8 oz.	Suet Pudding	12 oz.	10 oz.
	Thursday:-			**Thursday:-**			**Thursday:-**		
	Bread	8 oz.	6 oz.	Bread	6 oz.	6 oz.	Bread	6 oz.	6 oz.
	Potatoes...	8 oz.	8 oz.	Potatoes...	8 oz.	8 oz.	Potatoes...	12 oz.	8 oz.
				Cooked Beef, without bone	4 oz.	3 oz.	Cooked Beef, without bone	5 oz.	4 oz.
	Friday:-			**Friday:-**			**Friday:-**		
	Bread	8 oz.	6 oz.	Bread	6 oz.	6 oz.	Bread	6 oz.	6 oz.
	Porridge....	1 pint	1 pint	Potatoes...	8 oz.	8 oz.	Potatoes...	12 oz.	8 oz.
				Soup......	1 pint	1 pint	Soup......	1 pint	1 pint
				Saturday:-			**Saturday:-**		
	Saturday:-			Bread	6 oz.	6 oz.	Bread	6 oz.	6 oz.
	Bread	8 oz.	6 oz.	Potatoes...	8 oz.	8 oz.	Potatoes...	12 oz.	8 oz.
	Suet Pudding	8 oz.	6 oz.	Suet Pudding	10 oz.	8 oz.	Suet Pudding	12 oz.	10 oz.
SUPPER......	**Daily :**			**Daily :**			**Daily :**		
	Bread	8 oz.	6 oz.	Bread	8 oz.	6 oz.	Bread	8 oz.	6 oz.
	Gruel......	1 pint	1 pint	Porridge...	1 pint		Cocoa......	1 pint	1 pint
				Gruel......		1 pint			

THOMAS AUSTIN, M.A. (1854-1934)
Chaplain, H.M. Prison & H.M. Naval Prison, Bodmin

Thomas Austin was born in 1854 at South Malton, Devon. He was educated at St. Peter's College, Cambridge and received the degree of BA in 1878. He was ordained at Worcester (1880) and became Curate of Pirton & Croome D'Abitot and in 1882, became a Naval Chaplain.

His service started aboard *'Penelope'* and he was involved in the 'Bombardment of Alexandria', for which he was awarded the Egyptian Medal, the Alexandria Clasp and the Khedive's Bronze Star.

From 1883 to 1890, he served in five different ships, *'London'*, based in Zanzibar, *'Defence'* coastguard ship at Holyhead, *'Agincourt'* of the Channel Squadron and *'Revenge'* in the Mediterranean. He was chaplain on *'Malibar'*, which was a troopship on the Portsmouth to Bombay run.

From December 1890 to July 1893 he served as Chaplain of the Ascension Islands. He did another trip to Bombay on the troopship *'Crocodile'* in 1893-4, his last foreign posting and then stayed in the West Country, first on *'Defiance'* in Devonport, then at the Royal Marine Barracks and later the Royal Naval Hospital, both in Plymouth.

On the 13th November, 1907 he was appointed Chaplain of H.M. Prison and H.M. Naval Prison, Bodmin. He held this position until the Naval Prison closed in 1922.

He married Blanche Townsend Hemans in 1886 and died on the 14th June 1934.

Appointment of Thomas Austin to the Post of Chaplain, HM Prison, Bodmin. Signed by the Bishop of Truro, 1907.

Thomas Austin and Family, Ascension Islands. (1890-1893)

Photographs & details by kind permission of Margaret Nott of Camborne, his granddaughter

CHAPTER 15

Welfare of Prisoners

The welfare of the prisoners was the responsibility of the Chaplain, who was concerned with both religious instruction and education, and the Surgeon, who was responsible for the health of the prisoners. The objective was to improve both the spiritual and bodily health of the prisoners during their time in prison.

Education

Religious instruction, in the early days, consisted of daily chapel services and cell visits by the chaplain. This later changed to daily prayers and two services each Sunday. The cell visits were retained. Prisoners of non-established churches were visited by their own ministers. The books in the gaol, which were selected by the Chaplain, consisted of the Bible, prayer books and other moral and religious works. The main objective of the Chaplain was to get the prisoners to admit their guilt and repent and secondly, to teach the prisoners to read and write. There are a few numbers which give some indication of the size of the Chaplain's task.

State of Instruction of Prisoners								
Year	1832	1836	1837		1843		1846	
			M	F	M	F	M	F
Prisoners	684	130	373	100	474	138	428	155
Can neither Read nor Write	169	35	99	26	126	43	113	53
Can Read only	198	25	102	56	121	61	105	73
Can Read or Write, or both imperfectly	317	70	166	17	215	34	187	27
Can Read and Write perfectly			6	1	12	0	23	2

Of the prison population, 27.9% could neither read nor write (26.5% of males and 30.5% of females) and only 41 males and 3 females could read and write perfectly out of a population of 1,668 prisoners (3.2% males and 0.8% females).

The Chaplains' and Inspectors' of Prisons reports contain the following comments:

1829:[111] "A greater proportion of juvenile offenders...many of them were in a state of lamentable ignorance." A Sunday school and mutual instruction enabled many to read tolerably and almost all could repeat the Lord's Prayer, the Apostles' Creed and the Ten Commandments before discharge. Some of the adult prisoners were also instructed.

1831:[111] Prisoners willing to receive instruction but no real change of character.

1832:[111] All prisoners, except those prevented by sickness, have attended chapel daily. Several prisoners have availed themselves of the system of mutual instruction, and have been enabled to learn to read prior to their discharge.

1833:[111] A selection from liturgy and a chapter from bible read every morning to prisoners assembled in gaol chapel. Regular services held. On every occasion "the whole congregation was very orderly and attentive." Sunday school continued for juvenile offenders many of whom, "especially parish apprentices are... in a lamentable state of ignorance".

1834:[111] Juvenile offenders attending Sunday School have been enabled to read fluently before discharge.

1835:[20] The chaplain comes daily at 9 o'clock in the morning; he reads prayers; generally visits the wards afterwards, and converses, reads, or prays with the prisoners. He always has an interview with every prisoner shortly after his admission. He performs divine service, and delivers a sermon, twice on Sundays. He keeps a journal, which includes observations upon the character of the prisoners. A schoolmaster; who is not a prisoner, instructs the prisoners in reading on Sundays. On the week days a prisoner sometimes gives lessons in reading. The establishment is extremely well provided with religious works, which are supplied by the county on the order of the chaplain. The only other office which the chaplain has to perform elsewhere is divine service in the afternoon every Sunday at the County Lunatic Asylum, after the completion of his duties at the gaol.

Statistics of Religion, Matrimony, Celibacy and Education. Extracted from the Registers of Bodmin Gaol and House of Correction this 18th July 1836:—	
Total in custody	130
Religion—	
Established Church	118
Methodist	7
Roman Catholics	5
Married	63
Single	67
Instruction—	
Read and write	70
Read only	25
Neither read nor write	35
N.B. The 5 Roman Catholics are all foreigners; viz., 2 Frenchmen, 1 German, 1 Norwegian, and 1 Maltese.	
Very few miners come here; at present there are only nine. The smugglers are the best conducted of all the prisoners	

1837/8:[79] The chaplain since my last visit has had great reason to be satisfied with the conduct of the prisoners. He has met with many prisoners who have taken the sacrament before their admission. He keeps a copious journal, He has no other duty.

The chaplain performs divine service and preaches twice every Sunday, and once every Christmas-day, and Good-Friday, with prayers in the afternoons of those days. He reads prayers every morning at nine o'clock, visits the sick and those in solitary confinement. He administers the holy sacrament once in three months. He frequently visits the several wards of the prison for the purpose of exhorting the prisoners, and examines the juvenile prisoners as to the proficiency which they have made under the charge of the schoolmaster. He attends the general muster of the prisoners every Sunday morning, and distributes amongst them from time to time such religious books as they stand in need of. A Sunday-school is established at which he frequently attends; it is also constantly attended by a paid schoolmaster and by one of the turnkeys. When there are boys in the prison, and when a suitable adult prisoner can be selected to instruct them, they are daily assembled for that purpose.

Bibles and other religious books are placed in every ward throughout the prison, and are abundant.

1838:[112] A school had been formed in the prison, and many boys and men had been taught to read; but the prisoner who had the superintendence of the school had just been removed for misconduct and placed on the treadmill; and being unable to obtain another prisoner competent for the performance of the duties, the school had been suspended. The chaplain, in conclusion, urged the appointment of a permanent master to teach the prisoners.

1866:[28] The chaplain reads prayers every morning, gives two full services on Sundays, and administers the Sacrament once a month. He passes the mornings in visiting and instructing the male prisoners, and in the afternoon visits the females. On Saturdays he devotes his time to the debtors, and during the week frequently visits the school.

The schoolmaster has charge of the library, distributes the books, and instructs the prisoners from 10 to 12 a.m., and 1.30 to 5 p.m. daily. He also performs the duty of chapel clerk. The schoolmistress teaches daily from 2 to 4 p.m. There is a good supply of books, both of a religious and instructive character.

1868:[41] The chaplain states that since the new regulations on the subject of hard labour have come into operation it has been found impossible to assemble the male prisoners in chapel for religious instruction, and that from the same cause the male prisoners have not been able to avail themselves as much as heretofore of school instruction. The schoolmaster instructs the prisoners in the evening alter the hours of labour. A printed copy of the prison regulations is placed in every cell, and one of these regulations is that any prisoner may be visited by a minister of his own communion at proper and reasonable times.

1872:[100] Each uneducated adult receives on an average six hours instruction a week and juveniles eight hours.

From about 1870, all 'uneducated prisoners' received, on average, 6 hours secular instruction per week.[40,35]

Health

The surgeon usually attended daily, and whenever he was required. He inspected the general state of health of prisoners every Sunday and saw every prisoner on first admission. There was a male infirmary, containing 3 rooms, and a female infirmary consisting of 2 large rooms, 2 good cells, and a yard.

One of the duties of the Surgeon was to certify that every prisoner was physically and mentally capable of performing the tasks allocated to him. If a prisoner started to lose too much weight, the Surgeon would order extra food.

The Governor in his Quarterly report to the General Quarter Sessions of the Peace,[79] held at Truro on the 3rd April, 1838 stated: *In making this my quarterly report I regret to state that, during the past quarter, there has been more cases of sickness amongst the prisoners than for a very considerable time; it has been confined almost exclusively to the male prisoners convicted of felony, particularly those who have laboured constantly at the hand-mill, which has evidently produced much debility and consequent illness; but by timely application to the* **surgeon, who ordered such nourishing diet** *as he considered their cases required, the men are fast recovering, and those who were getting weak; but who were not on the sick-list, have, by an alternate change of labour,* **and some extra food,** *improved in their strength.*

The numbers of prisoners receiving extra diet in other reports were 14 (1866), 17 (1868), 32 (1872), 59 (1871), 20 (1874) and 43 in 1877.

In a few documents the numbers of sick prisoners for the year were recorded. However, different people reported the numbers in different ways and this gives the following incomplete data set. No real conclusions from these numbers are possible.

Cases of Sickness during the course of Year												
Year	1833	1834	1835	1837	1843		1846		1874		1877	
					M	F	M	F	M	F	M	F
Prisoners	678	549	455	534	519	141	472	160	600	132	663	141
Slight Indisposition	144		159	115	345	40	180	35	165			
Infirmary Cases			6		15	8	7	6	2	3	6	
Greatest number Sick at one time	5	4	6		11	2	6	6				
Greatest number in Infirmary				2								

Comments on prisoners' health, from various reports, are listed below:

Pre1828: The following statement was written in 1835.[20] The surgeon of this gaol has been attached to it for nearly 30 years. During the late governor's time the prisoners were much more unhealthy, and there were considerably more deaths than there have been since. At that time there were only two day-rooms, one in the gaol and the other in the bridewell, where the prisoners on each side were congregated together. The sleeping-rooms, which were originally intended for one, were always occupied by either three or five. There was a reservoir in the middle of each court-yard for the whole of the filth and deposits of the prison, which was removed about every six weeks by hand. The effluvia from this produced typhus, diarrhoea and dysentery, which carried off from six to eight yearly. The alterations that have been made by the present governor have entirely prevented (to use the surgeon's own words) a recurrence of these diseases – a circumstance the surgeon attributes to the cleanliness, to the regular dietary, and to the daily removal of all filth from every part of the prison by drains and a regular supply of water. There has not been a single death from any infectious disorder since the appointment of the present governor, and those few deaths which have occurred have been from diseases with which the prisoners were affected on being committed.

1829:[113] Favourable report on prisoners' health. Many cases of fever occurred but not infectious or of long duration. Main diseases brought to the prison by the vagrants. Twelve on the sick list, three of whom in the infirmary, none dangerously ill.

1830:[113] Favourable report. "The regular dietary, cleanliness and management of the Prison have prevented a recurrence of the fever which for so many years occurred at this Season"... "diseases principally venereal brought in by the Prisoners have been very much increased and there are several very bad cases on the sick list". As smallpox prevalent in neighbourhood all children and vulnerable prisoners vaccinated during last month.

1831:[113] Stated that more cases of sickness than previously, especially in June and July, with a "flu" epidemic.

1832:[113] Regarding health of prisoners, the introduction of the system of "Dietary and Classification", cases of fever have been reduced. Increased accommodation in the infirmary had been provided, but had not been occupied.

1832:[113] Because of the spread of cholera morbus and particularly because the disease might be introduced to the prison by vagrants from infected places, the governor, in conjunction with the Surgeon, had fumigated the gaol with the result that not one case of the disease had appeared, and the hospital had been empty for many weeks.

1832:[113] Presented most favourable report for years on prisoners' health, due to excellent management and "regular dietary". Principal diseases were among the vagrants.

1833:[113] Reported established "dietary" and extreme cleanliness resulted in not a single case of dangerous sickness among 738 persons committed.

1833:[113] Prisoners generally healthy, except during May when influenza prevailed. 144 cases of sickness during the year, only 5 at one time in the infirmary and no deaths. Mainly disease was amongst the vagrants.

1834:[113] Reported prisoners generally healthy, but several cases of fever during last three months, but no fatalities. Peter Mahon, convicted of misdemeanour, attacked with "virulent venereal ophthalmia in March last" which did not yield to "usual treatment" resulting in loss of his sight. Greatest number in infirmary at any one time was four.

The following is a list of diseases in the gaol of Bodmin in the county of Cornwall, from Michaelmas 1834 to Michaelmas 1835.	
Psora or Itch (principally vagrants)	29
Venereal	9
Fever	6
Dyspepsia	10
Pneumonia	53
Asthma	5
Diarrhoea	18
Rheumatism	5
Scrofula (tuberculosis of lymph glands)	14
Abscess	7
Ulcers	20
Ophthalmia (inflammation of the eye)	11
Total	**187**
There were many slight cases not entered as they were able to follow their occupations.	

1835:[113] Reported 165 cases of sickness, mostly slight. Gaol free at present of infectious disease. Two patients now in infirmary - Julian, a consumptive and Ankcorn with disease of the eyes.

1837:[79] The health of this prison was very good at the time of my inquiry; on account of the small size of the sleeping-cells, I ascertained this point by particularly questioning the prisoners. I found no patient neither in the male nor in the female infirmaries. I found two men and one child with the itch; and four or five men taking medicine. There was not much influenza last spring, nor had there been previously. There has been no scurvy since my visit. Colds and catarrhs are the chief complaints. There was some dysentery in 1837. I found some few of the prisoners with venereal affections. The cases most prevalent during the year were slight inflammatory affections and diarrhoea.

1838:[114] Chairman of the Cornwall Easter Sessions was sorry to say that the gaol had not been so healthy as it had previously been . . . the report of the governor attributed the illness to the use of the hand-mill now in the gaol. He (the Chairman) would only say that the hand-mill had been in use for four or five years before, and was not supposed to be injurious to the health of the prisoners. The working of it was rather easier than formerly, and the prisoners, during the last few years, were generally in good health. However there was no doubt from the opinion of the surgeon, who agreed with Mr. Everest (the governor of the gaol) that their health had been affected. He did not object to the prisoners being worked hard, or to their size being diminished, but it was not intended that their health should be injured. It was the opinion of the governor, that during the late inclement season, the spare diet and the hard labour had produced the sickness.

1842/3:[13] Five deaths in the course of the year. One lunatic transferred to Asylum.

1846:[14] One death. One lunatic transferred to Asylum.

1849:[23] Two deaths. One lunatic transferred to Asylum. One Pardon on medical grounds.

1850:[23] One death. One lunatic transferred to Asylum. One Pardon on medical grounds.

1855:[25] The infirmary contained four cases of sickness, one of which was likely to terminate fatally. The surgeon's kindness and attendance to the sick are highly spoken of.

1858:[26] The infirmary had not been occupied for many months before my visit, and there were at that time no sick persons except a single case of phthisis, which was considerably advanced at the time of the prisoner's reception. No deaths reported.

1865:[28] The surgeon reports that the health of the prisoners has been unusually good, and no epidemic has prevailed.

1868:[41] The surgeon visits and examines the prisoners daily, with rare exceptions. The health of the prisoners has been good, and no epidemic has prevailed but diarrhoea easily amenable to treatment.

1871:[99] The health of the prisoners has been generally good. Two cases of smallpox, occurring in females, were imported into the prison during the year, but by isolation, disinfectants, and the employment of nurses bearing strong marks of having had the disease severely, it was stamped out, and the prison has since been free of the disease

Six cases of imbecility and three of insanity, but not needing removal to an asylum, have been treated and discharged. Signs of unsoundness of mind were evident in all on their admission.

1872:[100] The general condition of the prisoners as to health has been good; the diet though punitive is quite enough to maintain the health and strength of the prisoners; and the clothing and bedding are sufficient. One prisoner received a pardon on medical grounds.

The daily average of cases treated in the infirmary was one. The daily average treated in their cells and excused labour was four, and the daily average treated and not excused labour was one.

1874:[40] The surgeon attends daily and oftener when necessary. He reports that the general health of the prisoners has been good; that there has been no epidemic. Light complaints are made with the view of obtaining an alteration of diet or a lightening of labour. Two males and three females have been treated in Infirmary during the year and 165 treated in their cells, of these one is on an average excused labour.

1877:[35] The surgeon attends once a day, oftener if necessary and he sees all the prisoners once a month. He states that the general health of the prisoners has been good and that there had been no epidemic disease.

Four (naval prisoners) received pardon on medical grounds. There were in all but six cases admitted into the infirmary, and during the year 72 prisoners were excused from all or part of their labour, some from infirmities existing on admission, others from temporary illness treated in cells.

1883:[31] Two attempted suicides both reported as feigned. Four Navy and two Army prisoners discharged on medical grounds.

1891:[103] One feigned suicide attempt.

1893:[104] Health and Conduct of the prisoners, male & female, has been good.

1901:[115] The general health of the prisoners has been good, only two prisoners admitted to infirmary during the year. No prisoner has been discharged on medical grounds. No death has occurred during the year.

The data in the table is contained in 29 reports, including 15 annual reports with 'no deaths' reported. After the drains were installed in 1828, the

Year	Name	Age	Sentence	Date of Admission	State of Health	Date of Death	Cause of Death

	Deaths in the Prison						
Year	**Name**	**Age**	**Sentence**	**Date of Admission**	**State of Health**	**Date of Death**	**Cause of Death**
Pre 1828	Death Rate 6 to 8 prisoners per year						
1829	Isaac Richards				Weak		
	Mark Nicholls						Killed in quarry
	Thomas Hugo		Debtor				Ruptured blood vessel
1830	William Walkey				poor		
1831	Brown		Vagrant				
	Robert Curnow						Sudden death
1832	John Pipey		Vagrant		poor		Typhus fever
1835	Henry Lander		Vagrant		poor		Consumption
	William May		Debtor		poor		
1842	W.R.	69	Debtor	26/7/1841	Bad	28/10/1842	Diabetes
	A.T.	80	2 weeks	14/11/1842	Bad	25/11/1842	Old age
1843	E.L.	40	8 m H.L.	13/9/1842	Bad	30/1/1843	Consumption
	T.J.	16	1 y H.L.	25/5/1842	Good	8/6/1843	Fever
	W.E.	17	2 m	14/6/1842	Good	25/7/1843	Fever
1845	John H.	49	4 m H.L.	10/7/1845	Bad	26/10/1845	Angina pectoris
1849	?						
	?						
1850	M.R.	43	18 m H.L.	23/4/1849	Bad	21/10/1849	Hepatitis Chronica
1877	?						Natural causes
	?						Natural causes
1883	?						Lung Disease
	?						Natural Causes
1894	Joseph Curtis	17	7 days HL	7/7/1894		9/7/1894	Suicide

death rate in the prison was very low. The number of deaths (23) is very small when the total population of the gaol, for the same report years, totalled approximately 16,000 inmates. This death rate is significantly lower than the rate in the general population probably because the people of Bodmin could not afford the services of a doctor or medicines.

There were claims by prison reformers that the 'silent system' would lead to a large number of mental health problems amongst the prisoners. In Bodmin, the following people were transferred from the gaol to the County Lunatic Asylum: J.M. (aged 39) in 1843, Joseph W. (29) in 1846, a female in 1849, a female in 1850, two prisoners in 1865, one female in 1872, 1 prisoner in 1883 and three female prisoners in 1901.

Three other cases of insanity in the gaol were recorded:

1858:[26] *One of the debtors was insane, but was within 4 days of his discharge*

1835:[20] *There is one insane prisoner at present here - a man aged 45, in custody one month, sent in for breach of peace and want of sureties. He was taken to sessions agreeably to commitment, and was directed by the court to be examined by two surgeons. They pronounced him insane.*

1837:[79] *I found here one insane prisoner, a man, aged 53, committed for want of sureties in a breach of the peace towards his wife, on the 16th of July last, for six-calendar months; he was evidently insane when brought to the prison, and is represented by his wife to have been so some time before.*

Discharged Prisoners' Aid Society

The Cornwall Prisoners' Aid Society was founded sometime between 1865 and 1874. It was in abeyance in 1883 but was re-established in 1885. The society gave assistance to prisoners when they were discharged from prison. Forty-nine prisoners received aid in 1874 and eighty in 1877. The Society was disbanded 1916

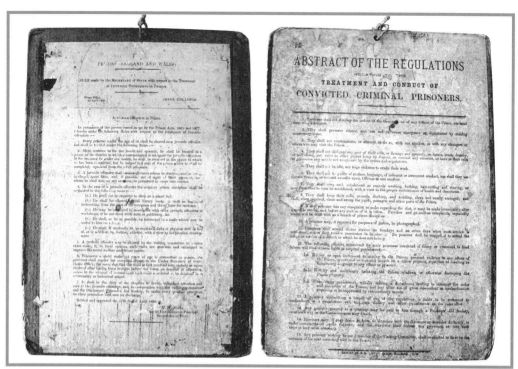

F.G.Stone Collection

'Rules & Regulations' Board, dated 1879, from the prison. On the reverse are the Rules for the Treatment of Juvenile Offenders.

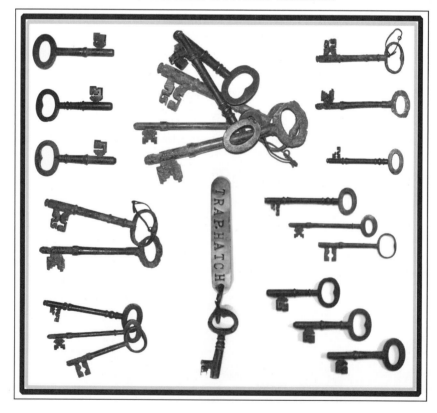

CHAPTER 16

Ins and Outs

This section deals with those people who must have liked life in the gaol, the re-offenders, and those who tried to leave the gaol, the escapers.

Re-offenders

The Victorians believed that their prison system was so harsh that after one visit, criminals would not want to return. Did the prison system achieve this objective?

Year	1830	1831	1835	1837	1843	1846	1865	1868	1872	1874	1877	1901
Committals	488	432	455	473	612	597	690	702	712	505	516	328
Re-offenders (M)			102	103	116	133	180	176	158	134	204	131
Re-offenders (F)			9	25	56	51	66	74	101	55	85	35
Total	115	89	111	128	172	184	246	250	259	189	289	166
% Re-offenders	24	21	24	27	28	31	36	36	36	37	56	51
Ratio M/F			11.3	4.1	2.1	2.6	2.7	2.4	1.6	2.4	2.4	3.7

The committals in the above table do not include debtors or naval prisoners. There were significantly more males recommitted than females. The very small number of females in 1835 seems unusual as, for the remaining years, the ratio of males to females averages 2.5 (range 1.6 to 4.1).

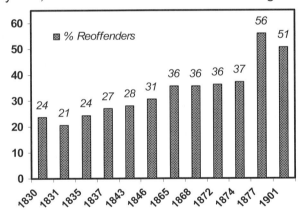

When the numbers of re-offenders is expressed as a percentage of the total committals for the year, it shows that recommittal rates were always over 20 percent and that they increased from the 1830s to the 1870s. In 1877, over half of the committals were previous inmates.

Data on multiple repeat offenders is available in four reports covering the years 1835-1846. In 1843, 116m and 56f were recommitted, 85 had been in the gaol once before; 40, twice; 17, three times and 30, four times or more.

	1835		1837		1843		1846	
	M	F	M	F	M	F	M	F
once	72		72	13	69	16	71	22
twice	28		16	5	22	18	25	11
3 times	6		8	5	7	10	14	4
4 or more	5		7	2	18	12	23	14
	102	9	103	25	116	56	133	51
Total	111		128		172		184	

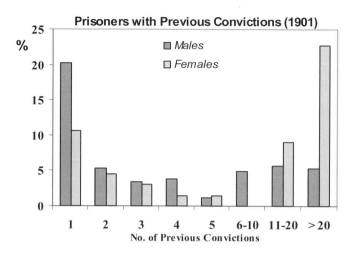

Prisoners with Previous Convictions (1901)

%

☐ Males
☐ Females

No. of Previous Convictions
1   2   3   4   5   6-10   11-20   >20

In 1901, 50% of males and 47% of females were committed for the first time. 20%(m) and 11%(f) had been in prison once before and percentages gradually decreased as the number of previous convictions increased from 2 to 5. However, a different group of multiple re-offenders then appears. For males, 16% (42) had between 6 and >20 previous convictions and for females, 32% (21) had been sent to prison more than 11 times.

There was a group of criminals who were not deterred by the life and conditions in the gaol or did they prefer to be in prison rather than out?

Case Histories: The following are examples of serial offenders at the end of the nineteenth century. The details have been provided by Malcolm McCarthy, of Padstow. The details have been transcribed from the Minute Books of Bodmin Magistrates Court.

Guildhall 3rd July 1896: Mayor CH Hext.

James Donovan and Mary Donovan: Drunk and disorderly at Town End.
Male defendant fined 10/6 and costs 6/6 or **21 days Hard labour** (Committed).
Female defendant fined 5/- and 6/6 costs or **7 days Hard Labour** (Committed).
Record produced by police against **James Donovan**

1891 January 31st	Stealing fowls	2 months
1891 October 31st	Common assault	28 days Hard Labour
1891 December 10th	Drunk etc	14 days Hard Labour
1891 December 10th	Assault on Police	14 days Hard Labour
1893 November 28th	Assault on Police	6 weeks Hard Labour
1894 March 24th	Drunkenness	Fined 5/-
1894 September 21st	Drunkenness	7 days Hard Labour
1895 March 25th	Drunkenness	7 days Hard Labour
1895 March 25th	Assault on Police	21 days Hard Labour
1895 April 22nd	Begging	28 days Hard Labour

Record produced by police against Mary **Donovan**

1890 November 19th	Found on enclosed premises	14 days Hard Labour
1891 February 10th	Hawking no certificate	14 days Hard Labour
1895 March 25th	Assault on Police	14 days Hard Labour

Guildhall Bodmin 18th October 1899: JMH Cardell

Bodmin Guardians V **Edith Rogers.** Refusing to work at Union on 18th October 1899

Thomas Whale (Master of Bodmin Union Workhouse) sworn: *This case has been a very troublesome one. She has been talked to by the Guardians and on Saturday last I had to report her again to the Guardians who instructed me that if she again misbehaved herself to give her into custody. Today she spoke of going out and Mr Whale my wife said "You shall go out as soon as you have cleaned your room". Afterwards it was found that she had hardly touched the room and refused to do the room anymore and began to curse and swear.*

Costs 9/6 paid (by the Guardians of the Workhouse?)   **10 days Hard Labour**

Guildhall Bodmin 6th March 1900: WA Bawden

Bodmin Guardians V **Edith Rogers.** Profane and obscene language 5th March 1900

Thomas Whale sworn. *Prisoner is in Workhouse Bodmin for maintenance at Common Fund, aged 27. Through yesterday all day she was going around house swearing and threatening what she would do to me. She had a wet5 towel at the time and said I will thrash you with this across your Bl..dy head. She threw a piece of cake at my wife who is Matron. The inmates generally are afraid of her. She used obscene language not fit to repeat.*   **14 days Hard Labour**

Guildhall Bodmin 25th June 1900: WA Bawden, JMH Cardell

Bodmin Guardians V **Edith Rogers.** Using profane and obscene language on 24th June 1900.

Thomas Whale sworn: *I am the Master of the Union Workhouse Bodmin, and the prisoner is an inmate. Last night about bedtime the women made a communication to me and I went into the Workhouse. Prisoner was in behind the door, she said "This hell of a place". She said D....n and swore she would not go to bed I had to bring her bed in another room. I ordered her to bed and she repeatedly refused to go. On Saturday she refused to go to the Hospital to scrub.*

Prisoner says: My reason why I called it a hell of a place is because of the women there. I have been put in the dark room on bread and water   **21 days Hard Labour**

Guildhall Bodmin 6th September 1900: WA Bawden, T Mudge

Bodmin Guardians **V Edith Rogers.** Profane language and refusing to work on 6th September 1900

Thomas Whale *I am Master of the Workhouse. Prisoner asked to go to her usual work, she said she would not go, so I told my wife to say nothing more I would send for the police. When I went up she was on the table swearing about the Workhouse, she said "To think I am in this hell of a place." She continued in the same strain.*

Costs 10/-   **One month Hard Labour**

Guildhall Bodmin 13th December 1900: J Treleaven, WA Bawden

Bodmin Guardians V **Edith Rogers.** Refusing to work on 11th December 1900

Thomas Whale sworn *Since prisoner came out of prison she has behaved herself well, but broke out again a few weeks ago. She burns holes in her apron, refuses to get up in the morning and refuses to work on the 11th.*

Costs 10/-   **Six weeks Hard Labour**

Guildhall 9th March 1896: CH Hext Ex Mayor

Sarah Jane Rawling. Vagrancy Begging 7th March.   Admitted **7 days Hard Labour**

Guildhall 1896: CH Hext

Sarah Jane Rawling. Vagrancy Begging.   Admitted **14 days Hard Labour**

Guildhall 6th April 1899: R Roscorla

Police **V Sarah Jane Rawling.** Begging in Castle Street on 5th April 1899. Pleads Guilty PC William Martin states: *He found prisoner begging in Castle Street and arrested her. Prisoner says she comes from Liskeard and admits previous convictions for begging.*   **7 days Hard labour**

Guildhall 1st May 1899: R Roscorla, J Stephens

Police V **Sarah Jane Rawling**. Vagrancy, begging on 29th April 1899. Pleads guilty and admits previous convictions. Treated as a rogue and vagabond for second offence as idle and disorderly person.   **One month imprisonment**

John Donovan was imprisoned 10 times in less than six years. Mary Donovan and Sarah Jane Rawling each had four terms. Edith Rogers was imprisoned five times in fifteen months just for upsetting the Master of the Workhouse.

Escapes

The following escapes or attempted escapes have been reported in Quarter Sessions records, in *'The West Briton'* newspaper (as Published in the series *'Life in Cornwall'* by R M Barton) and Inspectors of Prisons Reports.

1784:[116] Following attempts at escapes by prisoners at Bodmin Gaol, repairs to be carried out to the defective walls there.

1790:[117] Five militia men (in custody for not attending the 28 days required by the Militia Act), This Court highly approves of their behaviour while in custody, in preventing the escape of several convicts, and saving the lives of turnkeys and others assisting them: five guineas to be paid to the militia men, as a reward, by the vice-treasurer, out of County Stock. This order to be hung up in different parts of the gaol as an encouragement to others in a like situation.

1812:[118] Escape of two prisoners from Bodmin Gaol, August 27, 1812. George Kendall, a blacksmith, five feet ten inches high, aged 33 years, swarthy complexion, brown hair, grey eyes, a large scar on the left cheek, stout made, and one foot larger than the other. John Bayley, a travelling tinker, five feet five inches high, aged 33 years, grey hollow eyes, swarthy complexion, light sandy hair, lost two joints of his forefinger on the right hand. Whosoever will apprehend and lodge them in one of his Majesty's gaols, and give notice of the same to the gaoler of Bodmin Gaol, shall receive ten guineas reward, or five guineas for either of them.

1828:[119] Drew attention to insecure state of the bridewell, where several escapes had recently been made.

Pre 1829:[120] Parsons had previously escaped from Bodmin Gaol, having first stolen £5 from a keeper. He scaled the wall, visited a public-house, and returned to gaol of his own accord.

1831:[121] Escaped from Bodmin Gaol, early this morning, the under mentioned prisoners, charged with felony, viz.: James Medland, a native of Launceston, aged 34 years, 5 feet 9½ inches high, dark eyes, brown hair, fresh complexion, and rather bald on the top of his head; he had on, when he escaped, a fustian shooting jacket and trowsers, and a low crowned hat, with a broad brim. Thomas Hore, of St Austell, aged 27 years, 5 feet 6 inches high, gray eyes, brown hair, fresh complexion, has a scar on his right cheek, and also near the right eye; he had on, when he escaped, a fustian jacket, striped waistcoat and corded or fustian trowsers. John Burrows, of Bodmin, aged 45 years, 5 feet 8 inches high, gray eyes, sandy hair, fresh complexion, has a scar on his forehead, is freckled and has sandy whiskers; he had on, when he escaped, a long blue frock coat, blue waist-coat and trowsers, and a glazed hat. Whoever will apprehend the said prisoners and lodge them in any of his Majesty's gaols, shall receive 5 pounds reward, for each person apprehended, on application to Mr J. B. Everest, governor of the said gaol.

1832:[111] 20 prisoners were in irons for attempting to escape.

1833:[122] Escaped from the gaol at Bodmin, this morning, the 5th of December, 1833, four prisoners, viz.—John Walters, aged 41, 5 feet 6½ inches high, grey eyes, brown hair, sallow complexion, marked with ink on the left wrist and back of the left hand with a W and a heart; he is a native of Truro, and escaped in the county shirt only. Edward May, aged 32, 5 feet 9½ inches high, grey eyes, sandy hair, fresh complexion, bald on the top of the head, and sandy whiskers; he is a native of Plymouth and escaped in a county shirt and a blue flannel shirt only. Samuel Langley, aged 27, 5 feet 2½ inches high, grey eyes, brown hair, pale complexion, with a large mole between the shoulders; he is a native of Winkfield, in Berkshire, and escaped in the county shirt only. Thomas Jeffers, aged 27, 5 feet 7 inches high, grey eyes, dark hair, dark complexion, marked with ink on the left arm with a ship, an anchor and a sloop, and on the right arm with a sloop; mark of a wound on the right side of the face; he is a native of Bristol, and escaped in the county shirt only. A reward of five pounds will be paid on the apprehension of either of the above men, on being safely lodged in any of his Majesty's gaols. Langley and Jeffers were recaptured in a straw-shed near Liskeard a week later. They had posed as escaped smugglers to beg for food, and were suffering badly from exposure.

1836:[20] During eight years there have been five escapes all successful; one was of a woman; she escaped through the roof, which was only a few feet from the floor. Four other prisoners have so far escaped as to reach the outside of the prison but they were retaken. *(These numbers are not in agreement with other reports, see above).*

1838:[79] There have been none since my last visit. One person made an attempt, and got on the roof, but was retaken. He was a seafaring man.

1843:[13] No escapes.

1846:[14] Joseph P. (22), a debtor, escaped on the 3rd May, 1846. He was later retaken.

1855:[25] Two prisoners for trial made their escape from the sleeping berths in the gaol division of the prison some months before my visit, and have not been captured. This is not much to be wondered at, considering the flagrant faults of construction in the present building; but as a new prison is in the course of construction, there is good reason to hope that the high qualifications of the present governor will, in the course of a year from this time, have a more favourable field of operation.

1868:[41] No escapes.

The 16th (published in 1851), 24th (1859), 26th (1861), 31st (1866), 36th (1872), 37th (1873), 39th (1875) and 42nd (1878) Inspectors of Prisons reports make no mention of escapes. There were no escapes recorded in 'Commissioner of Prisons' reports, published in the years 1883, 1895, 1901 and 1916. The only escape reported from the New Gaol was:

1890:[86] Report from Visitors Committee to Home Office. 'An officer allowed a prisoner to escape through negligence.'

Details of an attempted escape in 1827 are contained in the following documents:[123]

Failed Escape Attempt on 28th April 1827

These several examinations were taken before me on this 30th day of April 1827. Joseph Pomery (*Clerk and Vicar of St. Kew. Justice.*)

The examination of Charles Smith a Prisoner in the Gaol of Bodmin in the County of Cornwall, who saith that since the Commitment of John Mortlake and Samuel Williams he has slept in the same cell with them. - That previous to the last Assizes he has heard several conversations between the said John Mortlake and Samuel Williams of their intention to endeavour to effect their escape in case they were found guilty and sentenced to be transported for life. That the fourth night after their return from the Assizes Mortlake proposed to examinent to fill a jacket with straw and put it in his Mortlake's bed that when the Turnkey came to lock up at night examinant and Williams were to say that there were three in the cell, which he and Williams refused to do. Mortlake and Williams then said that they would leave it 'till they were put on board the hulks. That on Saturday last in consequence of his suspicions that John Mortlake and Samuel Williams intended to attempt this escape this examinant wrote to Thomas Dungey one of the Turnkeys to be on his guard, which is hereunto annexed. That in consequence of this examinant information to Thomas Dungey he Dungey searched the cell where he found two pieces of iron now produced to him.

Received this of John Martin smuggler in Gaol. April 28 1827:

> '*Mr Dungey I would have you be very careful this night for Williams and Mortlake is up to roguery this night. I am afraid for hear them planing to come through the arch in the laundry room, so I think it best for to watch.*

Do you not say any thing about it till you see and then you can reprimand me at the time for not telling you you can say.'

O Smith

The examination of James Breuton a Prisoner in the Gaol of Bodmin in the County of Cornwall he saith that last Friday morning he saw Samuel Williams with an iron in the fire which he was sharpening the point of, that on Friday and Saturday last he saw Samuel Williams making a knife into a saw which he said was for the purpose of making rings of bone. That the iron and knife now shown him are the same he saw in the possession of Williams.

The sign of James Breuton

Thomas Dungey says that in consequence of a written information which he received last Saturday evening he went with assistance to search the cell of Samuel Williams and John Mortlake, he found two pieces of iron concealed under the straw of the bed, where Williams and Smith slept, Williams and Mortlake have since acknowledged that they put the irons there. On Saturday night he put Mortlake and Williams to sleep in separate cells. On Sunday morning when he went to let Mortlake out he found that Mortlake had a cleaver in his hand and threatened to cut down the first man that came to take him out and that in consequence of Examinant's threatening him Mortlake gave him the cleaver. - That last evening Mortlake and Williams gave up to him the two knives now produced.

Thomas (Dungey

On Saturday evening 20 April 1827, T Dungey received information that Mortlake and Samuel Williams had formed a scheme to escape. On T Dungey's making a search found an iron barr on the handle of a frying pan in the sleeping cell of Mortlake and Williams – Sunday morning - T Dungey went to Mortlake's cell with the intent to secure him in a solitary cell and found him armed with a cleaver and threatened the life of any man that should touch him; but after threats from T Dungey he at last gave up the cleaver and T Dungey put him in a solitary cell and Williams he put in another solitary cell.

In the evening Mortlake and Williams gave T Dungey two knives converted to saws – they both told T Dungey they intended by getting through the cell floor

T Dungey took from Williams pocket a … bottle of rum with which laudinum was to be put and given to Charles Smith a third prisoner to make him sleep while they were making the breach to escape.

James Chapple

1827 April 30

Visited the Gaol and in consequence of the above complaint, John Mortlake and Samuel Williams were ordered to be confined till a meeting of the magistrates.

Joseph Pomery ——

Published by kind permission of Margaret Nott of Camborne, granddaughter of Thomas Austin.
Documents given to Bodmin Town Museum collection: Accession Nos. 2008.10

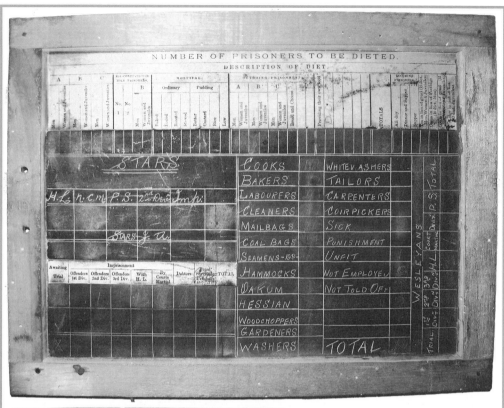

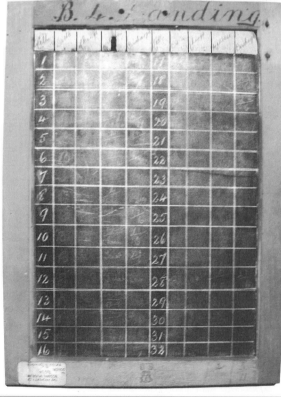

Warder's Tally Slate: Labelled 'B4 Landing', the top corridor in the Male Civil Prison. It showed the number of prisoners on that floor classified by type of sentence, for example, hard labour, court-martial, penal servitude, debtor and the class of prisoner, 1st, 2nd or 3rd Division. In addition, it recorded the numbers of prisoners on special diets, ill-conducted or idle prisoners, prisoners on hospital diets and incoming and outgoing diets. It also lists all of the different types of employment and trades. A separate section labelled 'Wesleyans' contained the numbers of different prisoner types. The reverse of the slate contained Cell No., Diet, Change (date of change to higher level in the 'four-stage system'?), Mattress and Discharge date.

Bodmin Town Museum

CHAPTER 17

Death Sentence and Executions

Death Sentences & Hangings (Western Circuit Assizes for 1816)		
Convicted of::	Death	Hanged
Breaking & Entering	26	1
Robbery Highway	14	1
Larceny (over 40/-) from house	13	
House Breaking	11	
Horse Stealing	8	
Sheep Stealing	7	
Forgery/Uttering	5	1
Naval Stores (over 20/-)	5	
Murder	4	4
Attempted Murder	3	
Burglary	2	
Cattle Stealing	2	
Rape (girl under 10)	2	2
Uttering/Counterfeiting	1	
Return from Transport.	1	
Total	**104**	**9**

National Statistics for 1822-1828			
Offence	Death	Hanged	%
Murder	110	93	84.5
Sodomy	14	11	78.6
Rape	56	27	48.2
Coining	33	12	36.4
Letters, Stealing Bank Notes	7	2	28.6
Arson	44	9	20.5
Murder, Intent to	154	31	20.1
Forgery	215	23	10.7
Robbery, Highway	971	72	7.4
Burglary	2011	83	4.1
Horse Stealing	911	37	4.1
Larceny, House	1171	23	2.0
Breaking, House	1181	21	1.8
Sheep, Stealing	754	12	1.6
Cattle Stealing	156		
Riot	50		
Transports at Large	46		
Sacrilege	36		
Felony, Armed	31		
Coins, Uttering	11		
Cattle, killing	3		
Larceny, Grand	3		
Larceny, Shop	3		
Letters, Threatening	3		
Piracy	2		
Felony, from Wreck	2		
Felony, Cutting Trees	2		
	7980	456	5.7

In the 1770s, it was estimated that there were over 240 offences for which the Assize Courts could order the death penalty but by the early 1800s the large majority of prisoners condemned to death were not executed.

The return from the Clerk of the Western Assizes, which included Cornwall, for the year 1816,[66] states that 487 persons were committed to the various gaols in the region for trial at the Assizes. Of these, 332 were convicted including 104 (31.3%) who were given the death penalty. The offences committed and the numbers of prisoners actually hanged are shown in the table. From this record, only 9 people were hanged of the 104 who had received the death sentence.

Similar figures are contained in national statistics. The average percentage of condemned prisoners executed in the years 1805–1811 ranged from 9.7% (1811) to 19.1% (1805). The national overall average for the years 1805–1811 was 15%.[77] The statistics for the years 1822 to 1828 are more detailed showing [76b] which crimes really led to the death penalty. The top of the list being murder.

The situation in Cornwall was very similar to the national picture. For example, at the Summer Assizes held at Bodmin on 7th August, 1820,[124] seven prisoners were sentenced to death but only one, Sarah Polgreen, who was found guilty of murdering her husband, was hanged. Five prisoners were sentenced to death for Larceny and the other for killing and stealing a sheep. They were probably transported, sent to hulks or sentenced to long periods in gaol.

Executions in Cornwall

Between 1735 and 1820, prisoners were hanged in Cornwall for a range of offences including murder, burglary, robbery with violence, sheep stealing, highway robbery, stealing (including a watch, a mare, an ox and wheat), killing animals, house and shop breaking, forgery and arson. Twenty-four of the sixty hangings were for murder. In the 1820s, Robert Peel's Prison Reform Acts greatly reduced the number of capital offences and further reforms meant that by 1860, few offences, including murder and treason, carried the death penalty. From 1821 to 1909, there were 20 hangings, 16 for murder and one each for arson (1825), highway robbery (1827), house breaking (1828) and bestiality (1834). This was the last hanging in Cornwall for an offence other than murder.

There were 60 confirmed executions at Bodmin between 1735 and 1909; 8 in Launceston (1735-1821); 2 in St Stephens (1767 and 1793) and 10 executions where the date or place has not been confirmed. The literature suggests that 8 of these were at Bodmin, one at Launceston and one not known.

Details of the 80 recorded executions in Cornwall are listed at the end of this section.

Places of Execution in Bodmin

The place of execution was moved several times during the gaol's history. Several versions of the 'Executions in Bodmin' list, with notes on the place of execution, have been published. Abstracts from two of the lists are compared below.

Bodmin Town Museum:

1785-1821:	*By gibbet in public on Bodmin Common,*
1825-1862:	*By drop gallows in public outside gaol.*
1878-1882:	*Gallows now screened from view.*
1901-1909:	*Scaffold and drop placed inside gaol.*

In 'Bodmin Gaol' by Alan Brunton:[125]

1785-1802:	*On Bodmin Moor (St Lawrence site).*
1802-1815:	*On Bodmin Moor or outside wall of the old gaol.*
1820-1862:	*Public hanging outside the wall of the gaol.*
1878-1882:	*Executed inside the new gaol in private.*
1901-1909:	*Executed in private inside the execution shed.*

The only agreements between the two lists are that the earlier hangings took place on Bodmin Common (near St Lawrence site), that some took place outside the gaol wall and that the last two executions were in the execution shed.

The Sherborne Mercury (August, 1796) states that the execution of Hoskin took place on Bodmin Common. The executions of Vanstone and Lee (1802) were the first by drop gallows in Cornwall. From the timings in the report, it would seem that the new drop was situated outside the gaol wall (Cornwall Gazette, 4th September, 1802). Further reports from the 1805 and 1812 executions state that the drop was *'erected without the prison wall'* and *'in front of Bodmin prison'*.

In the Quarter Sessions records for 1830/1831, the Governor reported a new execution drop was to be built over the gatehouse. This is confirmed by the painting, entitled *'An execution at Bodmin Gaol, 1841'* [22] and a much later newspaper report,[126] which states:

'Above the arched door of the gaol entrance was another, smaller door for the Chaplain, culprit and hangman to come through; outside of this were iron gratings (the trap) to walk on, with rails around to prevent the murderer from jumping off.'

Therefore, from about 1832 until the closure of the old gaol in 1860, executions took place above the gatehouse of the old gaol.

The Inspector of Prisons noted [27] in 1861 that:

'The apparatus called "the drop" for capital executions, which had inadvertently been so placed as to be nearly invisible from the exterior of the prison, had been ordered to be removed to a more suitable position.'

The details of the next hanging, that of John Doidge in 1862, is described in detail in *'The West Briton'*, dated 22nd August:[127]

About half-past eight on Monday morning, the carpenters commenced the erection, on the principal floor of the female department of the gaol, steps and a platform inside the southern wall of the prison—the platform being on a level with the grating floor of the drop on the exterior; and at ten o'clock these preparations were completed. The drop has the same southern aspect, and is nearly over the same site as that of the old gaol: and, consequently, the fields sloping down from the northern side of the street at the western part of the town—the "Bodmin highlands"— afford the same facilities for view of the dread spectacle that have been available to so many thousands at previous executions. We understand that it had been intended, in the building of the new gaol, to erect the drop at the northern part; but this purpose was abandoned because of the comparatively small assemblage of the public to whom the execution of a capital sentence could be made visible. [The female department was the building later known as the Naval Prison.]

An Act of Parliament of 1868 ruled that executions must be screened from the public. The next two hangings, those of Selina Wadge and William Bartlett, took place out of the public view but probably at the normal execution place. A report of the Bartlett hanging in 1882 states [128] that *'the drop was erected in an angle of the outside of the prison facing up the lane to Town Wall and down towards Dunmere. It was a wooden erection, looking at a distance like a roadman's hut. There was nothing else to be seen, but at 8 a.m. a black ball was run up by the big chimney, which spread out to be the black flag.'* The last two hangings, Giovanni (1901) and Hampton (1909) took place in the execution shed, which was built inside the gaol after 1882.

The Bodmin executions were carried out at the following places:-

1785-1802: By gibbet, on Bodmin Common (St Lawrence site).

1802-1828: By drop gallows outside wall of the old gaol.

1834-1856: New drop gallows above the old gaol gate.

1862: Drop placed on the outside of the South wall (new gaol).

1878-1882: As above but screened from public view.
1901-1909: Executed in private inside the execution shed.

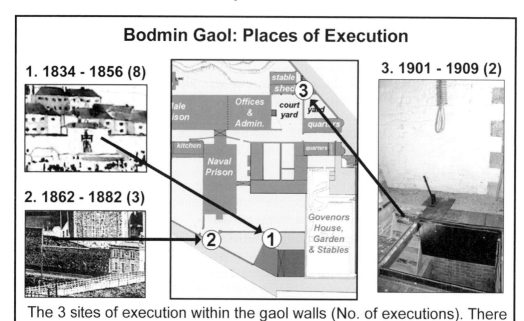

Bodmin Gaol: Places of Execution

1. 1834 - 1856 (8)

2. 1862 - 1882 (3)

3. 1901 - 1909 (2)

The 3 sites of execution within the gaol walls (No. of executions). There were 19 other hangings at the gaol but outside the walls (1802-1828).

New doors and mechanism, designed and fitted by Gary Ewart. The lever is original and was kindly donated to the jail by Mr Stephen Hall, owner of *'The Hole in the Wall'*, Bodmin.

Executions in Cornwall (1735 - 1909)

Year	Name	Age	Crime	Date	Place
1735	Henry Rogers		Murder of William Carpenter	6th August	**Launceston**
	John Sheel			7th August	**Launceston**
	Henry Fellows		Housebreaking	11th August	**Bodmin**
1736	John Notting		Murder of William Lowe	ca 12th May	**Bodmin**
	John Morris		Murder of Margery Plyn	Unknown	**Bodmin**
1739	Richard Cairn *		Murder of Richard Cressell	Unknown	*Bodmin*
1741	Richard Barnes *		Highway robbery	Unknown	*Bodmin*
	Abraham Mead *		Murder of Abraham Popjoy	Unknown	*Bodmin*
	John Harris *		Horse theft	Unknown	*Bodmin*
1742	Alice Warne *		Murder of male bastard child	Unknown	*Bodmin*
	William Francis *		Sheep stealing	Unknown	*Bodmin*
1743	John Pegrose *		Horse theft	Unknown	*Bodmin*
1745	Gabriel Mitchell		Murder of Daniel Oneal	Unknown	**Bodmin**
1746	Margaret Lukey		Murder of Alexander Mellows	Unknown	**Bodmin**
1748	John Boyens *		Murder of Grace Steplias	Unknown	*Bodmin*
1755	Grace Smith		Murder of female infant	11th August	**Bodmin**
1760	Francois Lafond		Highway robbery	19th May	**Bodmin**
	Antoine Dureau			20th May	**Bodmin**
1767	William Pearse		Stole from wreck	5th/19th October	**St Stephens**
1771	Catherine Burgess		Murder of female bastard	1st April	**Launceston**
	Ann Chapman		Murder of female bastard	9th August	**Bodmin**
1773	Richard Simons		Highway robbery	15th April	**Bodmin**
1776	Mary Penylegon		Murder of male bastard	29th March	*Launceston*
1777	Stephen Harris	22	Burglary	14th April	**Bodmin**
1785	Philip Randell	27	Burglary in Truro	7th March	**Bodmin**
	Robert Brown	33	Murder of John Newton	23rd March	**Bodmin**
	William Hill	33	Murder of John Pascoe	29th July	**Bodmin**
	John Richards	25	Highway robbery	7th August	**Bodmin**
1786	Thomas Roberts	34	Sheep stealing	6th April	**Bodmin**
	Francis Coath	45	Sheep stealing	20th or 26th April	**Bodmin**
1787	James Elliot	35	Highway robbery (of the mail)	10th April	**Bodmin**
	John Gould	23	Burglary at Budock	10th April	**Bodmin**
	William Congdon	23	Buglary at Rame	20th August	**Bodmin**
1788	James Kitto **	32	Burglary at Breage	August	**Bodmin**
1791	Michael J. Taylor	22	Stealing a mare	31st March	**Bodmin**
	John Carne ('*John Dash*')	23	Burglary	31st March	**Bodmin**
	James Symons	25	Stealing an ox	31st March	**Bodmin**

Year	Name	Age	Crime	Date	Place
1791	Ben Willoughby	20	Murder of Jas. Jones of Helston	2nd September	Bodmin
	John Taylor	26		2nd September	Bodmin
	William Moyle		Feloniously killing a mare	15th September	Bodmin
1793	Wm. Trevarevas (Trewarris)	25	Murder of Martha Blewitt	28th March	St Stephens
1795	James Frederick		Highway robbery of Thom. Leane	9th April	Bodmin
	Joseph Williams	28	Sheep stealing	27th August	Bodmin
1796	G A Selfcombe (Safehorne)	25	Murder of Peter Jacobus von Poulsma	23rd March	Bodmin
	John Hoskin		Stealing wheat in Redruth	11th August	Bodmin
1798	William Howarth	24	Stealing a purse containing 20 guineas	13th September	Bodmin
1801	William Roskilly	34	Burglary at Mawgan in Meneage	13th April	Bodmin
1802	Richard Andrews (Rowe) ***		Forgery and fraud	25th August	Bodmin
	John Vanstone	37	Burglary in the house of Walter Oke	1st September	Bodmin
	William Lee	60		1st September	Bodmin
1805	John Williamson	32	Breaking into the shop of Miss Tyeth	17th April	Bodmin
	James Joyce	27		17th April	Bodmin
1812	Pierre Francois LaRoche	24	Forging a £2 note	13th April	Bodmin
	William Wyatt	40	Drowned Isaiah Falk Valentine at Fowey	1st May	Bodmin
1813	Elizabeth Osborne	20	Setting fire to a corn stack	6th September	Bodmin
1814	William Burns	21	Murder of John Allen of Sennen	31st March	Launceston
1815	John Simms		Murder of Joseph Burnett	31st March	Launceston
1818	William Rowe, jn.	41	Sheep stealing	20th August	Launceston
1820	Sarah Polgrean	34	Murder of her husband by poison	12th August	Bodmin
	Michael Stephens	27	Killing a ram and stealing it	5th September	Bodmin
1821	John Barnicott	24	Murder of William Hancock, at Cury	2nd April	Launceston
	John Thompson	17		2nd April	Launceston
	Nicholas James Gard	42	Murder of Thomas Hoskin	10th September	Bod/Laun
1825	William Oxford	21	Setting fire to a corn stack	7th April	Bodmin
1827	James Eddy	29	Robbing Jane Cock with violence	19th April	Bodmin
1828	Elizabeth Commins	22	Murder of her male child	8th August	Bodmin
	Thomas Pring Coombe	21	Housebreaking, 2 cases	21st August	Bodmin
1834	William Hocking	57	Bestiality	21st August	Bodmin

Year	Name	Age	Crime	Date	Place
1835	John Henwood	29	Parricide	30th March	**Bodmin**
1840	William Lightfoot	35	Murder of Nevill Norway	13th April	**Bodmin**
	James Lightfoot	24		13th April	**Bodmin**
1844	Matthew Weeks	23	Murder of Charlotte Dymond at Roughtor	12th August	**Bodmin**
1845	Benjamin Ellison	61	Murder of Mrs Elizabeth Ruth Seaman	11th August	**Bodmin**
1854	James Holman	27	Murder of his wife Phillipa, at Crowan.	3rd April	**Bodmin**
1856	William Nevan	44	Murder of Serjeant-major Robinson	11th August	**Bodmin**
1862	John Doidge	28	Murder of Roger Drew, near Launceston	18th August	**Bodmin**
1878	Selina Wadge	28	Murder of her child at Altarnun	15th August	**Bodmin**
1882	William Bartlett	46	Murder of a child at Lanlivery	13th November	**Bodmin**
1901	Valeri Giovanni	31	Murder on the high seas	9th July	**Bodmin**
1909	William Hampton	24	Murder of Emily Tredrea at St. Erth	20th July	**Bodmin**

The above list of 'Executions in Cornwall' has been prepared from list researched by D J Mossop and published by Richard Clark.[129] The data is taken from Assize Books, Reprieves from the Secretary of State's Books supplemented as necessary by Sheriffs Cravings and Treasury Books: all of these documents are at the Public Records Office (National Archives). Data on execution dates was identified from local Newspapers. The details have been compared with a list of hangings (1785 -1909) published by L E Long in 'Executions in Bodmin'.[130] There is good agreement between the two data sets for hangings after 1785, except for 1788 James Kitto** which only appears in reference 129, and 1802 Richard Andrews (alias Rowe)*** in reference 130.

There are eight pre1750 entries, marked with *, which are classified as probable executions as no reprieve documents have been traced.

Trials and Executions

The Murder of Nevell Norway [131]

Mr Nevell Norway, a thirty-eight year-old timber and general merchant of Egloshayle visited Bodmin market on Saturday 8th February, 1840. At about 10 o'clock in the evening, riding his grey horse, he left Bodmin via the Wadebridge road. He overtook Mr Abraham Hamley of St Mabyn about a quarter of a mile out of Bodmin. They rode together as far as the turnpike gate at Mount Charles, about two miles from Bodmin, where the road to St Mabyn diverges from that to Wadebridge. They parted there.

Mr John Hick, farmer of St Minver, who had also been to the market, left Bodmin at a quarter past ten on the Wadebridge road. When he reached Clapper, about one mile from Wadebridge, he saw a light coloured horse galloping on before him, without any rider but with saddle and bridle. While trying to catch the horse, he met two people, one after the other, who thought it was Mr Norway's horse. He went, therefore, to Gregory, Mr Norway's carter, and together they went to the stable, where they found the horse at the gate. There were blood spots on the saddle.

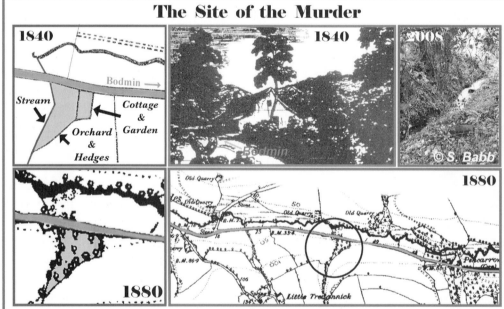

The Site of the Murder

The cottage, orchard and stream reported in 1840 newspapers, is clearly shown on the Tithe Map (1840). In later maps (ca 1880), the cottage has been demolished but the orchard, stream and shape of the plot have not changed. Today, the stream and the orchard are still present but the road is now much wider.

Thomas Gregory and Edward Cavell, who lived with Mr Norway, went down the Bodmin road towards Pencarrow Mill. When they came to a place called North Hill, there was an unoccupied lone cottage there on the right hand side of the road. On the Wadebridge side of the cottage, there was a small orchard and near the orchard a little stream coming down into the road. Mr Norway was found in the leat of water, lying on his back with his head towards the stream and his feet towards the road. He was quite dead. He was fully clothed, except for his hat, which was gone. They put the body on the horse and carried it back to Wadebridge. When the body was searched they found, in the pockets, a pocket book, containing £25 in notes, a silk handkerchief, a pair of saddle straps, a pair of drab worsted gloves, a watch and a penknife. No purse, keys or a writing-tablet, carried by the deceased, were found.

During the night and the next day, three different groups of people travelled to the crime scene. They included: Gregory; Cavell; Mr William Norway, Nevell's brother; Mr Tickell, the surgeon; John Menhennick Docking and several other friends and neighbours. They found the site of the murder, a pool of blood, opposite the cottage gate, some 30 feet from where the body was found and a trail of blood to the place where the body was found. During the several searches, they also found pieces of a broken button from Mr Norway's coat, his hat, a freshly broken hammer off a gun or pistol and footsteps of two persons in the orchard and the adjacent field. They did not belong to Mr Norway as they were nailed.

On Sunday morning, *Joseph Hamley, Esq.*, the coroner for East Cornwall, left Bodmin and went to Wadebridge, to hold an inquest on the body. A jury was summoned in the afternoon, and evidence given as to the finding of the body. The Coroner's Inquest was held on Sunday afternoon, at the *Ship Inn*, Wadebridge. The following gentlemen were sworn on the jury: *Wm. Pollard*, foreman, of Clapper, Egloshayle; *John Lakeman*, Egloshayle; *Morrish Wilton*, Egloshayle; *Thomas Martin*, Egloshayle; *Parmenas Menhennick*, Egloshayle; *Samuel West,* Egloshayle; *Roger Gill,* Egloshayle; *Gregory Brabyn,* St Breock; *John Wills,* St Breock; *James Mankin,* Egloshayle; *Robert Cleve,* St Breock and *James Rowell Rickard,* St Breock.

Evidence of the finding of the body was reported but the most important evidence was presented by *Trehane S Tickell, Esq.,* Surgeon, who described the injuries and cause of death: *'After the body was brought into the house, I examined it and found a general and severe injury of the head and face. There was a very severe wound on the chin, which must have been inflicted with very considerable force'.* He reported a long list of other injuries; damage to the lips, broken nose, a deep wound along the eyebrow, a wound from the eyebrow towards the temple, the whole of the front of the head and the left side was fractured, a further injury on the back of the head had driven parts of the skull into the brain. He concluded that any of the blows, i.e. to the brow, left side or back of the head could cause immediate death. These injuries must have been caused by different blows from a heavy blunt instrument, such as a heavy stick or the butt end of a gun or pistol. He considered that one injury was caused by the lock from a pistol, which he believed was used in the attack.

The jury delivered a verdict of wilful murder against some person or persons unknown.

As there was no police force at that time, the investigation into the murder was led by the Wadebridge magistrates, including *Capts. Hext* and *Rogers* and the *Revs. William Molesworth, Charles Hodgson,* and *Charles Lyne*, with the help of parish constables and a detective from London Police. A number of these people were later mentioned in the trial. They included, *Wm. Bray* of Bodmin, who was employed to make enquiries about the murder but was not sworn-in as a special constable; *Joseph Carveth*, constable of St Breock; *Charles Jackson*, officer of the London Police; *Mr Goddard,* constable of Stratton and *Henry Benody,* constable.

Bodmin Town Council held a meeting and decided to offer a reward for information leading to the arrest of the murderer; the money was willingly guaranteed by many Bodmin and Wadebridge townspeople. A number of placards were printed offering a reward of £100 for the apprehension of the murderer.

During the next few days, people came forward offering the names of possible suspects, included in the list was 'Lightfoot' of St Breock.

Wm. Roche, labourer of Lanivet, saw William Lightfoot watching Mr Norway pay a gentleman money from his purse in Bodmin at about 4 o'clock on the day of the murder.

John Harris, shoemaker of St Minver, on his way home from Bodmin at 9 o'clock on the evening of the murder, saw two men loitering between the uninhabited cottage and the stream. One man was dressed in a dark suit and the other in a smock frock. Later in Court, from their heights, dress and general appearance, he identified the men as the Lightfoot brothers.

Richard Eyre, blacksmith of St Breock, who lived in a dwelling connected to James Lightfoot's house, *'separated only by a thin partition, having some holes in it,'* went to bed between 9 and 10 o'clock and was awoken towards the morning, by two voices, the wife was crying and James Lightfoot went up and down the stairs wearing heavy shoes. He did not hear James Lightfoot coming home.

Richard Caddy of St Breock, at 11 o'clock on the Sunday, the day after the murder, he was in James Lightfoot's house and observed a large pistol on the chimney-piece. He has seen it often and had fired it off several times but, on this Sunday, there was no lock on the pistol. He asked James about the damage and James replied *"I shot at a cat on Wednesday and broke the screw that went through the lock."* He also claimed that he still had the lock.

Richard Caddy also stated that on the Saturday night he was at William Lightfoot's on the higher side of Burlawn. William Lightfoot came home at about 10 o'clock, his trousers were very wet from the foot up to above the knees. He said he had fallen and made himself wet. He was wearing a darkish jacket, no hat and no smock.

On Thursday, 13th February, William Bray and Constable Carveth searched the home of James Lightfoot. When asked about the pistol, James said that he had blown it to pieces last Wednesday week, firing at a cat. The pieces had been thrown away. On further questioning he said that he still had the barrel and took it down from a hole above an overhead beam in the kitchen. The barrel had contained powder but it had not been fired. Bray and Carveth left James at the house that night but returned around half past twelve, when they apprehended him and took him to Wadebridge.

William Vercoe of St Breock reported that on Friday (14th) he had a conversation with William Lightfoot and claimed that he had admitted that the pistol had a broken hammer and that he had told his brother to get rid of it.

William Lightfoot was later taken into custody on Monday 17th and was brought before Mr Molesworth at the Molesworth Arms in Wadebridge. He was cautioned but proceeded to make a statement, to which he later affixed his mark.

"I went to Bodmin last Saturday week, the 8th inst., and in returning I met my brother James at the head of Dunmeer Hill. It was just dim like. My brother had been to Egloshayle Burlawn to buy potatoes. Something had been said about meeting. My brother was not in Bodmin that day. Mr. Vercoe overtook us between the Turnpike Gate at the top of Dunmeer Hill, and Lane End. We came on the turnpike road all the way till we came to the house near the spot where the murder was committed. We did not go into the house, but hid ourselves in a field. We did not see Mr. Abbott's waggon. My brother knocked Mr. Norway down. He snapped a pistol at him twice, and it did not go off. Then he knocked him down with the pistol. I was there along with him. Mr. Norway was struck whilst on horseback. It was on the turnpike-road between Pencarrow Mill, and the directing-post towards Wadebridge. I cannot say at what time of the night it was. We left the body in the water, on the left side of the road coming to Wadebridge. We took some money in a purse, but I did not know how much. It was a brownish purse. There were some papers which my brother took and pitched away in a field on the left hand side of the road behind the house, at the head of the field, into some browse or furze. The purse was hid by me in my garden, and afterwards I threw it over Pendavy Bridge, the lower side of the bridge. My brother drew the body across the road to the watering. I threw away the purse last Friday. The contents of it were not examined. We did not know who it was before we stopped him. When my brother snapped the pistol at Mr. Norway, Mr. Norway said, "I know what you are about: I see you." We went home across the fields. We were not disturbed by any one. It was not above three or four minutes before we left him. The pistol belonged to my brother. I do not know whether it was broken. I never saw it afterwards, and I do not know what became of it. I never advised my brother to burn it; and I do not know whether it was soiled with blood. I did not see any blood on my brother's clothes. We returned together, crossing the river at Pendavey Bridge; and we crossed Treraven fields over Treraven ground, across a field or two to Burlawn village. My brother then went to his house, and I went to my own house. I think it was about eleven o'clock. I saw my brother again on the Sunday morning. He came up to my house. There was nobody there, I believe, but my own family. He said, "Dear me. Mr. Norway's killed." 1 did not make any reply. Richard Caddy and Jane Harvey were in my house when I came home on the Saturday night. I went to bed as soon as I came home, and Caddy, I believe, remained there for some time."

Further evidence was still being collected:

William Brown, farmer living at Tredennick, stated that on the morning of the 18th February, together with John Ellery, Phillip Bennett and a lad called Hawken, went in to his field called North Hill. This is the field behind the orchard and the abandoned cottage. At the top of the field about 100 yards from the orchard, he found the keys and a bundle of papers, some addressed to Mr Norway of Wadebridge. Most of the keys fitted locks at the Norway house.

On the 18th, *Joseph Goddard and Charles Jackson* took William Lightfoot to Bodmin in a chaise. They stopped at North Hill and *Goddard* asked the prisoner, where he had put the keys, the papers and the tablet. The prisoner told them that they were at the head of the field in a furze bush.

A similar exercise had been used by *Jackson and Constable Bonody* with James Lightfoot on the 14th February, when they had been taking him to be examined in Wadebridge. On this occasion, James admitted the crime but blamed his brother for the murder and the disposal of the keys and papers.

The tablet was found in James' house on the 26th February, when *Richard Harry, shoemaker,* went to the house to take possession of some furniture in payment for a bill for 21/-.

James Kitto, who had supplied James with flour in July but could not get payment, was paid a half-sovereign on the Wednesday after the murder.

The Trial of William & James Lightfoot for the Murder of Mr Nevell Norway
At the Crown Court on Monday 30th March, 1840.

WILLIAM LIGHTFOOT, AGED 36.   JAMES LIGHTFOOT, AGED 23.

Before 7 o'clock the Assize Hall was besieged by crowds making strenuous efforts to gain admission or, at least, to gain a sight of the prisoners.

At 9 o'clock, the Judge, Sir Thomas COLTMAN, took his seat and the prisoners were placed in the dock. They appeared more subdued than their last appearance before the magistrates; though, throughout the day, they showed a degree of levity and a lamentable indifference to the aweful judgement that was impending over them.

The highly respectable jury, composed of the following persons: *James Permewan* of Buryan, Forman; *George Bosustow* of Lugdvan; *Thomas Tremewan* of Sancreed; *Samuel Ivey* of Sancreed; *James Bosustow* of Cury; *John Varcoe* of St Keverne; *Richard Permewan* of Sancreed; *Thomas Ellis* of Madron; *Benjamin Angwin* of St Just in Penwith; *John Kemp(e)* of Madron; *William Nicholas* of Sennen and *William Veal Ellis* of Sancreed, were sworn in.

The Clerk of the Arraigns read the indictment:

"James Lightfoot, and William Lightfoot: you are indicted for feloniously murdering Nevell Norway, of the Parish of Egloshayle, on the 8ᵗʰ February, by striking and beating him on the head with a pistol, and a stick, giving him several mortal wounds of which he died. In another count, you James Lightfoot are indicted for murdering the said Nevell Norway, and you William Lightfoot for aiding and abetting in the murder. In another count, you, William Lightfoot, are indicted for murdering, and you, James Lightfoot for aiding and abetting."

Both pleaded *'Not Guilty'*.

The Prosecutors were Messrs. COCKBURN and ROWE. The prisoners were not represented by advocates.

The prosecution had a very strong case and a long list of witnesses. The prisoner, William Lightfoot, called two witnesses to support his claim that he was not in Bodmin at 4 o'clock on the day of the murder. *Mary Carveth* stated that it was a few minutes after 3 o'clock, when William left for Bodmin and therefore he could not be in Bodmin by 4 o'clock. However, this evidence was very weak because she went on to state that *she did know what Bodmin time was, but their time (at Burlawn) was 50 minutes faster than the Wadebridge town clock!*

The Learned Judge was very helpful to the prisoners during the trial. He explained statements and allowed them to ask questions. He also raised some points during his summing up:

a)   *Although it is right and proper to offer a large reward, as this is frequently the means of detecting criminals, it is apt to produce an over-zeal in giving evidence and in some cases, leads persons to exaggerate or pervert evidence.*

b)   *In referring to the evidence of Jackson, the police constable, and the means by which it had been obtained, the learned Judge remarked. "once a prisoner is taken up, and carried before a magistrate and remanded, it is quite beyond the duty of a constable to go into examinations of the prisoner." He gave Jackson a caution to his future conduct but ruled that the evidence (confession of James at North Hill) was admissible.*

c)   *The Judge mentioned the evidence of Thomas Dungey, turnkey at Bodmin Gaol. "He was going on with a statement of an examination he made of the prisoner James Lightfoot; but that I put a stop to, because I thought it an improper mode of getting evidence, for a gaoler, to go about from prisoner to prisoner in the gaol."*

When the case was handed to the Jury, within five minutes, they returned verdicts of *'Guilty'* against both prisoners. The learned Judge put on the black cap and passed the sentence of the law: ***"which is that you and each of you be severally taken hence to the prison from whence you came; and be taken from thence severally to the place of execution, there to be severally hanged by the neck till your bodies be dead. And that your bodies when dead be taken down and buried within the precincts of the prison in which you have been confined since your conviction according to the form of the Statute."***

The prisoners were returned to Bodmin gaol. Their behaviour, while in custody, was reported in newspaper articles: *Since their sentence, the Chaplain and the Rev. W. Molesworth have been indefatigable in their endeavors to excite proper feelings in the minds of the culprits. The fact is, their characters were incomprehensible. They seemed to have no sense of their awful situation. They told lies, after their condemnations, as readily as they did before, and with just as great an indifference. They ate, drank, and slept, as if there was nothing to press upon their minds. They saw their relations, their parents, their wives, their children, and parted with them without shedding a tear. They appeared callous, and they presented a passive resistance to all the earnest, energetic, soul-stirring appeals which were made to them by their religious instructors.*

During the last week, the two prisoners have made a confession, their authenticity is undoubted, for they are supplied by the Rev. F. Kendall, the Chaplain of the gaol, who kindly gave us every information he could consistently with the ends of justice.

The Execution of James & William Lightfoot
At Bodmin Gaol on Monday, 13ᵗʰ April, 1840.

By 9 o'clock, several thousand people had taken their places in the valley near the railway and in the adjoining fields. Soon after, the executioner, Mr Mitchell, a respectable dairy farmer from Ilchester, Somerset, came out on the drop and fixed the ropes, which passed over hooks in two cranes, branching from the wall. A portion of the raised path, immediately in front of the gaol, was very judiciously barricaded, not only to prevent any rush or pressure at the gateway, but also for the purpose of enclosing the place of burial appointed for the criminals, and of avoiding any unseemly disturbance near them in their last moments. A police force was stationed near this spot, consisting of the captain and sixteen other members of the Sheriff's troop, eight other constables of Bodmin and a policeman of Wadebridge. These arrangements were all conducted under the direction of the Acting Under Sheriff, Philip Protheroe Smith Esq., of Truro [132] aided by the Mayor of Bodmin, C. Coode Esq.

In accordance with the usual practice, a divine service was held in the Chapel. At ten o'clock, the condemned criminals entered the chapel, each stooping and lifting with his hand, the burden of the massive fetters in which his legs were bound. They took their seats together, in a recess which was screened from the view of all others in the chapel, except the Clergymen when standing at the altar. Presently, the body of the chapel was filled with male prisoners, in their prison dresses, of dark brown and yellow. In the gallery were the debtors, some inmates and part of the Sheriff's troop. In the centre of one side of the gallery is the reading desk, where the Chaplain Rev. Francis Kendall, took his place. He was accompanied by the Rev. W. Molesworth, Rev. Francis Cole, Rev. Nicholas Kendall and Rev. N. Kendall, jur. The Acting Under Sheriff, the Coroner and the Governor of the Gaol, John B. Everest.

The service concluded at about half past eleven, after the chapel had emptied, the two Lightfoots approached and knelt before the altar to receive the Sacrament.

By the time of the execution, the crowd had grown to an estimated 20,000-25,000. This included trains which were halted below the prison wall so that the passengers, estimated at 1,100, could watch the hangings without leaving the wagons.

Just before twelve o'clock, the prisoners were brought to the place of execution. The executioner then proceeded to place the ropes and put the caps on the prisoners. William Lightfoot then asked for the Rev. Francis Cole, who was in attendance with some other Clergymen, to come near, and spoke to him as follows: *"Tell my wife and family that I die happy, beg them to go to Church and keep the Sabbath; not to go in the way that I have gone, and brought myself to ruin. Tell them to avoid idleness, and get their living honestly, and pray that they may meet me in Heaven."* After which Mr. Cole turned to James Lightfoot, and asked him if he had anything more to say he, following up his Brother's words, answered, *"Say that I am happy. They (meaning his wife and child) must pray to God that we may meet in Heaven."*

Immediately after, the Drop fell, and their souls were launched into eternity.

> ## NEVELL NORWAY
> ### *Merchant of Wadebridge*
> ### AGED 39 YEARS
> WHO WAS MURDERED ON THE
> 8TH. OF FEBRUARY 1840.
> He left behind him a widow and six child
> ren unprovided for, but a subscription of
> Three Thousand five hundred pounds
> was made for their use: a noble testimony
> of the generous feeling of the Public, and
> of the high estimation in which his amiable
> and spotless character was held.
> ### *also*
> ### IN MEMORY
> of
> ## SARAH NORWAY
> Who survived her Husband six months
> SHE DIED THE 6TH AUGUST 1840
> ### AGED 36 YEARS
>
> Inscription on the gravestone of Nevell and Sarah Norway, who both died in 1840 and are buried in Egloshayle Parish Church.
> *This is a transcript from a photograph of the grave, taken by S. Babb.*

The documents on the following pages are new reproductions of contemporary broadsheets, relating to executions at Bodmin. (Refs: 133-136)

An Account of the

LIFE, CONFESSION, AND EXECUTION OF

Sarah Polgrean,

Who was convicted of causing the death of her late husband Henry Polgrean,

by poison, at the Summer Assizes, held at Bodmin on

Thursday the 10th of August 1820.

And who was executed at BODMIN, on Saturday the 12th.

Sarah Polgrean was born of poor parents, in the parish of Gulval, about the year 1786 or 1787. Her father was killed by an accident, in London. Her Mother deserted her when 4 months old, and left her chargeable to the Parish. She had no education, not being able to read or write. She was apprenticed at 9 years of age and during her apprenticeship yielded to the seduction of a fellow servant. After her time expired she lived in many places, but never settled in any of them; and about 10 years since she left Cornwall, to join her Mother at Dock, who was an indifferent character, and is since dead, She lived in Dock a few months, where she had some religious impressions, and married a soldier, who took her into the neighbourhood of London. Her husband and she parted by mutual consent, and she returned first to Dock, and afterwards to Cornwall, where she met with the late H. Polgrean, and married him.

She was convicted, on the clearest evidence, of purchasing arsenic, at Penzance, for the alledged purpose of poisoning rats, though it was proved the house had never been infested with them. The surgeons and other witnesses proved the illness of the deceased, and the prisoner's concealment of it: they also proved that he had died by poison, having examined the contents of the stomach, after the body of the deceased had been disinterred, although he had been buried eleven days. It was also proved that they had lived unhappily together, and that she had threatened to poison him. The deceased had been sick on the Friday evening, and was bled on Saturday by the Surgeon, in consequence of his dinner and supper disagreeing with him on the preceding day. This agrees with the evidence of the surgeon, who thought the poison had not been administered when the deceased was bled.

The judge recapitulated the evidence with great precision; and the jury without hesitation pronounced a verdict of GUILTY. — His Lordship then proceeded to pass the awful sentence of the law, and ordered the prisoner to be executed on Saturday morning, and her body to be given for dissection. — The wretched prisoner was so overwhelmed by her dreadful fate, that she seemed to be quite insensible, and was obliged to be supported during the time sentence was passing — she was carried out of the court.

The prisoner has confessed that she mixed the arsenic in a piece of butter, taken from a half pound, on Saturday afternoon, the 15th of July; that at supper-time she proposed to her husband to eat the piece already cut off, and buttered his bread with it, whilst she eat from the larger piece herself. She attributed her crimes to the want of a religious education, and her early seduction. She solemnly declared that she was not instigated to commit the crime by any man, and that his well-founded jealousy and her aversion to him induced her to do it. She expressed her free forgiveness of all whom she conceived to have injured her, lamented, after her trial, the expressions she had uttered towards some of the witnesses against her, and hoped that her end would be a warning to all who might be tempted to commit such crimes as hers, especially those of adultery and murder.

About a quarter past twelve she was drawn upon a hurdle to the drop, amidst an immense crowd of spectators, walked to the platform with a firm step, and for a few minutes joined very audibly in prayer. After this she sung a hymn with most extraordinary resolution, and begged all present to take a solemn warning from her untimely fate, shook hands with a man at the drop, and also with the executioner, gave the signal, and was launched into eternity.

Brougham, Printer, Falmouth.

Confession, Dying Behaviour,

AND

EXECUTION

OF

James Eddy

WHO WAS

HUNG AT BODMIN,

On Thursday, the 19th of April, 1827,

PURSUANT TO HIS

Sentence at the LENT ASSIZES, for Robbing and Violently Assaulting JANE COCK, on the King's Highway.

I am twenty-nine years of age, was born in the parish of Wendron, near the borough of Helston, in the county of Cornwall; am the son of an industrious miner, and one of ten children. When I was about ten years old I went into husbandry service, and until the age of nineteen I bore, a good character. From that period I became a miner at Crinnis, and still lived in fair repute till about twenty-five. I then stole a bundle of Laths, for which I was committed to the county Gaol, was tried at Sessions, and sentenced to six weeks imprisonment. After my discharge I went to St. Blazey, and then began bad habits,—smuggling—sabbath-breaking—adultery—drinking—pilfering—gaming—wrestling—&c, and thus got a bad name. In consequence of endeavouring to injure some excise officers with gunpowder, I left St. Blazey and went to live at Redruth. In February last I came up to St. Blazey on business, and on my return met Jane Cock, by whose evidence I am condemned to die, though I solemnly declare I never robbed her or intended to rob her. I forgive all my fellow-creatures, and humbly hope through the merits of Jesus Christ, to obtain pardon of my sins, and be received into His kingdom. I die in peace with all, and forgive all that swore against me."

Immediately after his condemnation at Launceston, he was removed to the Gaol at Bodmin, where he was attended by the Rev. Mr. Boor, the Ordinary, who was unremitted in his endeavours to awake him to a sense of his lost and fallen condition. We are happy to say, that his labours appear to have been successful, the unfortunate man having evinced a readiness to be instructed in divine things, about which he was before totally ignorant and unconcerned. The confession above was taken in writing from his own words, the day before his execution, at which time he appeared truly penitent and resigned. He married early in life, and has left a wife and three small children to lament his untimely end. The night before his execution, he slept soundly, and in the morning partook of a hearty breakfast.

After receiving the sacrament in the chapel, the unhappy man walked to the place of execution, at half past eleven. He then addressed, the multitude around in nearly the following words:—" I am come to the close of my life. I acknowledge that every word which the witnesses said on my trial was true, except what Jane Cock said; the only true word which she swore to was the day of the month. All the rest was false. 'Tis true we did break the seventh commandment; but I never robbed her. Thank God! I die innocent. This is a great relief to me. I confess I have been a great sinner, and I attribute my present fate to leaving my wife and family, and following other women. I never robbed Jane Cock; and I wish I could express to you the feeling the knowledge of my innocence gives me at this moment. I die happy."— The prisoner then knelt down, and devoutly joined in prayer, at the conclusion of which he again said:—"If any person here should see Jane Cock, I hope he will talk to her of the awful consequence that her words have brought me to. If she did lose seven shillings and her pocket, some person must have found it; and I hope, whoever has found it, will bring it forward, and clear my children from this disgrace. My earthly judge thought me guilty, but he could not see my heart. I forgive him; and I hope in a few minutes I shall be in the presence of that Judge who knows me innocent. God bless you all!!!"—He shewed uncommon fortitude throughout the dreadful period, and shook hands with several of his comrades whom he recognised among the crowd. At a quarter before twelve the drop fell, and after a few struggles the world closed on him forever!!!

The place of execution was crowded beyond any thing we had ever before witnessed; and, as usual, *disgraced* with an spectacle abundance of females, whose levity of demeanour ill-accorded with the appalling. We fear that such scenes add little to the cause of morality; instead of acting as warnings to the unprincipled and vicious, we have generally found them degenarate into wantonness and riot.

F. Symons, Printer, Bookbinder, and Stationer, opposite the New Market Place, Redruth

HORRIBLE
MURDER

Of Elizabeth Rous Seman,
Rosevean Road, Penzance,
Committed on Monday, July the 7th, 1845.

Just as we had finished our report of the festivities of Monday, we found it to be our duty to turn to a matter of the most tragical description. Whilst the thousands that were revelling in the joyous scene which we have elsewhere described—one of the most brutal and inhuman Murders must have been committed that has ever fallen to our lot to record.

In the present state of the proceedings, we forbear from furnishing our readers with the detailed evidence that was adduced, for obvious reasons; but we see no reason why we should not state briefly the particulars relating to this most diabolical act.

It appears, then, that a man residing in one of the Cottages situate in Rosevean Road, and nearly opposite the Catholic Chapel, called Benjamin Ellison, aged about 55, and of respectable appearance, called at the Temperance Hotel, in Prince's Street, kept by Capt. Edward Thomas, about eleven o'clock on Monday night, & asked for some refreshment. Subsequently he enquired if he could sleep there that night. He was answered in the affirmative, and asked how it was that he was going to stay out—why he did not go home. He replied that it was then too late—and requested to see a man called Wm. Eddy, who lodged at the Hotel. Eddy was sent for, and Ellison told him he had something important to communicate to him, and appeared rather restless—but he said nothing more than enquired of Eddy which place he preferred, Liverpool or Manchester. Eddy, in the course of conversation, asked Ellison how Mrs Seman was--(meaning the unfortunate woman who was afterwards found murdered, and with whom Ellison lived.) He said she was unwell, and then there was a pause in the conversation, which was broken by Eddy asking Ellison what it was he had to communicate to him; but nothing particular was said. Ellison appeared depressed in spirits & kept on examining and rubbing his hands. Shortly afterwards both retired to their respective places of rest.

Between five and six o'clock on the following morning, a son of Capt. Thomas's, at the Temperance Hotel, saw Ellison down stairs, who said that he wished to have his boots cleaned. He was requested to take them from off his feet for the purpose, but declined, and directed that they might be cleaned on. The boots were cleaned accordingly and the person who performed the task, represents the boots to have been very wet—as though they had been washed—but it rained pretty smartly on Monday night for some time.

He left the hotel before six o'clock, had his hair cut and got shaved—and in the course of the morning called at the house of a Mrs Hill, who resided in Rosevean Road, and informed her that his house had been broken

open and that Mrs Seman had been murdered. Mrs Hill exclaimed—Good God! and accompanied him to the fatal spot. There stretched out upon the floor lay the mutilated remains of the unfortunate woman—her face was covered by a gauze veil, and marks of blood were perceptible in all directions. Ellison said he would fetch the police, & requested Mrs Hill to make an alarm.

About nine o'clock, Ellison was again at the Temperance hotel—communicated the dreadful fact, and asked Capt. Thomas to go with him to Mr. Carne, one of the magistrates.

In the mean time, the police officers were on the *qui vive*—and used the necessary precautions to secure the man on whom suspicion rested. John Martin went to the Mayor's, and while there, an individual entered, who said his name was Ellison, upon which Martin took him into custody on suspicion.

As speedily as practicable, a Coroner's Inquest was held upon the body, before John Roscorla, Esq., Coroner, and a respectable jury, which occupied between 8 and 9 hours. During the whole of the time, the Hall was crowded—but we think it proper to remark that although the most intense interest was excited, there was none of that feeling exhibited against Ellison which we have often stated to have occurred elsewhere when prisoners have been examined upon similar charges.

Messrs. Millett and Borlase attended the Inquest on behalf of Ellison, who is stated to have said that a gold watch and wearing apparel to a considerable amount had been stolen from the dwelling—that deceased was in the receipt of an annuity—that she was about shortly to be married to a gentleman of title, and that she had agreed to settle an annual income upon him (Ellison) as soon as that event should take place.

After a short consultation, the jury returned a Verdict of *Wilful Murder* against Ellison, who was committed to Bodmin to await his trial on the charge at the next assizes.

We deem it proper to observe that neither the accused nor deceased were Cornish people—and that the awful deed cannot possibly owe its origin to anything connected with the proceedings of Monday. Ellison and deceased, we have been credibly informed, were both Teetotalers.

The prisoner left this town in custody at an early hour this (Wednesday) morning for Bodmin.

THOMAS, PRINTER, PENZANCE.

TRIAL & SENTENCE
OF THE SOLDIER,
William Nevan,
For the Wilful Murder of Serjeant-major Robinson.
Tried at Bodmin, on Monday, the 28th day of July, 1856.

WILLIAM NEVAN was indicted for the Wilful Murder of Benjamin Robinson, on the 1st of June, 1856. He was also charged with the same offence on the coroner's inquisition. The prisoner, when arraigned, and asked whether guilty or not guilty, replied "Not guilty, it happened by accident." The prisoner is an Irishman.

Mr. Collier stated the case for the prosecution. He had to call the attention of the jury to a very grave and solemn investigation into the circumstances attending the death of a brave officer in Her Majesty's service. The deceased was a serjeant-major of the name of Robinson, who had the charge of a number of pensioners acting as guard of some convicts in a vessel called the "Runnymede," lying in Plymouth Sound on the 1st of June and about to proceed to Swan River with those convicts. The prisoner was acting as Corporal under the deceased. It would appear from the evidence there had been a strong feeling, on the part of the prisoner, against Serjeant-major Robinson, who was a smart, active officer, and had found it his duty to remonstrate with the prisoner on several occasions, for not attending to his arms and some trifling deficiencies in duty. These remonstrances produced a strong effect on the mind of the prisoner, who had been heard to say, "if he finds fault with me again, I shall put a bullet in my musket and send it through his body." A day or two before the murder, the prisoner asked Major Russel to allow him to leave the ship, as he could not sail with Robinson. But the prisoner remained on board until Sunday, June 1st. In the afternoon of that day, serjeant-major Robinson had been parading the men, and amongst others had inspected the prisoner. A man named Sullivan was found to be missing. The serjeant-major told the prisoner to go and call Sullivan to him. The prisoner almost immediately after placed his musket on his hip, and fired. The piece was loaded with ball, and the unfortunate serjeant-major was shot in the abdomen, and said, "O my God, I am shot, I am dead." A pensioner, named Kinnard, seized the prisoner, who said "I have done it, I was driven to it."

Several witnesses were then examined for the prosecution, during which the prisoner appeared very anxious.

Mr. Coleridge then addressed the jury on behalf of the prisoner, in an able and eloquent speech of some length: He contended that the gun was discharged by accident and that the prisoner's story was true that it had caught in the hen-coop. Reviewing all the circumstances he confidently asked the jury for a verdict of acquittal.

The learned Judge summed up the evidence, and remarked on some of its features, and with regard to the alleged absence of motive, he said it was well known that many persons were found to take away the lives of others upon motives which to people in general appeared inadequate.

The jury then retired, and were absent about ten minutes, when they returned a verdict of "Guilty".

The Judge then put on the black cap and addressed the prisoner as follows: — William Nevan, you have been found guilty, after a patient trial, in which every thing that possibly could be urged in your defence has been done by the learned counsel who defended you. You have been found guilty of wilful murder, and it is my duty to state that I entirely concur in that verdict. I do not see how any other verdict could be properly returned on the evidence in this case. There has been placed in my hands a statement from a number of persons. I presume in the town of which you are a native. Any use to be made of it, shall be by forwarding it to the Secretary of State, who will take the pleasure of the Queen upon it. I only refer to it to beg you to place no reliance on it, but to take advantage of the short time you have to live, for to prepare for eternity. The sentence of the court is, that you be taken from hence to the prison whence you came, and that you be taken thence to a place of execution, there to be hanged by the neck till your body is dead, and that your body be buried within the precincts, of the prison; and may the Lord have mercy on your soul.

The learned Judge, in passing the latter part of the sentence, was quite overcome by his feelings. When the sentence was concluded, the prisoner exclaimed "The Lord look upon me." He was then removed from the bar.

Within the gloomy cell I lie,
Waiting my awful doom.
My spirits shrink with fear and dread,
My soul is fill'd with gloom.
What have I done? ah, dreadful deed!
His life I took away;
And I must answer for the crime,
The penalty must pay.
And must I die a felon's death?
Ah, dreadful thought indeed!
'Tis better die upon the field,
And for my country bleed.
The laurel ne'er will grace my brow,
Nor honour's medal wear;
The fatal rope is my sad lot,
A felon's name I bear.
'Tis hard to die—alas, so soon.
But I no warning gave;
With all his crimes upon his head,
I sent him to the grave.
Methinks I hear his piercing cry,
"My God-I'm shot- I'm dead !
He utter'd, when I fired there;
It fills me now with dread.
'Twas evil passions sway'd my mind,
And hatred that I bore.
That led me to commit the crime,
Which laid him in his gore.
On Sunday morn, when first I rose,
I thought not of the deed.

But vile temptations through the day,
To Murder did me lead.
When I the cruel deed had done,
What horror did I feel,
To see the blood stream from the wound
Which none on earth could heal.
I then was seiz'd and borne away,
Within a prison bound,
At length I was in Bodmin tried,
And soon was guilty found.
The Judge no hope could give to me,
But that I soon must die,
His good advice I now must take,
To heaven raise my cry.
Soon I shall hear the prison bell,
With solemn warning sound,
Telling the moments I shall live,
Are quickly passing round,
O may the living, warning take,
By my untimely fate,
And ne'er give way to evil thoughts,
No person ever hate.
Let no unguarded moment come,
Be watchful every day;
Had I--- l'd never come to this,
My life a forfeit pay.
When I'm suspended from the beam,
My quivering body view,
Resolve to shun your evil ways,
Begin your life anew

John O Harris, Printer, &c., Hayle

The LIFE, TRIAL, and EXECUTION of SELINA WADGE.

HER LIFE

Selina Wadge was executed at Bodmin Gaol yesterday August 15th. The unfortunate woman, who was about 28 years of age, was the daughter of an industrious labourer residing at Altarnun, a small village a few miles distant from Launceston. When about 22 years of age she formed the acquaintance of a young man, by whom she has an illegitimate child, and was confined at the Launceston Workhouse. Her parents took the child with them to reside, so as to enable their daughter to go into service, and she obtained a situation, and appeared to be leading a reputable life until three years since, when she again gave way to temptation and gave birth to a male child at the Launceston Workhouse. Her parents being unable to render her additional help she was compelled to live at the Workhouse with her two sons, but early in June last she left the Workhouse, and went home with her father and mother, hoping, so it is stated, that she would be able to earn a livelihood by going out washing. In this, however, she seemed to have failed. On the 21st of June last she left home for the purpose of meeting at or near Launceston a man named Westwood, who was coming from Morwenstow, and who, she expected was about to marry her. She took with her two children, and was conveyed to Launceston. The *sad* story of the remaining portion of her life is seen in the following.

HER TRIAL

CROWN COURT—Before MR. JUSTICE DENMAN.

On Monday, July 27th, 1878, Selina Wadge was indicted for the wilful murder of Henry Wadge, her child, two years old, at the Parish of St. Thomas the Apostle, on the 21st June last. Mr. Clark and Mr. Templer were counsel for the prosecution, and Mr. Massey defended the prisoner at the request of his lordship.

Mr. CLARK briefly explained the facts of the case to the Jury.

The following evidence was then taken: —

Mary Wakeham, residing at Altarnun, said she knew the prisoner who was a single woman with two children, one about five years of age and the other two years. The youngest child, a boy, looked well and healthy, but seemed weak on his feet. On Friday, the 21st June, she saw the prisoner with her two children about eight o'clock in the morning leaving Bank Gate in a waggon. On the following Monday she was shown the body of the deceased at the White Horse Inn, Launceston. Witness met the prisoner on Saturday, the 22nd June about six p.m., between Launceston and Pennygallon Gate, and at the time she had her eldest child with her. Prisoner told witness that deceased was in the town.

Cross-examined: Prisoner always behaved to the children like an affectionate mother. The deceased could not stand alone but was well fed and cared for generally.

William Holman, farmer, of Altarnun, said he knew the prisoner and her parents. He drove the prisoner and her children to Launceston, and she told him that she was going to see her man, James Westwood, who was coming from Stratton to meet her. He had occasion to pass the field where the well was whilst going to Launceston, and prisoner observed, "I see the well is railed off now." She left him at the entrance to Launceston, about a mile beyond the well, and went away towards the lower road. He did not see her again that day, but afterwards saw the dead body of the child at the White Horse Inn.

Cross-examined: Prisoner did not say where she was to meet Westwood. She simply said she was going to meet her man, who was coming from Stratton.

Richard Henry Langmail, a wggoner, stated that he saw the prisoner on the morning in question near a field where the well was situated. She had the two children with her.

Emanuel Chudleigh, said he farmed the field where the well was situated. The well was covered with boards and railed off, and the water was used for cattle. On the Thursday night he covered over the well after drawing some water, but the following day he observed that the boards had not been put down level with the well as he had left them. He also saw some froth on the water.

Janet Pethick, school-mistress at the Launceston Union, saw the prisoner in the Workhouse, who informed her that she had lost her other little boy. She also heard her say....................that it had gone quickly, the prisoner replied, "Yes, it had." On the 23rd of June the prisoner remarked, in answer to something said by Mrs. Downing, the Matron, "I did it, but he put me up to it." She was then asked who she meant by "he,"and she mentioned a name which witness could not remember.

Mary Ann Boundy, a widow, and sister of the prisoner, also an inmate of the Launceston Union, said that when the prisoner came to the Workhouse she told her "Harry was dead and that he died of abscess and the throat complaint." Prisoner further said, "I had a doctor to attend him, and we buried him between us. I had a coffin for the child, and John Train made it. He is buried near the church door." Prisoner told the nurse of the union a similar story.

Daniel Downing, master of the Launceston Union, deposed that the prisoner left the workhouse on the 8th June, and returned on the 21st. He spoke to her about the deceased, and she accused James Westwood of taking the child, and added that he put it in the well, and that he would have drowned the other boy, but she ran away with him. In answer to further enquires from witness prisoner said that Westwood afterwards went on to Bodmin, and she came on to Launceston.

Louisa Downing, matron of the Union, corroborated the last witness's evidence respecting the prisoner's statement about Westwood. Witness added that prisoner afterwards said, "Oh, Mrs. Downing, I did it, I put Harry in the water. There was no one with me at the time but little Johnny and he began to cry."
Cross-examined. Prisoner appeared fond of the children.

Mary Pooley said she heard the prisoner tell her mother that the reason she did not give Westwood in charge when he took the deceased away, was because she was afraid. The child Johnny made a statement to witness, and she in consequence of that went to prisoner in the presence of her mother and told her that Johnny had said "that mother put Harry in the pit, that there was no one there, and that deceased cried."

Jane Dennis, the next witness, stated that the prisoner told her she had buried the deceased; and Johnny said "it is in a pit, mother," whereupon the prisoner said "hold your noise or I'll give you a slap." The boy repeated it and she gave him a slap.

Police-Sergeant Barrett described his interview with the prisoner at the Union. She told him she met a man, and went to take a walk with him with her two children towards Tresmarrow-road. The man took up her little boy, and ran into a field with it, and then came out again, and said he had throw it in the pit and drowned it, where there were railings round. The man said that he would drown her and her other boy, and she then ran away with her boy. The man was Westwood and he lived in Stratton.

Harriet Parker, a family housekeeper at Launceston said prisoner *slept* at her house on the 21st June. She had only one child and she said that Harry had died at her mother's. She had had a doctor, but he told her (prisoner) the child would die and it did.

Superintendent Sherst gave evidence as to the finding of the body; and *Sergeant Roseveare* produced the clothes which the child was wearing when found.

James Westwood was then called. He said he had served 15 years in the Army, and was at present engaged as a farm labourer. He first made the prisoner's acquaintance on the 15th December last. He saw her on the 26th March, and then not again until the 29th June, when she was in custody. He had been working in the parish of Morwenstow during the week ending the 22nd June. Morwenstow was 28 miles from the spot where the child was found.

Mr. MASSEY: Were you engaged to be married to the prisoner?

Witness: Yes. No time was fixed, but I told her that I would marry her in the summer. Mr. MASSEY: Did you object to the children? Witness: Never. Mr. MASSEY: You always liked them, I suppose? Witness: I have always spoken of them in a kind and affectionate manner. I made no objection to them, and I never stated that they were an incumbrance. Mr. MASSEY: Had you not arranged to meet her anywhere during the week that you tell us you were working in the parish you speak of? Witness: I wrote her stating I would be near the turnpike gate on the Bodmin road, at 2 p.m. on the 22nd of June.

Mr. MASSEY: Will you swear it was not on the 21st? Witness: I will swear positively it was on the 22nd. I did not keep the appointment, as the work which I had to do prevented me from doing so. I wrote and told her so.

Mr. MASSEY: Did you know when you came here of the statements which the prisoner at the bar has made about you? Witness: I read of them in the papers. Mr. MASSEY: You knew, therefore, what she had said about you? Witness: I did. Mr. MASSEY: And you knew it was a question between you and her as to who had committed the deed? HIS LORDSHIP: That is hardly the question, because she makes two statements, one charging him, and the other charging herself. Mr. MASSEY: Very well, my lord. I shall have something to say about that bye-and-bye. (To Witness) At any rate you knew these statements were made, and you have taken no trouble to secure the attendance— HIS LORDSHIP: I do not think you can ask him that question. It is not his business to secure necessary witnesses for the prosecution. He is simply here himself as a witness.

Mr. George Wilson, surgeon, of Launceston, gave evidence to the effect that the death of the child was caused by drowning. There was no abscess or throat disease, and nothing else that could cause death.

P.C. Axworthy said the prisoner was in his custody during her remand on the 23rd of June. She asked him when the trial would take place, and he replied that he did not know. She then said that she was going away with James Westwood, and that he was going to marry her if she could rid of one of her children. She was very much affected, and after a pause she said "I tried to get in after it; I tried with a kibble. Oh! My poor mother; it will break her heart."

This closed the case for the prosecution, and Mr. Clarke briefly replied on the whole evidence.

Mr. MASSEY made an excellent defence on behalf of the prisoner.

HIS LORDSHIP then summed up at considerable length.

The Jury then retired to consider their verdict; and after an absence of nearly an hour returned into Court with a verdict of guilty, with a recommendation to mercy on the grounds that they think the murder was unpremeditated, and on account of her previous love for her children.

The CLERK of ASSIZE (to the prisoner): Selina Wadge, the jury have found you guilty of the crime of wilful murder. Have you anything to say why the Court should not give you judgment to die according to law?

PRISONER: (who seemed to be fainting): I don't understand.

Mr. CHAMBRE: Have you anything to say *why this* Court should not give you judgment to die, according to law?

PRISONER: Please have mercy on me.

SENTENCE

His Lordship then put on the black cap, and amidst profound silence passed the sentence of death, as follows: — Prisoner at the bar you have been found guilty upon evidence which it was impossible to resist, of throwing the body of your child, two years old, down a well. That could only have been done with one intention, which may possibly have been re....ed of speedily, but that it was an act of murder no twelve men of common sense could possibly doubt. With every disposition to strain every fact in favour of a prisoner, and especially a woman, under such a charge as this, the jury have, as honest men, found it impossible to resist a verdict of guilty. They have at the same time, accompanied that verdict with a recommendation to mercy, and in order such a recommendation may have full effect I desired to know the grounds upon which it was made. One ground is that they think the murder was unpremeditated, by which I understand them to mean that it was not long premeditated, and the other ground is on account of your previous kindness towards your children, which is established by the evidence of the witnesses. Whether that recommendation will or will not have any effect in staying execution, it is impossible for me to say. It is no business of mine. It rests not with me, but it rests with another power entirely. All I can say is that that recommendation shall be forwarded to the proper quarter. But my duty is — and that duty I do most strenuously perform, and with all the earnestness with which I can urge it upon you, in passing upon you the sentence of the law — to implore you not to rest upon a recommendation, but to take the readiest and most earnest means of preparing for death. The sentence of the Court is death, and I must pass in the ordinary form. It is that you be taken from hence to the place from whence you came, and thence to the place of execution; that you there be hanged by the neck until you be dead; that your body be afterwards buried within the precincts of the prison in which you are last confined after this your conviction; and may the Lord God Almighty have mercy upon your soul.

EXECUTION, 15TH. AUGUST, 1878.

Just before eight o'clock this morning a few little groups of people - almost without exception residents of Bodmin – formed near the prison at points of vantage on the surrounding eminences. There was one spot on Asylum Hill from which on the...................view these.............was immediately remedied. The scaffolding was erected in a narrow part of the south-west block of buildings; and it was an easy matter therefore, to suspend a piece of canvas from one wall to the other, and this effectually shut out the hideous erection from gaze. The ominous bell in the prison began to toll at a quarter to eight, and the few groups of spectators gathered at various points of vantage directed their gaze towards the prison buildings to catch the first sight of the black flag. A few minutes before eight that dark signal was seen gradually sliding up the tower over the chapel, and precisely at eight o'clock was shot up to its highest point, and the bell began to toll more quickly. When the drop was previously been tested by Marwood the rattling of the timbers could be very distinctly heard. No sounds however on this occasion reached those outside, but at a quarter past eight the bell ceased in token that it was all over.

Capt. Colvill visited the condemned woman in her cell at half-past seven in the morning. She was then quite resigned, expressed her penitence, and shook hands with him for the last time. At five minutes to eight the mournful procession which was to conduct her to the scaffold was formed and proceeded to the cell. On returning the Under Sheriff (Mr. T. Cornish) and the County Clerk (Mr. J.R. Paul) walked in front; then followed the Chaplain, reading the Burial Service; and behind him — just where the coffin would be in an ordinary funeral — came the condemned woman, accompanied by female warders; the Governor of the Gaol (Capt. Colvill) and the Gaol Surgeon (Mr. T.Q. Couch) bringing up the rear. The necessary arrangements which followed were

166

commendably expeditious. The prisoner was very neatly attired in her own clothing, and had much improved in appearance since her trial. She was sobbing as she walked along, and held a pocket handkerchief in her hand; but she was not otherwise visually affected. She walked on to the fatal drop with a tolerably *firm* step and without assistance. "God deliver me," she was heard to say, "from this miserable world;" and exactly on the stroke of eight — five minutes after she had left the condemned cell, Marwood drew the bolt; the body fell eight feet and death was instantaneous not a struggle or a groan being preceptible or audible. So instantaneously did she die that the handkerchief she carried to the drop never fell from her hand. After hanging the hour required by law, the body was cut down, and after the usual inquest, was buried in the precinct of the prison.

16th August, 1878. Published and Sold by E. T. CRABE, Bodmin.

I thank Anne Hicks of Bodmin for access to the original broadsheet and kind permission to publish the transcript.

HANGING A WOMAN

Selina Wadge was executed yesterday morning, at Bodmin Jail for the murder of her child, at Launceston, on the 21st of July last. The representatives of the press being refused admission to the prison, some difficulty was experienced In obtaining any reliable information of the circumstances attending the execution, but the scene appears to have been an unusually painful one, all the officers, including the Chaplain and Under Sheriff, being much affected. There had been no execution in the jail for 16 years previously. Up to 7 o'clock yesterday morning it was generally believed that a reprieve would arrive, but at that hour a communication was received by the Clerk of the Peace, to the effect that the Home Secretary could not see his way to interfere with the due course of the law. An hour later the unfortunate woman had paid the penalty of her crime, The Chaplain remained with her from 7:15 until the drop fell. She sobbed greatly as she walked from the cell to the scaffold, and on ascending the steps was heard to say, "Lord, deliver me from this miserable world." Marwood, the executioner, gave a drop of eight feet, and Wadge died without a struggle, grasping tightly in her hand a handkerchief. The accused, it will be remembered, threw her child down a well, and at her trial alleged that she had been induced to do to by a man named Westwood, who was courting her, and who, she said, promised to marry her if she got rid of the child. The jury who found her guilty recommended her to mercy, on the ground of her previous love for her children, and because they considered the murder was unpremeditated; but Mr. Justice Denman, in passing sentence of death, implored the accused not to rest upon the recommendation, although he would forward it to the proper quarter. Since then appeals from all parts of the country have been sent to the Home Secretary, praying for a remission of the sentence, but without avail. The execution was originally fixed for Monday last, but it was postponed till yesterday morning, as Marwood's engagements prevented him from coming earlier. After her condemnation Wadge received a letter from the man Westwood, who was a witness at her trial, begging for forgiveness. When his letter was read to her, her reply was: "Yes, he needed forgiveness for many things," or words to that effect. It is said that she made a statement to the Chaplain, which the reverend gentleman intends forwarding to the Home Secretary.

From the Liverpool Post, Aug. 16, 1878

Artefacts

Cornwall County Gaol 1837-1877   **Prisons Department 1877-1901**   **H M Prisons 1901-**   **H M Prisons 1901-**   **H M Naval Prison Bodmin 1901-**

Numbered bags (ca. 24 x 20 cm.), showing individual cell numbers and other canvas bags made in the Prison.

Restraint jacket. Each arm is ca.1.65 metre long to allow for wrapping around the prisoner and tying.

Thickness: ca.1"

ca. 27"

21"

Graffiti:
1. J Harrigan 1857 28 July 6yea(r ?)
2. M   Truro
3. J J Fenton Lanh(ydrock ?)
4. John D--w
5. James Hawken

Roof Slate. dated 1857 with signatures.

GOVERNOR'S HOUSE, BODMIN, CORNWALL.

Embossing Stamp for the Governor's House address.

Two views of a Warder's bell (40 x 30 cm.). Similar bells were placed in, or near, the Warder's rooms on each floor of the prison. A system of wires connected the bell to each cell on the floor.

When a prisoner required help in his cell, he would pull a small lever, which would ring the bell and activate an indicator outside the cell.

The mechanism is hand-made from brass and the bell is bell-metal.

The slate is in Bodmin Jail & 3 of the buttons in Bodmin Town Museum. All other objects are from the Frank Stone Collection.

168

CHAPTER 18

In their Own Words

The Editor's Description ¹³⁷

AN AFTERNOON IN BODMIN PRISON
-- : o : --
Four Hours Inside Without Hard Labour
-- : o : --
A WALK ROUND WITH THE GOVERNOR

On one of the hottest afternoons of the year I could have been seen applying for admission at the Prison gates with the necessary sanction in my hands. With the clanging of a big bell the door was opened, but before I had entered, the Rev. C.B. Simpson, who is so popular as the Prison Chaplain and who does so much for the help of prisoners on their discharge, joined me for the purpose of showing me the Prison Library, and of explaining its management. Having shown my permit to the gatekeeper, I was allowed beyond the second gate into the courtyard, and then had free access to the spacious hall upon each side of which are the Prison offices and from which the prison proper extends.

The Library and School

The Chaplain took me at once to his sanctum in which the various library books are shelved. Here it was not difficult to see that an admirable choice of reading matter had been made. From Cassell's Popular Educator on to such works as those of Scott and Thackeray and down to bound volumes of the "Strand", and the "Boys' Own" and the like, there is a fairly wide field of literature. Bodmin Prison not being a very large one the library is not of a very extensive character, but what it contains is good wholesome stuff, tending to the elevation of a prisoner who reads, and therefore to his future good conduct. The choice of the books lies principally with the Chaplain, but his list generally receives the assent of the Visiting Committee before the purchases are made. It was interesting to hear that one of the most popular books among the prisoners is Thackeray's "Newcomes."

The rule of the Prison is that no prisoners serving twenty-eight days or less can have the advantages of the library, but if the sentence extends beyond that, then after the twenty-eight days have been served one book a week can be obtained. When the third and fourth stages of the term have been reached two books a week are allowed. Naturally most of the prisoners who are entitled to the privileges of the library make use of them, and they are assisted in their choice of reading matter by the Chaplain. There is always in each prisoner's cell a Bible, a prayer-book, and a hymn book (A. and M.) and also what may be termed a moral suasion book (generally Bunyan's "Pilgrim's Progress" or the like.)

Somewhat connected with the library and the Chaplain's work is the school. Some, perhaps, will be surprised to learn that there is such a thing as a school in a prison. But it has long been recognised that one of the most potent factors in the diminution of crime is education, and hence the mental improvement of prisoners is not a point overlooked. All the prisoners between the ages of sixteen and forty who have a reasonably long sentence to serve are tested on admission by the Chaplain as to their mental attainments. If their education has already been of such a character as to make it unnecessary to carry them further they receive no attention from the schoolmaster, but where some attempt at advancement is thought advisable the prisoner is put in the hands of the clerk and schoolmaster - warder (Mr. Extence) who gives him two hours' instruction twice a week. At the end of his sentence the prisoner is again tested by the chaplain to see what progress has been made. Sometimes, of course, there are prisoners upon whom it would be absolute waste of time and energy to attempt any instruction and it is then in the power of the Chaplain to leave them alone. The age limit for instruction is fixed at forty because it is thought by the authorities that to attempt to impart further knowledge to a man after that age would be useless. Some of the prisoners occasionally express a desire for this or that educational book, one it may be desiring to increase his geographical knowledge, and another, perhaps with a mathematical turn, desiring a book of arithmetical problems. Whenever possible, the Chaplain complies with the request.

The Governor and Staff

The Governor of the Prison (Mr. W.R. Shenton) joined the Chaplain and myself in the library, and after the latter left me to attend to his duties elsewhere I went with the former to his offices and there had a very interesting chat about prison life and prison management, much of which will transpire as I continue my story.

But first let me have a personal word about the Governor. Mr. Shenton has been in the service of the Prison Commissioners for about forty years, and may fairly claim therefore to know the many intricacies of prison life. He has seen much of the seamy side of human nature, and has had perforce to often assume a severe and commanding attitude, but I should judge him after all to be the last man in the world to go beyond what was just and proper in the treatment of any fellow man. He is the son of an army officer, who was in what was known as the 14th Hussars. He was born at sea, and the first eleven years of his life were spent in India but he soon set foot on English soil, and there he has remained to this day. In 1862 he joined the prison staff at Gloucester as an assistant warder. Six years later he removed to Worcester as chief warder, and there remained till 1874 when he went to Lancaster, an old prison with many historic associations. In 1881 he was placed in charge of that prison and remained in that position until six years ago when he came to Bodmin to succeed Mr. Stevens, who had had as his predecessor a Mr. Parr, who was Mr. Shenton's predecessor at Lancaster.

Mr. Shenton speaks with no uncertain voice on the improvement in prison management during his forty years' service. The days of Charles Reade and of Howard have long since passed away, and in their place has come a system which, while seeing justice done is yet merciful and has as its chief purpose the checking of further crime by the ones fallen. I will not at this point give my impressions of what I saw, but suffice it to say that I was very agreeably struck with the system at present in vogue.

The staff at Bodmin Prison is a comparatively small one. It consists of the Governor, the Chaplain, the Medical Officer (Dr. Derry), the Storekeeper (Mr. Masters), the acting chief warder, and twelve warders and assistant warders. This refers, of course, only to the male prison. I will refer to the female prison later. The majority of the staff are engaged during the day, commencing at 6 a.m. At night there is always one warder patrolling the prison and two others sleep on the premises, so that they are within call at any moment. The warder who is patrolling has no keys with him, so that should a prisoner desire anything or the warder desire to enter the cell he cannot do so until he has called one of the sleeping warders who has charge of the keys. This seems a very safe precaution, as one warder by himself might easily be overpowered by a big, strong prisoner. The pay of the warders seems to be a reasonably liberal scale. They start at something about £60, are provided with a house (or extra pay in lieu of same) and uniform. They have to be at least 5ft. 7in. in height and a certain measurement round the chest.

The Stores and the Prisoners' Dress

Whilst sitting chatting with the Governor I could not help being struck with the large number of books in connection with the management of the prison standing on various shelves round the office. But when Mr. Shenton enlightened me a little as to the minuteness of the records to be kept and of the returns to be made to the Commissioners the need of these many books became more apparent. A further chat of five minutes with the storekeeper (Mr. Masters) afforded still more information. The merest detail in connection with the conduct of the prison has to be recorded, and in many instances in duplicate form. The stores are in the sole charge of the storekeeper, who has to account for all out-goings, even down to a single bootlace. When I speak of the stores I not only include the prisoners' wearing apparel, food and utensils; there are also included the raw material which they use in their labour and the goods turned out by them in their labour. In one of the main store rooms on the occasion of my visit there must have been hundreds (perhaps over a thousand) mail bags all ready to go out into use. Coal bags there were also in abundance and great bales of picked oakum.

The governor informed me that the labour done in the Bodmin prison was more remunerative last year that that of any other prison in the country – that is, of course, in proportion to the size of the prison. I believe I am right in saying that over £1,000 worth of goods were turned out from this prison last year as the result of the labour of the prisoners. This is somewhat accounted for by the fact that the prisoners are largely composed of naval men, who have been discharged from the service, and who are true to their designation as "handy men." I expressed a wonder as to what the Government could do with all the mail bags that must be constantly turned out in these establishments. The Governor, by way of reply, remarked that the recent war had made a big demand on prison made goods and consequently there was not such a flush as their otherwise would be. It must be understood in this connection that prisoners make a good deal of canvas stuffs used both in the Army and the Navy. The coal bags, for instance, are used very largely in the coaling of our big naval ships. In the store room set apart for the wearing apparel of the prisoners a very substantial reserve supply was noticeable. There are three grades of dress – the one in most general use is drab in colour, then there is the blue and the brown, which are worn by prisoners who are either in the second division or who are in some other way not herded with the common criminal. The men do not wear knee breeches, as is the custom at convict prisons, but are attired in trousers. Everything has on it the stamp of the broad arrow, and as far as I could see there was not a single thing in use in the prison but what was similarly branded. The shoes the prisoners wear are certainly not exactly dancing slippers, but they are what a good many well-to-do citizens cannot boast as having on their feet – they are all handsewn.

A Surprise

What surprised me most on passing from the prison offices to the prison proper (all under one roof) was to see several of the prisoners all working together outside their cells. They were engaged in what is known as association labour. This, I believe, is of only recent introduction. I had always understood that for hard labour sentences the prisoners had always to do their tasks in their cells, only having the one hour's exercise outside in the morning. But I was mistaken. Here were, perhaps, fifteen or twenty men sitting on stools (one in front of the other) working quietly on the making of mail bags. Talking is, of course, strictly forbidden, but there is the privilege of seeing one another at work and of seeing what is going on around. There is a kind of unspeaking association about it all. It must certainly be less unpleasant than being caged up in the cell all day with absolutely nothing to engage the attention but the work in hand. But this association labour is not participated in until 28 days have passed by. Thus those who only have a month or less to serve are engaged all the time in their cells. The first month of a sentence is always passed in solitude (with the exception of the daily exercise and service) this must naturally be the most trying part of a prisoner's term, for beside the solitude, there is the first fourteen days plank bed, the early horrors of confinement, and the very decided change in diet from what the prisoner has perhaps been accustomed to. Further, what is known as the hard bodily labour, such as picking oakum or making coal bags, comes in the earliest stages of the term.

The men engaged in the association labour on the ground floor were of the habitual criminal class, and the least intellectual in appearance. They were in charge of one warder who, standing at the head, could see all that was going on.

None of the prisoners are shaved close, and it cannot be said that the hair of several was kept back tight. Their beards are kept only as close as scissors will permit. When a prisoner's term is drawing to a close his hair is allowed to grow to the length customary to the man before he started his imprisonment. He does not, therefore, come out of the gaol with the brand on him.

The Cells and a Prisoner's Programme

The cells are all within the same four walls, there being three storeys with corridors are protected by high railings, and even if a prisoner jumped out over the intent to commit suicide he would undoubtedly fail, as wire netting is stretched right across to prevent his falling. There are in all one hundred and six cells, and on an average about eighty or ninety of these are daily in use. The cells are all alike. They are about fifteen feet by seven feet in size, well lighted and beautifully ventilated. They contain the prisoner's eating utensils, all of tin (except the wooden spoon), and shining like a mirror, his plank bed, with mattress rolled up and placed on a shelf, a stool, and the shelf for the Bible and other books he may have in use. In two of the walls, and immediately opposite each other, are two pairs of loop-holes into which the fastenings of the hammocks used to be placed. The hammocks, for sleeping purposes, are now, however, done away with. A gas burner stands low down just inside the massive door. At this period of the year the jet is never required. In the centre of the cell door is a kind of trap door (now not used), through which food and so on need to be passed. Above that is the spy hole for the warders on duty. This hole is covered when not in use by a moveable piece of iron, and in the centre of this is a hole about the size of a pin's head, through which the warder can look into the cell, but the occupant of the cell cannot see that he is being watched. On the outside of the door is placed all the particulars of the occupant of the cell, giving name, date of conviction, length of sentence, what character labour he has to perform and what class diet he is to receive. It need hardly be said that the window of the cell is protected on the outside of the glass by stout iron bars. Immediately inside the door is the handle to a bell which is fixed in the corridor outside. When the handle is pulled, a number printed on a piece of sheet iron springs out from the wall, thereby denoting in which cell the bell has been pulled.

Perhaps it will not be out of place if I give here an outline of the treatment of the prisoner from the time he enters the prison gates. When first received the necessary particulars as to name, age, crime, sentence, etc., are recorded, and in some cases (not, I believe, in those of a minor character) the Bertillon system of taking the impression of the thumb and other verifying marks is put into operation. This completed, the prisoner is passed on to what is known as the reception cells. Here he awaits a visit from the doctor, who certifies as to his ability for physical labour and as to his freedom from any infectious disease. Here he first dons the prison garb and his own clothes go on to the disinfector for treatment. A bath follows (all prisoners, by the way, have a bath once a week) and then he is ready to go on to the cell he will occupy for the remainder of his term in the main part of the building. He is provided with a printed card showing the rules of the prison, by which he is soon able to get an idea of the routine to which he will have to conform. At six the next morning the bell sounds out the order to rise. Half an hour is allowed for dressing and for putting the cell in order. Then work commences. It may be oakum picking (the work disliked most because of its arduous nature and because of its effect on the finger tips), or it may be coal bag making, or chopping wood, or some other task described as "hard bodily labour." At 7.30 breakfast in served. Following this the hour's exercise may be fitted in, and then there is a twenty-minutes service in the Chapel. By 9.30 the morning's work has commenced in dead earnest and continues till twelve, when there is an hour and a half's respite for dinner. The afternoon's labour continues till 5.45, at which time supper is served. If the prisoner has done his allotted task no further work is required of him after that time, but if he has failed to complete what it is considered he should have done he has to continue his work till 8.30 – the time for retirement. Those who have finished their work by supper time may use the time between then and 8.30 in reading or in meditating on their crime and its consequences. Day after day the same routine obtains, until Sunday comes, when the prisoner rises at seven instead of six, and of course does no work for the day. He attends Divine service in the morning and again in the afternoon, and he also has his hour's exercise. Under certain conditions prisoners who have earned the privilege are allowed to converse with each other while on exercise one day in the week.

Exercise, and the Garden.

The exercise yard is in the open. It consists of two rings. Those who are able-bodied and can walk briskly take the outer ring, and those who are somewhat handicapped take the inner. They are made to move at a good pace and cover about four miles in the hour. They are in charge of two warders who are so situated that they can see if there is any whispering or any other means of communication adopted. In cold or damp weather the men are provided with thick, warm capes, which they take from a rack as they go from the cells to the yard. In very wet weather the exercise is taken in doors.

Some of the prisoners get their daily exercise in the garden. This stands at the higher side of the prison buildings and commands a good view of the whole. Those known as the "star men" generally get the privilege of working the garden. They are men who have never been convicted before and whose previous reputation was good and whose antecedents had irreproachable characters. These men, though they may have long sentences and may be sentenced to hard labour the same as any common felon, are not placed in association with the habitual criminal – a very wise discrimination being shown.

A large proportion of the vegetables used in the prison are grown on the prison grounds. Most of the space is devoted to potatoes, as this is the vegetable most largely in use. Along the edges of the beds, however, the prisoners are encouraged to grow flowers, and I noticed a beautiful lot of sweet Williams growing in this way as I walked around. Even roses are under the care of some of the prisoners, and as beautiful a lot as could be seen in any gentleman's garden were in full bloom in one of the yards on the day I visited the prison. They numbered one less after I had gone from the prison, but that, as Rudyard Kipling would say, is another story. I will only add that it was taken from the tree and placed in my coat in full view of the Governor. It wouldn't do for people to have the idea that I had committed a felony in a prison!

The Cook-House and Diet.

The cook-house was one of the most interesting parts of the building which I visited (and I believe there was not a part I was not most courteously shown). The room is splendidly lighted from a skylight in the roof, and it has ample space, was beautifully cool even on the very hot day I was there, and so clean that a spot of dirt could not be detected anywhere. It was shortly before supper time when I was there, and three prisoners ("star men") in charge of a warder were busy preparing their comrades' last meal for the day. In one of the big boilers porridge was being prepared and ladled out into the tin cans in a spoon which would certainly be a trifle superfluous for a small family, but which is doubtless essential in an establishment like the Bodmin Prison. Another boiler contained gruel, the difference between this and porridge being simply one of the amount of meal put into the mixture. Gruel is thinner than porridge. In the third boiler there was an inviting lot of cocoa standing, all ready to be served up. It is made from identically the same cocoa as is used in the Navy, and no purer cocoa can be found anywhere. I drank about half a cup of it, and as a bit of a connoisseur in cocoas, I readily admit that the drink was most palatable. On the table by the side stood a sample of the dinner which had been served that day. It consisted of haricot beans, potatoes and a slice of fat bacon. It was not quite the kind of dinner one would expect in a Parisian restaurant, but there was certainly plenty of it, and possibly it is far more easy of digestion that a good deal of the stuff we who enjoy our liberty trouble our stomachs with. I next sample the bread. It is all of the whole meal order, brown in colour, but yet wholesome and palatable. I have eaten much white bread that I liked less. Each prisoner gets a thick chunk of it in addition to the other courses of his meal. The character of the diet varies according the term of the prisoner and according to medical instructions. Whatever food the doctor says a prisoner must have that food is given to him. The plainest fare always comes at the beginning of the sentence and it slightly improves as the term proceeds. Cooked meat is generally given for Thursday's dinner, and Australian preserved meat on the Sunday. Breakfast and supper generally consist of so much bread and either gruel, porridge, or cocoa. Plain though the fare is, it has the redeeming quality of abundance. Seeing the big allowances being made out on the day of my visit I could hardly understand how any prisoner could complain of being hungry. The gruel was being served in a good sized tin, and into the top of that another tin was made to fit in which the bread was placed. A dozen or so of these allowances were being placed on a wooden tray ready to be carried to the various cells.

With regard to the prisoner's diet and as to his fitness for certain degrees of labour the medical officer is the guiding power. If a man complains that he cannot eat this or that food he is seen by the doctor, and future treatment is guided by the officer's decision. Every consideration, too, is shown prisoners in the case of sickness. In the ordinary course of things the doctor visits the prison twice daily, and it is only for a man to say he is unwell and Dr Derry is called at once. But woe be to the man if he is malingering. Neither the Governor nor any of the warders take it upon themselves to decide this point. It is not for them to say whether a man is shamming or whether he is in earnest. Be it any hour of the day or night the doctor is sent for if a prisoner makes an urgent request. And it is interesting in this connection to remark that only one prisoner has died during Mr Shenton's governorship. The prison hospital is provided with all necessary appliances, but on the occasion of my visit there were no patients.

With respect to communication with the outside world, no prisoner is allowed to receive or send any letter until after two months of his sentence have expired. He is then entitled (if he has not forfeited the privilege through breach of discipline) to send one letter and receive one letter per month. He is also entitled to one visit from a friend during the same time. But should his friends live at a considerable distance or be otherwise prevented from paying the visit, the prisoner may send and receive one extra letter in lieu thereof. All these communications are, of course, read by the Governor, before they leave the prison or get into the hands of the prisoner.

The Chapel

The prison chapel is an interesting building. It is divided into four sections. On one side there is the space for the women, coming next there is a space for second-division men, "star" men and prisoners of that class, then comes the place for the habitual criminal, and on the other side is the portion allotted to the naval prisoners, who come from the prison in which they are located (and which is completely separate in management from the civil prison) to worship with the other prisoners. Each portion is partitioned off to such a height that no section can see the other. The arrangement of the building, however, is about to undergo structural alteration, for at present only half of the worshippers are able to see the altar. This is to be obviated by the erection of a gallery at the back which will be occupied by the naval men. The Chaplain and Governor have their places high up in a gallery at the front where they can see all and be seen by all. The singing is led by a large harmonium – a new instrument recently installed in the place of one out of date and, perhaps, out of tune. The organist is Mr Banfield Whale. The singing is generally very hearty and harmonious, accounted for in some measure by the number of ex-naval men in the congregation. Those prisoners professing some other religious persuasion than the Church of England are not bound to attend the services in the Chapel, but as a rule they all like to be present. The service is one of the few green spots in a barren desert and none of them care to miss the chance of a nibble. Within the past few months the Rev. W.T. Gill has been appointed by the Commissioners as Chaplain to prisoners owning association with Wesleyan Methodism and he visits the prison periodically. The Roman Catholic priest also pays periodical visits.

Other Details

I went into what was once the treadmill room, the glory of which has for some time departed. In other words the old wheel has been sold, the Governor "having no further use for it." Public opinion had cried out against the treadmill and as public opinion paid the piper public opinion had its way. For this no one thanks public opinion more than the unhappy prisoner. The maximum amount of money that a prisoner can earn during his term is 10s., but by good conduct he can secure a reduction of his sentence. Sentences of six months or under are "strictly nett" but when they get beyond that a reduction of one quarter can be earned on the remaining period beyond the first six months. Thus a prisoner with a twelve months' term could get a quarter reduction on his last six months. When his term has expired he is released about 7.30 a.m., in time to catch the first train out of town. The authorities pay his fare to the place from whence he came, or if the application is considered a reasonable one to any other place he may desire. He is told to go to the station and a warder in plain clothes meets him there, sees him in the train and gives him his ticket.

There are carpenters' and engineers' shops attached to the prison, and in these some of the prisoners whose previous training may have fitted them for it are engaged. Some really first-class work is done by the men, and some of the mail bags which I was privileged to closely examine showed most careful and precise stitching.

The execution yard is fortunately very seldom called into use. Within the past twenty years there has been but one execution, and that was of an Italian sailor for murder committed on the high seas. This is in striking contrast to the nine cases of the death sentence during Mr. Shenton's term at Lancaster. And this reminds me that the hoisting of the black flag will be seen no more. By order of the authorities (as already announced in the Press) notices affixed outside the prison are to be substituted for the older form of acquainting the public that a death sentence has been carried out.

There is a very complete and efficient system at the prison for dealing with an outbreak of fire. The alarm is given by a bell, and the warders at once rush to where the appliances are kept in the hall and can get them in working order in the course of three or four minutes. Hydrants are placed at convenient parts of the prison and the force of water is sufficient to deal with any outbreak at the most remote corner.

Debtors and men who have refused to pay for the maintenance of their wives or children receive somewhat more considerate treatment in prison than the ordinary felon. But they all have to do some work. They are, however, allowed fuller use of the library and certain other privileges. Men on trial are not compelled to work nor are they bound to put on the prison garb. Most of them, however, prefer to have something to occupy their time, and after they have earned between three and four shillings in the week what they make beyond that amount can be devoted to their own use. They can utilise it in their defence, or have meals and newspapers from the outside; but in some cases the prisoners prefer that it should be sent to their wives and families to help maintain them during the bread-winners' compulsory incarceration.

The female prison, which comes under the supervision of the Governor, is in charge of a warder-acting-matron (Miss Curnick) and one assistant. Entrance to it must be effected through the main prison yard, and the cells, thirteen in number, are simply an extension from the main building, with a dividing wall. On the occasion of my visit there were nine cells being occupied. It is very seldom that the sentences on the women extend beyond six months, and on one occasion during Miss Curnick's three years at the prison there were no females for her care. Their hard labour consists in washing, knitting, mending and so on. They do all the washing of the prison, except in the case of the very heavy articles, when male prisoners are called in to assistance. The hours and diet of the female prisoners partake pretty much of the character of that obtaining in the male section. Both the matron and her assistant sleep in the prison, and though they do not keep watch at night there is no fear of their not hearing any alarm should it be given, or any call should it be made.

Impressions

And now by way of conclusion let me give as briefly as possible my impressions of what I saw and of what I was told. One thing was very forcibly borne home upon me, and that was that hard labour prisons are not by any means such terrible institutions as some of us have generally imagined. I don't for one moment mean to suggest that life inside is pleasant; it certainly cannot be; but it is not associated with that torture, both of body and mind, which is the generally accepted idea. Discipline, and very rigid discipline there is, some confinement there is, monotonous work there is, the plainest of food there is, but none of this is torture. In fact, I can quite understand a certain type of man after he has been in prison for some considerable time leaving his new home with certain regrets.

Though I visited the Bodmin prison the hottest day so far this year the building (go in any part you like) was beautifully cool. The ventilation must be well-nigh perfect. Each cell, too, has its ventilators, so that whether engaged in the corridors or in their own cells the prisoners cannot complain of a stuffy atmosphere. In winter the building is heated by hot air. There is an abundance of light, too, go where you will. The roof of the main building is centred with glass, and in each cell the window is sufficiently large to admit plenty of light; in this respect the cells are much better off than the storekeeper's apartments. Of course, everything is perfectly clean; floors, cells, utensils, garden, cookhouse: they are perfect in this respect.

The treatment which a prisoner will receive during his incarceration depends very much upon himself. If he settles down to his work and to the routine of the establishment with a set determination to make his term as pleasant as he can for himself, in the circumstances, he will find there will be many little ways in which he can lighten his punishment. But if, on the other hand, he sets himself up in defiance, endeavours to do as little as possible and to give the warders as much trouble as he can, he will find that he is making his time doubly hard. Because if prison laws are not obeyed, the breaking of them carries with it its punishment. All cases of insubordination, shirking of work and the like, come before the Governor, and he has considerable discretionary power. In the case of extreme punishment, the Visiting Committee as well as the Governor consider the matter, and when flogging is decided on the decision goes before the Prison Commissioners for consideration before it is carried out. Flogging in hard labour prisons, however, is extremely rare. It is only allowable in cases of mutiny, escape, and assaults on prison officers.

Prison life must undoubtedly bear most severely in the earliest stages of the term, for it is then that the great change from freedom to confinement, from perhaps rich food to plain, and it may be from comparative leisure to continuous work is the most keenly felt. One can get used to almost anything, and I can readily believe that the second year of a two years' sentence can be borne with comparative indifference. I hope the strain in which I am writing will not induce to crime, simply because the punishment is not so terrible as some have imagined. But I should be untrue to the impression I formed if I said otherwise. It may be argued that I cannot speak with the experience of a prisoner. I cannot; but I was not four hours in Bodmin prison, and afforded every facility for seeing everything, without getting some idea of what prison life is like.

And the effect of prison life upon the prisoner? Well, the best answer to that is to be found in the number of re-convictions and in the number of those who must be described as habitual criminals. Unfortunately there are a very large number in this class, but then I would argue that this is due more to their nature than to the effect of their first term of imprisonment. It is almost impossible to keep some men from crime, and the only way in which it can be done is to confine them within the four walls of a prison. But fortunately, there is another side to all this. There is a type of man who has fallen once, but who is not by nature really vicious or criminal. Here prison acts as a decided corrective. Every incentive is given to the man during his incarceration to look with some hope to his life after he leaves the prison. If he be but poorly educated he is taken in hand by the chaplain and schoolmaster and every effort made to make him more fit to honestly fight life's battles when freedom is once more his. Such books and advice will be given him as will help him to have a clearer sense of what is right and wrong, and he will be in every way encouraged in the thought that because he is once a prisoner he need not of necessity be one again. Handicapped he certainly is (that is inevitable after the first fall) but the prison authorities do their best to minimise that as much as possible. And here the merits of the Discharge Prisoners' Aid Society are readily seen. Deserving men on their release are provided with monetary assistance or clothes, and in many instances situations are found for them. It is not always the assistance is appreciated, but the hon. Secretary (the Rev. C.B. Simpson) ofttimes receives gratifying evidence of the good work the Society has accomplished.

As I took my departure it was gratifying to learn on the testimony of the Governor that the amount of crime in the county of Cornwall is much below the average of the other counties. Not more than about half of those detained in the Bodmin Prison are as a rule Cornishmen. The majority of the remainder are naval and military men who have been discharged from the service in addition to a term of imprisonment.

'Bodmin Guardian' 25th July and 1st August 1902

The Prisoner's Description [138]

LIFE IN BODMIN GAOL

A correspondent sends us the following notes as the result of his six months' imprisonment, remarking that Bodmin Gaol bears a pretty good name amongst criminals for humane treatment.

After a brief record of his admission a new comer receives a pretty brown loaf weighing ¾lb. and a ¼lb. of potted meat, which strangely enough is described on the official printed dietary as "preserved by hot air." A bath precedes a change of clothes and a medical examination. Then supper is the order, this meal consisting of a pint of gruel and 8oz. of bread, the poor unfortunate being awarded an orange coloured badge, bearing his official number, which he has to wear at all times.

Equipped with clean sheets, a pillow slip, and devotional books, he is introduced to his new place of abode, a tiny apartment, in which he finds done up into a neat roll, blankets and coverlet, there being also in the cell a gallon can of water, a washing bowl, a slop pot, a salt cellar, a wooden spoon, some cleaning rags, and brickdust for shining up the metal vessels, and a very small handbrush for sweeping the floor of the cell. Having taken possession a prisoner may turn in as soon as he pleases. At six o'clock next morning a thing like an intoxicated sheep bell yells a discordant summons to arise, and a few minutes later an officer unlocks the doors to enable the man to put out any waste paper, or make any application, say, for the doctor; or, if on remand, for permission to write to a friend or "my solicitor." Cleaning and tidying up and scrubbing follows. At 7.30 breakfast trots from cell to cell, and about an hour later the bell goes for chapel. Then for the first month the prisoner works alone in his tiny abode until 12 o'clock, when dinner is served, and soon after five what is described as supper is handed round. Then comes another hour's work, and a period which prisoners may devote to themselves till the bell rings out for bed at eight o'clock.

It is no cursory personal examination, by the way, prisoners have to face. They are inspected while perfectly nude in order that not only height and weight, but tattoo marks, scars, and birth marks may be recorded for future use, if necessary. Men who have been awarded a substantial sentence, are also photographed before they leave the gaol, some twice, and various impressions of their thumb and fingerprints are taken.

WORK AND MONEY

For the opening few days, a week roughly, the delinquents are kept at oakum picking, concerning which there is always plenty of grumbling at their not having done enough. For the first month the work is usually coal bag making. After a month matters brighten up a bit, and the men are allowed to have a library book, which is changed once a week, while they are usually employed on the lighter work of making canvas mail bags, in company with other prisoners, although they are not allowed to converse. A captive also begins to amass money now in the form of a gratuity for the second four weeks, always provided his industry and conduct have been up to high water mark. In his third month the prisoner gets

178

a "rise" from 1s. to 1s. 6d., the following month to 2s. and the following to 2s. 6d. A man may write and receive a letter after completing two months, and at the end of his third month he may have a visit of twenty minutes' duration from a friend. Then, if his industry and conduct have kept good, he is permitted a visit of thirty minutes' duration every fortnight.

At the end of the fourth month a man becomes eligible for any special work in or about the prison, work for which he may by reason of his occupation or aptitude be specially fitted, such as shoe-making, tailoring, carpentering, white-washing, or painting, each of which employment is a considerable relief from the monotony of mail bag manufacture. For the first fourteen nights all adult male prisoners, not over 60 years of age, have to sleep on the plank bed. On Sundays there are two services in chapel with sermons, Holy Communion being celebrated seven or eight times during the year. If a prisoner is of a different religious persuasion to the Church of England he is not compelled to attend Divine service, but is allowed visits from a minister of his own denomination instead.

All inmates are permitted, if they choose, an hour's walking exercise in company with other prisoners. There are various forms of punishment, such as the docking of gratuities, and reducing the diet to 1lb. of bread and water for three days. At the close of the second month the library book is changed twice a week. Prisoners are supplied with clean underclothing every seven days, and leave to bath once a fortnight.

The opportunities for writing and receiving letters are afforded for the purpose of enabling prisoners to keep up a connection with their respectable friends, and not that they may be informed of public events. All epistles are read by the prison authorities, and must be legibly written without being crossed. Any of an objectionable tendency or containing slang are suppressed. Matters of special importance may be communicated at any time by letter to the Governor, who will inform the prisoner they concern if he deems it expedient. In case of misconduct the privilege of writing and receiving letters may be forfeited for a time, but granted again on subsequent good conduct. Nothing in the way of books, money, food, tobacco, or clothes is allowed to be sent to prisoners. Persons attempting to clandestinely communicate with or introduce any article to or for prisoners are liable to fine or imprisonment, and any man undergoing sentence concerned in such practices runs the risk of severe punishment.

'Bodmin Guardian' 15th September 1905

The Governor's Report (1901)

As regards the working of the Prison Act 1898, I have received no offenders of the first division, and but four sentenced as "second division". Remission of sentence was granted as a reward for industry in forty cases: the privilege is still much appreciated, and is a great incentive to good character and hard work. The provision of part payment of fines has only been taken advantage of by one prisoner, the majority being too poor to pay. The privilege of associated labour has not been abused, except in a few cases. It still conduces to more efficient work under proper supervision. Conversation at exercise has been allowed; all prisoners have availed themselves of it with two exceptions, who asked to be excused. It can, in my opinion, as now limited be safely conceded without danger to discipline or risk of contamination. The conduct of the officers during the last year has been good, and the discipline well maintained. The conduct of the prisoners has been satisfactory. There have been no offences of a serious nature and no case of corporal punishment. There were no escapes or attempts at escape. Hard labour during the first 28 days was enforced by means of coal-sack making and picking oakum. After that period it consisted of cutting out and making mail-bags, coal sacks, seamen's bags, bolster cases, hammocks, and cases, palliasses, tents; also firewood chopping, gardening, oakum picking, labouring, and the usual employment in the service of the prison. The female prisoners have been employed at washing, knitting, and needlework. The condition of the existing buildings and fences is satisfactory. The following alterations and repairs have been carried out, viz: - The chaplain's room papered and painted; a new washing boiler fixed in the laundry; the cover plates to inspection holes of cells have been perfected; the filters at Fair-wash have been cleaned; a pair of large light doors have been fixed to screen off the execution pit; all the cells, air shafts, etc., have been cleaned and whitewashed. The exterior work of the governor's, chaplain's, and principal warder's quarters and front entrance gate have been painted. The old mortuary has been removed from the van shed: new lead valleys have been laid on main roof over female prison: all the extraction flues from the cells have been cleaned; new concrete floors have been laid down in the scullery, larder, and coalhouse of the principal warder's quarters: a part of the principal warder's quarters has been whitewashed and papered: three new w.c.'s have been fixed in the male prison: a new washing boiler has been fixed in the chaplain's quarters, and the ceiling of the drawing-room re-plastered: the governor's and chaplain's stables have been whitewashed: the drawing-room in the chaplain's quarters has been re-decorated, and the basement floor cleaned and whitewashed. The arrangements in case of fire have been tested monthly and found to be in proper working order. The supply of water is adequate. The clothing and bedding in store have been sufficient. The supplies by the contractors were equal to the samples, and punctually delivered. The dietaries have been good and wholesome. The garden has been cultivated, with the result that the produce has been very satisfactory, the vegetables being nearly sufficient for the prison use. The flowers grown in various parts of the prison have been much appreciated. The progressive stage system has worked well, and has been carried out in conformity with the rules. The rules relating to juveniles have been strictly carried out. The "star" class prisoners have been separated and kept apart from all other prisoners. The rules laid down for the government of the prison have been complied with, excepting in such cases as have been specially reported to and brought under the notice of, a Commissioner.

Reported in 'Bodmin Guardian' 10th October 1902

The Poet's Description (undated)

John Bull's famous Cornish Inn;
or,
Bodmin Jail, both out and in.

In Bodmin's pretty country town—
  Though not a place of great renown—
There is a spot remembered well,
  Where stands Bull's famous branch hotel.

Wheel and oakum, tread and tease,
  So wearisome and slow;
Crank and jobbing, turn and greaze,
  And round the ring they go.

Regardless of expense 'twas built,
  Outside there's neither show nor gilt;
But if you go you'll get a cell,
  At John Bull's famous branch hotel.

Blue dress for those who are untried
  And brown for those who have been tried;
But in these togs they look queer coves,
  Just like pork hams stuck o'er with cloves.

A pris'ner's life's a dreary one,
  No talk, nor knocking to and fro;
And while at Bull's all sport is done
  At theatre, market, fair or show.

All things are bleak at that hotel,
  And not for you my honest swell;
But he who's morally impure—
  May be turned out a perfect cure.

The doctor tries to keep them whole;
  The earnest parson strives to sow
The Word into each darkened soul,
  Though seldom grows a holy glow.

The morning service in the hall
  Have sacred charms for one and all;
The Sunday rest they pleasant find,
  With sound-sence books to store the mind.

The breakfasts, suppers, are quite light,
  With Adam's ale they can't get tight;
The bill of fare's not fare for Bill,
  Who likes his pipe and loves his gill.

For victuals they've variety—
  Brown bread of fairest quality,
Porridge, gruel and stirabout;
  Six months cures corpulence and gout.

They've also bacon, beans and beef—
  Too good you say, for rogue or thief—
Soup, cocoa, spuds and suet duff;
  But here's the pinch—there's ne'er enough.

An ounce of bacon once a week,
  Make many play at hide and seek;
The half-pint soup goes quickly o'er—
  In vain the dish is licked for more.

Tin washing basin, plate and pan,
  Tin mug, meat dishes, water can;
Comb, brush and soap, salt-box and spoon,
  And prayers hung up for morn and noon.

But there are neither knives nor forks,
  Though plenty screws but not for corks;
Bracelets, but not for Ladies' wrists,
  Badges, but not for honest breasts.

"System of progressive stages,"
  Mean a scale of marks and wages;
For first month there is no reward:
  "The next a bob without the "Hard."

The other two are really bricks,
  For both combin'd bring three and six;
Though if they one or two stretch did,
  There's nothing more than half a quid.

The nightly movements on the plank
  Are something sim'lar to the crank;
It's round and round from night till morn,
  And glad to rise though sore and worn,

The treadwheel's spirit-breaking task,
  Like night-mare in a half-closed cask;
Or pickles, sweets, dessert and cake,
  When jaws and ev'ry tooth does ache.

For breach of rules—handcuffs behind,
  Belt, birch, eight inches, dark confined;
The penal pound, with Adam's wine,
  The canvas dress, the cat-o'-nine.

When on triangle getting bashed,
  Which means tied up and being lashed,
They think—while screws are taking chops—
  Of glass, and pipe, and fancy shops.

Those dear, familiar sounds we hear—
  The crow of cock and caw of crow—
Mind of sweet liberty so near
  To that grim den of silent woe.

The worst's the pack of wolfish screws,
  Whose looks do cut, whose words do bruise;
Though flesh breaks down, with hard, rough fare:
  The wounded spirit's worst to bear.

Those who have been to that famed place
  May know to some there's no disgrace;
For there are some who get a trip
  To Bull's hotel for giving lip.

Take this advice before we part—
  Be thou a stranger, friend or foe—
Do what is right, where'er thou art,
  Lest Cornwall County Jail you know.

PETER S. SINCLAIR.

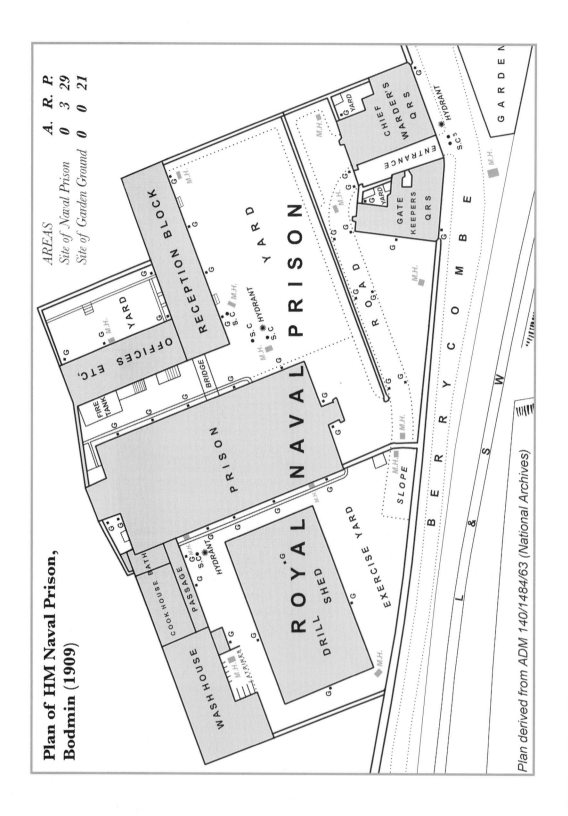

Plan of HM Naval Prison, Bodmin (1909)

AREAS   A. R. P.
Site of Naval Prison   0   3   29
Site of Garden Ground   0   0   21

Plan derived from ADM 140/1484/63 (National Archives)

CHAPTER 19

Naval Prisoners at Bodmin[140]

In the early 1870s, the Royal Navy in Devonport had a problem with naval prisoners. The main naval prison, situated at Lewes, Sussex, was too far away and as there was no similar institution in the west country, the Navy was forced to send prisoners to the local municipal prison at Devonport. During the six months ending 31st May 1873, 197 seamen, marines and boys were committed to Devonport Borough Gaol.

In June, 1873, Captain A. Heneage of H.M.S. "Royal Adelaide" and Dr. William T. Domville, Deputy Inspector General of Hospitals and Fleet, R.N. Hospital, Plymouth carried out an Official Inspection of the prison. The Report, which ran to 21 sections, was highly critical of Devonport and they suggested that a ship-of-the-line be moored in the harbour and fitted as a floating naval prison until a new building, based on Lewes (with respect to discipline and diet) could be arranged.

This adverse report was summarised in a letter from Admiral the Hon. Sir Henry Keppel, G.C.B. to the Secretary of the Admiralty, dated 29th July 1873. An extract is shown below:

Sir,

I HAVE the honour to request that you will be pleased to direct their Lordships' attention to the accompanying unsatisfactory report on the Devonport Borough Prison, showing that our men return to duty physically deteriorated, from insufficient dietary, and morally, by faulty discipline in points of cleanliness and occupation, and by association with the rogues and vagrants of a large district.

I have reason to believe that offenders do not view imprisonment in this gaol with much disfavour, except as regards their limited dietary.

The response from the Admiralty, dated 13th September 1873 contained the following paragraph: *"As no naval establishment could be brought into use at Devonport as a prison for a considerable period, it appears necessary that you should communicate with the magistrates respecting all the improvements which it is possible to make in the Borough prison, and come to some arrangement in regard to enforcing stricter discipline, observing that my Lords decidedly object to any naval prisoners being confined in any but separate cells, and I am to direct that you will take the necessary steps accordingly."*

Over the next few months, several letters were exchanged between the Admiralty, the Admiral and the Magistrates responsible for Devonport. Gaol. On the 29th December 1873, Captain F. A. Herbert, H.M.S. *"Cambridge"* and Captain A. Heneage of the *"Royal Adelaide"* visited the gaol for another inspection and gave the Governor a list of propositions. The list and the response of the Magistrates was:

1. THE two upper wards should be kept entirely for the use of naval prisoners, and they should be at all times kept separate from the civil prisoners. - *they regret that they find it impracticable to assent to it in its entirety.*

2. A cell never to have more than one prisoner. - *they assent so long as any cell in the prison is unoccupied.*

3. With regard to the dress, the frieze jacket, trousers, waistcoat, and cap. The articles supplied to prisoners to be thoroughly cleaned by washing before issue. - *it is found that the exterior woollen articles are not susceptible of frequent washing.*

4. The prisoners on entry and discharge should always be weighed, the same noted, and a return forwarded to the ship or barrack to which the men belong. – *assent.*

5. No prisoners committed for a period not exceeding three months to be permitted to perform any labour except that which can be performed in their cells. - *In their view, such a rule would be prejudicial to the health of the prisoner, and also inconvenient in carrying out the discipline of the gaol.*

6. Naval prisoners not to be allowed to take their exercise with civil prisoners. – *assent.*

7. Naval prisoners when taking their exercise not to be allowed to converse with one another. – *assent.*

8. That the cleanliness of their persons be strictly enforced: their shirts and socks to be changed twice and their flannels once a week. - *the magistrates will assent to it if it should still be thought to be essential, but I am to state that the governor of the gaol is directed to order clean clothing for prisoners in all cases where it is necessary.*

As it was becoming obvious that the discussions with Devonport would be protracted and that no new naval prison would become available in the near future, Admiral Keppel instructed his inspecting officers Herbert and Heneage to visit the Cornwall County Gaol at Bodmin. Their detailed report (page 194) was sent to the Admiral on the 10th January 1874. During the next month the following letters were sent to the Admiralty.

REPORT of Inspection of the CORNWALL COUNTY GAOL at BODMIN.

"Royal Adelaide" at Devonport,
Sir,   15 January 1874.

WITH reference to your letters L. M. M. of the 13th September and 3rd November last, I have the honour to report that propositions for the better government of naval prisoners in the Devonport Borough Prison are now in the hands of the magistrates, but as some time may elapse before I am favoured with their decision, I beg leave to submit the report of Captains Herbert and Heneage on the Cornwall County Gaol at Bodmin.

2. There is no question as to the superiority of this gaol in every point, even if the suggestions made respecting the borough prison be adopted. The latter refer only to separate cells, increased cleanliness, and the isolation of naval from civil prisoners, as far as circumstances will admit, but the difficulty remains that there is no hard labour, no deterring punishment, and the dietary is not equal to that of the Cornwall County Gaol, although the charge for subsistence, 1s. a day, is the same in each establishment.

3. The Bodmin station is 27 miles distant by rail from Plymouth, and the fare is 2s. 3d. third class. The gaol is situated about 3½ miles from the station, and the custom as regards civil offenders is to march them from the station, the escort returning by omnibus from Bodmin at a charge of 1s. a head.

4. Should their Lordships approve of the future imprisonment of naval prisoners in this gaol, they would be sent twice a week in charge of the Metropolitan Police, as

provided for by paragraph 3, page 31, of the Port Orders, and Article 56 of the same would be amended accordingly.

5. I regret to state that offences against discipline, to a degree insuring imprisonment, appear to be wilfully committed by a certain class of men in the "Royal Adelaide," when under orders for draft to a foreign station, and in ships when on the eve of departure, the object being to remain in the port where, owing to the number of men waiting draft in comparison to the work to be done, they have easy and pleasant times. My letter, No. 53. of the 12th, instanced no solitary case, that of a man sent three times in six months to the Devonport Borough Gaol; but I will venture to say that the discipline of the Cornwall gaol is not such as to render it probable that offenders will again wilfully seek its walls.

I am, &c.
Admiral Henry Keppel,

To The Secretary
of the Admiralty, London.

Reception of Prisoners in the Cornwall County Gaol, at Bodmin.

"Royal Adelaide," in Hamoaze,
6 February 1874.

Sir,

WITH reference to your letter L.M.M., of yesterday, requesting to be informed whether naval prisoners will be received in the Cornwall County Gaol at Bodmin, I have the honour to reply in the affirmative, and enclose a list of such persons sent since the lst November last.

2. The gaol has accommodation for 200, while the average number of civil prisoners amounts to 90 only, thus leaving an ample margin for naval offenders.

3. The governor, Captain Colville, is a military officer of upwards of 20 years' service, most of which in the capacity of adjutant, and therefore understands the characters of the men with whom he has to deal, and takes an interest in enforcing a strict and proper discipline.

4. It is rather early yet to report on the benefit derived from the adoption of this prison, but the fact that the "Fantome" sent five grave cases of leave-breaking to the Devonport Borough Gaol and two to Bodmin, while the "Modeste", commissioned on 1st January, has not yet sent a single case, leads to a favourable impression as regards the deterrent effect of the new establishment on this class of offenders.

5. I should be glad to know whether the Cornwall County Gaol may now be adopted in lieu of the Devonport Borough Gaol, observing that, in the meantime, commanding officers are acting on the following general signal, viz.:—
"Pending issue of general order, prisoners for Cornwall County Gaol are to be sent to the superintendent of police at dockyard, on Tuesdays and Fridays, at 8.30 a.m., taking dinners with them. Warrants to be dated on those days, and to provide for release on corresponding days."

6. Considerable expense will be saved by sending the prisoners in parties twice a week, the escort returning with released prisoners on the same days.

I am, &c. Henry Keppel, Admiral.

The following letter confirmed that Bodmin Gaol should replace Devonport Borough Gaol for naval prisoners. (* date should be 1874)

The Secretary of the Admiralty to Admiral the Hon. Sir H. Keppel, G.C.B.

Sir,   Admiralty, 11 February 1875*.

WITH reference to previous correspondence, and to your letter of the 6th instant, respecting the reception of prisoners in the Cornwall County Gaol at Bodmin, I am commanded by my Lords Commissioner of the Admiralty to acquaint you that **this gaol may now be adopted in lieu of the Devonport Borough Gaol for naval prisoners**, and that they approve of the arrangements you have made.

I am, &c.
(signed)   Robert Hall.

A few weeks later on the 2nd April, 1874, the Naval Inspectors visited Bodmin and produced a detailed report. Admiral Keppel's letter to the Admiralty and the full report are reproduced below:

"Royal Adelaide", in Hamoaze,
Sir,   8 April 1874.

WHEN their Lordships last visited this port I had the honour of directing their attention to the unsatisfactory condition of the Devonport Borough Prison. Their Lordships having subsequently been pleased to approve of my suggestion that naval prisoners should, for the future, be sent to the Cornwall County Gaol at Bodmin, I have now to enclose the copy of a report of the inspection made of that establishment on the 2nd instant by Captain A. C. F. Heneage and Deputy Inspector General Domville, **by which it will be seen that the discipline and arrangements of that establishment leave little to be desired.** I may add that the deterrent effect of this gaol on offenders is daily becoming more marked; at present I can only draw a comparison between harbour ships for the month of March, my order to use the gaol being only dated the 13th February last.

In March 1873, 11 naval offenders were sent to Devonport Borough Gaol.

In March 1874, one naval offender was sent to the Cornwall County Gaol.

2. With reference to paragraph 12 of the inspecting officers' report, I request their Lordships' authority to sanction an increase in the meat ration for the reason and to the extent therein stated.

I have, &c.

The Secretary of the Admiralty.   (signed)   *Henry Keppel,* Admiral.

H.MS Royal Adelaide

Admiral of the Fleet The Hon. Sir HENRY KEPPEL, C.G.B.

Cornwall County Gaol.—Report of its Inspection.

Sir,   Plymouth, 2 April 1874.

IN pursuance of your memorandum of the 31st ultimo, we, on the above date, visited the County Gaol at Bodmin, and have the honour to submit the following report of our proceedings, commencing with the several subjects to which our attention was specially directed.

2. *Dormitories* or *corridors,* from which the several cells of the prisoners opened, clean, well ventilated, and of equable temperature, thermometrical observations being duly noted to ensure the same.

3. *Solitary cells* dry, and ventilation good.

4. *Personal cleanliness* was attended to, and facilities are now afforded by which every naval offender has a warm bath weekly. Water is laid on to each cell, and the prisoners can at all times perform ordinary ablution.

5. *The clothing* was fairly clean and sound, but an improvement will be made in this respect on the receipt of new clothing already ordered.

6. The prisoners are employed strictly in accordance with the labour chart annexed, and no exemption is made in any case except from sickness, or the exhibition of debility on the part of any prisoner, when the attention of the medical officer is at once given to him, and he certifies as to the amount or suspension of labour at the wheel, and under these circumstances alone can the exemption take place.

7. The hours appropriated to treadwheel labour are eight, but the actual time on the wheel during the day is four; intervals of fifteen minutes being observed for alternate labour and rest. While unemployed the prisoner sits in a small compartment at the rear of his compartment at the wheel, which effectually prevents any oral communication, and also shuts out from sight each prisoner, after being marched at intervals, in single file, to the wheel gallery. A warder sits upon an elevated platform, regulates the relief by sound of clock, and effectually checks any intercourse, even a glance from right or left being a punishable offence.

8. *The wheel labour* is not lost, the whole of the flour used in the prison being ground by it.

9. *The wheel* is placed in a well-aired and well-lighted gallery, the latter being effected by a glass roof, allowing the solar rays to permeate the apartment, to obviate much of the pallor usually coincident with incarceration.

10. *The prisoners* are inspected by the medical officer of the prison on, or soon after, admission, and previous to commencing hard labour.

11. Our attention, according to your direction, was specially given to the case of the late William Anstice. During his imprisonment he never exhibited the slightest evidence of disease, never complained, and was at all times cheerful and ready to perform the task allotted. On the day of discharge he had a warm bath, which was a source of pleasure to him, and the attendant warder describes him as running up the stairs afterwards with unwonted alacrity. Speaking from a medical point of view, it is not improbable that the inclemency of the weather on the day of discharge may have contributed to the fatal termination. The temperature of the atmosphere on the 10th of March was only 37 degrees, that of the prison on the same day 59 degrees. His weight, registered on admission, was 133 lbs.; on discharge, 139 lbs; showing an increase of 6 Ibs.

12. The important question of dietary was discussed with the Governor, who expressed himself as ready to meet any improvements, but that the change must greatly depend upon the character and amount of alteration, insomuch as it might become a question for solution, not only by the justices, but also of the Secretary of State. We questioned several of the prisoners as to the satisfaction of hunger, and in no instance was any grievance elicited. We respectfully submit, however, that it is a question of

quality and nutrition rather than of quantity, and. having regard to the importance of maintaining the physique of our seamen and marines, recommend an addition of eight ounces, making 10 ounces in all, on the days of meat issue, viz.. Sunday, Tuesday, Thursday, and Saturday. By this arrangement an approximation to Lewes dietary will be made, an excess of two ounces for those days over Lewes, but recommended as the meat here supplied is Australian, samples of which we tasted and found most excellent in flavour, and the apparent retention of its nutritive qualities, no other meat has been in use for several years, with most beneficial results.

We strongly urge an addition to the food supply, as it will be found on reference to the "Report of the Health of the Navy for 1870," pages 48 and 49, that men returning from the naval prison at Malta were more incidental to disease than others, and the records of the hospital at this station, that treatment in hospital has not been unfrequent after prison.

13. Association of prisoners is at variance with the prison regulations, and is in no instance permitted: the strictest observance of this system being carried out, whether at labour or at rest. The slightest recognition or glance from one prisoner to another bringing its penalty.

14. Chapel is attended daily, when each prisoner enters and passes to his own compartment, hidden from the sight of all, excepting the prison officials. Roman Catholics have the benefits of religion from a priest, who also attends the prison.

15. The question of communication with friends was brought to our notice, and the irregularity of letters being forwarded from ships in contravention of your orders upon this subject. As a matter of course they are not delivered. The same rule applies to newspapers.

16. We have finally to express our admiration of the extreme order and cleanliness which pervaded every part of the establishment, reflecting great credit upon Captain Colville, the governor, and his subordinates.

We conversed with the prisoners, and questioned them as to their treatment, but not a single complaint upon this ground was elicited. The disciplinary treatment, however, appeared to have told, and a sense of shame and contrition was well apparent. They thoroughly realised the fact that acts subversive of good order and authority had alone led to their punishment, and that the penalty was being inexorably carried out without favour or affection.

Their manner was strongly in contrast to the levity and superciliousness of demeanour witnessed at the Devonport Borough Gaol; and it is our belief that the punishment, as carried out at the Cornwall County Gaol, with firmness, but devoid of harshness or oppression, will exert a deterrent influence throughout the service.

We have, &c.

(signed)   *Algernon Heneage,* Captain.
William T. Domville,
Deputy Inspector General of
Hospitals and Fleets.

To Admiral the Hon. Sir H. Keppel, G.C.B.,
      Commanding, Devonport

The Inspectors, the Admiral and the Lords of the Admiralty were all very happy with the hard labour and discipline at Bodmin but the old problem they had at Devonport, that is, the poor state of prisoners returning to their ships caused by poor diet, was also happening at Bodmin.

188

Diets and the Condition of Naval Prisoners
The diet and the weight and condition of the returning prisoners was a major issue.

Devonport Borough Gaol
The following table shows the differences in diet between the Naval Prison, Lewes and Devonport Borough Gaol (6th May, 1873).

Comparative Scale of Diet between the Naval Prison at Lewes and the Borough Gaol at Devonport, calculated for a term of 28 Days, with Hard Labour.										
Prison	**Oatmeal**	**Bread**	**Milk**	**Soup**	**Beef**	**Veg.**	**Potato**	**Indian Meal**	**Gruel**	**Cheese**
	Ibs.	*Ibs.*	*pints*	*pints*	*Ibs.*	*Ibs.*	*Ibs.*	*Ibs.*	*pints*	*Ibs.*
Naval Gaol, Lewes	14	19	8	8	4	1	8	11¼	-	-
Devonport Gaol	-	32	-	-	-	-	9	6	56	½

The Lewes diet is more varied and contains beef, vegetables, soup and milk in addition to the bread and potatoes. The oatmeal and Indian Meal (Cornmeal), possibly with milk, was made into porridge or gruel.

Devonport reported the weight of prisoners at the beginning and end of their sentences. They had all been on the above Devonport diet.

Quarter	Days	Prisoners			Average gain/loss	Range
		Number	**Wt. Gain**	**Wt. Loss**		
					lbs.	*lbs.*
4Q 1872	90	7	4	2	0	+3 to -5
1Q 1873	"	6	3	2	0.8	+6 to -3
4Q 1872	42	6	1	5	-1.3	+2 to -4
1Q 1873	"	7	0	7	-3.3	-2 to -5
4Q 1872	35	6	2	4	-1.1	+1 to -5
1Q 1873	"	6	2	4	-0.3	+4 to -6
4Q 1872	21	5	0	5	-2.8	-1 to -6
1Q 1873	"	5	0	5	-3.8	-3 to -5
		48	12	34		

They reported on 48 prisoners, 24 for September to December, 1872 and the same number for January to March, 1873. Over the sentence 12 prisoners gained and 34 lost weight. The average loss for the 1872 set was 13 ounces (0.81lb.) and for the 1873 group it was higher at 25 ounces (1.56lb.). However, when the losses in weight are compared with the length of sentence, those serving 21 days lost the most weight in both groups (-2.8 and -3.8 lbs.) and those serving 90 days had returned to their original weight (0 and +0.8 lbs.). On this data, it seems unlikely that the observed weight loss was due to diet and was probably caused by the change in life style.

Bodmin Gaol

<table>
<tr><td colspan="8">Comparative Scale of Diet between the Borough Gaol at Devonport and the County Gaol at Bodmin, calculated for a term of 28 Days, with Hard Labour.</td></tr>
<tr><th>Prison</th><th>Bread</th><th>Soup</th><th>Beef</th><th>Potato</th><th>Indian Meal</th><th>Gruel</th><th>Cheese</th></tr>
<tr><td></td><td>lbs.</td><td>pints</td><td>lbs.</td><td>lbs.</td><td>lbs.</td><td>pints</td><td>lbs.</td></tr>
<tr><td>Devonport Gaol</td><td>32</td><td>-</td><td>-</td><td>9</td><td>6</td><td>56</td><td>½</td></tr>
<tr><td>Bodmin Gaol</td><td>28</td><td>12</td><td>2</td><td>28</td><td>-</td><td>56</td><td>-</td></tr>
</table>

In a comparison of the two diets, Bodmin includes soup, beef and extra potatoes in place of the Cornmeal and cheese at Devonport. It is closer to the diet used at Lewes.

H M S	Days	Prisoners			Average gain/loss	Range
		Number	Wt. Gain	Wt. Loss		
					lbs.	lbs.
"Royal Adelaide"	60	4	1	3	-2.5	7 to -6
"	48	1	0	1	-3.0	
"	42	4	0	4	-7.5	-6 to -8
"	39	5	0	5	-7.0	-3 to -11
"	35	2	0	2	-9.5	-3 & -16
"	29	4	0	4	-6.5	-5 to -9
"	28	1	0	1	-6.0	
"	26	1	0	1	-14.0	
"	22	3	1	2	-2.0	1 to -4
"	21	1	1	0	+2.0	
"Implacable"	29	1	0	1	-6.0	
"Topaze"	36	1	0	1	-5.0	
"	29	1	0	1	-4.0	
"Indus"	42	1	0	1	-12.0	
"	30	2	0	2	-2.0	-1 & -3
"	22	3		2	-3.3	0 to -5
"	21	2	1		+0.5	+1 & 0
"	15	2	0	2	-3.0	-1 & -5
"	12	2	0	2	-2.5	-2 & -3
		41	4	35		

This data was reported to Admiral Keppel on the 1st October, 1874 and covers men released from Bodmin Gaol between the 15th June and 30th September, 1874. Of the 41 prisoners with full data, 4 gained weight and 35 lost weight. The average loss per prisoner was 4.8 lbs. significantly higher than the prisoners released from Devonport in 1873. The indication in the Devonport data, that after 90 days in gaol, the weight tends to return to normal is not shown in the above return but the maximum sentence at Bodmin was 60 days.

In addition to weighing the prisoners, in many cases there were Medical Officer's reports on the prisoners' condition, either before, after release or both. There is data on 50 prisoners. Before prison, 34 were classified as 'good', one 'fair', one 'weak' and there were no comments on the remaining 14. On release, 38 prisoners from all ships except '*Indus*', 5 were rated 'good', 8 'fair', 2 'sick', 3 'debilitated', 18 'lean & pallid' and 2 with no report. For H.M.S. "Royal Adelaide", the Staff Surgeon, John Bernard, and the Captain, Algernon Heneage, signed the following report (dated 1st October, 1874):

'The total number of men sent to prison was 47, those who returned from prison (to H.M.S. "Royal Adelaide") were 35. Of the latter 14 were fit for duty, 14 recommended for light duty and 7 admitted to the sick-list. The complaints of those admitted to the sick-list were:- Scabies; Syphilis; Diarrhoea and Debility; Variocele (chickenpox) and Debility and three cases of Anemia.

Those men who were put on the sick-list, and who were recommended for light duty, presented, as a rule, a worn, emaciated, and pallid appearance, and were quite unfit to perform the ordinary duties of a seaman. This debilitated condition showed that the amount of animal food which they had received in prison was not sufficient to enable them to undergo their sentence with impunity to their health, or to perform their duties efficiently on their return from prison.'

The report from *"Indus"* for the same date was quite different. Twelve prisoners were sent to Bodmin Gaol, 11 were classified 'good' and one was 'weak'. When they were returned to the ship after their sentence, the Staff Surgeon, William Richardson, and Captain R V Hamilton, certified 11 of them as 'good' and the original weak Stoker 2nd Class was still classified as weak, even after losing twelve pounds. They queried the accuracy of the weighing machine as it was borrowed from the steelyards and could not be relied on. All the prisoners from this ship were given the same health classification before and after their stay in Bodmin Gaol even though 9 of them had lost weight. It would appear that the classification of health was totally subjective and depended on the individual surgeon.

EXTRACT of a LETTER from Admiral the Hon. Sir H. Keppel, to the Secretary of the Admiralty.
BODMIN GAOL.
REPORT on effect of Dietary in, and Comparison with, Devonport Borough Prison.
"Royal Adelaide," Hamoaze,
Sir,   19 October 1874.
WITH reference of the 10th September last, informing me, that the question of **sending naval prisoners to Bodmin Gaol will be finally settled on receipt of my report on the effect of the present dietary,** and at the same time the necessity for an additional constable, will be taken into consideration.
I have now to inclose for their Lordships' information, Returns, showing the condition of prisoners on rejoining their ships, by which **an increase in the meat ration to the extent recommended in the inspecting officers' report, would appear to be desirable,** with reference to the strict discipline and labour imposed in the Bodmin Gaol,

and if it is intended that the men should return with their strength unimpaired; at the same time, my impression is, **that the men rapidly regain their condition on release, and that the temporary falling off may be attributed as much to the irksome nature of the life in confinement as to the dietary, which is superior, I fear, to that on which many labouring men in England support both health and strength.**

The reply from the Secretary of the Admiralty, dated 31st October, 1874, **confirmed Bodmin as the Naval Prison** and ordered a 5oz. increase in the meat ration in each case where it is allowed to naval prisoners. (This increased the meat ration from 2lbs. to 7lbs. per 28 days.)

Did the move to Bodmin Gaol reduce the number of Offenders?

It was Admiral Keppel's belief that the tough 'Hard Labour' system at Bodmin would reduce the number of offenders and re-offenders. To check this, returns were compared between Devonport, 1873 and Bodmin, 1874.

The offences were classified into four groups: Breaking Leave (BL); Desertion (Des.); Insubordination and Drunkenness (I/D) and Theft (Th.). The overall result show a significant decrease in the number of offenders, 120 against 157, a drop of 24 %. In three of the four 'Offence' groups there were reductions of between 25% and 71% but the number of desertions almost doubled from 16 to 30 (+88%).

Total Prisoners sent to Gaol between 1st April and 30th September, 1873 & 1874										
H M S	**Devonport 1/4 - 3/9, 1873**					**Bodmin 1/4 - 3/9, 1874**				
	BL	Des.	I/D	Th.	Total	BL	Des.	I/D	Th.	Total
"Royal Adelaide"	46	9	8	1	64	10	6	3	1	20
"Indus"	12	0	1	0	13	22	2	4	0	28
"Cambridge"	2	0	2	0	4	0	1	0	0	1
Training Ships	1	2	2	1	6	5	1	2	0	8
Channel Squadron	12	1	15	1	29	8	3	0	0	11
Troop Ships	6	0	1	0	7	9	2	2	0	13
Other Ships	10	4	5	3	22	17	11	0	1	29
1st Reserve Ships	9	0	2	1	12	3	4	3	0	10
Total	98	16	36	7	**157**	74	30	14	2	**120**
% Change						-25	+88	-61	-71	**-24**

The results from the flagship, "Royal Adelaide", were best with 'Breaking Leave' reduced from 46 to 10, Desertion (9 to 6) and Insubordination and Drunkenness (8 to 3) giving a total reduction of 78%. Keppel's explanation for this change stated:

'On the old system men repeatedly broke their leave with a view to avoiding draft to foreign stations, but **now foreign service is preferred to Bodmin Gaol**, and as the establishment becomes better known, its discipline will be found to exercise a more marked deterrent effect year by year.'

The returns from 'other ships' reported a doubling of 'Leave Breaking' and 'Desertion', from 14 committals to 28 and the Channel Squadron reduced 'Insubordination / Drunkenness' from 15 cases to zero. There is an explanation for the large increase in committals from "H M S Indus": Short sentences in Bodmin Gaol have been awarded in grave cases of leave breaking, whereas, under the former system, **men were confined to the cells on board as a more severe punishment than that involved in a short term at the Devonport Prison.**

From June 1874, the 'detached squadron' was in port and sent a return. The committals from this squadron were 24 (LB), 7 (I/D) and 4 (Th.) a total of 35 in less than four months. They must not have heard about the severity of imprisonment in Bodmin Gaol!

The issue of Bodmin Gaol being used for naval prisoners was finally settled in a letter from Admiral Keppel to the Clerk of the Magistrates of Devonport. An extract from the letter, dated 26 October 1874, is produced below:

'The impression conveyed by a study of the reports on the rival prisons has been confirmed in favour of Bodmin by the fact that a much better tone prevails in the force under my command since offenders have been sent to that establishment. This is most marked in the "Royal Adelaide," the principal depot for seamen at this port, whence the committals during the last six months were one-third of the number formerly sent during a corresponding period to the Devonport Borough Gaol.

*Under these circumstances I cannot recommend a return to a system I have condemned, and **I have therefore urged the Lords Commissioners of the Admiralty only to abandon the Bodmin Gaol in favour of a naval prison under our own jurisdiction, as such a system is preferable to the association of offenders against naval law with civil criminals, and the feeling in the Service is that the time has arrived for such a change.'***

COURT MARTIAL ON BOARD THE "*ROYAL ADELAIDE*" ON THE OFFICERS OF THE "*AGINCOURT*"

Reporting visiting Cornwall County Gaol (10th Jan 1874)

IN accordance with your directions, we have visited the Cornwall County Gaol at Bodmin, and carefully inspected that establishment as to its suitableness for the imprisonment of men and boys of the Royal Navy, and find as follows:—

The cells are large and well ventilated; the fittings suitable and kept in good order. Both the occupied and empty were clean.

The solitary cells, which are only used for the confinement of prisoners for prison offences, are the same dimension as the others, but have no light, are separated from the other cells, and have double doors, so that little or no sound can reach them.

The workrooms for the men are cells fitted up for the purpose; thus at all times keeping the prisoners separate.

There is a treadmill, which prisoners sentenced to hard labour have to work; the number of hours is shown on the enclosed scale of punishments.

The only naval prisoner is a seaman of the "Royal Adelaide," sentenced for a period of three months, who had undergone six weeks' hard labour. He was, at the time we visited the gaol, employed looking after the boiler. He appeared in good condition and clean in his person, although his clothes, from the nature of the employment, were not so.

The dietary, of which a Table is enclosed, appears sufficient, and was of good quality. The meat is the Australian preserved beef, supplied in 4-lb. tins, and merely warmed, so that none of its nutritious qualities are lost. The bread is made of flour ground by means of the treadmill. Vegetables and other necessaries are bought in the open market.

The discipline is evidently good, judging to the respect shown to the governor by the warders, and the manner in which the prisoners carried out the various orders they received.

The gaol is capable of containing 200 prisoners.

The average number lately confined there being 80, thus allowing room for a large number of naval prisoners.

In comparing it with the Devonport Borough Gaol, we find that it has the following advantages: —

That a regular system of hard labour is laid down, which is such that in cases of short sentences it must have a more deterring effect than imprisonment such as is carried out in the Devonport Borough Gaol.

That although naval prisoners will not be entirely separated from civil ones, the arrangements and surveillance is such as to prevent the possibility of their communicating or learning anything about their fellow prisoners.

There is a chaplain attached to the gaol, who has been there for several years, and devotes himself to his duties. The school is under his immediate direction.

Daily prayers are held in the chapel (which is divided into cells), and a regular service on Sundays.

A surgeon is also attached to the gaol.

Great care is taken of the clothing, which is of three different sorts; that for misdemeanours and naval and military offences being different to that of felons. Every attention seems to have been paid to its being thoroughly cleansed, if previously worn by other prisoners.

There are baths, in which the prisoners are thoroughly cleansed before being placed in prison clothing, and every prisoner is obliged to take one once a month.

In conclusion, we beg to remark that the treatment of prisoners at the Devonport Borough Gaol, being that of a reformatory nature, would not be likely to have so deterrent an effect as one where hard labour is carried out, especially on prisoners committed for short periods, and in our opinion is more suited for offenders against the civil than the naval and military law.

CHAPTER 20

Establishment of H. M. Naval Prison, Bodmin [37]

In a letter from the Admiralty to the Secretary of State at the Treasury, dated 18th December 1879, the Lords Commissioners of the Admiralty accepted an offer to convert part of the Borough Prison at Plymouth into a Naval Prison, on the understanding that the cost of making the separation would be £1500, to be paid out of naval funds. The proposed change would accommodate 56 naval prisoners and would include the building of a new Governor's house, accommodation for warders, new latrines, toilets and workshops. The Admiralty noted that if the number of prisoners exceeded 56, a new wing or an extension of the existing cells would be needed.

This conversion never happened. A much later document (Prison Commissioners Minute No. 78037, dated 16th April 1888) gave the following explanation:

Bodmin Prison – It was first proposed to let the Admiralty have a part of Plymouth Prison for a naval prison, on condition that they would give up possession after a twelve months notice. To this they demurred and suggested that (1) a two year notice should be given to them and (2) that all funds expended by them in improvements and extensions should be repaid to them.

The Home Office agreed to No.1 but the Treasury vetoed No.2. The Admiralty agreed to this. Consequently, it was decided to give the Admiralty a part of Bodmin Prison instead of Plymouth.

On 8th December 1880, the Admiralty instructed the Commander-in-Chief at Devonport to visit Bodmin Prison and to enquire into the accommodation that could be supplied. The Governor was instructed by the Prison Commissioners to accompany the C-in-C and to give him all the information he required. During the following year the Home Office was pressing the Admiralty for a decision on using part of Bodmin Prison as a Naval Prison but no action was taken.

Three years later, in March 1884, the Home Office sent the following letter to the Prison Commissioners:

Re: Admiralty

Make suggestions as to the provision in England of accommodation for Naval prisoners, who are to return to the Service, and, ask that a plan be transmitted to them shewing what portion of Bodmin Prison, containing no less than 60 cells could be transferred to them.

This order from the Home Office led to discussion among the Prison Commissioners about the numbers of cells that should be given over to the Naval authorities and those retained by the Civil Prison. It was suggested that up to 150 cells should be given up and only 83 retained as civil. It was also proposed that the spare cells could be given up to house both Naval and Military prisoners. It was pointed out that '*At the last return (September 1883?) there was in Bodmin, 122 males of which 50 were naval and marine.*' *This leaves 72 males including soldiers and 11 females.* From these numbers it was suggested than the Civil Prison should retain 100 cells for males and 20 for females.

To help the Commissioners, the actual prisoner returns and vacancies on the first twelve Tuesdays of 1884 were compiled. The results showed that the average population consisted of 35 males (civil), 11 females (civil) and 81 males (naval & military). This left about 30 male cells and 48 female cells empty. There were also 20 male and 5 female cells reserved in the Debtors block for debtors but these sleeping-cells were smaller than certified cells for prisoners.

It would appear that the objective of the Prison Commissioners was to reduce the size of their section of the prison to a minimum and thus save money. However it was pointed out that the Admiralty needed prison places for two different types of prisoner, that is, those discharged from the service and those returning to the service.

Date	Cells	Prisoners			Empty Cells *	
1884		M	F	Navy/Army	M	F
1st January	234	35	14	79	36	45
8th "	230	26	10	79	41	49
15th "	230	35	13	81	30	46
22nd "	230	34	13	86	26	46
29th "	230	32	12	83	31	47
5th February	230	28	11	87	31	48
12th "	230	42	10	87	17	49
19th "	230	41	13	84	21	46
26th "	230	42	11	87	17	48
4th March	230	43	11	79	24	48
11th "	230	36	10	79	31	49
18th "	230	28	10	66	52	49
Average		35.2	11.5	81.4	29.8	47.5

* Number of empty cells for criminals. It excludes 20 male & 5 female cells reserved for Debtors.

These two groups had to be housed in different institutions. In addition, the navy did not like sharing accommodation with soldiers. The Lords of the Admiralty also confirmed that they only wanted space for 60 prisoners in the new Naval Prison.

The Prison Commissioners decided to offer the Admiralty the Female prison and a large part of the Debtors prison. The Admiralty requested several new buildings and that additional buildings and services be transferred from the Civil authorities.

The following plans are two alternative schemes, both dated August, 1884.

196

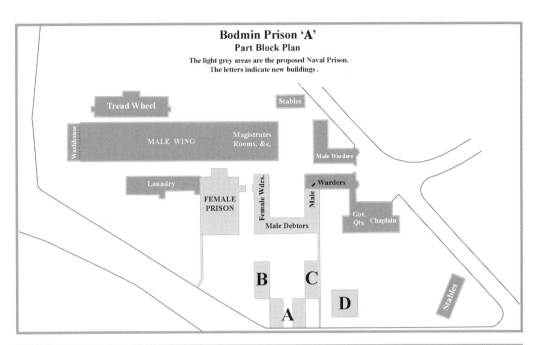

Bodmin Prison 'A'
Part Block Plan

The light grey areas are the proposed Naval Prison.
The letters indicate new buildings .

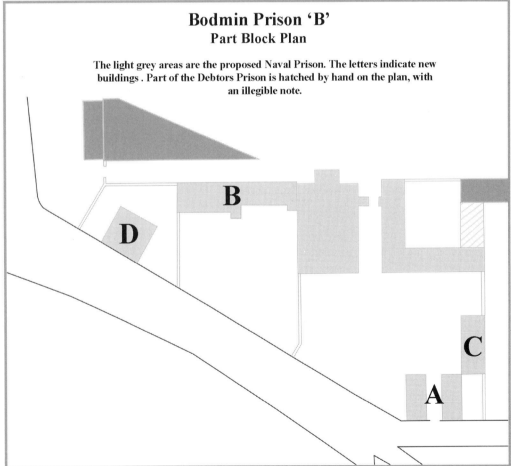

Bodmin Prison 'B'
Part Block Plan

The light grey areas are the proposed Naval Prison. The letters indicate new buildings . Part of the Debtors Prison is hatched by hand on the plan, with an illegible note.

The two different schemes, the costs involved and the final outcome of the discussions, as judged by later documentation, is contained in the table.

Building		Scheme 'A'	Scheme 'B'	Cost (£) 'A'	Cost (£) 'B'	Outcome
1	A	Gatekeepers lodge, reception, entrance and inner & outer gates		600	600	Built
2	B	Kitchen and Laundry (New)	Convert old female laundry	1000	600	Scheme B adopted
3	C	Offices for Governor, Clerk, chaplain etc.and stores		600	600	Set up in Debtors prison
4	D	Governors Residence (Civil Gov. Garden)	Governors Residence (near New Female wing)	1800	1800	Build on Flax Moor. Not Built.
5		WC's, Latrines, Coal Store.		200	200	Built onto building B
		Total		**4200**	**3800**	
Prisoner labour would reduce the totals to £3,050 and £2,730						

The use of prison labour would significantly reduce the building costs but it was thought unlikely that sufficient labour would be available. The scheme could be completed by contractors in twelve months but using prison labour it would be considerably longer.

The above information only covers the new buildings and major alterations. The were several other costs involved:

Naval Prison: (1) Cleaning and improving the interior of cells - £150
(2) Opening corridors and the lower ground floor - £250
(3) Joining the two naval prison blocks - £750
(4) Improving the Debtors sleeping cells - £100

Civil Prison: (1) Cut off cells for females at the end of the male block; Form rooms for female officers; New entrance and stairs; Convert washhouse into laundry/drying room; make passage from female prison to chapel; Make arrangements for Debtors/civil process prisoners in main block - £350
(2) Build wall to divide Civil from Admiralty Prison - £50

On 4th June 1885, the Prison Commissioners reported that: *'(the Admiralty) avail themselves of the offer of part of this* (Bodmin Prison) *as a Naval Prison, request the Prison Dept. to get on with the required alterations as* specified & charge to Naval Estimator & ask to be informed about date of completion as contracts for certain new buildings will be entered into by the Admiralty.'

Mr. W Stevens, Chief Warder in Charge, reported to the Home Office, *"I have this day, 15th August, 1887 handed over the Naval Prison buildings to the Superintending Civil Engineer"* (Mr. Frederic G Fisherden, Director, Admiralty Works Department, Devonport). The Naval Prison finally opened on 4th April, 1888, some thirteen years after the Hon. Henry Keppel called for a local Naval Prison.

The transfer of parts of the Civil Prison to the Admiralty did not go smoothly. In April 1888, a minute of the Prison Commissioners noted that '*There appears to be some objection to the Naval Governor seeing the Civil Prisoners from his seat in the gallery*'. There were several suggestions to solve the problem, including having separate services for the civil and naval prisoners, moving the naval governor's seat to the floor from the gallery and rebuilding the partitions in the gallery. This problem was addressed in a letter from the Admiralty to the Prison Commissioners but the letter also contained the following statement: '*The Admiralty submit that the prison should be considered as having been handed over to them for use as long as required and not as the Prison Commissioners suggest 'on loan''*.

Sir Edmund du Cane, Chairman of the Prison Commissioners, commented: '*It is absolutely necessary that there should be a clear understanding with the Admiralty in these matters, for the doctrine they lay down is quite inadmissible. Not only have we naturally all the rights of control over the prison which arise from its being our property and the duties which arise from the local authority being a contingent interest for which we are responsible, but we have to be careful of its security and general well being of the prison of which we retain possession. On no other terms than that of our retaining full power to secure our interest in the building set apart from Naval prisoners could it have been assigned for that purpose, and the confidence we had that reasonable and harmonious action was to be anticipated is shown in the whole course of the proceedings and especially in allowing the Naval prison authorities access inside our part of the prison for Divine Service.*

It seems to be forgotten that the prison was handed over instead of Plymouth Prison and of course on the same conditions as were laid down in that case though, naturally, it was not thought necessary to repeat them when the change was made.

As regards the proposed alteration of the seat for the Naval Governor we make no objection, but must be allowed to do the work ourselves, it being in our Chapel'.

These sentiments were formalised in a letter, shown on the next page, drafted by du Cane, dated June, 1888 (78037/89) from the Home Office to the Secretary of The Lords Commissioners of The Admiralty.

Letter from the Home Office to the Admiralty, June 1888

With reference to your letter of 7 April last enclosing a plan of a proposed improved entrance to the seat of the Naval Governor in Bodmin Prison Chapel, I am directed by the S. of S. to acquaint you for the Lords Commissioners of the Admiralty that he has no objection to this alteration being carried out, on the condition that the work be done by the Prison Commissioners the Chapel not forming part of the building handed over as a Naval Prison.

With regard to the first part of your letter the S. of S. is unable to concur with Their Lordships in the views expressed in that letter, as to the terms on which the prison has been handed over to the Admiralty, or as to their exclusive powers with regard to alterations of the part occupied by them.

Even if it were otherwise desirable the S. of S. has not the power, by reason of the tenure on which he holds the prison himself to allow the occupation of any part of it by the Admiralty otherwise than as a loan, on the same terms as were agreed on, in the case of Plymouth Prison for which Bodmin Prison was afterwards substituted.

I am also to point out to you that in consenting, on the recommendation of the Prison Commissioners, to afford the Admiralty the accommodation they desired, by permitting a part of Bodmin Prison to be appropriated as a Naval Prison, the S. of S. as well as the Commissioners assumed that they might rely on the willingness of the Admiralty to satisfy them, when necessary, that nothing would be done which might injuriously affect the responsibilities of the Prison Department or the interests they have charge of, but that harmonious action might be relied on between the departments and that the consideration which has been shewn for Naval interests would be fully reciprocated.

It would, otherwise, have been impossible to entertain the proposal that buildings so closely connected with the Civil Prison, and on which security and welfare must necessarily somewhat depend, should be, even temporarily placed beyond the direct control of the Prison Department and it was never supposed that there would be any objection on the part of the Admiralty to consult the Prison Commissioners and obtain their concurrence before undertaking any work or making any alterations in the buildings.

Arrangements such as are proposed have, for some years, been in force with the War Department, in regard to the occupation as Military Prisons of parts of several Civil Prisons, without giving rise to any difficulty, and the S. of S. trusts that the Admiralty may consent to follow a similar course.

Block Plan of H M Prison and H M Naval Prison, Bodmin (1888)

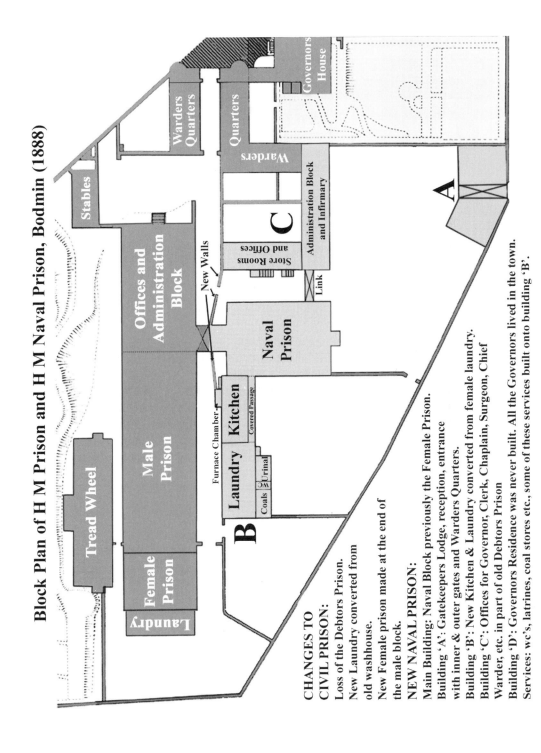

Tread Wheel

Female Prison

Laundry

Male Prison

Offices and Administration Block

Stables

Warders Quarters

Quarters

Warders

Governors House

Store Rooms and Offices

C

Administration Block and Infirmary

Link

New Walls

Furnace Chamber

Laundry

Kitchen

Covered Passage

Coals | WC | Urinal

B

Naval Prison

A

CHANGES TO
CIVIL PRISON:
Loss of the Debtors Prison.
New Laundry converted from
old washhouse.
New Female prison made at the end of
the male block.

NEW NAVAL PRISON:
Main Building: Naval Block previously the Female Prison.
Building 'A': Gatekeepers Lodge, reception, entrance
with inner & outer gates and Warders Quarters.
Building 'B': New Kitchen & Laundry converted from female laundry.
Building 'C': Offices for Governor, Clerk, Chaplain, Surgeon, Chief
Warder, etc. in part of old Debtors Prison
Building 'D': Governors Residence was never built. All the Governors lived in the town.
Services: wc's, latrines, coal stores etc., some of these services built onto building 'B'.

WILLIAM SOWDEN (1847-1936)
Warder, H.M. Naval Prison, Bodmin

William Sowden was born in 1847 at Antony *(Carbele)*, Cornwall. He was the youngest of the three children of Thomas Sowden and Mary Sowden Rodd.

On his 18th Birthday, 25th April, 1865, he joined the Royal Navy and signed-on for 10 years and, in 1875, he signed for a further 10 years. He was described on his service record as being 5' 5½" tall, with dark brown hair, brown eyes, dark complexion with a wound on left thigh. Details of his service record from 1865 to 1873 are missing. After 1873, he served on 11 ships, which included: *'Achilles'* Jan. 1873 – Mar. 1874; *'Defence'* from Feb. 1876 – Dec. 1879; *'Ganges'* Jan. 1880 – Apr. 1882 and his final ship *'Agincourt'*, from Oct. 1883 – Apr. 1885, when he left the service.

He was promoted from A B Seaman to Ships Corporal, 2nd Class on 29th Jan. 1876 and to Ships Corporal 1st Class on the 1st Dec. 1878. The position of Ships Corporal is unusual, it is best described as 'Ships Policeman', he would have been responsible for discipline and he would have reported to the Master-at-Arms. This job explains his short periods of service on a number of other ships including *'Cambridge'*; *'Duke of Wellington'* and *'Revenge'*. From 1873 to 1885, he spent seven periods of service on the flagship, *'Royal Adelaide'*, ranging from 3 days to three months. This could be connected with discipline problems on the ships or being present or giving evidence at Courts-Martial, which were held on the *'Royal Adelaide'*. The service on the *'Royal Adelaide'* could also include the transfer of convicted naval personnel from the Court to serve their sentence at Bodmin Gaol.

It is not known when he became a warder at Bodmin but it seems likely, given his previous experience, that he joined when the Naval Prison opened in 1888.

William was married to Anne Amelia Robert Selley in 1876 at Antony and they had ten children. He lived in Cornwall until 1927, when he went to live with his daughter Frances at llford, Essex. He died there on 3 February 1936 and he was brought back to Bodmin and buried with his wife in a family grave.

"It was during his time on HMS Ganges that according to his daughter Maud he liked a drink and was pushing one of the babies in a wicker pram along the quay at Mylor Bridge having imbibed overmuch when he managed to totter over the edge, pram and all! The cold water sobered him up and he was able to get both himself and the baby to safety but it shocked him so much that he never drank again and became a founder member of the temperance group, 'The Band of Hope' in Bodmin. He didn't smoke either according to Maud. He was by all accounts a very good living and sincere man."

Photograph by kind permission of Jan Carey, great granddaughter of William Sowden. Supplied by Gary James of Bodmin.

CHAPTER 21

Life in the Naval Prison [141, 142]

From the 1st November,1873, the county gaol had been used for the detention of navy and army personnel. In his letter to the Clerk of the Magistrates of Devonport, dated 26th October 1874, Admiral Keppel stated that Bodmin Gaol would only be abandoned in favour of 'a naval prison under our own jurisdiction'. It was in April 1887, some twelve years later, that a Naval Prison was set up by Admiralty Warrant. This resulted in the division of H.M. Prison, Bodmin into two separate prisons, H.M. Civil Prison and the new Naval Prison.

Under the 'Naval Discipline Act' only prisoners who were to remain in the service, were imprisoned in the naval prison. Those prisoners, whose sentence included dismissal from the navy, had to be held in a civil prison. This explains the presence of naval prisoners in the civil gaol even when the Naval Prison had space.

The stated philosophy of the prison system at that time was that every prisoner should be made to feel, during the whole period of his confinement, that his state and condition in prison was worse than when he is on active service. This meant a very hard life for the prisoners. They worked hard, received basic food, were frequently reminded of their sins by the Chaplain, discipline was severe and their daily life was ruled by the 'silent system'. The governor was instructed to make arrangements that prevented all intercourse or communication between prisoners, by word or sign, so far as the business of the prison or the labour of the prisoners will permit. When working in groups, always under the supervision of an officer, communication was strictly confined to the work on which they were employed. The main objective of this regime was to prevent re-offending.

The prisoners arrived at the prison any day except for Sunday, Christmas Day and Good Friday. They would be wearing prison travelling dress or, if in uniform, would carry the following clothes; cap, jacket, trousers, shirt, pair of socks, pair of boots, braces, a flannel waistcoat, cotton or flannel drawers and a greatcoat or cloak. Every prisoner was placed in a reception cell so that he may be strictly and minutely searched with all possible regard being paid to decency, his clothes would be cleaned or purified, if required. An inventory of his possessions would be made, he would take a bath, his hair would be cut close and he would dress in prison uniform. If his sentence was greater than one month, his whiskers, beard and moustache would be clipped but not so as to disfigure him. The following morning the prisoner would be weighed, examined by the Medical Officer and was read the rules relating to the conduct and treatment of prisoners.

Every prisoner was confined in a single cell. Each cell was certified by the inspector of Naval Prisons to be of the correct size, lighted, warmed, ventilated and furnished with a means of communicating with an officer at all times. The number or mark of each cell was contained in the certificate - any changes to the cell rendered the certificate, and therefore the cell, invalid.

Prisoners wore a complete prison dress with proper marks or badges distinguishing the progressive stage to which he belonged. Every prisoner had to wash himself carefully at least once a day, and his feet at least twice a week. Each Sunday and Thursday they would be issued with a clean shirt and socks. The prisoner was responsible for all items given to him from the prison stores, any damage or loss of the items, would be paid for by the prisoner on return to his ship. The prisoners were responsible for keeping their cells, utensils, clothing and bedding clean and neatly arranged. They also had to clean and sweep the yards, passages and other parts of the prison as directed. All prisoners were compelled to attend the morning and evening Divine Services on Sundays and to take religious instruction from the chaplain, except for prisoners of denominations other than the Established Church. They had to take instruction from a minister of that church. Each prisoner was given a Bible and Prayer Book approved for the denomination to which he belonged. Prisoners were also instructed in reading, writing and arithmetic.

Prisoners and Offences

At this time, very few prisoner details have been found. One return for 1st November 1873 to 6th February 1874 contains a list of 29 unnamed prisoners. The offences include; Desertion (11), Breaking Leave (8), Breaking out of ship and absence (6), Insubordination (3), Disobedience of orders (1), Drunk/asleep on duty (1), Smuggling liquor into ship (1) and Theft (1).

The Naval service records for individuals are now available on the National Archive website. The record for one sailor, Martin Nesbitt, contains sufficient information for his story to be told:

'Martin Nesbitt, born in Liverpool on 26th January, 1861, joined the Navy on the 10th July 1877, with the rank of Boy 2nd Class. (the £5 paid to him in Michaelmas 1877 was probably a joining award or gratuity). He served on 'Impregnable' until 25th July 1877 and then moved to 'Ganges'. He was promoted to Boy 1st Class on the 23rd October, 1878 and then things went bad. He ran away from his ship on the 21st December 1878 at Falmouth. He was found and sent to the 'Resistance' on the 19th June 1879 and moved back to 'Ganges' on the 29th June. The sentence was 90 days in gaol (probably at hard labour) and to be 'Discharged from the Service' as 'objectionable'. The other information on the record 'Date and Period of Engagement':- on reaching his 18th birthday he automatically started his 10 years of Navy Service. His service below the age of 18 did not count towards the 10 years. He received a gratuity of £2.10. 0d at Xmas 1878, when his adult service started. Whether this was paid before he ran away or when they caught him is not obvious!'

Rating.	Ship.	Offence.	Date of Committal.	No. Days.
Return of Naval Prisoners sent to the Cornwall County Gaol at Bodmin				
Ordinary	"Royal Adelaide"	Desertion from "Agincourt"	1 Nov. 1873	60
Able bodied	ditto	ditto "Hector"	1 Nov. 1873	90
Ordinary	ditto	ditto "Aurora"	15 Jan. 1874	30
Ordinary	"Valiant"	Breaking leave, disobedience of orders, and insubordination.	16 Jan. 1874	28
Ordinary	" Fantome "	Breaking out of ship, and absent 84 hrs.	17 Jan. 1874	42
Ordinary, 2nd class	ditto	ditto 202 hours	19 Jan. 1874	42
Stoker, 2nd class	"Indus"	Desertion from "Asia"	19 Jan. 1874	30
Gunner, R. M. A.	"Valiant"	Absence without leave, and breaking out of ship.	22 Jan. 1874	42
Ordinary	"Royal Adelaide"	Insubordination	22 Jan. 1874	42
Ordinary, 2nd class	ditto	Breaking leave	22 Jan. 1874	21
Ordinary	ditto	ditto	24 Jan. 1874	35
Private, R. M.	ditto	Desertion from "Sultan"	26 Jan. 1874	42
Private, R. M.	ditto	ditto "Agincourt"	26 Jan. 1874	60
Ordinary	"Ganges"	ditto "Reindeer"	28 Jan. 1874	60
Able bodied	"Modeste"	Insubordination	28 Jan. 1874	30
Gunner, R. M. A.	"Achilles"	Breaking out of ship, absence, in possession of comrade's coat.	28 Jan. 1874	42
Ordinary	"Royal Adelaide"	Breaking leave	28 Jan. 1874	28
Ordinary, 2nd class	ditto	Desertion	29 Jan. 1874	90
Ordinary	ditto	Quitting boat when on duty, and absence.	29 Jan. 1874	28
Ordinary	ditto	Breaking out of ship, and absence.	29 Jan. 1874	42
Ordinary, 2nd class	ditto	Desertion	29 Jan. 1874	60
Ordinary	ditto	Breaking leave	3 Feb. 1874	42
Private, R. M.	"Achilles"	Drunk and asleep while sentry	3 Feb. 1874	21
Able bodied	"Royal Adelaide"	Desertion from "Salamander"	6 Feb. 1874	61
Ordinary	"Royal Adelaide"	ditto "Duke of Wellington"	6 Feb. 1874	43
Cook's mate	"Implacable"	Smuggling liquor into ship	6 Feb. 1874	40
Cook's assistant	"Cambridge"	Breaking leave	6 Feb. 1874	29
Private, R. M.	"Achilles"	ditto	6 Feb. 1874	15
Private, R. M.	ditto	ditto	6 Feb. 1874	15

Period of Sentences awarded for Desertion are founded on previous character of Deserters, and circumstances under which the Desertions took place.

Employment of Prisoners

Prisoners were not employed on Sundays, Christmas Day, Good Friday and other days appointed as Public Fasts or Thanksgivings.

When naval prisoners were first imprisoned in the gaol they were employed under the same labour system as the civil prisoners. This 'five stage' system is very detailed and complex. In practice, for hard labour it meant 8 hours on the treadwheel and 2 hours rope picking. By gaining points for good behaviour they could progress through the stages, by the seventh month (stage 4), treadwheel was down to 4 hours and 'other employment', 6 hours. There were different diets for each stage and secular books and schooling were allowed at stage 3.

The following description of the treadwheel labour is taken from a Naval Inspector's Report: *The hours appropriated to treadwheel labour are eight, but the actual time on the wheel during the day is four; intervals of fifteen minutes being observed for alternate labour and rest. While unemployed the prisoner sits in a small compartment at the rear of his compartment at the wheel, which effectually prevents any oral communication, and also shuts out from sight each prisoner, after being marched at intervals, in single file, to the wheel gallery. A warder sits upon an elevated platform, regulates the relief by sound of clock, and effectually checks any intercourse, even a glance from right or left being a punishable offence.*

Labour Table for Convicted Prisoners 1874.					
Time	Class	Hard Labour First Class	Hard Labour Second Class	Not Hard Labour	Restrictions
14 days or less	1	Consists of work at treadwheel, shot drill, crank, hand cornmill, stone breaking, rope or oakum beating, mat making, with heavy looms. May be placed on treadwheel, crank, hand cornmill, or stone breaking, eight hours; two hours' rope picking, ¾lb.	Consists of oakum or coir picking, mat making, cleaning the prison, chimney sweeping, oakum packing, digging, pulling down buildings, bricklayers' or masons' labourers' work ; ten hours' rope picking, 4½ lbs., if not at treadwheel or other labour of second class above.	10 hours' oakum picking, 7lbs.; 1 hrs. airing	If previously convicted, to sleep on plank bed, whole period, without mattress.
> 14 days less than 1 month.	2	Ditto	Ditto	Ditto	Ditto
> 1 month less than 2 months	3	Eight hours' treadwheel. &c.; two hours' rope picking, ¾lb	Ditto	10 hours' oakum picking, 6½lbs.; 1 hrs. airing	If previously convicted, no slates, or secular books, or schooling advantages.
> 2 months less than 6 months.	4	Up to end of third month, 8 hours' treadwheel, &c., and 2 hours rope picking, ¾lb: after third month, six hours treadwheel, and 4 hours other labour of second class.	Six hours rope picking, 3lbs. or other labour of second class, as above.	10 hours' industrial labour or other employment.	Ditto
Greater than 6 months.	5	Seventh up to end of 12th month, four hours' tread-wheel, six hours' other employment, remainder of sentence. two hours' treadwheel, &c.; eight hours' other employment.	Four hours' rope picking, 2 lbs., six hours' other employment of second class, as above ; two hours' rope picking. 1 lb. ; eight hours' other employment of second class.	Ditto	Ditto

Four Stage System

The 'Five Stage System' was later refined to a 'Four Stage System'.

Hard labour of the first class consisted of work at the shot drill, crank, capstan, stone breaking, oakum picking and any other bodily labour as may be appointed. This type of hard labour was any boring, repetitive task, which had no useful purpose. It was designed, in addition to the silent system, to break the spirit of the prisoners. Second class hard labour was defined as any bodily labour which may be appointed but it should be to the best advantage of the public service. A few prisoners of the second hard labour class, as a reward for industry and good behaviour, could be employed in the necessary services of the prison but not as warder or messenger. They were also eligible for special employment for which their services were required. The Medical Officer examined every prisoner to see if he was mentally and physically fit for the work assigned. He also, from time to time, would examine the prisoners and report the names of *those 'whose health is endangered by a continuation of hard labour of a particular kind'.*

Prisoners with sentences of over 28 days entered the four stage progressive system, which was associated with length and type of work and privileges. The time spent in each stage was governed by a system of marks. A prisoner earned 6, 7 or 8 marks each working day depending on his industry. On Sunday, he was awarded with the average number of marks earned during the previous week. He remained in the first stage until he had earned 28 x 8 (224) marks. The same number of marks was required for the transitions from stage 2 to 3 and 3 to 4. The prisoner would remain in the 4th stage until his release. Any prisoner, who was idle, misconducted himself or who was inattentive to instruction, was liable to forfeit stage privileges, be detained in the stage for longer or be placed in a lower stage for a specific period.

The 1892 'Regulations for Naval Prisons', describes the rules for each of the four stages. First class hard labour was only used in stage 1 and was replaced by second class hard labour for stages 2, 3 and 4. The length of the working day was gradually reduced from 10 hours (stage 1) to 8 hours (stage 4). In stage 1, the prisoner slept on a plank with no mattress, was not allowed books in his cell, lessons, exercise, library books, letters or visits. These privileges were gradually introduced in the higher stages.

1892	!st Stage	2nd Stage	3rd Stage	4th Stage
Work (hrs./day)	10	9	8.5	8
Type of Work	1st. Class h. l.. Strict separation	2nd. Class h. l.. Strict separation	2nd. Class h. l. Strict separation	2nd. Class h. l.. Strict separation
Bed	Plank	Mattress (5 days)	Mattress (6 days)	Mattress
Books in Cell	No	School / Religious	School / Religious	School / Religious
Lessons	No	No	3 hr./week	6 hr./week
Exercise	No	Daily	Daily	Daily
Library Books	No	No	Yes	Yes
Letters	No	No	No	1in + 1out
Visits	No	No	No	30min. Month
1900				
Work (hrs./day)	10hr.	10hr.	10hr.	10hr.
Type of Work	Hard labour. Strict separation.	Less hard labour. Some association.	Less hard labour. Some association.	Less hard labour. Some association.
Bed	Plank (14 days)	Mattress	Mattress	Mattress
Books in Cell	School / Religious	School / Religious	School / Religious	School / Religious
Lessons	No	Yes	>4hr./week	>4hr./week
Exercise	No	Daily	Daily	Daily
Library Books	No	1/week	2/week	2/week
Letters	No	No	1in + 1out	1in + 1out
Visits	No	No	20min. Month	30min. Month

In 1900, the regulations were changed to bring them into line with the regime in the Civil prison. The working day was 10 hours for all prisoners but hard labour was still restricted to stage 1. The plank was replaced by a mattress after the first fourteen days. The privileges, including library books, receiving and writing letters and visits were introduced at an earlier stage.

The scheme is a daily plan for Naval Prisons which have no treadwheel or crank (1892). The scheme demonstrates the improvement in prison life for those who have progressed in the four stage system.

	WEEKDAYS
A.M.	
5.45	Bell rings to warn Officers to duty.
6.00	Officers come on duty. Prisoners rise, empty slops, spread out bedding to air, &c.
6.30	Labour commences. 1st stage prisoners pick oakum in cells 2nd, 3rd, and 4th stages, labour.
8.00	Labour ceases. Prisoners to cells for breakfast. Stow bedding, &c. Officers to breakfast, except patrols.
8.50	Officers return to duty. Patrols to breakfast.
8.55	Bell for prayers.
9.00	Prayers.
9.30	Labour recommences. 1st stage prisoners
	Pick oakum in cells 9.30 to 10.15
	Shot drill 10.15 to 11.45
	Other stages.
	Exercise 9.30 to 10.00
	Labour 10.00 to 11.45
11.45	Labour ceases. Prisoners to cells for dinner.
12.00	Prisoners dinner. Officers to dinner, except Patrols.
P.M.	
1.00	Officers return, to duty. Patrols to dinner till 2. Labour recommences. 1st stage prisoners
	Pick oakum in cells 1.00 to 2.30
	1st stage prisoners
	Shot drill 2.30 to 4.00
	1st stage prisoners
	Pick oakum in cells 4.00 to 5.35
	2nd, 3rd and 4th stages,
	Exercise 1.00 to 1.30
	2nd, 3rd and 4th stages,
	Labour 1.30 to 5.35
4.00	Night duty Officers to tea, returning at 5.45.
5.35	Labour ceases. Prisoners to cells for

6.00	Officers go off duty, except those on night duty. Labour recommences in cells picking oakum.
	1st and 2nd stages 6.0 to 7.45
	3rd stage, 3 nights a week 6.0 to 7.45
	3rd stage, 3 nights a week 6.0 to 6.45
	4th stage 6.0 to 6.45
6.45	School for 3rd and 4th stages.
	3rd stage, 3 nights a week 6.45 to 7.45
	4th stage, every night 6.45 to 7.45
7.45	Labour and school cease. Task performed in cells given out, cells cleaned, beds made.
8.00	Prisoners to bed. Lights out.
	SUNDAYS
A.M.	
6.15	Bell rings to warn Officers to duty.
6.30	Officers come on duty. Prisoners rise, &c.
8.00	Prisoners' breakfast. Officers to breakfast, except Patrols.
9.00	Officers return to duty. Patrols to Breakfast.
9.55	2nd, 3rd, and 4th stage prisoners, exercise.
10.25	Bell for Divine Service.,
10.30	Divine Service.
12.00	Prisoners' dinner. Officers to dinner, except Patrols.
P.M.	
1.30	Officers return to duty. Patrols to dinner.
2.25	2nd, 3rd, and 4th stage prisoners, Exercise.
2.55	Bell for Divine Service.
3.00	Divine Service.
4.00	Prisoners to cells.
4.30	Night Duty Officers to tea.
5.00	Prisoners' supper.
5.30	Officers go off duty. Those for night duty return.
8.00	Prisoners to bed. Lights out.

The first stage prisoners worked from 6.30 to 8.00, 9.30 to 11.45, 1.00 to 5.35 and 6.00 to 7.45. The only breaks from the repetitive hard labour were for meals. The higher stage prisoners had more varied work, apart from the evening oakum picking, and two half-hour exercise periods a day. In addition, the 3rd and 4th stage prisoners had the evening school lessons. Sunday, apart from the two Divine Services, was a rest day for all.

The early County Gaol and later, Naval Prison, Regulations, contain 'Shot Drill' as an option for Hard Labour. In the *'Time Table of Daily Duties'* it is included for 1st Stage prisoners.

Shot Drill

Shot exercise performed with a 24lb shot. The shot was placed in two lines, or in the form of a rectangle, from six to eight paces apart. The men fell in, each with a shot in front of him. On a given word, the men stoop and lift the shot, so that the elbows and shot should be level with the hips, and move briskly to the next position. On a signal, the shot is placed on the floor, the man comes to attention, and, on command, marches back to his original position. This procedure is repeated for a period of 1.5hrs. The maximum for shot exercise is 3 hours per day.

The whole of this exercise was timed. For example, if the shot was placed six paces apart, the shot was moved at a rate of 5 per minute. This meant that 1,800 paces were marched with the shot and 1,800 paces without shot in one hour.

This exercise was changed to a punishment by increasing the shot weight to 32lbs. and changing the routine so that the prisoner did not march back to his original position but always continued to the next position. In the above example, this meant that the prisoner carried the shot for 3,600 paces in one hour.

Prisoners were permitted in warm weather to remove their jackets. If a prisoner stopped during the exercise, he was to continue for 10 minutes, for each stop, after the class was dismissed, unless the Medical Officer certified that it was unavoidable.

Table showing the Distance each Man must march in moving Shot.				
Number of Paces between the Shot.	Number of Shot moved in a Minute.	Number of Paces per Hour marched with a Shot.	Number of Paces marched per Hour without a Shot.	Whole Distance marched in the Hour. (Paces.)
3	6	1,080	1,080	2,160
4	6	1,440	1,440	2,880
5	4	1,200	1,200	2,400
6	4	1,440	1,440	2,880
5	5	1,500	1,500	3,000
6	5	1,800	1,800	3,600
Shot exercise may be made more severe, either by increasing the weight of the shot to 32 lbs., or by working, as in Exercise No. 4, the prisoners always having a shot in the hand when moving.				

The Naval Prison Dietary (1892 & 1900)

The following tables contain the prisoners' diets for use in Naval Prisons in England. The diet basically consisted of a breakfast consisting of oatmeal and milk, a dinner of pea or lentil flour with milk and supper of bread and milk. The basic diet was augmented, for prisoners on hard labour, by the addition of meat meals, which consisted of beef without bone, potatoes or bread, soup thickened with oatmeal and seasoned vegetables. The number of beef dinners and the quantity of some items was dependant on the length of the sentence.

SCALE 1	SCALE 2
Dietary for first 28 days for all Prisoners undergoing hard labour, except those sentenced to 6 months or more, who will commence on Scale 2.	Dietary for after 28 days for all Prisoners undergoing hard labour, including those sentenced to 6 months or more, who will commence on this Scale.
Breakfast **Daily** { 8oz. Oatmeal / ½ pint milk	**Breakfast** **Daily** { 8 oz. Oatmeal / ½ pint milk
Dinner { **Tuesday Thursday** { 8oz. beef without bone, 1lb. of potatoes or 8 oz. bread, 1 pint of soup containing 1oz. of oatmeal, 2 oz. of vegetables seasoned with pepper / salt. **Other days** { 9oz. pea or lentil flour. / ½ pint milk	**Dinner** { **Sunday Tuesday Thursday** { 8 oz. beef without bone, 1lb of potatoes or 8 oz. bread, 1 pint of soup containing 1oz. of oatmeal, 2 oz. of vegetables seasoned with pepper / salt. **Other days** { 9oz. pea or lentil flour. / ½ pint milk
Supper { **Tuesday Thursday** { 8 oz. bread / ½ pint milk **Other days** { 12 oz. bread / ½ pint milk	**Supper** { **Sunday Tuesday Thursday** } 8 oz. bread / ½ pint milk **Other days** { 12 oz. bread / ½ pint milk

SCALE 3	SCALE 4
Dietary after 56 days for all Prisoners undergoing hard labour, including those sentenced to 6 months or more, who will come on to this scale after 28 days.	Dietary of Prisoners not employed at severe hard labour.
This scale is the same as Scale 2 with the following changes: Breakfast: 10 oz. Oatmeal on 4 days. Dinner: 12 oz. of pea or lentil flour on 4 days. On Sunday, prisoners in the fourth progressive stage may have 10 oz. of beef without bone before cooking, instead of 8 oz.	**Breakfast** **Daily** { 8 oz. Oatmeal / ½ pint milk **Dinner** **Daily** { 6 or 9 oz.* pea or lentil flour. / ½ pint milk **Supper** **Daily** { 8 or 12 oz.* bread / ½ pint milk * The lower quantity is for prisoners sentenced to less than 56 days. The higher numbers for sentences above 56 days. If the sentence exceeds three months, one meat dinner per week may be allowed to men placed on this scale.

When it is deemed necessary for the health of prisoners, the Medical Officer may substitute bread for oatmeal, or pea or lentil flour. 10 oz. bread for 8 oz. oatmeal. 12 oz. bread for 9 oz. of pea or lentil flour and 8 oz bread for 6 oz. of pea or lentil flour.

210

The dietary shows the increase in the meat ration for naval prisoners over civil prisoners. In the last chapter, the issue of the state of naval prisoners on release and the corresponding diets were discussed. The Lords of the Admiralty ordered a 5oz. increase in the meat ration in each case where it is allowed to naval prisoners. In the above diet it was increased by 6 ozs. An identical dietary was published in 1900.

Punishment Diet in Naval Prisons

The standard punishment diet was 1 lb. of bread daily and any quantity of water that the prisoner wanted. This diet was limited to 3 days, for longer periods the following diets were used:

No. 1 SCALE:
When given for more than three days it consists of (a) 1 lb. bread *per diem* with water and (b) the ordinary diet of the prison, for alternate equal periods not exceeding three days in duration. Thus, if the prisoner was sentenced to the No.1 scale for twelve days, he would be on bread and water for a total of six days, the bread and water days alternating with the ordinary diet in periods of one, two or three days, at the discretion of the Governor. The No. 1 scale may be ordered for any single term not exceeding 18 days. The prisoner will not work on the bread and water days.

No. 2 SCALE
For prisoners not tasked at any labour: *Stirabout Diet.*
> Breakfast: Bread, 8 ounces.
> Dinner: 1 pint stirabout, containing 2 oz. oatmeal;
> 2 oz. pea or lentil flour; salt; potatoes 8 oz.
> Supper: Bread, 8 oz.

When the No. 2 scale is ordered for a period exceeding 21 days, it is to consist of the No.2 diet for the first three weeks and after the fourth week. During the fourth week the prisoner is to receive the ordinary prison diet. The entire period for which the No.2 diet is ordered is not to exceed 42 days.

No. 3 SCALE
For prisoners performing a daily task of labour:
> *Full Stirabout Diet.*

As No. 2 scale, except Dinner: 1½ pint stirabout containing 3 oz. oatmeal and 3 oz. of pea or lentil flour; salt; potatoes 8 oz. and bread 8 oz.
When the No. 3 scale is ordered for a period exceeding 42 days, it is to consist of the No.3 diet for the first six weeks and after the eighth week. During the interval of 14 days the prisoner is to receive the ordinary prison diet. The entire period for which the No.3 diet is ordered is not to exceed 84 days.

Prison Offences and Punishments

The Naval Prison Rules (1892) contained the following 'Principles to be observed in the award of punishments':

Experience having shown that discipline is not better maintained by commonly resorting to severe punishments, such punishments should be reserved for use when milder means have been tried unsuccessfully, and when it is necessary to apply them on particular occasions.

It should also be borne in mind that many prisoners who have for the first time been brought under prison discipline are liable to commit offences from imperfect knowledge or understanding of what is required of them, and these offences, or the repetition of them, may be better prevented by instructing them, and causing the Officers to clearly and patiently explain the regulations or orders to which they are expected to conform, than by the too ready resort to the infliction of punishment.

The Rules also stated that no punishments should be awarded except by the Governor or one or more Visitors and that no prisoner should be punished until he has heard the charges and evidence against him.

The Governor had the power to hear complaints against prisoners accused of the following offences against prison discipline:-

1. Disobedience of the prison regulations;
2. Common assaults by one prisoner on another;
3. Cursing and swearing;
4. Indecent behaviour;
5. Irreverent behaviour in Chapel;
6. Insulting or threatening language to any Officer or prisoner;
7. Absence from Chapel without leave;
8. Idleness or negligence at work;
9. Wilful mismanagement of work.

The Governor could award the following punishments:—

1. Confinement in a punishment cell. *Not to exceed 24 hours.*
2. Reduction of diet. *Limited to No.1 diet for 3 days, No.2 for 21 days and No.3 for 42 days. The highest level being reserved only for the gravest kinds of misconduct.*
3. Degradation to a lower stage. *Not to exceed 14 days.*
4. Prolongation of period in a stage. *Not to exceed 14 days.*
5. Deprivation of stage privileges.
6. Placing in irons, or other mechanical restraint. *This includes Handcuffs, Loose Canvas Restraint Jacket, Leg Chains or Cross Irons, Body Belt or Light Steel Connecting Chains. If the restraint was used for over 24 hours a written order from a Visitor was required, stating the cause for the restraint, the time that the prisoner was to be kept in irons and, in the case of handcuffs, whether they are to be kept in front or behind.*

The Visitors could award the following punishments:—

1(a) Imprisonment for offences under Sect. 82 Naval Discipline Act.
This section covered interruption of a Prison Officer in the execution of his duty, or aiding or inciting any person to assault, resist or interrupt any

such Officer. *This case was heard before at least three of the Visitors or two Justices of the peace. The sentence was up to 6 months, with or without hard labour, provided that the sentence together with former sentence should not exceed a total period of two consecutive years imprisonment.*

(b) Corporal punishment.
The following offences rendered prisoners to corporal punishment:—
Mutiny, or open incitement to mutiny in the prison; Personal violence to any Officer of the prison; Aggravated or repeated assault on a fellow prisoner; Repetition of insulting or threatening language to any Officer or prisoner; Wilfully and maliciously breaking the prison windows, or otherwise destroying the prison property; When under punishment, wilfully making a disturbance tending to interrupt the order and discipline of the prison; And any other act of gross misconduct or insubordination requiring to be suppressed by extraordinary means.
Corporal punishment was inflicted with a cat-o'-nine tails or, in the case of a boy under 18, with a birch rod, and the instruments in both instances had to be of a pattern approved by the Admiralty. The punishment should not exceed 25 lashes or strokes.

The Visitors could also award:—

2 (a) Confinement in a punishment cell. *Not to exceed 14 days.*
(b) Degradation to a lower stage. *Not to exceed 28 days.*
(c) Prolongation of period in a stage. *Not to exceed 28 days.*

By 1900, the number of prison offences had increased to seventeen.

1. Disobeys any order of the governor or of any other officer, or any prison regulation.
2. Treats with disrespect any officer or servant of the prison, or any visitor, or any person employed in connexion with the prison or works.
3. Is idle, careless, or negligent at work, or refuses to work.
4. Is absent without leave from divine service, or prayers, or school instruction.
5. Behaves irreverently at divine service or prayers.
6. Swears, curses, or uses any abusive, insolent, threatening, or other improper language.
7. Is indecent in language, act, or gesture.
8. Commits a common, assault upon another prisoner.
9. Converses or holds intercourse with another prisoner without authority.
10. Sings, whistles, or makes any unnecessary noise, or gives any unnecessary trouble.
11. Leaves his cell or other appointed location, or his place of work, without permission.
12. In any way disfigures or damages any part of the prison, or any article to which he may have access.
13. Commits any nuisance.
14. Has in his cell or possession any article he is not allowed to have.
15. Gives to or receives from any prisoner any article whatever without leave.
16. In any other way offends against good order and discipline.
17. Attempts to do any of the foregoing things.

All the above punishments were still used and, in addition, the governor could deprive an idle prisoner of his mattress for three days. Some offences could now result in forfeiture of seven days remission.

For the more serious offences, including personal violence to a fellow prisoner: grossly offensive or abusive language to any officer or servant of the prison; wilfully or wantonly breaking the prison windows, or otherwise destroying the prison property; when under punishment, wilfully making a disturbance tending to interrupt the order and discipline of the prison; any other act of gross misconduct or insubordination requiring to be suppressed by extraordinary means or escaping or attempting to escape from prison; the Visitors could order the same punishments as in 1892 but the severity of the punishments was increased. For example, the limits on reduction of diet had changed to: Diet No.1 for 15 days; No.2 for 42 days and No.3 for 84 days. Corporal punishment was still available for serious offences, for example mutiny, but the Admiralty had to be informed. The maximum number of strokes inflicted on the prisoner had increased from 25 strokes to 36.

Discharge of Prisoners

A prisoner was discharged from prison at 7 a.m. on the day on which his sentence expired, except when that happened on a Sunday, Christmas Day or Good Friday, In that case, he was discharged on the previous day at an hour that would enable the Officer in charge of him to return to his duty on the same evening. Before his discharge a prisoner was examined by the Medical Officer and his state of health recorded. He also examined prisoners about to transfer to another place of confinement. In this case he would certify that the prisoner was free from malignant or infectious disease and in a fit state to be moved. On his discharge to his Ship or Division, a report on the prisoner's conduct was made to his Commanding Officer.

Part of a Civil Prison discharge document recording two naval prisoners who were D.S. (discharged from the Service). *Bodmin Town Museum*

The prisoner would receive the letters sent to him during his time in custody with his other property, unless the Visitor should approve of the Governor withholding them on account of their content.

214

CHAPTER 22

Closure of the Prisons

In the early twentieth century, although the gaol was still occupied by vagrants and people gaoled for non payment of fines, the number of serious criminals committed was falling rapidly. In 1901, there was only one woman in the female prison and by 1908, there were no female warders employed. Female prisoners were cared for by the wives of the warders.[128] The female part of the gaol was closed on the 31st March, 1911, when the female prisoners were sent to Plymouth.[143]

With the outbreak of the First World War, both criminals and prison staff were encouraged to join the services in the war effort. This further reduced the need for the prison at Bodmin. On the 21st March, 1915, the Secretary of the Prison Commission, wrote to the Admiralty: *'I am desired by the Prison Commissioners to inform you that owing to the low number of persons now being committed to prison they have made arrangements to temporarily close the establishment at Bodmin on the 1st June next. In these circumstances the Commissioners will be glad to know whether the Admiralty would like to have the loan of the building as a naval prison.'* [144]

The Admiralty declined the offer even though Mr. Brandreth, the Deputy Governor of the Naval Prison, highlighted some problems with the closure: the capacity would have to be reduced to 90 cells as the other cells would be required for manufacturing purposes, which were being carried out in the civil buildings; the 'Chapel problem', although the naval prisoners entered the chapel gallery by a direct route from the Naval Prison, the Chaplain entered from the Civil prison; and all the heating and lighting was supplied from the civil prison.

The Admiralty was not convinced that they could afford the extra cost of taking over the civil section and the old practice of separating naval prisoners into those who were to remain in Service being segregated from those dismissed the service was breaking down. Prisoners remaining in the service after serving their sentences were being sent to civil prisons in Ipswich and Canterbury, rather than the Naval Prison at Bodmin. The civil prison was closed in June 1916. Prisoners were later sent to Plymouth or Exeter.

The gaol was used for storage of documents of national importance during WWI. The Bodmin Research Project quotes from a letter dated 28th April, 1919, from Anthony Story Maskelyne, Assistant Keeper of Public Records.

'Upon information personally conveyed by the Permanent Head of the Office of Works 7th December 1917 to the Deputy Keeper of the Public Records, of facts in possession of the Government as to German designs upon London, the Master of the Rolls sanctioned the removal of the bulk of the Records to places of safety. That various prisons then vacant were put at the disposal of the

Record Office; that Bodmin was selected and a small Committee sat to decide what should be sent there; that the three first out of 24 pantechnicon van loads arrived via LSWR in charge of Mr. Joseph Pratt, 5 Feb 1918, consigned to the care of an Assistant keeper of Public Records sent down to receive them. The last van loads left Bodmin on their return journey 25th Feb 1919. The selection sent consisted both of State Papers and Records. The heating was cut off from the Prisons, the climate was not a suitable one, but it is considered that while traces of mildew are in evidence, the books and rolls have suffered no permanent damage'.

There are reports that claim that great works of Art and the Crown Jewels were stored in Bodmin Prison but *'The Tower of London'* website states that the Crown Jewels only left London during the Second World War. The index[145] listing all of the medieval and state records, included the Domesday Book, which were stored in the prison contains details of 3,418 bundles, about 19,600 items. Some details of this very important collection are contained in Appendix 9.

The Naval Prison continued for a time and in 1919,[146] over fifty out of 100 naval men who appear to have given trouble in North Russia were lodged in the gaol. According to the men's version, they had been sixteen hours in action without food, protested in some form and were court-martialled at Murmansk. Some were sentenced for up to five years imprisonment.

The Naval Prison was handed back to the Prison Commissioners on the 31st March, 1922.[147] The caretaker of the Civil Prison, ex Chief Officer Green, was instructed to take over the Naval Prison on behalf of the Commissioners.

PRISON (ENGLAND AND WALES).

40 and 41 Vict., c. 21.

Order made by the Secretary of State for the discontinuance of Bodmin Prison.

WHEREAS the number of prisoners confined in Bodmin Prison (being the only prison within the County of Cornwall) is usually very small:

AND WHEREAS there are other prisons which can be conveniently used for the confinement of prisoners from the County of Cornwall:

NOW, THEREFORE, in pursuance of the powers vested in me by the above Act, I, the Right Honourable Sir William Joynson-Hicks, Baronet, one of His Majesty's Principal Secretaries of State, do hereby, for the reasons aforesaid, order that the said Prison at Bodmin shall be discontinued from this date.

(signed) W. Joynson Hicks

147788/33.
WHITEHALL.
18th March, 1927.

Little happened to the buildings until, in April, 1926, Mr. G J C Harrison, MP, asked a question of the Secretary of State about the future of the prison. At first the Commissioners suggested keeping it but later in the same year they asked the Secretary of State to discontinue the prison by Order under Section 33 of the *Prisons Act 1877*. They claimed that there was no likelihood of the prison being required and that maintenance would become a considerable charge on public funds.

A new arrangement for prisoners was in place. All Cornish prisoners were housed in Plymouth and when Plymouth became over-crowded, non-Cornish prisoners were transferred to Exeter, which had ample surplus accommodation. The Order for discontinuance of Bodmin Prison was issued on the 18th March, 1927.

The Home Office offered the prison to Cornwall County Council, who were the former prison authority, at the statutory price of £11,186.8.0. The response was that *'the Council cannot entertain such an offer.'* The sale of the prison was arranged by the 'Directorate of Lands of the War Office and Air Ministry'. On the 9th March, 1928, one bundle of Deeds, and one roll of drawings were delivered by hand to the Comptroller of Lands at the War Office. The Deeds consisted of about 70 documents, including leases, conveyances and agreements dated from 1758 to 1924. Twenty of the documents, dated 1917 to 1924, were agreements for the renting of the Naval Quarters, Governor's House, Chaplaincy, Warder's Quarters (No.1 to No.6) and a few of the allotments. There were over 60 individual drawings and plans of parts of the prison on large drawings (numbered 1, 2, 4, 5 and 6).

When preparing documents for the sale, several issues were raised by the *Directorate of Lands*. Most queries related to fixtures and fittings in the rented houses, agreements with regards to water and gas charges and tenancy agreements but one serious issue was the removal of the remains of executed criminals buried within the prison area. Most of the queries were settled by the Prison Commissioners but they stated that *'No record can be found of executed prisoners having been buried in Bodmin Prison'.* This statement is untrue. By law, executed criminals had to be buried inside the prison walls and there are several reports of graves being present in a closed-off section of the garden.

The auction sale of the Prison, as 19 separate lots, was organised by D. Ward & Son and took place at the Royal Hotel, Bodmin at 3pm on Thursday 7th February, 1929. All lots were sold and the auction raised a total of £4,340.

G. R.

By Direction of the Prison Commissioners

PLAN, PARTICULARS AND CONDITIONS OF SALE
of the Important FREEHOLD Property comprising

H.M. PRISON

Two Residences, Eight Dwelling Houses
and Allotment Land

situate at

BODMIN, CORNWALL

which, unless previously disposed of by private treaty, will be

OFFERED FOR SALE BY PUBLIC AUCTION

in 19 Lots

by

Messrs. D. WARD & SON, F.S.I.

at THE ROYAL HOTEL, BODMIN, at 3 p.m. on Thursday, the 7th day of February, 1929, subject to the General Conditions of 1925 issued by the Law Society, as adopted by the Incorporated Law Society of Plymouth, and to the following Special Conditions.

Lot	Description	Sold to:	For:
1	Gaol & Land	Mr. A.S.Lee	1050
2,3	Governors & Chaplains Houses	Mr. G. Hellen	1250
4	Naval Quarters	Mr. J.H. Harney	300
5,18,19	Naval Quarters + 2 allotments	Capt. S. Warne	275
6	No. 1 Quarters	Mr. E. Dangerfield	250
7	No. 2 Quarters	Mr. W. Williams	220
8	No. 3 Quarters	Mr. J.C. Morrison	235
9	No. 4 Quarters	Mr. A. James	220
10	No. 5 Quarters	Mrs. M.J. Peters	230
11	No. 6 Quarters	Mr. W. Bound	230
12-17	Allotments	Mr. A. Jago	80
Total			**£4,340**

Mr. E Dangerfield rented No.1 Quarters from 31st July, 1922 at a rent of 7/9d per week. On 15th October 1927, he was employed as caretaker of the prison and lived rent free. He bought the property in the sale, however, as the prison had now been sold, his employment was terminated on the 31st March 1929, the completion date.

The Prison buildings were sold to Mr. A S Lee of Ipswich for 1,000 guineas (£1,050). The Governor's House and the Chaplaincy raised £1,250, the Naval Villas and the six Warder's houses (£200-300 each) were sold individually and became private residences. Mr. Lee intended to demolish the prison buildings, sell the valuable slate, stone, granite, lead, fixtures and fittings and to make use of the cleared site.[148] The roofs and floors were removed from all buildings, except for the administration building, and all fittings including the slate galleries, cell doors, the pews and all other contents of the buildings were removed and sold.

(F.G. Stone Collection)

Bodmin Gaol ca.1930.
The roof of the Debtor's Prison and a section of the main wall have been removed. The slates on the 'Old Quarters' are being taken off but the main blocks still seem to be intact.

Attempted demolition of building walls was not a success, the lime mortar used in the building had fused with the granite stones and rather than breaking to give clean usable stone blocks, it resulted in useless pieces of rubble. There are reports that explosives were used but again this gave no useful saleable building materials. This failure to make a profit from the stone resulted in the main buildings still being present today.

Mr. Lee decided to open the buildings to the public and organised 'mock hangings',[149] this was not popular with some locals who considered such exhibitions in bad taste.[150]

The chapel was converted into a games room and was used by Bodmin Badminton Club in 1930.[151]

The OLD PRISON, BODMIN

GREAT ATTRACTION!

MOCK EXECUTIONS

will be carried out 4 times Daily, 11 - 30 a.m., 2 p.m., 4 and 6 p.m.

☞ **Come and See how it is Done.**

Just Discovered—TWO DUNGEONS

ADMISSION : ONE SHILLING (Tax Paid).

ALL THE OTHER ATTRACTIONS AS USUAL.

Executions will Start on
WHIT-SATURDAY, JUNE 7th, 1930.

Sir,

May I ask for the favour of a small space in your paper to lodge a strong protest against a poster which is being displayed on our public hoardings advertising "mock executions" at the Old Prison.

That "the last dread penalty of the law" should be burlesqued in this manner is an offence against all the canons of public decency and can only call forth the severest condemnation of all right-thinking persons.

I trust that public opinion will express itself so strongly that this disgraceful and indecent exhibition will be prevented and that those who are responsible for the idea, and who are, presumably, hoping to make financial gain out of it, may be made to feel thoroughly ashamed of themselves.

JOHN B. WILKINSON   County School, Bodmin.   June 2nd, 1930.

Sir ,

With reference to the letters in last week's "Guardian" I would like to point out that there is no difference between the mock executions and a real execution with the exceptions that a dummy is used in the former. As the £100 we gave to the Bodmin Hospital, Bodmin Ambulance and Nursing Association was not objected to, why raise a storm? Until those who have written have actually seen it, it is absurd for them to protest against such a thing taking place.

JAMES LEE   The Prison, Bodmin.   June 10th, 1930.

The next owner, Mr. George Smith, used the site for several different types of business, including a haulage company and a scrap yard. The chapel was converted into the '99 Club', which was decorated in a harem theme with paintings by Gordon Quest of Newquay. The Club seems to have been a success during and after WWII. The site was sold in the early 1950s, when Mr. Smith's haulage company was bought by Pickfords.

The Downbeat Band at the 99 Club c. 1947.
(L to R: F. Angove (snr.), W. Hankey, G. Males, C. Knight & R. Weary)
G. Ellis Collection (D2263)   *Published by kind permission of The Cornish Studies Library.*

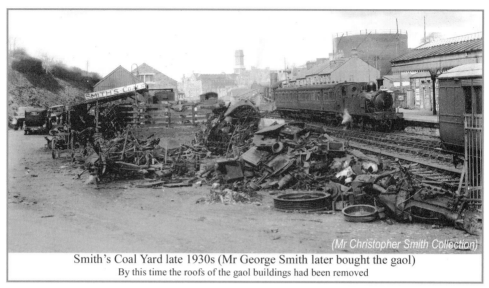

Smith's Coal Yard late 1930s (Mr George Smith later bought the gaol)
By this time the roofs of the gaol buildings had been removed

(Mr Christopher Smith Collection)

The prison has had a number of owners during the last fifty years including Mr. & Mrs. Dobell, Mr. Kenneth Allen, Mr. G Morecombe, Mr. Mason, Mr. Terry Gilhooly and, the present owners, the Wheten family. The gaol has been used for many purposes over this time but they may be classified into two groups. Firstly, some of the buildings and the land has been used for workshops and small businesses and secondly, the administration block has been used for entertainment and the tourist industry. The site has been used by other groups, for example, the Fire Brigade (1930s), Bomb Disposal Unit (1940s) and Civil Defence (1960s).

After 1960, the old prison garden contained several workshops and was later developed into a housing estate. The main exercise yard was separated and sold to a local building firm. The Bodmin Jail Night Club occupied the chapel in the 1960s & 70s.

Mr. Gilhooly used part of the civil block as a tourist attraction with exhibits based on the stories of some of the major criminals who had been executed in Bodmin Gaol and a bar and restaurant in the main building.

THE CORNISH GUARDIAN, THURSDAY, OCTOBER 2, 1969

BODMIN JAIL NIGHT CLUB & CASINO

OLD BODMIN PRISON. Bodmin 2999

TONIGHT, FRIDAY AND SATURDAY:
PAUL DANIELS
Must be one of the best comedians and magicians in the business.
Also STRIPTEASE by
FARINA

☆ DANCING every night to **Bob Cooks Trio**

Come to Cornwall's gayest Night Spot—the only place in Cornwall where you can see two different first-class Cabaret acts twice nightly, seven nights a week, and DANCING! Admission: Tonight and Friday —
4/- members, 6/- guests
Sat., Sun. and Mon.—
6/- members, 8/6 guests
Tue. to Fri. inclusive—
4/- members, 6/- guests
RESTAURANT
open every night

SUNDAY NIGHT AND ALL NEXT WEEK:
Another big attraction to the club — Radio and TV Star (who you all must know)—
VINCE EAGER
Also STRIPTEASE by that well-known
MAI LOO

Special attraction on Monday next:
ROD MASON and The Tamar Valley Jass Band

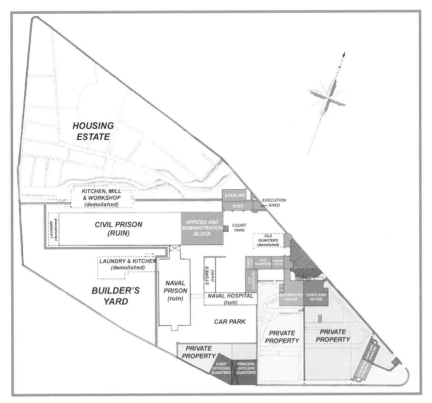

The above plan shows the site in 2009, it includes the housing estate, the builder's yard, the Governor's House, Chaplaincy and Naval Villas, which are all privately owned. The state of the various prison buildings, named as in the 1929 sale plan, is indicated. The only buildings still used are the Offices and Administration section of the main block, part of the old quarters, the main gateway building and the stables/shed. The lower two levels of the civil block contains prison related exhibits and are open to the public. The ruined naval block is also open for public viewing. The two laundry buildings, kitchens, and half of the old quarters were demolished sometime after 1929.

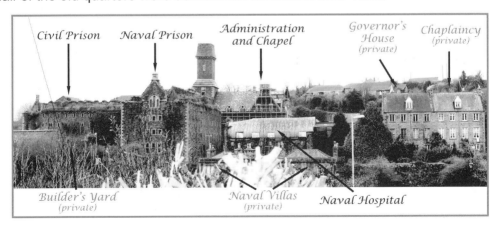

Recent Changes to the Jail

Plenum tower: *Centre:* Image shows the extensive damage at the top of the tower. *Left:* Getting to the top & *right:* After the repairs.

Major Changes to Restaurant and Bars: *Top left:* Refurbishment of the main bar. *Top Right:* New lounge and Cocktail Bar. *Other Images:* The logo and views of the new *'La Scala'* Art Deco style restaurant created in the old prison chapel. The balconies above the curved entrance are the original seating areas for the Governor and his Staff.

The Future of the Jail

Bodmin Jail [152] is a unique heritage asset which had been allowed to decay until the Wheten family bought the site in the Summer of 2004. They are ploughing all the revenue from entrance fees and profits from the shop and business back into the Jail with a ten-year plan to revive the site. This will include replacing roofs and renovating internal structures and cells to their original state. It will also incorporate a Museum of Cornish Life, covering the last three centuries.

No. 98.

5 Geo. IV. c. 83, sec. 3.

Commitment of an Idle and
Disorderly Person.

To the Constable of the County of Cornwall, and to the Keeper of His Majesty's Prison at Bodmin, in the County of Cornwall.

DIVISION OF
~~East~~ NORTH,
COUNTY OF
CORNWALL
(*to wit*).

Whereas *& Joel Henry Lucas*
of *no fixed residence*
in the said County, was this day duly convicted before the undersigned, one of His Majesty's Justices of the Peace in and for the said County of Cornwall, of being an Idle and Disorderly Person within the intent and meaning of the Statute of the Fifth Year of the reign of His late Majesty King George IV., chapter 83; for that he the said *Joel Henry Lucas*
on the *20th* day of *November* in the year of our Lord One thousand nine hundred and *seven* at *Pipers Pool*
in the Parish of *Trewe...*
in the said County, unlawfully ~~did aid and counsel and procure — Louis to do or commit a~~ did wander abroad [or place himself] in a certain public place [or street, highway, court or passage] there called — *Pipers Pool* to beg alms, contr'y to the Form of the Statute in such case made and provided, and was by me, the said Justice, adjudged and ordered to be committed for the said offence to His Majesty's Prison at Bodmin aforesaid, there to be kept to *hard labour for the space of* *Ten days*.

This sentence to commence from this date.

Thompson

These are therefore to command you, the said Constable of the County of Cornwall, to take the said *Joel Henry Lucas*
and him safely convey to His Majesty's Prison at Bodmin aforesaid, and there to deliver him to the Keeper thereof, together with this Warrant; and I do hereby command you, the said Keeper, so receive the said *Joel Henry Lucas* into your Custody in His Majesty's Prison, there to imprison him and keep him to *hard labour for the space of* *Ten days*. and for so doing this shall be your sufficient Warrant.

Given under my Hand and Seal this *20th* day of *November* in the Year of our Lord One thousand nine hundred and *seven* at Launceston, in the said County.

Shaw & Sons, Fetter Lane, E.C.
(7376—06)

Thompson

A Committal Document, dated 1907.
(Found by Ken & Beryl Allen under the floorboards in the mid-1960s, when they owned the Jail.)

Appendix 1:

Sir John Call, Bart., J.P., M.P. (1732-1801)

SIR JOHN CALL, Bart., celebrated as a military engineer, was born in 1732. Having gone to India, he was made, before he had reached his twentieth year, chief engineer at Fort St. David, a situation which he held till in 1757, he was made chief engineer at Madras, and soon after of all the Coromandel coast. He accomplished the reduction of Pondicherry and Vellore. During a great part of the war with Hyder Ali in

1767-68 Call accompanied the army into the Mysore country, and whilst he was there the Company advanced him to the third seat in the Council, and he was strongly recommended by Lord Clive to succeed to the government of Madras on the first vacancy. But news reached him of the death of his father, and he made up his mind to return to England. He had managed to scrape together a very considerable fortune and he desired to spend the rest of his days in the enjoyment of it. He embarked on February 8th, 1770, after a service of nearly twenty years, and he landed at Plymouth on July 26th.

He bought Whiteford, in the parish of Stoke Climsland, and greatly enlarged the house. In 1771 he was appointed Sheriff of Cornwall, and in March, 1772, he married Philadelphia, third daughter of Wm. Battye, M.D., a somewhat distinguished physician living in Bloomsbury.

Call became a banker, a manufacturer of plate-glass, and a copper-smelter. He designed and saw to the execution of the Bodmin Gaol in 1779. He was elected M.P. for Callington in 1784, and retained his seat till 1801. On July 28th, 1791, he was created a baronet, and granted as his arms, *gules, three trumpets fessewise in pale, or*; as crest, a *demi-lion ramp, holding between the paws a trumpet erect, or.*

By his wife he had six children. In 1785 he purchased the famous house of Field-Marshal Wade, in Old Burlington Street. He became totally blind in 1795, and died of apoplexy at his residence in town on March 1st, 1801.

Call was one of those admirable, self-made men who have been empire-makers in the East, and, better than that, have been makers of the English name as synonymous with all that is powerful and true and just. He well deserved the title accorded to him. He was a man of whom Cornwall may be proud, and it needed no trumpets in his arms and fictions about the origin of his family to make the name honourable.

The authorities for the life of Sir John Call are Playfair's *British Family Antiquity*, 1809; Clement R. Markham's *Memoir on the Indian Surveys,* 1878; H. G. Nicholl's *Forest of Dean*; and *Neota,* by Charlotte Hawkey, 1871, *The Imperial Dictionary of Universal Biography,* 1863 and S.G. Baring-Gould's *Cornish Characters and Strange Events,* 1908 & 1925.

The grant of the baronetcy to Sir John Call, dated 1795, is now in the Museum of the Royal Institution of Cornwall, at Truro.

Appendix 2:

Haden Warm-air Stove System

On two of the diagrams relating to the warming and ventilation system used at Bodmin Gaol, the machines are referred to as 'Patent'. This is Patent No. 9259, granted 15th August, 1842,[45] entitled *'Warming and Ventilating Buildings'*. Parts of the specification, describing the machine are reproduced below:

My Invention of Improvements in Apparatus for Warming and Ventilating Buildings consists in the adaptation or application to the external sides of stoves, grates, or other warming apparatus, of certain metallic plates or zigzag pieces, which, being cast on to or otherwise fixed to the sides of the stove or grate, increase the extent and effect of the heating surfaces and cause currents of air to pass with considerable rapidity in close contact with these heated surfaces, the air thereby becoming warmed, and which warmed air may then be conducted to any room or apartment that may require its temperature raised.

The Figures show a close stove of a rectangular form, the surfaces of the top and four sides of the stove are furnished with projecting plates of metal a, a, a, a, which may be straight and ranged in angles, or bent or curved in any way that may be thought most desirable. These plates vary in projecting depth from one inch to twelve inches or more according to the size of the stoves, and they may be arranged in any directions and at any angles with reference to the sides that may be found most convenient. The sides of the stove being furnished with any number of these plates and arranged in any convenient manner, as said, the stove may be covered or surrounded with a casing of any suitable material, which, as it must touch the outer edges of the projecting plates a, a, a, a, will form a number of zigzag channels. Through these channels atmospheric air is conducted from below through apertures made for that purpose. As metals of all descriptions are known to be good conductors of heat, the projecting plates which are connected to the sides of the stove soon become heated by the fire within, and the air being obliged to pass in narrow streams between these plates soon becomes warmed.

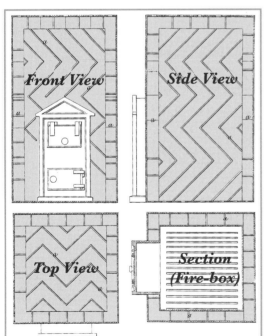

The air to be warmed is admitted to the apparatus through suitable holes or apertures made at the lower part of the casing or in its bottom, and which air in passing up the narrow channels becomes warmed, and ultimately escapes at the upper part through similar holes or flues, or may be conducted off to some other apartment. Pure atmospheric air may be supplied to the apparatus by means of pipes or flues leading from the outside.

Appendix 3:

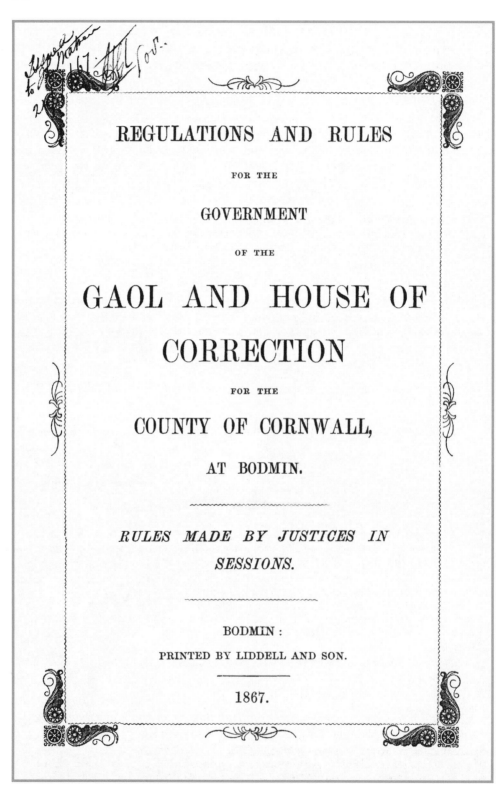

REGULATIONS AND RULES

FOR THE

GOVERNMENT

OF THE

GAOL AND HOUSE OF

CORRECTION

FOR THE

COUNTY OF CORNWALL,

AT BODMIN.

RULES MADE BY JUSTICES IN SESSIONS.

BODMIN :

PRINTED BY LIDDELL AND SON.

1867.

RULES MADE BY JUSTICES IN SESSIONS.

VISITING JUSTICES.

MEETINGS AND INSPECTIONS
1.   The Visiting Justices shall meet at the Prison on such day after the Quarter Sessions as may be ordered; and once at least in each quarter shall carefully examine the several Books kept by the Governor and others, as directed in the Act.

They should take into consideration the Report made by their predecessors, and the Orders of the Quarter Sessions thereon; and make convenient arrangements for securing the frequent visiting of the Prison, and a General Meeting of the Visiting Justices at least once a month. At such Meetings it will be proper for them to visit the several Departments, Cells, Infirmaries, Yards, Solitary or Punishment Cells, &c.

TO ACQUAINT THEMSELVES WITH ACTS OF PARLIAMENT AND RULES
2.   They shall make themselves acquainted with the provisions of the several Acts of Parliament relating to Prisons, and with the additional Rules of the Prison, as well as with the duties of the Officers; and shall strictly enforce on the Officers the due execution of their duties as laid down by the Rules.

TO REGULATE THE SCALE OF FINES
3.   They may regulate a Scale of Fines, to levied by the Governor* upon the subordinate
Officers, for misconduct or negligence in the performance of duties: the Fines so levied to form a fund for the benefit of Subordinate Officers, according to such Rules as may be approved by the Visiting Justices.
The term Governor is to be held to include that of Keeper, Gaoler, or Chief Officer of every Prison, by whatever name designated.

TO ATTEND TO REPORTS IN WRITING.
4.   They shall attend without delay to any Report in writing which they may receive from the Governor, Chaplain, or Surgeon, as to the mind or body of any Prisoner being likely to be injured by the discipline or treatment to which he or she is subjected; and should give such directions thereon as they may deem expedient, reporting the same to the next Quarter Sessions.

TO CONTRACT FOR SUPPLIES.
5.   They shall, as far as practicable, invite competition in supplying the Prison with different articles by Public Advertisement or Tender; and enter into such Contracts for any period not exceeding twelve months, as they deem advisable.

TO EXAMINE ACCOUNTS.
6.   They shall examine all Bills and Accounts after they shall have been certified by the Governor.

USE OF IRONS.
7.   All occasions of the use of irons or mechanical restraint to be reported to a Visiting Justice, but in any case where it is deemed necessary to use irons or mechanical restraint for longer than twenty-four hours, an Order in writing from a Visiting Justice, specifying the cause thereof, and the time during which the Prisoner is to be kept in irons, or under mechanical restraint, shall be preserved by the Governor as his Warrant.

NOTICE OF PENALTIES.
8.   The Visiting Justices shall cause to be affixed in a conspicuous place outside the Prison a Notice, setting forth the Penalties that will be incurred by persons committing any Offence in contravention of the Prison Act.

POWERS RESPECTING PRISONERS COMMITTED TO CLOSE CONFINEMENT.
9.   A Visiting Justice may see any Person committed by lawful authority to close confinement, and may hear or receive any representation from him as to his treatment, and inquire into the same; but he is not to hold any communication with him unconnected therewith.

MINUTE BOOK.
10.   They shall keep a Book, to be called "The Visiting Justices' Minute Book," in which shall be entered all their proceedings; the Minutes of each Meeting to contain the names of the Visiting Justices present, and to be signed by the Chairman.

VISITING JUSTICES' ORDER BOOK.
11.   They should keep another Book, to be called "The Visiting Justices' Order Book," in which should be entered all Orders by the Visiting Justices.

TEMPORARY APPOINTMENT TO FILL VACANCY.
12.   In the case of the absence, death, resignation, or removal of any of the Superior Officers, the Visiting Justices shall nominate a person to fill the vacant office during such absence, or until the

appointment of a permanent Officer by the Justices in Sessions assembled.

PRISONERS UNDER SENTENCE TO PENAL SERVITUDE TO BE KEPT AT HARD LABOUR
13.   The Visiting Justices may direct Prisoners under Sentence of Penal Servitude, or Prisoners against whom Sentence of Death is recorded, to be kept to Hard Labour of the first class, unless certified by the Surgeon to be unfit for such Hard Labour, when they shall be employed at Hard Labour of the second class, if fit.

MISCELLANEOUS.

KEYS OF GATE TO BE DELIVERED TO THE GOVERNOR AT NIGHT.
14.   When the Prison is locked for the night, the Keys of the Gate shall be delivered to the Governor, who shall keep them in his custody until the time for unlocking in the morning.

COUNTY PROPERTY TO BE MARKED.
15.   All articles of County Property in the Prison shall be marked, whenever practicable, with the County mark.

GENERAL RULES. OFFICERS.

OFFICERS TO ATTEND DIVINE SERVICE.
16.   The Subordinate Officers shall be recommended by the Visiting Justices, but appointed by the Justices in Sessions assembled.

17.   The Officers shall, as far as practicable and consistent with the performance of their duties respectively, punctually attend Divine Service in the Chapel with the Prisoners whenever it is performed.

THE GOVERNOR.

CONDUCT TO PRISONERS.
18.   He shall exercise his authority with firmness, temper, and humanity; abstain from all irritating language, and not strike a Prisoner. He shall enforce similar conduct on the Subordinate Officers.

VISITS OF LEGAL ADVISERS.
19.   Prisoners shall be permitted to see their legal advisers, (by which is to be understood Certificated Attorneys or their authorized Clerks,) on any Week Day, at any reasonable hour, and in private if required.

      Any person presenting himself for admission as the Clerk of an admitted Attorney, shall, in the absence of his Principal, produce to the Governor in such case a written authority from his Employer, or some other proof satisfactory to the Governor of his being properly authorized; and the Legal Adviser or his Clerk shall name the Prisoner whom he wishes to visit.

VISITS TO PRISONERS UNDER EXAMINATION.
20.   He shall allow Prisoners committed for examination to see their friends and relatives at reasonable hours, unless a Visiting or Committing Magistrate shall have issued an order to the contrary; or unless he shall know any sufficient reason why any person should not be admitted; in which latter case the name of the applicant, together with the name of the Prisoner whom he applied to visit, and the date of the refusal, shall be entered in his Journal.

VISITORS TO PRISONERS COMMITTED FOR TRIAL.
21.   He shall allow Prisoners committed for trial to see their relations and friends at reasonable hours twice a week, without any order, or oftener by an order in writing from a Visiting or Committing Magistrate, unless a Visiting or Committing Magistrate shall have issued an order to the contrary; or unless he shall know any sufficient cause why any person should not be admitted; in which latter case the name of the applicant, together with the name of the Prisoner whom he applied to visit, and the date of the refusal, shall be entered in his Journal.

VISITORS TO CONVICTED PRISONERS.
22.   He shall not allow Convicted Prisoners to see their relations and friends until after the expiration of the first three months of their imprisonment; but subsequently to that period, he shall allow them to receive visits once in the course of each successive three months. In case of sickness, or other special circumstances, however, he shall allow Convicted Prisoners, and Prisoners committed for non-payment of Penalties, or for want of Sureties, to see their relations and friends at other times; such special circumstances to be entered in his Journal.

LETTERS TO PRISONERS
23.   He shall allow Prisoners committed for examination or for trial to send and receive letters, unless a Visiting or Committing Magistrate shall have issued an order to the contrary, or unless he shall know a sufficient cause why any such letter should not be sent or received; in which latter case he shall record the fact in his Journal. He shall, under the same restrictions, allow Convicted Prisoners to send and receive one letter in the course of each quarter of a year.

INSPECTION OF LETTERS AND PARCELS.

24.　　　He shall inspect every letter to or from a Prisoner under charge or conviction of any Crime, except such letters as are addressed to a Visiting Justice, or other proper authority; and in every case where he shall deem it necessary to withhold a letter either to or from a Prisoner, he shall record the fact in his Journal, and shall without delay lay such letter before a Visiting Justice for his decision.

　　　He may also inspect any letter to or from a Debtor, when he has reason to suspect that it refers to any escape, or infringement of discipline; entering his having done so in his Journal, and marking the letter with his initials.

TO PAY OVER FINES RECEIVED.

25.　　　In case of the payment of any fine or penalty by a Prisoner, he shall immediately pay over the same to the person authorized to receive it, notifying such payment in his Journal.

CHAPLAIN AND RELIGIOUS INSTRUCTION OF PRISONERS.

VISITS TO FEMALE DEPARTMENT.

26.　　　When visiting Female Prisoners, the Chaplain shall be attended by the Matron or one of the Assistant Matrons.

TO SUPERINTEND SCHOOLS.

27.　　　The Chaplain shall direct the disposal of the time of the Schoolmaster and Schoolmistress, and the Course of Instruction to be pursued by them; and he shall superintend the Schools, and frequently visit them and examine the Prisoners as to their progress.

　　　No adult Prisoner shall be compelled to attend School against his inclination; but on the contrary, the permission to receive instruction shall always be treated as a boon.

SURGEON.

VISITS TO FEMALE PRISONERS.

28.　　　When visiting the Female Prisoners, the Surgeon to be attended by the Matron or one of the Assistant Matrons.

WINE, &C. AND TOBACCO CAN BE ORDERED BY THE SURGEON.

29.　The Surgeon can sanction the admission of wine, malt liquor, or spirituous liquor, or tobacco, for the use of any convicted Criminal Prisoner, entering in his Journal the name of such Prisoner, and the quantity of such wine, malt liquor, or spirituous liquor for issue to him. (This is not to apply to any stock of spirituous liquor kept in the Prison for the use of the Infirmary, and under the control of the Surgeon.)

BEDDING.

30.　　　The Surgeon may order the bed-clothes to be aired, changed, or washed, as often as he may consider requisite.

HAIR CUTTING OF FEMALE PRISONERS.

31.　　　The Surgeon may order the hair of a Female Prisoner to be cut, if necessary on the ground of health.

MAY DIRECT SUPPLY OF FLANNEL.

32.　　　The Surgeon may direct the supply of flannel to Prisoners in such cases as he may deem necessary.

TO GIVE DIRECTIONS IN CASE OF INFECTION.

33.　　　The Surgeon shall give directions in writing for separating Prisoners having infectious complaints, or being suspected thereof; for cleansing, disinfecting, and white-washing any apartments occupied by such Prisoners; and for washing, disinfecting, or destroying any infected apparel or bedding.

TO EXAMINE PRISONERS ON RECEIPT.

34.　　　He shall examine every Prisoner before he is passed into the proper Ward.

TO MAKE HIMSELF ACQUAINTED WITH REGULATIONS

35.　　　He shall make himself thoroughly acquainted with the Regulations of the Prison, and its various details.

MATRON.

TO ATTEND GOVERNOR.

36. The Matron shall attend the Governor when visiting the Femles' Prison, or, during detention by other duties, cause him to be attended by one of the Assistant Matrons.

　　　When the Chaplain or Surgeon visits the Females' Prison, the Matron will also attend, or cause one of the Assistant Matrons to attend him at such visit.

TO SEARCH VISITORS IN CASES OF SUSPICION.

37.　　　Should there be any grounds for suspicion in the case of Female Visitors to any Prisoner, the

Matron, or some other Female Officer the Governor may direct, will search such Visitor. Such search not to be in the presence of any Prisoner, or of another Visitor.

EFFECTS OF PRISONERS RETAINED BY MATRON.

38.   The Matron shall take charge of all monies or other effects brought into the Prison by any Female Prisoner, or sent to the Prison for her use, which she is not allowed to retain. The Matron shall keep an Inventory of them in a separate Book.

SUBORDINATE OFFICERS GENERALLY.

REPORT BOOK.

39.   Each Subordinate Officer shall be provided with a Book for Reports relating to the condition of his department, and the conduct of the Prisoners under his charge; which he is to lay before the Governor daily.

NAMES OF SICK PRISONERS TO BE REPORTED.

40.   Subordinate Officers shall, without delay, report to the Governor the names of the Prisoners who desire to see the Surgeon, or appear out of health, or who desire to see the Governor, the Chaplain, or the Visiting Justices.

STRICTLY TO CONFORM TO RULES AND OBEY THE GOVERNOR.

41.   Subordinate Officers shall strictly conform to the Rules of the Prison, obey the directions of the Governor, and assist him in maintaining order and discipline.

INSTRUCTION BOOK.

42.   The general and special duties of each Subordinate Officer shall be inserted in a Book, to be kept by the Officer.

SCHOOLMASTER AND SCHOOLMISTRESS

APPOINTMENT AND HOURS OF ATTENDANCE

43.   A person duly qualified to give elementary instruction, and, in the larger Prisons, at least one Schoolmaster and Schoolmistress shall be appointed, and more than one where requisite. Their hours of attendance shall be regulated by the Visiting Justices.

TO REPORT PRISONERS' PROGRESS TO CHAPLAIN.

44.   They shall, from time to time, make, Reports in writing to the Chaplain as to the conduct and progress of the Prisoners; such Reports to be filed, and a minute of them made in the Chaplain's Journal.

PRISONERS.

PRISONERS ON RE-COMMITTAL TO SLEEP ON PLANK BEDS.

45.   Prisoners on re-committal to Prison shall sleep on Plank Beds, without Mattresses, (having a rug and sufficient blankets,) during the first month of their imprisonment; provided the Surgeon first examine such Prisoners, and certify that it will not be injurious to their health so to do.

         While under punishment for Prison Offences, any Prisoners, not exempted by the Surgeon, may be placed upon Plank Beds, without Mattresses.

CLOTHING AND BEDDING.

46.   The following articles shall form Dress of Male Prisoners, viz.— Jacket, Waistcoat, Pair of Pantaloons, Stock or Neckerchief, Shirt, Pair of Stockings, Pair of Shoes, Pocket Handkerchief, Cap, Belt or Flannels, when the Prisoner has been in the habit of wearing them.

CLOTHING OF FEMALE PRISONERS.

47.   The following articles shall form the Dress of Female Prisoners, viz.— Dress or Jacket, Petticoat, Pair of Stockings, Shift, Neckerchief, Pocket Handkerchief, Cap, Pair of Shoes, Other necessary articles, Stays, when the Prisoner has been in the habit of wearing them.

BEDDING.

48.   The following articles of bedding shall at least be always supplied, viz.—Hammock or Bedstead, Mattress and Pillow, A sufficient number of Blankets, Coverlet; except in cases where a Plank Bed is ordered, when a Coverlet and Rug only shall be supplied.

HARD LABOUR, 1ST CLASS.

49.   Hard Labour of the 1st Class shall consist of work at the Treadwheel, Shot Drill, Crank, Hand Corn Mill, Stone Breaking, Rope or Oakum Beating, Mat Making with heavy Looms, or such other like description of hard bodily Labour as may be hereafter appointed by the Justices in Sessions assembled, with the approval of the Secretary of State for the Home Department.

HARD LABOUR, 2ND CLASS.

50.   Hard Labour of the 2d Class shall consist of work at Oakum or Coir Picking, Mat Making,

Washing, Cleaning the Prison, Chimney Sweeping, Oakum Packing, Needlework, Mangling, Wringing, Knitting, Digging, Pulling down Buildings, Bricklayer's or Mason's Labourers' Work, Excavating Work, Rolling Gravel Walks or Roads. Also the following Handicrafts or Trades, viz. — Tailors, Shoemakers, Bricklayers, Masons, Paviors, Painters, Plumbers, Carpenters, Brushmakers, Smiths, Coopers, Tinmen, Millers, Bakers, Printers, Bookbinders, Basket Makers, Engineers, Stokers, or such other description of bodily labour as may hereafter be appointed by the Justices in Sessions assembled, with the approval of the Secretary of State for the Home Department.

PRISONERS SENTENCED TO HARD LABOUR FOR 14 DAYS AND UNDER

51.   Prisoners sentenced to Hard Labour for terms not exceeding fourteen Days may be kept at Hard Labour of the 2d Class during the whole period of their Sentences.

MISDEMEANANTS OF FIRST DIVISION.

52.   No Prisoner shall be placed in this Division except by order of the Judge or Court before whom he is tried.

NOT TO BE PLACED IN COMMON RECEPTION CELL.

53.   He shall be placed in a Reception Cell other than the common Reception Cell.

TO RETAIN MONEY OR EFFECTS NOT IMPROPER OR DANGEROUS.

54.   He shall be searched on admission by the Governor, who shall take from him any dangerous weapon or article calculated to facilitate escape, but who shall permit him to retain or subsequently to receive any money and effects, (subject to examination,) provided that in the opinion of the Governor they are not improper or dangerous.

NOT TO BE PLACED WITH ANY OTHER DIVISION.

55.   He shall not be placed with any other Division of Prisoners.

CLOTHING.

56.   He shall be permitted to wear his own clothing.

MAY MAINTAIN HIMSELF.

57.   He shall be permitted to maintain himself, and to receive at reasonable hours any food, clothing, bedding, or other necessaries, but subject to examination, and under such limitations, to be judged of by one or more Visiting Justices, as may be requisite for preventing extravagance or excess. He shall be permitted to procure for himself wine, not exceeding one pint, or malt liquor, not exceeding one quart, in the course of each twenty-four hours.

DIET.

58.   He shall, if unable to maintain himself, be provided with such diet as any two or more Visiting Justices shall direct.

NOT REQUIRED TO WORK.

59.   He shall not be required to do any work, to clean his apartment or make his bed, or to perform any menial office; but his apartments shall be cleaned, his bed made, and his meals brought to him by an Officer or Servant of the Prison; at his own request, however, he may be supplied with, or may at his own expense procure any employment, and materials and tools for the same, which the Governor may deem safe and not inconvenient.

AIR AND EXERCISE.

60.   He shall be allowed to exercise in the open air, either alone or with other Prisoners of this Division. In either case he shall be attended by an Officer of the Prison, if deemed necessary by the Governor.

BOOKS AND NEWSPAPERS.

61.   He shall, at his own expense, be permitted the use of Books or Newspapers which are not of an objectionable kind, to be judged of by one or more Visiting Justices.

VISITORS.

62.   He shall be permitted to see his friends in his apartment between the hours of nine in the morning and six at night; an Officer of the Prison to be present at such visits, unless his, presence shall be dispensed with by an Order in writing by a Visiting Justice. Such Officer shall be responsible that no prohibited or otherwise improper communication, either verbal written, takes place between such Prisoner and his friends; and he shall report, without delay, to the Governor any attempt to evade this regulation.

LETTERS.

63.   He shall be permitted to write, send, or receive letters or other papers; but before they are sent by such Prisoner, or received by him from any Visitor, or in any other manner, they shall be examined by the Governor; who in the event of his deeming any such letter or paper to be improper, shall withhold, and

forthwith lay the same before one or more Visiting Justices for their directions thereon, recording the fact in his Journal, and marking the letter with his initials.

ABUSE OF RULES.

64.   If he shall disobey or abuse any of the Rules of the Prison applicable to this Division, he may be punished, in accordance with the Prison Rules.

DEBTORS. Debtors under 12 & 13 Vic. c.101, s.3.

TO BE PLACED IN A RECEPTION ROOM, AND EXAMINED ON ADMISSION.

65.   They shall be placed on admission in a Reception Room, by an Officer appointed for the purpose, where they shall be examined, but not in the presence of any other Debtor, in order to ascertain that they have no dangerous weapons or articles calculated to facilitate escape, spirituous liquors, tobacco, or other prohibited articles; after which examination they shall be placed in the Class to which they belong, and the Cell or Room, or part of the Cell or Room they are respectively to occupy, shall be assigned to them.

TO MAKE BEDS, &C.

66.   They shall make their Beds, and clean their Sleeping-cells, Day-rooms, and Airing-yards, every morning. They shall also keep the furniture and utensils appropriated to their use clean and neatly arranged in the intervals between their meals. They shall be required to keep themselves clean and decent in their persons, and to conform to such regulations for that purpose as the Governor may lay down.

MAY PURCHASE FOOD, &C. WHEN NOT RECEIVING PRISON ALLOWANCE.

67.   They may, when not receiving any allowance from the Prison, receive from their friends, or purchase food or clothing; but no Debtor of this class shall be allowed to receive or purchase more than one pint of malt liquor in any one, day of 24 hours. Articles of food shall only be received between the hours of eight in the forenoon and four in the afternoon, and shall be subject to the inspection of the Governor or Subordinate Officers, and to such restrictions both as to quality and quantity, as the Visiting Justices may deem proper, in order to prevent extravagance and waste.

NOT ALLOWED TOBACCO, SPIRITS, OR WINE.

68.   They shall not be allowed the use of tobacco, spirituous liquors, or wine under any pretence whatever, unless by a written order of the Medical Officer, specifying the quantity, and for whose use; and no beer, cider, or other fermented liquors shall be admitted for their use, except in such quantities, in such manner, and at such times, as may be allowed by the Rules.

TO ATTEND DIVINE SERVICE.

69.   They shall attend Divine Service when performed, unless prevented by illness, or other reasonable cause, to be judged of by the Governor; but no Debtor so exempted from attendance shall be permitted to leave his Ward or Room during Divine Service.

VISITS OF FRIENDS AND LEGAL ADVISERS.

70.   They shall, as a general rule, be allowed to see their friends and relations on three days in the week, the hours of visiting to be fixed by the Visiting Justices, and subject to such regulations as may be necessary to prevent improper communication, especially between persons of different sexes, and to prevent the introduction of forbidden articles. Any exceptions which may be made to the regulation for restricting visits, either in consequence of the illness of the Debtor, or other reasonable cause, to be determined by the Governor, shall be recorded, with the grounds of such exceptions, in the Governor's Journal.

No visit shall be allowed from a person of bad or suspicious character, to be judged of by the Governor, who shall record the grounds of such exclusion in his Journal.

They shall be allowed to see their legal advisers at all reasonable hours, and in private, if required.

MAY WRITE AND RECEIVE LETTERS.

71.   They may write to and receive letters from their relations and friends, but the Governor, if he deem it necessary, may inspect and withhold any letter to or from any Debtor, when he has reason to believe that it relates to an escape, or attempt at escape, or any breach of the Rules of the Prison; and whenever he shall open or withhold a letter, he shall mark it with his initials, record the fact in his Journal, and report it to the Visiting Justices.

TO BE DIVIDED INTO TWO CLASSES.

72.   They shall be divided into two Classes wherever the construction of the Prison will admit of it. The First Class to be comprised of those who maintain themselves, and the Second Class of those who are destitute.

NOT TO BE PLACED IN SEPARATE CONFINEMENT OR CLOTHED IN PRISON DRESS, OR MIX WITH CRIMINALS.

73.   They shall not be placed in separate confinement, nor be clothed in a Prison Dress, but be strictly

confined to the Wards and Airing-yards appropriated to their use.

They shall not be permitted to mix or communicate with Prisoners either under charge or convicted of any crime or offence.

DEBTORS RECEIVING PRISON ALLOWANCE TO HAVE DIET AND BEDDING.

74.   Debtors unable to maintain themselves shall be provided with the following articles of Diet and Bedding:— *For Diet, see Prison Scale. Bedding.*— Bedstead, Mattress, and Pillow, and a sufficient number of Blankets, a Rug, and a pair of Sheets.

SURGEON MAY DIRECT EXTRAS.

75.   The Surgeon may direct the supply of such additional allowance of food to Debtors who do not maintain themselves, as in particular cases may appear necessary to him for the preservation of health, inserting the particulars thereof in his Journal.

GOVERNOR EMPOWERED TO HEAR COMPLAINTS, &C.

76.   The Governor or Keeper has power to hear complaints against Debtors touching any of the following offences:— that is to say, disobedience of the Rules of the Prison; assaults committed by one Debtor confined in such Prison upon another, when no dangerous wound or bruise is given; profane cursing and swearing; any indecent behaviour, and any irreverent behaviour at Chapel; and may punish such offences by ordering any offender to close confinement in the Refractory or Solitary Cells, and by keeping such offenders upon bread and water only, for any term not exceeding three days.

FEMALE DEBTORS.

77.   The foregoing Rules for Male Debtors shall extend, as far as they can be applied, to Females.

PRISONERS UNDER SENTENCE OF DEATH.

NO STRANGERS ADMITTED AFTER SENTENCE OF DEATH HAS BEEN PRONOUNCED. Cir. Home Office, 2dJune, 1845.

78.   No person, excepting the proper authorities, shall be admitted into the interior of the Prison, on the occasion of a Condemned Sermon, nor during the performance of Divine Service after Sentence of Death has been pronounced.

The foregoing Rules and Regulations for the Government of the Gaol and House of Correction for the County of Cornwall, at BODMIN, *having been submitted to me, I hereby certify my approval thereof.*

(Signed)

GATHORNE HARDY.

Whitehall, 18th May, 1867.

Gathorne Gathorne-Hardy, 1st Earl of Cranbrook (1814-1906), Politician
Gathorne Gathorne-Hardy, 1st Earl of Cranbrook, was a Conservative politician who held office in every Tory government between 1858 and 1892. He served as Home Secretary (1867-8) and as Secretary of State for War (1874-8).

Appendix 4:

Quarter Sessions Sentences for 1812, 1822 & 1832

Name	Indicted:	Details	Sentence
1812			
Hawken, Samuel	assault	Sally Peake	2m gaol + 5/-
Vean, James	assault	Sally Peake	2m gaol + 5/-
Bartlett, James	taking	6lbs hay	3m gaol
Bray, Gregory	taking	a pound of bacon	3w hard labour
Chapman, John	taking	gallon of wheat	2y hard labour + 2 public whippings.
Chipmas, Richard	taking	12 apples	1w gaol
Cunningham,Henry	taking	tablecloth,stockings,shirt, shoes	3m hard labour
Reed, Thomas	taking	fowling piece & parts	3m hard labour + public whipping
Reed, Thomas	taking	brass pan	3m hard labour + public whipping
Vennard, Thomas	taking	cotton shirt	2m hard labour
Hawke, Elizabeth	taking	2 silver teaspoons	1m hard labour (pleaded guilty)
Jewell, Mary	taking	leather shoes	14d gaol
Morgan, Mary Ann	taking	two foreign coins(dollars)	3m hard labour
1822			
Cock, Ambrose	assault	Jane Doidge	1m gaol +10/- gaol until paid
Cock, George	assault	Betsey Rickard	14d gaol + 5/- gaol until paid
Tanson, John	assault	Elizabeth Larke (aged 9) carnal know.	12m hard labour + whipping
Webber, Wilmot	assault	William Austin	1m gaol
Mallett, James	begging		6w gaol + private whipping
Barnett. John	taking	items of clothing	1m hard labour + public whipping
Boase, Simon	taking	1 lb candles	1m hard labour + private whipping
Cadwell, John	taking	10 gallons of coals	6m hard labour
Cock, Richard	taking	calico bag, a pound of almond comfits	1w gaol. To be whipped
Crews, William	taking	over 120 pieces of wood	3m gaol
Darke, Henry	taking	2 blankets, counterpane	4m hard labour
Davies, Samuel	taking	elm wheel	1m gaol
Fullam, Edward	taking	trousers, dog,hatchet, pair of shoes	6m hard labour
George, Nicholas	taking	check apron	2m hard labour
Gribble, Richard	taking	2x200 lbs copper ore	9m hard labour
Hancock, Richard	taking	10 gallons of coals	6m hard labour
Holman, James	taking	calico bag, a pound of almond comfits	1w gaol. To be whipped
Honey, James	taking	worsted stockings	3m hard labour
Houghton, Joseph	taking	2 coats	1m gaol + private whipping
Jenkin, Enoch	taking	100 turves	14d hard labour
Jenks, John	taking	5 promissory notes(£1), 1 gn.	4m hard labour
Keet, John	taking	bushel of coals	14d hard labour
Lean, James	taking	calico bag, a pound of almond comfits	1w gaol. To be whipped
May, Thomas	taking	over 120 pieces of wood	3m gaol
Moses, Henry	taking	2lbs snuff and a bladder of snuff	3m gaol + private whipping
Prideaux, James	taking	calico bag, a pound of almond comfits	1w gaol. To be whipped
Smeeth, John jun	taking	10 deal planks	3m hard labour
Sowden, Nathan	taking	piece of silver	6m hard labour + private whipping
Stephens, George	taking	2 shawls, handkerchief	4m hard labour
Thomas Dunstan	taking	waistcoat	3m gaol. 'privately whipped'
Vivian, James jun	taking	50lbs copper ore	6m gaol
Warren, Henry jun	taking	calico bag, a pound of almond comfits	1w gaol. To be whipped
Wilson, Thomas	taking	5 promissory notes(£1), 1 gn.	acquitted
Woolcock, William	taking	4 gallons potatoes	1m hard labour
Younis, John	taking	items of clothing	1m hard labour + public whipping
Matthews, Julia	assault	Maria Jordan	14d gaol
Bolitho, Ester	keeping a disorderly house		acquitted

Name	Indicted:	Details	Sentence
Bolitho, Sally	keeping a disorderly house		6m gaol
Farr, Elizabeth	keeping a disorderly house		3m gaol
Haly, Mary	keeping a disorderly house		3m gaol
Downing, Ann	taking	5lbs lard	14d gaol
Huges, Elizabeth	taking	blanket, items of clothing	1w gaol
May, Ann	taking	blanket, items of clothing	1w gaol
Deeble, Bridget	vagrancy	incorrigible rogue	6m gaol
Thomas, Jane	vagrancy		1m solitary confinement

1832

Name	Indicted:	Details	Sentence
Ball, Thomas	assault	Henry Angwin, constable	1m hard labour
Gribble, Thomas	assault	2 constables in execution of their duties	6m hard labour
Hambly, William	assault	intent to ravish Ann Williams	12m hard labour
Holman, Thomas	assault	with intent to ravish	2y hard labour
Hunkin, Joseph	assault	intent to ravish & beating Emma Ford	2y gaol (guilty of assault only)
Lucas, John	assault	Nathan Sturge	1m gaol
Luney, Ezekiel	assault	Henry Angwin, constable	1m hard labour
Morcomb, John	assault	2 constables in execution of their duties	12m hard labour
Rogers, John	assault	2 constables in execution of their duties	6m hard labour
Thomas, Stephen	assault	parish constable	6m hard labour
Whitford Joseph	assault	2 constables in execution of their duties	6m hard labour
Roberts, Charles	false preten.	goods	6m hard labour
Williams, John	false preten.	five shillings	6m hard labour
Bennett, John James	receiving	receiving three £5 notes	6m hard labour
Waters, William	receiving	see Treweek, John	transported seven years
Allen, George	stealing	20lbs rope	1m hard labour
Allen, James	stealing	two barn door fowls	custody until end of sessions
Allen, Joseph	stealing	two barn door fowls	1m hard labour
Andrewartha, John	stealing	100lbs copper ore	9m hard labour
Austin, James	stealing	3 pecks barley & bag	6m hard labour
Baker, Thomas	stealing	two geese	1m hard labour
Bias, Joseph	stealing	a sheet	6w hard labour
Bowles, William	stealing	2 sacks & silver meat spoon	6m hard labour
Bray, Alexander	stealing	100lbs copper ore	9m hard labour
Bray, William	stealing	4 shirts, cravat & handkerchief	4m hard labour
Burdon, Richard	stealing	two geese	1m hard labour
Burnard, Robert	stealing	two gallons apples	14d hard labour (pleaded guilty)
Candy, John	stealing	20lbs copper & 10lbs copper	2m hard labour
Clift, Joseph	stealing	4 barn-door fowls	14d hard labour + whipping
Cock, John	stealing	5lbs. Gingerbread	1m hard labour
Cole, Nicholas	stealing	£5 note	4m hard labour
Coom, Richard	stealing	2x 60lbs tin ore and 60lbs black tin	3m hard labour
Cuming, Henry	stealing	five ganders & two geese	9m hard labour
Dingle, John	stealing	watch, watch chain & key	acquitted
Donovan, Michael	stealing	2 sacks & silver meat spoon	6m hard labour
Dymond, Thomas	stealing	8 gallons barley	1m hard labour
Elliott, James	stealing	10 pairs leather shoes	3m hard labour
Elliott, Joseph	stealing	two hazel roots	1w hard labour (pleaded guilty)
Endean, Richard	stealing	a counterpane	3m hard labour
Fish, John	stealing	glass rummer & teaspoon	1w hard labour
Friggins, John	stealing	horde collar & harness	3m hard labour
Giles, Henry	stealing	4 brass bearings & 80lbs brass	12m hard labour
Halse, John	stealing	five ganders & two geese	9m hard labour
Hamilton, Henry	stealing	five ganders & two geese	9m hard labour
Henning, James	stealing	2 guns, powder horn,2 barrels & a stock	6m hard labour
Hodge, William	stealing	faggot of wood	1w hard labour
Inch, John	stealing	3 furze faggots & oak pole	1m hard labour
Jacobs, John	stealing	2x 60lbs tin ore and 60lbs black tin	3m hard labour
Jory. Ralph jun	stealing	30 qrt Madeira wine,2 qrt. Ale, 30 bottles	12m hard labour

Name	Indicted:	Details	Sentence
Lawrence, John	stealing	wood faggots & 50 oak poles	3m hard labour
Lee, Thomas	stealing	pair of leather shoes	3w hard labour (pleaded guilty)
Lewis, Andrew	stealing	silk shawl & handkerchief	3m hard labour
Llewellyn, James	stealing	9 bottles & 9 qts. porter	1m hard labour
Lobb, John	stealing	40lbs flour, sack, loaf barley bread	12m hard labour
Martin, Josiah	stealing	20 gallons potatoes	1d gaol
Menhenniott, Richard	stealing	2 sacks wheat, 2 sacks & 24 gal.wheat	12m hard labour
Nicholas, William	stealing	tin box, medal 2 keys & a thimble	1m hard labour + private whipping
Old, John	stealing	a watch	12m hard labour
Pascoe, Robert	stealing	a gun lock	14d hard labour
Pearce, John	stealing	5 sheaves & quantities of wheat and straw	3m hard labour
Pearce, Stephen	stealing	sledge hammer,2 shovels, 2 water barrels	12m hard labour
Perriman, Martin	stealing	shirt	3m hard labour
Prinn, William	stealing	4 brass bearings & 80lbs brass	12m hard labour
Rowling, Thomas	stealing	mutton, bacon,pigs fat,barley meal, etc.	6m hard labour
Rule, John	stealing	cock, hen & 2 barn-door fowls	2m hard labour
Sarah, Richard	stealing	20 gallons potatoes	3m hard labour
Sarah, Richard	stealing	pair of breeches	3m hard labour following previous
Scawn, John	stealing	a gander	1m hard labour
Smith, Thomas	stealing	pick & mattock	1m hard labour
Sowden, Peter	stealing	two geese	6m hard labour
Stanbury, Benjamin	stealing	2 mattocks, pick,lock & vat cage	3m hard labour
Stephens, Jacob	stealing	quantities of oats	1w gaol
Stephens, Richard	stealing	2 candlestick (iron & brass), snuffers	2m hard labour
Stoddart, William	stealing	bed sheets & bed curtains	12m hard labour (pleaded guilty)
Strange, James	stealing	a sheet	6w hard labour
Strongman, Henry	stealing	3 halfcrowns	1m hard labour + 2 private
Teague, William	stealing	two barn door fowls	1m hard labour
Treweek, John	stealing	2 sacks wheat, 2 sacks & 24 gal.wheat	12m hard labour
Vivian, Joseph	stealing	watch, watch chain & key	6m hard labour + private whipping
Watts, Hugh Bawden	stealing	brown silk umbrella	14d hard labour (pleaded guilty)
White, John	stealing	shirt, waistcoat,trousers, jar, beer & cider	4m hard labour
White, John Guiham	stealing	two waistcoats	3m hard labour
Williams, Joseph	stealing	two barn door fowls	1m hard labour
Williams, Thomas	stealing	a duck	1w hard labour
Willoughby, Oliver	stealing	two barn door fowls	1m hard labour
Wills, Thomas	stealing	4 barn-door fowls	14d hard labour + whipping
Wilson, James	stealing	10 pairs leather shoes	acquitted
Worth, Frederick	stealing	a wheel	1m hard labour
Hugh, Duance	assault	Richard labour Lobb, constable	6m hard labour
Lucas, Mary Williams	assault	Nathan Sturge	acquitted
Brown, Charlotte	false preten.	goods	12m hard labour
Bennett, Margaret	stealing	three £5 notes	6m hard labour
Burden, Ann	stealing	3lbs mutton	6w hard labour
Chappel, Martha	stealing	blanket	1m gaol
Collins, Mary Ann	stealing	£1.13s.	6m hard labour
Ellis, Jane	stealing	a turf	14d hard labour
Hancock, Elizabeth	stealing	several coins	14d hard labour
Harris, Mary	stealing	8ozs. Worsted	3m hard labour
Key, Elizabeth	stealing	3yds lace	14d hard labour
Lampshire, Betsey	stealing	haberdashery, soap, soda, tea & snuff	6w hard labour
Rowling, Elizabeth	stealing	mutton, bacon,pigs fat,barley meal, etc.	6m hard labour
Selkirk, Elizabeth	stealing	linen sheet, feather bed,10lbs feathers	14d hard labour
Stacey, Ann	stealing	piece of printed cotton	6m gaol (pleaded guilty)
Tregea, Sophia	stealing	pair of leather shoes & 2 pattens	1m in gaol
Triggs, Elizabeth	stealing	poker, tongs & fire shovel	2m hard labour
Watts, Jane	stealing	100yds ribbon	12m hard labour (pleaded guilty)
Wills, Jane	stealing	20lbs bacon	6m hard labour

236

Appendix 5:

List of Staff Employed in Bodmin Gaol					
Name	Title	From	To	Born	Recorded in:
Alford, Beatrice A	Assist. Warder			1876	C1901
Angwin, William	Engineer	pre 1861	post 1871	1822	C1861, C1871
Angwin, William H	Clerk	pre 1873	post 1881	1846	K1873, C1881
Arnold, James	Warder	pre 1871	post 1881	1826	C1871, C1881
Austin, Thomas	Chaplain	Nov-07	1922	1854	C1911, K1914
Bacon, Charles J	Warder			1832	C1891
Barker, Joseph	Clerk	pre 1883	post 1891	1849	K1883, C1891
Barraball, Wm.	Warder			1872	C1911
Beard, John	Turnkey	1779	1786		QS1779
Beard, William	Watchman			1796	C1851
Bennett, William J	Assist. Warder			1844	C1901
Blight, Henry	Assist. Warder			1872	C1901
Boor, Leonard Jarvis	Chaplain	1822	1835		QS1823, QS1835
Bound, Walter	Watchman			1839	C1861
Bound, Eliza	Assist. Warder			1837	C1881
Bramble, John Thomas	Warder			1810	C1851
Brandreth, Comm. Thos.	Governor Naval	1910	1922	1866	C1911, K1914
Bray, William H	Clerk			1842	C1871
Bricknell, William	Baker			1829	C1861
Browett, Henry Leonard	Governor Civil	pre 1906	1916	1859	K1906, K1914
Burch, William	Clerk/Store			1850	C1901, K1902
Cartwright, M B	Governor Naval	1890	1890/1		BG 7/1/1922, p4
Chapman, Samuel E	Ward/Clerk/Sch.	pre 1900	post 1914	1870	C1901, K1914
Chapple, Frederick	Governor Civil	1827			QS1827(Oct.)
Chapple, James	Governor Civil	1779	1827		QS1827
Climo, Samuel	Warder		pre1911	1852	C1901
Collins, Thomas	Warder (Hosp.)	1865	1883	1824	C1871, C1881
Colvill, Hugh George	Governor Civil	ca.1860	post 1878	1822	C1861, PO1873
Copp, Samuel R	Assist. Warder			1874	C1901
Corney, Philip	TK/Messenger	1786	1835	1835	QS1786, QS1835
Curnick, Lucy	Acting Matron			1852	C1901, K1902
Dangerfield, Edward	Asst.Warder (N)			1862	C1911
Davey, Thomas	Warder / Miller	pre 1861	post 1871	1830	C1861, C1871
Derry, Barth. Gidley	Medical Officer	pre 1889	post 1914	1846	K1889, K1914
Doidge, Richard Amos	Warder	2/1889	1916	1860	C1891, C1911
Duncan, Jas. H	Governor Civil				Cal.QS 1903

Name	Title	From	To	Born	Recorded in:
Dungey, Ann	Matron	1840	post 1871	1808	C1841, C1871
Dungey, Edna Ann	Assist. Matron			1836	C1861
Dungey, Mary	Matron	1863	1883	1841	C1871, C1881
Dungey, Mary Ann	Matron	1831	post 1843	1806	C1831, C1841
Dungey, Thomas	Turnkey	1790			QS1790
Dungey, Thomas	Prin. Turnkey	1819	post 1851	1790	QS1828, C1851
Edmonds, Joseph	Chief Warder (N)	pre 1891	post 1914	1859	C1891, K1914
Edwards, Cyrus	Warder / miller			1846	C1881
Elston, Wm. Henry	Prin. Warder (N)			1859	C1911, K1914
Everest, John Bentham	Governor Civil	1828	1860	1782	QS1828, C1851
Everest, Wm. Frederick	Chaplain	pre 1861	post 1883	1818	C1861, K1883
Every, Peter	Third Turnkey	1828			QS1828
Extance, Edwin Albert	Clerk/School			1870	C1901, K1906
Fayrer, Joseph	Chaplain	1812	1822		QS1812
Fisher, Joseph J J	Assist. Warder			1860	C1901
Gearing, Warren S	Chief Warder (N)	pre 1891	post 1901	1846	C1891, C1901
Goff, Daniel	Chief Warder				K1906
Green, John	Chief Warder			1856	C1911, K1914
Guard, Wm. B	Warder			1854	C1901, C1911
Hamley , William	Surgeon	pre 1797	1810		QS1797, QS1810
Hamley, Joseph	Surgeon	1805	post 1847	1783	QS 1810, IR1847
Harris, William	Turnkey	pre 1831	post 1841	1771	C1831, C1841
Harrison, George	Warder	pre 1851	post 1861	1811	C1851, C1861
Hawke, William	Turnkey	1779	1786		QS1779
Hawken, Thomas	Warder	pre 1900	post1911	1874	C1901, C1911
Heal, James	Porter / Warder			1828	C1871
Hellen, John	Warder			1830	C1871
Hewett, John	Turnkey	1786	1790		QS1786
Hill, Sampson Francis	Watchman	1839	post 1847	1814	C1841, IR1847
Hill, William	Turnkey.	1827	post 1847	1786	C1831, IR1847
Hodges, William	Temp warder			1834	C1891
Holman, James	Gate porter	1828	post 1871	1805	C1831, C1871
Holman, Richard	Second Turnkey	1828			QS1828
Hoskin, Edward John	Assist. Warder			1843	C1881
Jacobs, William	Principal Warder				K1902
Jago, Thomas	Watchman	pre1861	post1881	1826	C1861, C1881
James, John	Clerk/Store (N)	pre 1889	post 1891	1850	K1889, C1891
Jane, Charles	Cook / Baker			1849	C1881

Name	Title	From	To	Born	Recorded in:
Johnstone, Comm. P C	Governor Naval	1891	1910	1843	C1891, K1906
Kemp, Alfred R	Ass. Warder (N)			1852	C1891
Kendall, Francis J H	Chaplain	1835	1845	1805	QS1836
Kendall, Nicholas	Chaplain	1845	post 1851	1810	IR1847
Kernick, James	Warder			1855	C1891
Lane, Maj. E W	Governor Civil	pre 1881	1883	1832	C1881
Leach, Edmund	Governor	1779	1780		QS1780
Lethbridge, John	Chaplain		1797		QS1797
Lockyer, Thomas H	Warder (N)	pre 1891	pre1911	1845	C1891, C1901
Luscombe, Samuel Geo.	Clerk/Store. (N)				K1906
Makin, Chas. F.	Warder			1881	C1911
Marshall, Adelaide	Matron				K1906
Martin, John	Gate Keeper	1831	post 1861	1795	C1841, C1861
Martin, John N	Officer	pre 1861	post 1871	1834	C1871
Mayell, James	Principal Warder			1819	C1871
McAdam, Cuthbert	Chaplain (Cath.)				K1897
McElroy, Alphonsus	Chaplain (Cath.)				K1914
McIlwaine, Captain G S	Governor Naval	1890	1890		BG 7/1/1922, p4
McNeile, Comm. Malcolm	Governor Naval	1887	1890		K1889
Menehini, Felix	Chaplain (Cath.)				K1889
Morgan, Moses	Chaplain	1797	1810		QS1802
Morris, Elizabeth	Assist. Warder			1857	C1891
Mules, Mrs			post 1831		QS 1829, C1831
Nichol, James	Warder			1852	C1891
Northey, John W	Sch. / master				C1871
Osborn, John M	Assist. Warder			1828	C1861
Osborn, William	Turnkey/ Warder	1840	post 1861	1797	C1841, C1861
Parr, Mr	Governor	1883			NA T1/15534
Pascoe, Joseph	Turnkey			1800	C1841
Perkyns, Ernest J	Artisan Warder			1879	C1911
Peter, Jane	Assist. Matron	1844	post 1871	1812	C1851, C1871
Peter, William	Clerk / School.	1843	post 1851	1815	IR1847, C1851
Phillips, Louisa	Warder			1864	C1891
Plummer, George Thos.	Chaplain	1810	1812		QS1810, QS1812
Quiller-Couch, Thomas	Surgeon				K1883
Rainford, Robert	Chief Warder			1833	C1881
Ranger, James	Messenger			1835	C1851
Richards, Alice M	Warder			1864	C1901

Name	Title	From	To	Born	Recorded in:
Richards, George J	Assist. Warder	pre 1891	post 1901	1863	C1891, C1901
Rundle,Thomas	Warder Naval			1864	C1911
Sandford, George H	Warder (N)			1849	C1891
Scobell, Peter Edward	Surgeon	1797	1803		QS1797, QS1803
Shaftain, George	Gate Porter			1824	C1881
Shenton, Wm. Repulsa	Governor Civil	1896	post 1901	1842	K1897, C1901
Simmons, Harriet	Assist. Warder		post 1883	1837	C1881
Simpson, Charles B	Chaplain	pre 1891	post 1901	1849	C1891, C1901
Smith, Aloysius	Chaplain (Cath.)				K1906
Sowden, Henry	Warder	pre 1881	post 1891	1832	C1881, C1891
Sowden, William	Ass. Warder (N)	pre1891	pre1911	1848	C1891, C1901
Statham, Samuel P H	Chaplain	post 1901	pre 1914		K1906
Stevens, Mary A	Acting Matron			1850	C1891
Stevens, William	Governor Civil	ca.1883	1896	1841	K1889, K1893
Titford, Albert J	Warder / Cook	pre1891	post1911	1853	C1891, C1911
Towner, Henry	Warder Naval			1865	C1911
Triscott, Wm. George	Prison Officer			1877	C1911
Tucker, James	Miller / Turnkey	1836	post 1851	1815	C1841, C1851
Walker, Osborne	Schoolmaster	pre 1891	post 1902	1851	C1891, K1902
Ward, Thomas D.	Warder			1881	C1911
Wellington, Avis	Assist. Warder			1846	C1881
Wellington, Thomas	Warder	pre 1871	post 1881	1828	C1871, C1881
Wells, Charles	Assist. Warder			1868	C1901
Wheale, Benjamin	Baker			1845	C1871
Whetter, Joseph	Debtor's Turnkey	1842	post 1847	1816	IR1847
White, Augustine H	Chaplain (Cath.)				K1893
White, Elizabeth	Matron's Assist.			1829	C1861
White, Thomas	TK /Shoemaker	1828	post 1851	1800	C1841, C1851
White, Thomas	ReceivingWarder			1829	C1861
White, Wm. Thomas	Prin. Warder (N)	pre 1891	post 1906	1850	C1891, K1906
Winter, Wm. W	Prin. Warder (N)			1845	C1891
Worth, Joseph	Engineer			1848	C1881

C = Census. K = Kelly's Directory of Cornwall or Cornwall & Devon. IR = Inspector of Prisons Report: QS = Quarter Sessions Records. PO = Post Office Directory BG = Bodmin Guardian. Cal. = Calendar. NA = National Archive.

Appendix 6:
Single Day Prisoner Counts (*& Annual Averages*)

Year	Felons			Bride.			Debtors			Criminals			Navy	Army	Total			Grand Total	Ref.
	M	F	T	M	F	T	M	F	T	M	F	T			M	F	Juv.		
1779						13	12	1	13									**26**	*2*
1782						8	12	2	14									**26**	*2*
1787			5			24			18									**47**	*2*
1803	7	6	13			20			12									**45**	*91*
1814	19		19	16	4	20			-									**39**	*19*
1830																		**185**	*20*
1830	58	15	73	44	22	66	19	0	19						121	37	9	**167**	*95*
1831																		**119**	*20*
1831							14	0	14	93	27	120			107	27	6	**140**	*82*
1831	39	2	41	66	15	81	12	0	12						117	17	3	**137**	*95*
1832																		**149**	*20*
1832	32	7	39	56	14	70	9	1	10						97	22	7	**126**	*95*
1833																		**151**	*20*
1833	42	10	52	52	10	62	6	2	8						100	22	6	**128**	*95*
1834																		**116**	*20*
1834	38	6	44	44	9	53	18	1	19						100	16	3	**119**	*95*
1835																		**130**	*20*
1835			36			54			14								1	**105**	*113*
1836	19	8	27	71	13	84	18	1	19						108	22		**130**	*20*
1838	40	7	47	39	21	60	22	2	24						101	30		**131**	*79*
1841										111	20	131			111	20	6	**137**	*82*
1843							24	2	26	82	28	110			106	30	11	**147**	*13*
1846							8	0	8	84	28	112			92	28	14	**134**	*14*
1850	58	12	70	34	4	38	13	1	14						105	17	10	**132**	*23*
1851										86	19	105			86	19	8	**113**	*82*
1855							5	0	5	69	17	86			74	17		**91**	*25*
1858							15	2	17	78	32	110			93	34	1	**128**	*26*
1860							7	2	9	67	30	97			74	32		**106**	*27*
1861									11			49					1	**61**	*82*
1864															72	12		**84**	*28*
1865							5	0	5	69	25	94			74	25		**99**	*28*
1868									5	55	22	77						**82**	*41*
1871							1	1	2	66	13	79			67	14	0	**81**	*100*
1871																	10	**93**	*82*
1872							2	0	2	61	22	83			63	22	5	**90**	*100*
1873										59	15	74			59	15		**74**	*40*
1874										65	19	84			65	19		**84**	*40*
1876							3	0	3	40	21	61	40		83	21		**104**	*35*
1876																		**101**	*36*
1877										43	11	54	29		72	11		**83**	*35*
1877												103	(23)					**103**	*36*
1878										79	15	94						**94**	*36*
1878										98	25	123	(28)					**123**	*36*
1881										52	9	61	47	35	134	9	0	**143**	*82*
1883										*110*	*12*	*122*						*122*	*31*
1885										*87*	*7*	*94*						*94*	*102*
1891										*33*	*4*	*37*						*37*	*103*

Year		Criminals			Navy	Army	Total			Grand Total	Ref.
		M	F	T			M	F	Juv.		
1891	*(Civil Prison)*	24	3	27	16		40	3	1	**44**	82
1891	*(Naval Prison)*				27	14	41			**41**	82
1895		*58*	*5*	*63*						*63*	*104*
1901		*66*	*4*	*70*						*70*	*33*
1901	*(Civil Prison)*	28	1	29	44	2	74	1	0	**75**	82
1901	*(Naval Prison)*				69		69			**69**	82
1911	*(Civil Prison)*	46	0	46	4					**50**	82
1911	*(Naval Prison)*				20					**20**	82
1916		*28*	*0*	*28*						*28*	*39*

Annual Committals (*& Total Prisoners*)

Year	Criminals			Debtors			Vagrants	None Payment of Fine	Navy and Army	Grand Total	Ref.
	M	F	T	M	F	T					
1803										**85**	*91*
1805										**105**	*15*
1820			**383**			**70**				**453**	*16*
1829										**378**	*15*
1830			**488**			**67**	55			**610**	*79*
1831			**432**			**32**	81			**545**	*79*
1832			**443**			**34**	207			**684**	*79*
1833			**502**			**60**	116			**678**	*79*
1834			**405**			**52**	92			**549**	*79*
1835			**354**			**49**	52			**455**	*79*
1836			**354**			**48**	82			**484**	*79*
1837			**384**			**61**	89			**534**	*79*
1838			**400**			**66**	99			**565**	*79*
1839										**293**	*15*
1843	474	138	**612**	45	3	**48**				**660**	*13*
1846	441	156	**597**	31	4	**35**				**632**	*14*
1849	658	173	**831**	37	0	**37**				**868**	*23*
1850	465	141	**606**	47	7	**54**				**670**	*23*
1854	492	157	**649**	35	2	**37**				**686**	*25*
1855	409	155	**564**	50	3	**53**				**617**	*25*
1858	569	241								**810**	*26*
1860	507	227								**734**	*26*
1865	539	151	**690**			**74**				**764**	*28*
1868	521	181	**702**			**193**				**895**	*41*
1871	581	209	**790**	90	12	**102**				**892**	*99*
1872	525	187	**712**	77	20	**97**				**809**	*100*
1874	373	132	**505**						227	**732**	*40*
1877	390	139	**529**	11	2	**13**			262	**804**	*35*
1883										*899*	*31*
1901	262	66	**328**							**328**	*33*
1900										*516*	*33*
1908							482			**936**	*65*
1909			**271**				508	119		**898**	*65*
1916										*180*	*39*

Appendix 7:

PRISONERS in the Gaol and House of Correction of Bodmin on the 12th of July, 1850.

Name	Age	Nature of Offence.	Commitment	Trial	at	Sentence.
MALES CONVICTED OF FELONY.						
1 F. B.	22	Stabbing	16 Oct 1848	26 Mar 1849	A	20m h. l.
2 J. B.	23	Ditto	3 Mar 1849	26 Mar 1849	A	18m h. l.
3 J. L.	21	Arson	16 May 1849	25 July 1849	A	12m h. l.
4 J. R.	29	Receiving stolen property	13 June 1849	25 July 1849	A	12m h. l.
5 R. T.	25	Burglary	21 June 1849	25 July 1849	A	12m h. l.
6 W. C.	41	Stealing clothing, 2 charges	2 Aug 1849	16 Oct 1849	S	12m h. l. (1m Sol.)
7 B. J.	20	Stealing sheep, 2 charges	28 Sept 1849	16 Oct 1849	S	12m h. l. (2w sol.)
8 W. B.	38	Stealing a sheep	26 Nov 1849	1 Jan 1850	S	18m h. l. each.
9 J. S.	37					
10 J. D.	17	Stealing £30-14s. from house	28 Nov 1849	1 Jan 1850	S	9m h. l.
11 W. W.	34	Receiving stolen property	5 Jan. 1850	23 Mar.1850	A	9m h. l.
12 B. L.	23	Stealing a fowl	8 Jan. 1850	23 Mar.1850	A	4m h. l.
13 R.S.C	58	Stealing potatoes, &c.	21 Jan. 1850	23 Mar.1850	A	12m h. l.
14 J. M.	40	Stealing two watchcases	12 Feb 1850	23 Mar.1850	A	12m h. l.
15 W. L.	26	Stealing potatoes	19 Feb 1850	23 Mar.1850	A	6m h. l.
16 T. S.	19	Stealing earthenware	5 Mar 1850	23 Mar.1850	A	9m h. l.
17 J. W.	44	Stealing121bs. of beef.	5 Mar 1850	23 Mar.1850	A	6m h. l.
18 D.P.	26	Stealing wood	13 Mar 1850	23 Mar.1850	A	12m h. l.
19 J. P.	22	Assault and robbery	14 Mar 1850	23 Mar.1850	A	18m h. l.
20 G. C.	29	Stealing a pair of trowsers	20 Mar 1850	23 Mar.1850	A	4m h. l.
21 J.W.H.	17	Stealing a jacket	23 Mar 1850	9 Apr 1850	S	6m h. l. (2w Sol.)
22 W. C.	33	Stealing timber	23 Mar 1850	23 Mar 1850	A	6m h. l.
23 J. L.	23	Stealing shoes, &c.	25 Mar 1850	23 Mar 1850	A	12m h. l.
24 J. T.	25	Stealing clothing	30 Mar 1850	9 Apr 1850	S	12m h. l. (2w Sol.)
25 J. H.	33	Stealing barley	6 Apr 1850	9 Apr 1850	S	4m h. l.
26 T. R.	24	Stealing clothing	9 Apr 1850	2 July 1850	S	4m h. l.
27 R. P.	40	Stealing ducks	16 Apr 1850	2 July 1850	S	6m h. l.
28 R. R.	23	Stealing a shirt	20 Apr 1850	2 July 1850	S	3m h. l.
29 T. B.	53	Stealing beef suet	22 Apr 1850	2 July 1850	S	1m h. l.
30 T. C.	17	Stealing a coat	29 Apr 1850	2 July 1850	S	6m h. l. (1m Sol.)
31 T. B	51	Stealing a quilt	11 May 1850	2 July 1850	S	1m h. l.
32 S. I.	19	Stealing a waistcoat	18 May 1850	2 July 1850	S	3m h. l.
33 W. B.	40	Stealing ducks	20 May 1850	2 July 1850	S	6m h. l.
34 W. B.	26	Stealing a duck	25 May 1850	2 July 1850	S	2m h. l.
35 A. R.	49	Stealing hay	27 May 1850	2 July 1850	S	1m h. l.
36 J. S.	36	Stealing a duck	28 May 1850	2 July 1850	S	3m h. l.
37 F. T.	37	Stealing oats, &c.	31 May 1850	2 July 1850	S	6m h. l.
38 R. K.	32	Stealing clothing	31 May 1850	2 July 1850	S	6m h. l.
39 J. T.	22	Housebreaking	14 June 1850	2 July 1850	S	6m h. l.
40 J. W.	21	Stealing a waist coat.	19 June 1850	2 July 1850	S	2m h. l.
41 H. H.	27	Stealing turves, and assault.	29 June 1850	2 July 1850	S	1m h.l.+ 2m h.l.
42 S. H.	25	Stealing chicken	29 June 1850	2 July 1850	S	5m h. l.
43 H. E.	28	Stealing apples and wood	S. in Court.	2 July 1850	S	3m h. l.
44 G. H.	19	Steaking wheat	S. in Court.	2 July 1850	S	3m h. l.
45 S. L.	51	Stealing hams, &c.	S. in Court.	2 July 1850	S	6m h. l.
46 J. H.	18	Stealing money from person	15 June 1850	2 July 1850	S	10 years trans.
47 J. M.	26	Stealing ducks	15 June 1850	2 July 1850	S	10 years trans.
48 J. B	15	Stealing bacon, &c.	29 Jan 1850	23 Mar 1850	A	12m h. l.
49 J. L.	15	Stealing a pair of shoes	19 Mar 1850	23 Mar 1850	A	4m h. l.
50 J. L.	16	Stealing a rope	28 May 1850	2 July 1850	S	2 m h. l. each
51 W.K	16					

Name	Age	Nature of Offence.	Commitment	Trial	at	Sentence.
FEMALES CONVICTED OF FELONY						
1 A.R.	38	Stealing money from person	20 Nov 1849	1 Jan 1850	S	9m h. l.
2 A. J.	17	Stealing money from person	6 Jan.1850	23 Mar 1850	A	6m h. l.
3 A. G.	37	Stealing a pair of boots	16 Jan 1850	23 Mar 1850	A	4m h. l.
4 M.J.F.	16	Stealing an umbrella	21 Jan 1850	23 Mar 1850	A	4m h. l.
5 E. D.	24	Stealing a looking-glass	27 Feb 1850	23 Mar 1850	A	18m h. l.
6 H. C.	48	Receiving stolen property	S. in Court	23 Mar 1850	A	18m h. l.
7 A. C.	22					12m h. l.
8 N. T.	50	Stealing candles	S. in Court	23 Mar 1850	A	4m h. l.
9 M. J.	39	Stealing milk	27 June 1850	2 July 1850	S	2m h. l.
10 M. C.	29	Stealing beef, &c.	1 July 1850	2 July 1850	S	3m h. l.
PRISONERS CONVICTED UNDER THE JUVENILE OFFENDERS ACT.						
1 C. E.	12	Stealing a pair of snuffers	1 July, 1850	Summarily		3m h. l.
2 W. S.	13	Stealing a brass tap	9 July, 1850	Summarily		1m h. l. (whipping)
MALE PRISONERS CONVICTED OF MISDEMEANOUR.						
1 B. D.	25	Assault with intent to rape	26 Oct. 1848	26 Mar 1849	A	2 years h. l.
2 W. G.	50	Forging an order	11 Dec 1849	26 Mar 1850	A	6m .
3 T. M.	47	Assault with intent to rape	1 Jan 1850	23 Mar 1850	A	2 years h. l.
4 R. H.	20	Assault with intent to rape	16 Jan 1850	23 Mar 1850	A	6 m h. l.
5 J. W.	53	Breach of the peace ...	5 Feb 1850	Summarily		12m or sureties
6 J. N .	24	Assault	12 Feb. 1850	23 Mar 1850	A	12 mouths h. l.
7 W. B.	61	Assault with intent to rape	S. in Court	23 Mar 1850	A	9m .
8 J. M.	25					
9 E. W.	39	Uttering counterfeit coin	28 Mar 1850	9 Apr 1850	S	6m h. l. each.
10 G T.	27					
11 J. R.	56	Fraudulently removing	16 April 1850	Summarily		6m h. l. or £30-10.
12 H. P.	62	Fraudulently removing	16 April 1850	Summarily		6m h. l. or £21-12s.
13 E. S.	24	Disobeying an order (bastardy)	10 May 1850	Summarily		3m or £2-12s.
14 J. W.	50	Smuggling tobacco	20 May 1850	Summarily		6m or £100
15 W.T.	46	Smuggling tobacco	20 May 1850	Summarily		7m or £100
16 T. M.	26	Disobeying an order (bastardy)	1 Jun 1850	Summarily		3m or £1-11s.
17 J. C.	60	Vagrancy	3 Jun 1850	Summarily		3m h. l.
18 WHT.	25	Assault	6 Jun 1850	Summarily		2m or £2-11s.
19 J. H.	38	Incorrigible rogue	10 Jun 1850	2 July 1850	S	2m h. l. (whipping)
20 W. J.	24	Disobeying an order (bastardy)	10 Jun 1850	Summarily		2m or £2/6/8.
21 W. S.	37	Nonpayment of taxes	10 Jun 1850	Summarily		till he pays £9/16/8.
22 T. M.	54	Refusing to maintain family	14 Jun 1850	Summarily		1m h. l.
23 R. W.	40	Breach of peace	18 Jun 1850	Summarily		12m or surities.
24 J. J.	18	Assault	19 Jun 1850	Summarily		2m or £2/10/0.
25 W. J.	19	Assault (2 charges)	19 Jun 1850	Summarily		2m or £2/10/0; 1m h. l. or £2/8/3.
26 F. D.	19	Assault (3 charges)	19 Jun 1850	Summarily		2m or £2/10/0 ; 1m h. l. or £2/8/3; 1m h. l. or £2/10/0.
27 —	ca.60	Vagrancy	21 Jun 1850	Summarily		1m h. l.
28 G. F.	24	Disobedience in Union	22 Jun 1850	Summarily		1m h. l.
29 W. M.	24	Assault	1 July 1850	Summarily		3m h. l.
30 W. T.	24	Vagrancy	2 July 1850	Summarily		21d h. l. or pay £1
31 J. S.	49	Fraudulently removing	21 Jun 1850	Summarily		6m or £45.
32 W. M.	56	Vagrancy	2 July 1850	Summarily		21d h. l.
33 T. F.	18	Vagrancy	4 July 1850	Summarily		14d h. l.
34 R. L.	34	Refusing to maintain family	6 July 1850	Summarily		3m h. l.
35 WSD.	15	Furious riding	9 July 1850	Summarily		1m h. l. or £3/2/9.

244

Name	Age	Nature of Offence.	Commitment	Trial	at	Sentence.
FEMALE PRISONERS CONVICTED OF MISDEMEANOUR.						
1 E. T.	21	Breach of peace	25 Apr 1850	Summarily		12m or surities.
2 M.A.T.	25	Breach of peace	25 Apr 1850	Summarily		12m or surities.
3 E. C.	16	Vagrancy	16 May 1850	Summarily		3m h. l.
4 J. U.	20	Breaking glass	2 July 1850	Summarily		1m h. l., or 12/6d.
5 M.T.	32	Disorderly in a Union	9 July 1850	Summarily		14d h. l.

Name	Age	Nature of Offence.	Commitment
MALES PRISONERS FOR TRIAL AT ASSIZES			
1 G. S.	27	Stealing 12s. 6d.	11 July, 1849
2 W. G.	21	Arson	7 May, 1850
3 R. H.	62	Rape	30 May, 1850
4 G. B.	45	Housebreaking	8 Jun 1850
5 B. H.	26	Stabbing	18 Jun 1850
6. C. G.	11	Burglary	19 Jun 1850
7 J. A.	33	Stealing a jacket	3 July 1850
8 C. P.	22	Stealing a lamb	3 July 1850
9 R. B.	26		
10 S. H	30	Stealing 3 grates and 101lbs.of lead	5 July 1850
11 J. A.	26		
12 W. L.	35	Stealing wood	8 July 1850
FEMALES PRISONERS FOR TRIAL AT ASSIZES			
1 H. G.	17	Burglary	19 June 1850
2 J. M.	27	Stealing money from the person.	5 July 1850
3 E. V.	20	Stealing a brooch, &c.	8 July 1850

Name.	Age.	Court	Warrant.	Debt.			Sentence.
MALE DEBTORS							
1 W. L.	59	Exchequer	18 Aug. 1849	55	14	0	
2 T. W.	47	Exchequer	18 July 1849	288	0	0	
3 T. S.	61	Queen's Bench	6 Oct 1849	44	3	11	
4 T. A.	65	Exchequer	3 April, 1850	31	5	7	
5 J. M.	36	Queen's Bench	22 May 1850	36	4	7	
6 C.A.W.	36	Queen's Bench	24 Apr 1850	58	18	8	
7 S. K.	32	Stannaries of Cornwall	19 Apr 1850	79	19	4	
8 E.J.J.	40	Queen's Bench	6 Jun 1850	144	6	0	
9 W. J.H.	22	County Court Plymouth	24 May 1850	24	0	4	40 days from the 21st June, 1850.
10 J. R.	72	Queen's Bench	23 Feb 1850	125	3	0	
11 C. K.	24	Exchequer	25 Jun 1850	28	7	0	
12 R. P.	62	County Court Launceston	26 Jun 1850	15	11	6	30 days from the 28th June, 1850.
13 W. D.	29	Queen's Bench	3 July 1850	168	0	0	
FEMALE DEBTORS							
1 A. P.	67	Chancery	15 Feb 1850	Contempt			

Appendix 8:

Notes on Gaol Budgets

In the early days, the prisoners' labour was used commercially to make profits, which were distributed among the prisoners, the Keeper, in lieu of fees, and the County, towards the cost of the prison. This was only a profit on the prisoners' labour and did not cover the total running costs of the institution. In fact, the gaol was costing the County quite a lot of money.

In 1795, the Quarter Sessions Court noted that the expenses for the gaol were increasing but that no accounts had been received from Chapple since 1781. They ordered accounts to be prepared indicating costs for the subsistence of prisoners, repairs to buildings, expenses in conveying prisoners, fees for discharge, punishment etc., salaries and accounts of prisoners' labour. The Court also called upon Chapple to explain the use of advances made to him to purchase materials for the employment of prisoners.

The Report on Bodmin, Falmouth and Launceston Jails sent to Paul Hoare on the 12th March 1821 (ref CRO AD272) contains the following statement: *There appears to be no account kept of the amounts of earnings and the gaoler would not admit that he could furnish any satisfactory information on this point. I observed that the gross amounts of earnings in 1800 and 1803 were £36.19.8 and £28.4.4, a regular account having been then kept.*

EXPENDITURE:	1843			1901		
	£	s	d	£	s	d
Prison diet for year	875	6	4	261	3	5
Extra by order of surgeon	18	6	5			
Medicines				13	6	0
Clothing	147	8	11	129	1	1
Furniture and bedding	56	18	1			
Straw	10	5	2			
Beer and spirits	7	17	11			
Light, Water, Cleaning Materials						
Soap	17	18	0	320	2	7
Fuel	164	1	5			
Candles & oil	62	12	1			
Stationery and printing	17	17	0			
Books (moral & religeous)	5	10	6			
Salaries, fees and emoluments	1156	8	0	2066	12	3
Rent, rates and taxes	15	17	8			
Pensions to retired officers	15	0	0			
Removing to assizes/QS	87	0	10			
Removing transported convicts	125	13	0			
Sundries	215	15	11			
Repairs in and about prison	613	6	7			
Grand Total	**3613**	**3**	**10**	**2790**	**5**	**4**

The expenditure for the year 1843 is shown in the table, this covers all aspects and costs for the gaol. As a comparison, the costs for 1901 are not complete as they only cover the cost of staff and the maintenance of the prisoners, that is, food and clothing, etc. and not the cost of the buildings and services. The two totals are not comparable.

The reports for some years include the total cost of the gaol, the salaries, the diet and the annual cost per prisoner and the weekly diet.

Between 1835 and 1877, the annual cost was between £2,369 and £3,737, with both diet and salaries increasing with time. The annual cost per prisoner increased from ca. £21 in 1835 to

Year	Total Cost			Diet			Salaries			Cost / Prisoner			Diet / week	
1835	2678	14	8	618	12	8	1056	18	0				2	0½
1837	2368	9	5	580	3	1	1056	18	0	20	18	2	2	1
1843	3613	3	10	875	6	4	1156	8	0				3	0
1846	3211	16	10¼	972	19	6	1156	8	0	24	6	8	3	4¼
1855	3525	6	9¼	1347	10	5½	1249	16	0					
1858										26	9	11		
1860										32	0	6		
1865	3271	1	9							31	14	6¾	2	0¾
1868	3545	18	10							33	4	10	2	5
1872	3384	18	4							36	15	9	2	2¾
1874	3737	15	6							41	1	5	2	1¾
1877	3618	0	8				1720	16	8	33	10	0	2	0½
1901	2790	5	4	261	3	5	2066	12	3	39	17	3	1	5
1901 Local Prisons Average Cost										25	2	5		
1901 Cost including Buildings and Services										30	9	0		

£41 in 1874. After the County Gaol became H.M. Prison in April 1878, most budgets are only quoted nationally. The exception is 1901 when some data was produced for each local prison. The maintenance and staff costs for Bodmin were £2,790/5/4, giving a cost per prisoner of £39/17/3, much higher than the national local prison figure of £25/2/5. When the cost of buildings and services are included the national average increased to £30/9/-.

Allowing for these costs the actual cost per prisoner in Bodmin increases to ca. £48. The cost of the diet was between 10p and 17p per week, except for 1901, when it was only 7p. It is possible that at this time most prisoners were vagrants and drunks and they only received the cheap, gruel and bread diet.

The gaol did receive some cash from various sources. The early earnings are repayments for the subsistence of other peoples' prisoners, that is, from the military, local boroughs and the Treasury for Transports. The large number in 1855 is reported as *'Amount received from the Treasury for the maintenance of convicted prisoners.'* The profits from the sale of goods were for selling oakum to the Royal Navy, flour from the treadwheel labour, sold to the Asylum and brush and mat making.

RECEIPTS:	1837			1843			1846			1855			1868			1872			1874			1877		
	£	s	d	£	s	d	£	s	d	£	s	d	£	s	d	£	s	d	£	s	d	£	s	d
Subsistence of military prisoners		5	6	21	8	9		8	0	3	18	6												
Maintenance of convicts by Contract	55	13	0	26	10	0	58	14	0	675	16	8												
For removal of transports				88	13	0	141	14	1	67	6	9												
Subsistence of transports				1	1	0																		
Subsistence of Revenue prisoners				22	16	8																		
Profit from sale of goods													84	2	7	92	14	3	171	16	8	203	8	1
Estimated Value of Work done for Prison																462	6	9	289	15	2	337	3	0
Total	55	18	6	160	9	5	200	16	1	747	1	11	84	2	7	555	1	0	461	11	10	540	11	1

	No. of Prisoners	Estimated Value of Work			Profit per Prisoner		
		£	s	d	£	s	d
1883	122	818	5	6	6	14	2
1885	94	692	6	0	7	7	4
1891	37	280	4	3	7	11	6
1895	63	319	11	11	5	1	5
1901	70	1333	16	6	19	1	1

Between 1868 and 1872, the authorities started to estimate the value of work done in the service of the prison. This was extended during the time after nationalisation and in 1901 the Government was estimating the value of the work to be over £1330 and reporting it as a profit per prisoner of £19/1/1. However the same document noted *'As the work on which prisoners are employed is principally for Government, only a small portion of the amount is actually received in cash.'*

Even with these estimates and the actual production of goods for the Services and Government, at no time in the history of the gaol did it make a profit. It was paid for by the people of Cornwall and later by Central Government.

It would appear from the following letters, that over the years, the Governors of the Gaol had some difficulties in recovering prisoner maintenance charges from the Boroughs.

Letter from Governor Chapple to John Tippett, jnr. of Helston (undated). [153]

Sir,

Above is the particulars of my Claim on the Parish of St. Keverne and I'll thank you if you'll be so good to desire the managers to remit me the amount. (£11-5-2)

Enclosed you have the order, I have this morning served John Golifer alias Golier with a copy of the same.

I am Sir your very Obidient Servant

James Chapple

Letter from Gov. Colvill to F V Hill, Mayor of Helston, dated 1st April, 1878. [154]

Sir,

I beg to hand you on the other side hereof, the Quarterly account for the subsistence of Prisoners committed from the Borough of Helston with <u>arrears</u> amounting to £24-10-0. As the prisoners are now the property of Her Majesty, it is requested that the above amount be forwarded forthwith to enable me to close the <u>Borough Account</u> with the <u>County</u> and to give credit for same at the Easter Sessions.

Yours Truly

H G Colvill

Employment of Prisoners and the Value of their Earnings during the Year ending 31st. March, 1901										
Description of Employment.	Daily Average Number of Prisoners.			Value of Prisoners' Labour.			Total.		
	Males.	Females.	Total	£	s.	d.	£	s.	d.
IN MANUFACTURES :									
Bed, bolster, rnattress, pillow makers &c.	4		4	109	3	9			
Bookbinders	1		1	14	3	9			
Hammock makers	3		3	129	10	0			
Labourers, &c.	1		1	14	13	0			
Mail-bag makers	20		20	460	0	0			
Needleworkers, &c.		1	1	18	8	6			
Oakum pickers	5		5	8	9	10			
Sack makers & menders	4		4	208	4	0			
Tailors, &c.	1		1	28	13	6			
Wheat grinders	10		10	17	6	6			
Wood choppers	1		1	9	9	2			
Total	**50**	**1**	**51**				**1,018**	**2**	**0**
IN BUILDINGS, &c.:									
Carpenters, labourers, and painters.	2		2	54	16	6			
Total	**2**		**2**				**54**	**16**	**6**
EMPLOYMENT in the ordinary service of the prison: :									
Bakers	1		1	31	0	0			
Cooks	2		2	62	0	0			
Cleaners and jobbers working in the prison	5	1	6	97	6	6			
Gardeners				17	11	0			
Stokers	1		1	14	6	6			
Washers	1	1	2	38	14	0			
Total	**11**	**2**	**13**				**260**	**18**	**0**
Total NON-EFFECTIVE :									
Awaiting trial	2		2						
Not told off at unlocking .	1	1	2						
Total	**3**	**1**	**4**						
GRAND TOTAL	**66**	**4**	**70**				**1,333**	**16**	**6**

Appendix 9:

Records Removed from the PRO to Bodmin Prison

Important state records from the Public Records Office were stored in Bodmin prison from February 1918 to February 1919.[145] The collection consisted of 3,418 bundles. A bundle contained any number of documents from a single letter to a large group of rolls or books. About 19,600 items were stored.

The collection not only contained one-off items, for example, the Domesday Book, but more importantly it consisted of the day-to-day documentary records of the government of England from the 12th century onwards. The two main departments of medieval government were the *Chancery,* responsible for producing royal charters, letters, treaties and records and the *Exchequer*, the financial department, which was responsible for the receipt and issue of the King's revenue. Its records consist of a large number of accounts, tax assessments and surveys of land tenure, There are also many records generated by the medieval courts, including the judicial arms of the Chancery & Exchequer.

Examples of the medieval records include:

Pipe Rolls *(accounts of royal income)*: From 1129 to 1832 (676 rolls).

Inquisitions *(inquiries after the death of a tenant of the crown to confirm the lands held and who should succeed. NB at this time all land was crown property):* Reigns of Henry III to Richard III (after 1216 to 1483).

Legal Records *(Common Pleas - civil cases and King's Bench – criminal cases)*: From late 12th century.

Scutage *(tax levied on knights' fees in lieu of military service)*: 1214 - 1338 (13 rolls).

In Tudor times, the *Chancery* and *Exchequer* were replaced by Secretaries of State, their documents were called State Papers. These collections contained records from Henry VIII (1509) to James I (1624). Later State Papers were indexed as Domestic, Foreign and Foreign Office Protocols.

One such archive was State Papers Foreign, Entry books *(copies of letters)* covering 1571 to 1783. It consisted of 271 bundles and volumes.

There were several sets of State Papers, which were indexed as miscellaneous series. They included: Treaty Papers (1577-1780); Royal Letters (1564-1780); Ciphers (Elizabeth I to 1791) (67 volumes); archives of British Legations (1568-1871) (345 volumes) and Treaties (1579-1780).

Other records in the list included: the Gloucester Cartulary (c1100-c1400); Papal Bulls; Privy Council Registers (from 1540) and many books.

One small but special archive was the Coronation Rolls, which provide a record of the accession and details of the coronations. Earliest roll, Edward II (1308). In 1918, there were 15 rolls stored at the prison. Two additional rolls have since been added for George VI (1937) and Elizabeth II (1953).[155]

References & Notes:

1. *'Imperial Dictionary of Universal Biography'* (Pub. Mackenzie), Vol. XI, **1863,** p939. *(AC)*
2. *'The State of Prisons by John Howard'* (Pub. J M Dent & Sons), **1929.** *(AC)*
3. A Brodie *et al* in *'English Prisons'* (Pub. English Heritage), **2002**, p35. *(AC)*
4. John Howard in *'The State of Prisons in England ...'*, (Printed by Wm. Eyres), **1777.** *(BTM)*
5. Document: CL/1236. *(CRO)*.
6. Document: QS/1/3/404-422. *(CRO)*.
7. Document: QS/1/4/56 & 57. *(CRO)*.
8. 18 George III. cap.17, **1778.** *(BTM)*.
9. Engraving **1779**: Drawer 59; Set 2; No. 36. *Sir John Soane's Museum, London.*
10. OS Map by R K Dawson. Published in *'Report from Commissioners: Municipal Corporation Boundaries. Bodmin.'* **After 1832.** *(AC)*
11. S.Baring-Gould in *'Cornish Characters and Strange Events'*, 2nd Series, **1925**, p196. *(AC)*
12. Document: QS/1/12/150-3. *(CRO)*
13. 9th Report of the Inspectors of Prisons, III Southern & Western District, *Parliamentary Papers,* **1844**, [542.] XXlX. *(AC)*
14. 12th Report of the Inspectors of Prisons, III Southern & Western District, *Parliamentary Papers,* **1847- 48**, [908.] XXXV. 1. *(BL)*.
15. Cyrus Redding in *'An Illustrated Itinerary of the County of Cornwall'* (Pub. How and Parsons), **1842.** *(AC)*
16. Returns from all the Gaols, &c., *Parliamentary Papers*, April **1821.** *(AC)*
17. Document: QS/1/11/614-657. *(CRO)*
18. Report of the *'Bodmin Research Project'*, **1986.** (Bod.L)
19. *'Report printed by order of the Honourable Court of Aldermen of the City of London, 1815'* as reported in *'Bodmin Guardian'*, 20th October, **1927.** *(BTM)*
20. 2nd Report of the Inspectors of Prisons, III Southern & Western District, *Parliamentary Papers,* **1837**, [89.] XXXll. 659. *(BL)*
21. The Tithe map of 1840 for Bodmin Town & Bodmin Borough has been digitised and correlated with the apportionment details by J M & W H Johnson.
22. Document: AD 194/1/pages/187. *(CRO)*
23. 16th Report of the Inspectors of Prisons, III Southern & Western District, *Parliamentary Papers,* **1851**, [1346.] XXVll, 699. *(AC)*
24. S J Pocock in *'Behind Bars. A Chronicle of Bodmin Gaol'* (Pub. S J Pocock), **1998.** *(AC)*
25. 22nd Report of the Inspectors of Prisons, III Southern & Western District, *Parliamentary Papers,* **1857**, (Sess. 1), Vll. 401. *(BL)*
26. 24th Report of the Inspectors of Prisons, Southern Districts, *Parliamentary Papers,* **1859,** (Sess. 1), Xl. 169. *(BL)*
27. 26th Report of the Inspectors of Prisons, Southern Districts, *Parliamentary Papers,* **1861,** XXlX. 1. *(BL)*
28. 31st Report of the Inspectors of Prisons, Southern Districts, *Parliamentary Papers,* **1866,** XXXVll. 1. *(BL)*
29. *'Particulars for the Sale of H M Prison, Bodmin'*, D Ward & Sons, Plymouth, **1929.** *(BTM)*
30. P J C Davies. Personal Communication.
31. 6th Report of the Commissioners of Prisons (Part ll), **1883.** *(AC)*
32. Report of the *'Bodmin Research Project'*, **1986,** p103. (Bod.L)
33. Report of the Commissioners of Prisons *(For the Year Ending 31st March, 1901)*, **1901.** *(AC)*
34. L E Long in *'An Old Cornish Town'*, (Pub. Bodmin Books Limited), **1975.** *(AC)*
35. 42nd Report of the Inspectors of Prisons, Southern Districts, *Parliamentary Papers,* **1878,** XLI. 1. *(BL)*
36. 1st Report of the Commissioners of Prisons, **1878.** *(AC)*
37. Archive: PCOM 7/6 (C314637), **1880-1888**. *(NA)*

38. Kelly's Directory of Cornwall, **1889**. *(see ref: 83)*

39. Report of the Commissioners of Prisons *(For the Year Ending 31ˢᵗ March, 1916)*, **1916.** *(AC)*

40. 39ᵗʰ Report of the Inspectors of Prisons, Southern Districts, *Parliamentary Papers,* **1875,** XXXVII. 1. *(BL)*

41. 33ʳᵈ Report of the Inspectors of Prisons, Southern District, *Parliamentary Papers,* **1868-69,** XXIX. 1. *(AC)*

42. 2ⁿᵈ Report of the Surveyor-General of Prisons, **1847.** *(AC)*

43. Document: WSRO 1325/39, page 111. **1858.** *(W&SRO)*

44. Document: WSRO 1325/39, page 156 & 162. **1861.** *(W&SRO)*

45. *'British Patents 1617 to 1889'* (CD. *Pub. MFIS Ltd.)*: Specifications. 'Patent Office'.

46. C. Tomlinson *'Warming and Ventilation' (Pub. Crosby Lockwood & Co.),* **1886.** *(AC)*

47. (a) Document: QS/HD/354. November 1853.*(CRO)*
    (b) Notice: *'West Briton'* 18ᵗʰ Nov. 1853 *(CSL)*

48. Ordinance Survey Map, **1881.** *(BTM)*

49. *'Bodmin Research Project, research Material – Maps'.* **1986.** (*Bod.L)*

50-56. Acts of Parliament cited in *'Meet the Prisoner'* by John A. F. Watson, *(Pub. Jonathan Cape),* **1939**: *(AC)*
    1779, 19 Geo. III, cap. 74: **1782,** 22 Geo. III, cap. 64: **1784,** 24 Geo. III, cap. 55: **1791,** 31 Geo. III, cap. 46: **1815,** 55 Geo. III, cap. 50: **1823,** 4 Geo. IV, cap. 64: **1835,** 5 & 6 Guil. IV, cap. 38.

57-61. Acts of Parliament (held in Statute Books by BTM):
    1839, 2 & 3 Vict., cap. 56: **1865,** 28 & 29 Vict., cap. 126: **1869,** 32 & 33 Vict., cap. 62: **1869**, 32 & 33 Vict., cap. 71: **1877,** 40 & 41 Vict., cap. 21.

62. Act of Parliament: **1898,** 61 & 62 Vict., cap. 41. *(BTM)*

63. *'Regulations and Rules for the Government of Gaol…',***1867.** *(BTM)*

64. Kindly provided for publication by Malcolm McCarthy of Padstow.

65. 'Whispers and Echoes' in *'Bodmin Guardian',* 8ᵗʰ October, **1909.** *(BTM)*

66. Commitments,Trials, Convictions &c. Returns from General Sessions for 1816. *Parliamentary Papers, 24ᵗʰ February,* **1817.** *(AC)*

67. Document: RP/245. 15ᵗʰ April, **1817.** *(CRO)*

68. Document: R/5579. 2ⁿᵈ July, **1867.** *(CRO)*

69. Document: RO/6297. 20ᵗʰ & 21ˢᵗ October, **1903.** *(CRO)*

70. Document: A/1/85. 22ⁿᵈ March, **1794.** *(CRO)*

71. Document: RP/236. 8ᵗʰ August, **1803.** *(CRO)*

72. Document: CF/4439. 17ᵗʰ August, **1829.** *(CRO)*

73. Document: D70. 16ᵗʰ March, **1869.** *(BTM)*

74. Document: CF/4441. 10ᵗʰ November, **1905.** *(CRO)*

75. Documents: D119. Calendars dated **1913 - 1920.** *(BTM)*

76. (a) Return of Persons Committed to Gaol for Trial at the Assizes and Sessions in England and Wales, 1805-11. *Parliamentary Papers, 26ᵗʰ February,* **1812.** *(AC)*
    (b) Return of Persons Committed to Gaol for Trial at the Assizes and Sessions in England and Wales, 1822-2. *Parliamentary Papers, 23ʳᵈ February,* **1829.** *(AC)*

77. Return of Persons Committed to Gaol for Trial at the Assizes and Sessions in England and Wales. Nature of Crimes 1810-11. *Parliamentary Papers, 5ᵗʰ March,* **1812.** *(AC)*

78. Cornwall Record Office holdings may be searched at www.a2a.org.uk.

79. 4ᵗʰ Report of the Inspectors of Prisons, III Southern & Western District, *Parliamentary Papers,* **1839,** [200.] XXII. 215. *(BL)*

80. Convicts. Two Reports of J H Capper, (Superintendant of Ships…employed for the Confinement of Offenders.). Dated July 1829 and January, 1830). *Parliamentary Papers, 17ᵗʰ February,* **1830.** *(AC)*

81. Sidney & Beatrice Webb, *'English Prisons under Local Government'* (Pub. Longmans, Green & Co.), **1922,** p180. *(AC)*

82. Census data was collected from the following sources:
- 1831: Bodmin Register, **1831.** *Bodmin Library.*
- 1841: Cornwall Online Census Project. *(///freepages.genealogy.rootsweb.com)*
- 1851: Transcript. *Bodmin Library.*
- 1861: Cornwall Online Census Project. *(///freepages.genealogy.rootsweb.com)*
- 1871: Microfiche. *Bodmin Library.*
- 1881: www.familysearch.org
- 1891: Cornwall Online Census Project. *(///freepages.genealogy.rootsweb.com)*
- 1901: www.1901censusonline.com
- 1911: www.1911census.co.uk

83. Directories may be searched at *www.historicaldirectories.org* (University of Leicester)

84. Bodmin (Cornish) Guardian: bound volumes from 1901 to ca.1977 held at BTM.

85. Document: QS/1/11/339-369, 15th April **1828.** *(CRO)*

86. Document: HO 45/9695/A49760. *(NA)*

87. Ledger of 'Brewer's Outfitters & Uniform Makers', Bodmin. *(Bodmin Jail)*

88. Document: QS/1/4/258. *(CRO)*

89. Document: AD/272 'Report on Bodmin, Falmouth and Launceston Gaols'. **1821.** *(CRO)*

90. Pat Munn in 'The Cornish Capital' *(Pub: Bodmin Books Ltd)* 1977, p3. *(AC)*

91. James Neild, *'Remarks on Prisons, Lunaticks, &c.',* Gentleman's Magazine, **1804,** p610. *(Bod.L)*

92. Kelly's Directory of Devon & Cornwall, **1893.**

93. Document: QS/1/11/525-528. *(CRO)*

94. Tony Philp, *'A Social History of Bodmin Union Workhouse',* (Pub. BTM), **2005.** *(AC)*

95. Quarter Sessions Records: QS/1/11/668-71 (**1830**); QS/1/12/74 (**1831**); QS/1/12/209-12 (**1832**); QS/1/12/329-32 (**1833**); QS/1/12/434-6 (**1834**). *(CRO)*

96. Data from the *Office of National Statistics.*

97. Document: QS/1/10/474-8. **1823.** *(CRO)*

98. Document: QS/1/12/190-6. **1832.** *(CRO)*

99. 36th Report of the Inspectors of Prisons, Southern Districts, *Parliamentary Papers,* **1872,** XXXI. 1. *(AC)*

100. 37th Report of the Inspectors of Prisons, Southern Districts, *Parliamentary Papers,* **1873,** XXXII. 1. *(AC)*

101. John A. F. Watson in *'Meet the Prisoner' (Pub. Jonathan Cape),* **1939,** p49. *(AC)*

102. 8th Report of the Commissioners of Prisons (Part ll), **1885.** *(AC)*

103. 14th Report of the Commissioners of Prisons (Part ll), **1891.** *(AC)*

104. 18th Report of the Commissioners of Prisons (Part ll), **1895.** *(AC)*

105. Document: QS/1/10/347-372. **1822.** *(CRO)*

106. Document: KL/24/3. **1824.** *(CRO)*

107. Document: QS/1/11/467-487. **1829.** *(CRO)*

108. R. M. Barton, *'Life in Cornwall in the Early Nineteenth Century' (Pub. Dyllansow Truran),* **1997,** p162. *(AC)*

109. Sidney & Beatrice Webb, *'English Prisons under Local Government' (Pub. Longmans, Green & Co.),* **1922.** *(AC)*

110. R. M. Barton, *'Life in Cornwall in the Mid Nineteenth Century' (Pub. D. Bradford Barton, Ltd.),* **1971,** p104. *(AC)*

111. Quarter Sessions Records: QS/1/11/525-8 (**1829**); QS/1/12/75-6 (**1831**); QS/1/12/209-12 (**1832**); QS/1/12/329-32 (**1833**); QS/1/12/434-6 (**1834**). *(CRO)*

112. Reference 110, p53.

113. Quarter Sessions Records: QS/1/11/525-8 (**1829**); QS/1/11/668-71 (**1830**); QS/1/12/76 (**1831**); QS/1/12/150-3 (**1832**); QS/1/12/209-12 (**1832**); QS/1/12/329-32 (**1833**); QS/1/12/434-6 (**1834**); QS/1/12/520-3 (**1835**). *(CRO)*

114. Reference 110, p45.

115. 'Bodmin Guardian', 10th October, **1902.** *(BTM)*

116. Document: QS/1/6/1-34 (**1784**). *(CRO)*

117. Document: QS/1/6/146/1-158/1 (**1790**). *(CRO)*

118. Reference 108, p33.

119. Document: QS/1/11/370-97 (**1828**). *(CRO)*

120. Reference 108, p181.

121. Reference 108, p207.

122. Reference 108, p237.

123. Documents: *'Pomery Letters'. (BTM)*

124. Document: X/369/1 (**1821**). *(CRO).*

125. Alan Brunton, *'Bodmin Gaol'* (Pub. Bodmin Gaol), 1995. *(AC)*

126. 'Bodmin Guardian', 7th February, **1929,** p6. *(BTM)*

127. R. M. Barton, *'Life in Cornwall in the Late Nineteenth Century'* (Pub. D. Bradford Barton, Ltd.), **1972,** p97. *(AC)*

128. 'Bodmin Guardian', 3rd July, **1908,** p5. *(BTM)*

129. http://www.capitalpunishmentuk.org

130. L.E.Long, *'Executions in Bodmin & other Essays'* (Pub. Bodmin Books),**1985**. *(BTM)*

131. Information taken from *'Cornwall Royal Gazette'* (14th February; 6th March; 3rd April; 17th April) and *'West Briton and Cornwall Advertiser'* (14th February & 3rd March), **1840.** *(BTM)*

132. Document: MEN/154. (*RIC*)

133. Document: X/106/36. *(CRO)*

134. Document: X/106/42. *(CRO)*

135. Document: X/106/40. *(CRO)*

136. Document: X/369/3. *(CRO)*

137. 'Bodmin Guardian', 25th July & 1st August, **1902.** *(BTM)*

138. 'Bodmin Guardian', 15th September, **1905**. *(BTM)*

139. Reported in 'Bodmin Guardian', 10th October, **1902**. *(BTM)*

140. *'Bodmin Gaol as a Naval Prison', Parliamentary Papers,* 25th February **1876**. *Bodmin Jail.*

141. Document: HC/CL/JO/10/169/218. *'Naval Prisons Regulations',* **1892**. *House of Lords Record Office.*

142. Document: HC/CL/JO/10/198/105. *'Naval Prison Regulations, revised to bring into agreement with Local Prisons'* **1900**. *House of Lords Record Office.*

143. 'Bodmin Guardian', 2nd June, **1911,** p5. *(BTM)*

144. Document: ADM 1/8451/64. **1916.** *(NA)*

145. Archive: *'List of Records removed from the PRO to Bodmin Prison',* OBS1/888/40, **1918.** *(NA)*

146. 'Bodmin Guardian', 5th December, **1919**. *(BTM)*

147. Archive: *'Closure and Disposal of HM Prison, Bodmin.'* PCOM 7/7 (C337725), **1922- 1929**. *(NA)*

148. 'Bodmin Guardian', 14th February, **1929,** p4. *(BTM)*

149. 'Bodmin Guardian', 5th June, **1930,** p14. *(BTM)*

150. 'Bodmin Guardian', 12th June, **1930,** p7. *(BTM)*

151. 'Bodmin Guardian', 5th November, **1931,** p4. *(BTM)*

152. www.bodminjail.org

153. Document: P/99/16/A/1. **N.D.** *(CRO)*

154. Document: RO/5551. **1878.** *(CRO)*

155. Archive*: 'Coronation Rolls',* C57, **1308-1953.** *(NA)*

Sources are shown in brackets after each reference. Abbreviations are:- The National Archive (NA); The British Library (BL); Cornwall Records Office (CRO); Cornish Studies Library (CSL); Bodmin Town Museum (BTM); Author's Collection (AC); Bodmin Library (Bod.L); Wiltshire and Swindon Records Office (W&SRO); Royal Institution of Cornwall (RIC).

Index:

Administration of Gaols:
  Gaol Acts 1823,1835, 47-8
  Prison Acts, 1865, 1877, 1898 , 49-50
  Rules for the Government of Gaol, 50, 227-33
Artefacts, 134, 142, 168, 223
Austin, Rev. Thomas (Chaplain), 124
Browett, Leonard (Governor), 64
Budgets, 246-9
Buildings County Gaol:
  Design and Buildings of First Gaol, 13-15
  Expansion of Gaol 1779-1854, 19-24
  New Bodmin Gaol (ca.1860), 25-6
  Changes in Buildings 1860 -1929, 33-5
  Buildings in 1929, 28-31
  Position of the Old Gaol, 43-4
Building Plans & Layouts:
  First Bodmin Gaol, 16-18
  Position of the Old Gaol, 45-6
  Buildings 1860 & 1880s (Possible layout), 36
  Buildings Naval Prison (Proposals 1884), 197
  HM Prison & HM Naval Prison (1888), 201
  HM Prison 1929, 27
Call, Sir John. Bart., 13, 224
Chaplains, 72
Chapple, James (Governor), 70
Cells:
  Description, 37
  Lighting, 37
  Number, 34-5, 196
  Special, 38
Closure of the Prisons, 215-6
Committal Document, 223
Courts in Bodmin:
  Assizes, 54-5, 58-9
  Petty Sessions, 51-2, 59
  Quarter Sessions, 52-3
Deaths in the prison, 132
Death Sentence & Hangings, 143
Diets and Conditions (Naval Prisoners):
  Devonport & Bodmin Gaols, 189-92
Diets for Prisoners, 115-123
  Rules for Dietaries 1878, 119-22
  Dietary for 1911, 123
  Naval Prison for 1892 & 1900, 210-11
Discharged Prisoners Aid Society, 133

Documents stored in the Prison (1918), 250
Doidge, Richard A (Warder), 64
Dungey Family (Warders/Matrons), 73
Eddy, James. Execution of, 159
Employment of Prisoners:
  County Gaol & HM Prison, 101-5
  HM Naval Prison, 205-6
Employment (Hard Labour):
  Hand Corn Mills, 113-4
  Oakum Picking, 114
  The Crank, 112
  Treadwheel, 102-3, 109-11
  Shot Drill (Naval Prisoners), 209
Escapes, 138-40
  Failed Escape 1827, 140-1
Establishment of Naval Prison, 195-201
Everest, William Bentham (Governor), 70-1
Executions, 143
  List of Hangings (Cornwall 1735-1909),147-9
  Places of Execution in Bodmin, 144-6
Gaol Registers, (Prisoner Details), 88
Governors, 71
Governors, Naval, 72
Haden Warm-air System, 39-42, 225
Howard, John (Prison Reformer), 5-6
  Gaols in Cornwall (pre1776), 7-10
  Proposed Improvements in Prisons, 10-12
Inspection of Prison (1874), 187-8, 194
Keppel, Hon. Sir Henry (Admiral), 182
Life in HM Naval Prison, 203
Life in HM Prison:
  Editor's Description (1902), 169-77
  Governor's Report (1901), 179-80
  Poet's Description, 181
  Prisoner's Description (1905), 178-9
Lightfoot, Wm. & James. Execution, 154-7
Matrons, 73
Naval Prison (Prisoners & Offences), 204-5
Naval Prisoners in County Gaol, 183-6
Nevan, William. Trial & Sentence, 161-2
Norway, Nevell. Murder of, 150-4
Polgrean, Sarah. Life, Execution, 158
Population: Prisoners
  'Single Day' Numbers, 75-6, 241-2
  Numbers Committed, 77-8, 242

Population: Prisoners (continued)
  Population on 12th July, 1850, 86-7, 243-5
  By Sex and Age, 78-9
  By types of prisoner, 80-1
  Changes in gaol population, 82-5
Population: Staff
  Numbers & Accommodation, 65-9
Prison Offences & Punishments:
  Civil, 98-100
  Naval, 212-14
Prison Rules & Regulations:
  1782, 90
  July 1832, 94-5
  Late Victorian, 96-7
  Naval 1892 & 1900, 212-4
Re-offending Rates, 135-8
Sale of the Prison, 217-8

Seman, Elizabeth Rous: Murder of, 160
Sentences:
  Hard Labour, 61
  Length of Sentences, 82
  Penal Servitude, 63
  QS sentences for 1812, 1822 & 1832, 234-6
  Solitary Confinement, 61
  Transportation & Hulks, 61-3
  Whipping, 60-1
Sowden, William (Naval Warder), 202
Staff members, List , 237-40
Surgeons & Medical Officers, 74
System of Progressive Stages, 106-7, 206-8
Wadge, Selina: Life, Execution, 163-7
Welfare of Prisoners:
  Education, 125-7
  Health, 128-133

Key Dates:

Cornwall County Gaol at Bodmin	1779-1878
County Bridewell for Minor Offenders	1779-1865
County Prison for Debtors	1779-1868.
HM Prison, Bodmin	1878-1916 (Males)
	1878-1911 (Females)
HM Royal Naval Prison	1887-1922.

I persuade myself that my readers will excuse the insertion of several tables here which I have before given in my last publication, as this book may fall into the hands of some who have not the other in their possession. And may I not indulge the hope that, many years after I shall be dead and forgotten, these tables, being of a public nature, will be occasionally reviewed, and may have inferences drawn from them which will, in their consequences, contribute to alleviate the miseries of mankind, and add something to the general stock of happiness among the human race?

John Howard